The Journal and Selected Letters of William Carey

Collected and Edited by
Terry G. Carter

SMYTH & HELWYS
PUBLISHING, INCORPORATED MACON, GEORGIA
WWW.HELWYS.COM

Smyth & Helwys Publishing, Inc.
6316 Peake Road
Macon, Georgia 31210-3960
1-800-747-3016

Terry G. Carter, editor

Library of Congress Cataloging-in-Publication Data

Carey, William, 1761–1834.
[Selections. 1999]
The journal and selected letters of William Carey /
collected and edited by Terry G. Carter.
p. cm.
Includes bibliographical references and index.
1. Carey, William, 1761–1834 Diaries.
2. Missionaries—India Diaries.
3. Missionaries—England Diaries.
4. Carey, William, 1761–1834 Correspondence.
5. Missionaries—India Correspondence.
6. Missionaries—England Correspondence.
7. Missions—Theory.
I. Carter, Terry G. II. Title.
BV3269.C3A3 1999
266'.61'092—dc21
[B] 99-14798
CIP

ISBN 978-1-64173-403-5

The Journal and Selected Letters of William Carey

Contents

ACKNOWLEDGMENTS

The monumental task of gathering, editing, and compiling numerous source materials into a useable volume always requires a team approach. I am constantly reminded of my dependence on others to complete this work. Statements of gratitude are not only deserved, but earned by several key people.

First, I offer my appreciation to my wife, Kathy, for her invaluable assistance in keeping things in order while I was doing research in the Angus Library at Regent's Park College, Oxford. Her encouragement kept me going when reading one more yellowed, original Carey letter seemed unbearable. A special thanks is also due the Regent's Park College Librarian, Sue Mills, for her long term support of the project. Over two years ago I commenced a correspondence with Sue and learned quickly to depend on her expertise. I am also grateful for the kind help delivered by Jennifer Thorp, Archivist at Regent's Park. Her able assistance during the research phase advanced the accomplishment of the goal. I also appreciate the deciphering ability of both Jennifer and Sue. Carey's handwriting is worse than mine, but between the three of us a rendering was usually possible.

Others contributed to the project and deserve recognition. Dr. Paul Fiddes and Dr. Ben Elrod originally conceived the idea and communicated it to me. Dr. Fiddes kindly worked with me to finalize the arrangements. The student workers at Ouachita Baptist University also warrant a note of appreciation. I thank Kevin, Erin, Bill, Aaron, and Tracy for their patient proofing of the text and Ryan Hankins and Kevin Miles for their invaluable help with details in the final production of the work. Thanks also to Randy Garner whose generosity in loaning me a laptop computer for the Oxford research was a genuine blessing.

A word of gratitude is due the publisher, Smyth & Helwys, for having enough vision to believe this collection will enhance the study of Christian missions history. Thanks also to Jackie Riley for her patience with a new writer and professionalism in editing the work.

For permission to make and print transcriptions of these documents, I am indebted to Regent's Park College, Oxford; the Baptist Missionary Society; and the Carey Family Association, especially its secretary, Kay Carey, and to Judy Peters, representing the family in Australia.

My hope is that *The Journal and Selected Letters of William Carey* will provide insight to students of missions for years to come.

Introduction

The History of Christian missions is the story of God employing individual believers or groups of believers to spread the Gospel message around the world. A few of those believers distinguished themselves for their courage, ingenuity, and commitment to God and the task. In some ways all missionaries are "mission trailblazers," since they carry out their mission in their own way and in a specific setting. Each missionary is in reality, as every minister (lay or professional), unique. No one does missions exactly like David Brainerd, David Livingstone, or Albert Schweitzer. They each exhibited unique methods, styles, and gifts.

However, some missionaries make their reputation by setting the stage, opening new doors, trying untried strategies and methods, and exemplifying the boldness and devotion that becomes a model for those who follow. William Carey earned that sort of distinction and the title "Father of the Modern Mission Movement." His vision for the world, and particularly India and its neighboring nations, became the standard for missionaries for two centuries. Several of his methods—for example, bivocationalism, education, translation and publication, and missions support—have been copied by succeeding generations.

Missions historians have not ignored Carey's contributions and achievements. Study of his life and debates and arguments over his methods have filled volumes and articles. Biographies such as *William Carey* by S. Pearce Carey (1923), *William Carey; a Biography* by Mary Drewery (1978), and *Faithful Witness: The Life and Mission of William Carey* by Timothy George (1991) tell Carey's story in different ways. Each of these works relies on the primary source materials, such as Carey's journal and his personal correspondence. These biographies interpret Carey and his work and help us to see the man through various lenses.

But what about Carey's version of his story? Can we ever really get to know the man and his dream of missions? What has been lacking in Carey scholarship is a collection of Carey's writings. As valuable as biographies are, hearing from the missionary personally is equally important. In fact, how much more valuable a biography might be if accompanied by a source book of Carey's own thoughts on missions? During his forty years of mission work, Carey wrote voluminous letters to the Society, his friends (Fuller, Ryland, Sutcliffe, etc.) and his family detailing his work and struggles and often sharing his heart. No doubt, due to the fact that Carey had *many* thoughts and wrote them often resulting in a mass of material, a collection of this sort has been slow to make an appearance. Nevertheless, the value of a work consisting of Carey's journal and letters is indisputable to the student of missions and missions' history.

HISTORY OF THE PROJECT

Allowed some personal liberty, I will share how the project became mine. Ouachita Baptist University, the Christian liberal arts university where I teach, has prided itself in its ever expanding international programs and study opportunities. Two or three years ago our then President, Dr. Ben Elrod, visited Regent's Park College to investigate some academic possibilities. He returned to Arkansas amazed at the amount of archival information on Carey that Regent's Park holds and that it remained unedited and unpublished. Having discussed the possibility of the project with Dr. Paul Fiddes, Principal of Regent's Park, Dr. Elrod passed this chore to me. Feeling that Carey's letters and journal represented invaluable information on the man and missions, I pursued the project with pleasure. This volume represents the fruit of that pursuit.

METHODOLOGY

As all publications, especially collections, are limited and selective, this work will not prove the exception. The work features representative letters that inform the reader concerning William Carey, the missionary. By nature, personal correspondence is encumbered with information that readers, even the most interested, would find dull and mundane. Imagine someone reading 300 pages of your personal correspondence without benefit of editorial culling. Information about the weather, obscure people and events would soon grow tiring.

An author must decide focus before attempting the massive task of compiling and editing copious letters. The spotlight in this case was simple. Carey was a missionary first and foremost—often to the exclusion of other important roles. Therefore, the editorial selection of letters and most often excerpts of letters centers on Carey's view of missions. What did William Carey think about missions' strategy and support? How did he daily carry out the role of missionary, and what were his feelings about that role and others involved in it? What was life in India like, and how did Carey's family fit into the missions' lifestyle? This compilation of Carey's letters allows Carey to speak for himself and gives insight into these questions.

Letters randomly compiled lead to confusion and frustration for the reader. Organization becomes an essential aid in order to get the greatest benefit from a large number of letters. In view of this, Carey's correspondence is categorized according to mission topics. Admittedly, in some cases the categories may seem forced but invariably have reason to appear where they are. All care has been taken to keep context clear. Some may wish that other categories had been chosen, but as the work focuses on missions as it relates to Carey the categories follow that line of thought. Several excerpts give unique insight into Carey as a person, a Christian, and a missionary.

Sequence also plays an important role in the organization of a collection. In addition to categorization, the letters must be placed in each category in some sequence. After considering several options, the chronological method prevailed based upon the concept of development. Did Carey's thought concerning missions' strategy, support, or approach to the work change over a period of time? Did experience or circumstance cause him to alter his views? These questions are important and can be answered if one studies Carey's view of missions from early to late life. This approach is not without risk as common themes within a category may not appear together. Nevertheless, the number of divisions within the work make it easier to pinpoint general themes, and additional help is found in the Index.

At the risk of contradiction, the journal demands a different approach. A journal represents day to day experience and movement, whereas letters are more disjointed and speak to specific situations and times. Carey's journal exists as a single volume written over a two year period. It chronicles the first two years of Carey's life as a missionary and gives a unique glimpse into the early struggles of a missions in a foreign country. Consequently, the journal is not divided into categories but appears in its entirety and serves as the introduction and foundation for the letters section.

A caveat may be in order. Journals and diaries consist of some very exciting stories and details, but often the day to day life story translates as humdrum and repetitive. Carey's journal is a prime example. To keep the contextual fiber of the story, however, reading the entire journal is important. Most missionaries experience times of excitement, joy, fear, sadness, success, failure, and struggle punctuated by more extensive times of ordinary daily life that lack that "on-the-edge" sense. Yet, exciting times occur in the midst of everyday life. To get a realistic picture of mission life, one must see the mundane with the exhilarating.

AN EDITOR'S CONCERN

As you will see in reading his letters, William Carey often complained about the misuse of his correspondence by people in England. The Baptist Missionary Society used the excerpts of Carey's letters to tell the story of missions to the constituents at home who were "holding the ropes" for Carey and his associates. Publication of the letters by some members of the Society did not always happen with total objectivity. This displeased Carey and caused him to react.

Carey to the Society (undated)

> Private correspondence, as you well know, is always accounted sacred, and ought to be so; consequently no person had a right to make such use of my private letters, much less to publish them or any parts of them, without my consent. Had I been applied to, I could never have been commissioning them to make me say just what they pleased; and accordingly those Gentlemen have, by publishing garbled extracts from them, grossly and deliberately misrepresented me.

Carey was no doubt correct in suspecting some men in England of taking his letters out of context to make them say what he did not say. This causes an editor of Carey's letters to take great care in allowing the author to speak for himself with integrity. Authorial intent, although not always easy to determine, as a hermeneutical principle weighed prominently on the mind of the editor. Objectivity as the ultimate goal, as difficult as that is, remained a priority. Perhaps these goals guarded the editor throughout the process.

In addition to this concern, one wonders if Carey would approve of such a work at all. He plainly declared in correspondence his desire concerning published work about himself.

Carey to Sisters, Aug. 18, 1828

> I lately received two Letters from Poor Dear Morris. His Spirit is anything but what it should be. He wants me to furnish him with materials for a History of the Mission and my own Biography. I think him the last man who should write the History of the Mission, and as to my life, no one has materials on which to found one, and certainly no one ever shall with my consent. I intend to reply to him and tell him so.

I must believe Carey's reluctance was due to his own natural humility, a trait common to many great missionaries and ministers. The biographers and I possess no privilege of asking permission from the "Father of Modern Missions," but we defend our pursuits by citing Carey's importance to Christian history and the story of its expansion into new lands. We need men like Carey to teach us.

EDITORIAL NOTES

Upon the first reading of Carey's journal and letters one realizes there are major editorial issues to address. Carey took little notice of the details of writing and grammar that normally help the reader follow and comprehend. His spelling is inconsistent. Punctuation is sporadic and without standard. He seldom used periods, opting instead for dashes (-) or semicolons to separate sentences. Sentences are regularly lengthy, disjointed,, and laborious. Paragraphs rarely break the thought; the text just continues. Capitalization appears randomly—at least from the editor's point of view. As in most personal correspondence and diary writing, subjects change quickly and sometimes defy connection to a central theme. What kind of editorial approach works with material like this?

Unsure of what the best approach might be, the editor selected a method that hopefully provides clarity without altering Carey's intent.

(1) Carey's method of capitalization seems to be random, but it is impossible to determine his rationale. In order to retain as much of the original Carey as possible, this capitalization generally remains intact.

(2) Carey's spelling of personal names and places presents a more difficult problem. Uniformity is nonexistent in both the journal and letters. At times the spelling is so awkward identification becomes virtually impossible. Andrew Fuller complained to Carey about this inconsistency.

Fuller to Carey, Sept. 6, 1797

> . . . You desire us to keep to your spelling in what we print. We will endeavor to do so but you do not always spell alike. Sometimes you write Moonshee, & sometimes Munshi, and sometimes Moonshi. If the trumpet give uncertain sound, who can prepare for the battle? - You must allow me again to remind you of your pronunciation. I never knew a person of so much knowledge as you profess of other languages, write English so bad. You huddle half a dozen periods into one. Where your sentence ends you very commonly make only a semi-colon instead of a period. If your Bengal N.T. sh(ould) be thus pointed I sh(ould) tremble for its fate. . .[1]

Carey's letters scream for an editorial standard to be applied. The biographies written by Pearce Carey and Mary Drewery serve as the standard for this work. A list of names and places compiled into a spell check data base act as the consistency mark for the work. Due to the inability to decipher, some proper names and places cited by Carey will appear as in the original. The reader should approach these words with an understanding spirit.

(3) Punctuation for Carey might be described as chaotic art. As Fuller noted, all manner of punctuation appears interchangeable. In the letters this issue is addressed directly to provide a more readable text and to enhance comprehension. In an attempt to maintain authorial intent, sentence divisions and punctuation have been applied. In addition, paragraphs are imposed—no doubt artificially at times—when a break in thought is perceived.

(4) The journal is treated differently from the letters. Since it appears in one volume with context and meaning more apparent, very little editorial license seemed necessary. Aware that this inconsistent approach might confuse, the editor preferred to leave the journal as pristine as possible. A literal reading of the journal promotes a grasping of Carey's true style and method of recording his thoughts and the events of his life and work. The journal is contained in a single volume, which the format of this book may obscure. In order to gain a sense of the original page-by-page account, Carey's pagination is noted by parentheses and italics within the text of the journal.

(5) This work seeks to allow Carey to speak for himself regarding Christian missions. Extensive commentary muddles that attempt and is held to a minimum. Chapters and categories are introduced when necessary and occasional transitional thoughts appear designated with *{italics}*. As already noted, categorization is designed to aid the reader and serve as quick reference for study of the letters. If the reader requires more help, a good biography of Carey read in conjunction with the letters and journal would be the best approach.

(6) Citations of the material present an unusual dilemma. There are over 450 segments of letters in the work and citing each letter would prove to be quite redundant and tedious, not to mention occupying as much space as a chapter in the book. However, scholarship demands a recognition of source. All the material included in the book is housed in the Angus Library, Regent's Park College, Oxford, which includes letters belonging to Regent's Park and the Baptist Missionary Society. The journal is found in a bound version, and the letters and a transcription of the journal are stored in boxed collections. The bibliography is designed to act as a citation of the letters. The letters are listed by recipient and date according to the box designations. For instance, Carey to Dyer, June 15, 1819 is listed under Box IN 13 (1 of 2) that can be found in the Angus archives of Regent's Park College. For the most part, original letters were consulted. However, a bound volume containing several typed transcripts of original letters from Carey to Ryland resides in the Regent's Park collection as well. The originals are housed in the Northamptonshire archives and Dr. Rachel Watson, an archivist in Northamptonshire, verified the accuracy of the transcripts

The editor recognizes the unusual nature of a blanket citation in the bibliography. However, given the fact that all the materials used in the book are found in the same library and in the same collection, prudence allows this departure from the norm and unburdens the reader. The bibliography contains a complete list of letters cited in the work. I must again offer my gratitude to the librarian, Sue Mills, and the archivist, Jennifer Thorp, for their professional and expert help with this project. In addition, their ability to decipher Carey's less than perfect penmanship was essential to the completion of the work.

The Journal and Selected Letters of William Carey should serve as a resource for the serious student of missions as well as interested lay people. As a companion to one of the good biographies mentioned, the collection permits the student to compliment the story of William Carey with primary source material. Surely Carey expresses some points concerning missions and his part in the work better than we can. This volume aspires not to replace good biographies on Carey, but rather to enhance and animate them.

NOTE

[1]Mary Drewery, *William Carey: A Biography* (Grand Rapids: Zondervan, 1978) 102.

THE JOURNAL OF WILLIAM CAREY

1793-1795

William Carey set out to keep the Society informed of his important work. His first attempts included not only correspondence, but also a daily journal of activities and feelings. As those prone to record daily life discover, keeping a journal requires time and discipline. Carey maintained the discipline from June 13, 1793 to June 14, 1795, journaling the trip to India and the first days on the field. This daily account furnishes valuable information pertaining to the difficult task of beginning mission work in a new and sometimes hostile field. Impressions, attitudes, struggles, and relational insights fill the journal pages. Reading Carey's journal gives the reader a sense of the missionary and his daily task.

Carey discontinued the journal approach after 1795. Evidently the time required and the demands of the work precluded this effort. From that point on, he included some journaling in his letters.

Carey to Sutcliffe, Nov. 27, 1800

> I must write my letters journal wise to all my correspondents. By that method I may be able to supercede the keeping a journal which I cannot regularly do. I finished a letter in this way last to brother Fuller - now I begin one to you.

Read the journal as Carey meant for it to be read - gleaning the experience of a brand new missions' endeavor - bold and exciting. Remember the journal retains much of its original form and style and contains few editorial changes in order to avoid destroying Carey's intended impact. Surely he desired the pages to not only inform but to encourage, excite, and enlist others to the work. Perhaps it still will.

1793

June 13

After being prevented from going on the "Oxford" (by reason of the abominable East India Monopoly) we embarked by divine providence in the *Cron Princess Marie*, a Danish ship commanded by Capt. Christmas, an Englishman, at five in the morning from Dover - and by night were off Beachy Head. This I hope was a day of Joy to my Soul. I was returned to take all my family with me and to enjoy all the Blessings which I had surrendered up to God - this is an Ebenezer which I raise to God and hope to be strengthened whenever I reflect upon it.

14

Sick as were all my family and incapable of much reflection. We are off the Prall Point this Evening.

15

Still sick, - in the Bay of Biscay - Lat. 47 N. Long. 3 W.

16

Lord's Day, a little recovered - met for Prayer and Exhortation in my cabin - had a dispute with a French Deist - Lat. 46 12 N. Long. 5 W. *(end of page 1)*

17-22

All this Week nothing of moment occurred. We meet every morning and Evening for family prayer, and meet with innumerable civilities from every body on board, but have most awful proof of the [Awful] effects of human depravity when heightened by bad principles - the Old Deist (Barnard) is one of the most daring presumptuous wretches that ever I heard - Calm the last five days.

23

Lord's Day, had two publick meetings; Mr. T. preached once, and I once. In the Morning we had but one person more than our own family - in the Afternoon we had three, viz. The Surgeon and two of the Passengers - God grant that it may be useful.

24-25

Fell in with the Trade wind in lat. -39. N. and the next day passed the Island of Madeira. It was in sight greatest part of the day - A French privateer, hoisted English Colours and pretended to be bound to Sierra Leone.

26

Nothing material - Lat. by Observation at Noon 30. 30 -

27

Passed Palma, one of the Canaries - saw Gomara, and Fero but by reason of strong Squalls could not see Teneriff. *(end of page 2)*

28

A very heavy swell so that the Ship rolled much and some of us were Sick again - for this week past have seen Shearwaters & Mother Carey's Chickens - and the 16th vast number of Porposses were seen and a Calm succeeded on the 24 saw a number of flying fish - have begun to write Bengali - & read Edwards' Sermons - Perlegs Cowper's Poems - mind tranquil & serene - I have of late found my mind more impressed than ordinary with the importance of the work upon which I am going - God grant that I may feel it more & more.

29

This Day about 3 o'clock in the Afternoon passed the Tropic of Cancer - the Heat is very moderate and has been all the Voyage the Thermometer at 72 - and has never been more - I find some delight in reading, and in preparing for my Work by writing the Bengali - only however because it relates to my great Work.

30

Lord's Day - a pleasant & profitable Day - our Congregation Composed of Ten persons - but no good done yet - Lat. 21. 5 -

July 1

But little wind - had a long Conversation with the Deist to day - but never found a man so hardened and determined to turn Scripture into Ridicule as him - Oh how dreadfully depraved is human Nature.

2

Nothing remarkable - Calm within, and without the Thermometer at 86 - in the Lat. of the Cape Verd Islands - *(end of page 3)*

3

A pleasant and profitable Day - Good Wind -

4

But little Wind - Busy day.

5

O - but happy within - yet a most unprofitable Creature - I have need to read the Word of God more & above all I want an heart to feed upon it -

6

Nothing remarkable.

7

Lord's Day - a pleasant and I hope profitable one; our Congregation increased by one - had much sweetness and enjoyment of God.

8-9

Barren and Cold - and full of grief - Calms and Squalls, a Whale passed by us on the 8th Lat. on the 9th - 10 N. -

10-21

Contrary Winds by which we were much detained and prevented from making much progress - was very ill owing to a Bilious Complaint, and obstructed perspiration which is very dangerous in hot Countries - find my mind somewhat drawn out to God - but in general quite spiritless - on the 21 passed the Line - and the whole day was spent by the Sailors in mirth - but my soul was sad.

22

A wretched day full of Chagrin - discontent and pride no heart for God nor for divine things spent the day in reading - but to no purpose - *(end of page 4)*

23-Aug. 2

Last night passed the Tropic of Capricorn - this time has been filled up with various exercises of mind, I have in general reason to mourn that I have no more of the spiritual warfare maintained in my soul - and no more communion with God - I feel myself to be much declined upon the whole in more spiritual exercises of religion - yet have had some pleasant exercises of Soul - and feel my heart set upon the great work upon which I am going - sometimes I am quite dejected when I see the impenetrability of the Hearts of those with us - they hear us preach on the Lord's Day - but we are forced to witness their disregard to God all the Week - O may God give us greater success among the Heathen - I am very desirous that my Children may pursue the same Work and now intend to bring up one in the study of Sanskrit, and another of Persian - O may God give them grace, to fit them for the work - I have been much concerned for fear the power of the Company should oppose us - but tho we have spent much time in contriving - we have at last concluded to apply to them for Land to settle upon - and leave the success with God. *(end of page 5)*

20

Nothing very material having occurred since we passed the Tropic of Capricorn, I have not written any account, but this day we are off the Cape of Good Hope - we expected to have gone in there, on account of which I had written to friends in England some time since, but now having some hopes in arriving in Bengal, before the breaking up of the Monsoon we pass by - I have some reason to regret this as I had hopes of persuading one of the ministers there to engage in a Correspondence with England - but the Lord is wise - I have reason to lament over the barrenness of Soul - and am sometimes much discouraged for if I am as dead and stupid how can I expect to be of any use to the Heathen - yet I have of late felt some very lively desires after the success of our undertaking - if there is anything engages my heart in prayer to God it is that the Heathen may be converted, and that the Society which has so generously exerted itself may be encouraged, and excited to go on with greater vigour in the important undertaking - my Wife thro mercy is well satisfied with our undertaking, and we are all now in remarkable good Health - Our Course was by the Islands of Trinidada - Saxenburg - Tristhan da Cunha and there from Lat. 27 S. Long. 29 W. - due E to this place. *(end of page 6)*

25

A very pleasant day - had much enjoyment in further worship but about half past one on Monday morning was awakened by the violent motion of the Ship, and in about half an hour was in formed that she had carried away her main top and fore top masts - I went upon deck where a dreadful sea presented itself, the Masts and Rigging hanging over the side and the Ship violently rolling & pitching and I thought she must have gone down - but thro mercy all were preserved.

29

All day a hard Gale.

Nov. 9

From the time of my last Journal to now nothing of so much importance occurred as to be worth recording - I think that I have had more liberty in prayer, and more converse with God than for some time before - but have notwithstanding been a very unfruitful creature, and so remain - for near a month we have been within 200 miles of Bengal, but the violence of the Currents set us back when we have been at the very door. I hope I have learned of the necessity of beating up in the things of God, against the Wind and Tide when there is occasion - as we have done in our voyage: We have had our Port in view all along and there has been every attention paid to ascertain our situation by Solar, and Lunar Observations - no opportunity occurred that was neglected; O that I was but as attentive to the Evidence of my state as they to their situation - a Ship sails within Six Points of the Wind, that is if the wind blow from the North a Ship will sail E.N.E. upon Tach, and *(end of page 7)* W.N.W. upon the other if our course is North one must, therefore, go E. N. E. a considerable way then W. N. W. and if the Wind shifts a point the advantage is immediately taken now though this is tiresome work, and (especially if a Current sets against us) we scarce make any way. Nay sometimes in spite of all that we can do we go backwards instead of forwards, yet it is absolutely necessary to keep working up - if we ever mean to arrive at our port. - So in the Xn Life we often have to work against Wind & Current, but we must do it if we ever expect to make our Port -

To Day was the first time of an interview with the Hindus. Two Boats came to sell us Fish, and Mr. T (Thomas) asked the men in one of them whether they had any Shastras - their answer was, "We are poor men - those who have many Cowries - (or are rich) read the Shastras but we do not know them - I like their appearance very much. They appear to be intelligent persons tho of the lowest caste - rather beneath the middle stature and appeared to be very attentive to whatever we said to them - we have not yet been ashore - but on Monday we intend, God willing to go - O may my Heart be prepared for our Work - and the Kingdom of Christ set up among the poor Hindus -

1794

Jan. 13

For these two months past I have seen nothing but a continual moving to and fro. For three weeks we were at Calcutta selling our Venture, but the great expence into which Mr. T. had inadvertently given of Servants, &ct. filled my mind with anxiety and wretchedness, and the continual Hurry of Business took up all my time and preyed upon my Soul, so that with the prospect of worldly Poverty & the want of a sense of divine things filled me with constant discontent and restlessness of mind - we, therefore, went *(end of page 8)* on excursion into the Country when we had the offer of either Buying or renting an House at Bandel; we thought at first of purchasing but the time approaching when we must pay, and money not being at Hand, we changed our minds, and from that moment my mind was fully determined to go up into the Country, and build me an hut, and live like the Natives; Mr. T. had entertained thoughts of settling [in his profession] at Calcutta [on account of his

Creditors] but upon my determination to go up the country he resolved not to leave me -

One day, however, he went to Calcutta and while he was there he was informed by Capt. Christmas that the Company had been looking out for a person of Botanical Ability to superintend the Botanical Garden - I being advertised of this went to Calcutta but found the station disposed of already - Mr. T. having determined to reside there; I enquired of a Banian, whether Land could be procured near Calcutta, who informed me that it might - I went, therefore, and we brought our Families down to Calcutta again - he in expectation of settling there and I in expectation of having Land to settle upon. Upon our arrival I found that I had only been trifled with about Land, and that no free Land could be got now, the Banian offered me to live in his garden House till some could be got - - at which House I now am at Manicktolla; and have sent a trusty old Native to procure Jungle Land at Debhatta; about 16 Case or 32 Miles from Calcutta to the Eastward, where if I succeed I intend to Build a Bungalow, or straw House, and cultivate about 50 or an 100 Biggahs of Land - the Uncle of Ram Ram Boshu - being Zemindar in that place I have hope of succeeding, but have had much trial for both Faith and Patience - I shall be 32 Miles from Mr. T [and]

My Family have been much afflicted with the Flux - my Wife and Sister too, who do not see the importance of the Mission as I do, are continually exclaiming against me, and as for Mr. T. they think it hard indeed that he should live in a City in an affluent manner, and they be forced to go into a Wilderness and live without many of what they call the necessaries *(end of page 9)* of Life, (Bread in particular) - but] I not only am convinced of the impossibility of living in Calcutta, but also of the importance of an missionary being like, and living amongst his people - the success of future missions also lies near my Heart, and I am fearful lest the great expence of sending out my Family - should be a check upon the zeal of the Society; how much more if I should now live upon an European Plan, and incur greater charges, now I see the Value of Faith in some Measure, and think I feel more than ordinary sweetness in the Word of God - O may I again taste the sweets of Social religion which I have given up, and see in this Land of Darkness, a people formed for God -

15-16

On the first of these days I received an account that I may have as much Land as I please for three Years, for nothing, and after that to pay a small Rent per Annum - [I therefore went to Mr. T. to consult him, and to obtain money - when I found that my all was expended, and that Mr. T. was already in debt - I was much dejected at this. I am in a strange Land, alone, no Christian Friend, a large Family - and nothing to supply their Wants - I blame Mr. T. for leading me into such Expence at first, and I blame myself for being led; tho I acceded to what I much disapproved of, because I thought he knew the Country best; and was in earnest to go and live up the Country, and that for a Week or two while we sold our Venture it would be a greater expence to have a separate house, and servants than for us to live together - I am dejected, not for my own sake but my Family's and his, for whom I tremble, he is now at the certain Expence of *L*400 per Annum and unless he has speedy practice, he must be irrecoverably involved - I must borrow 500 Rupees if I can - with which I intend to build an Hut or two, & retire to the Wilderness -]

There are many Serpents & Tigers, but Christ has said his followers shall take up serpents & etc. unhurt - in the Evening poured out my soul to God; but still my Burden continued - The next day had a pleasant time in prayer to God in the morning [but afterwards the abusive treatment I received from her who should be an help to me quite overcame my spirits, I was vexed, grieved, and shocked, I am sorry for her who never was hearty in the undertaking, her health has been much impaired, and her fears are great, tho five parts out of six are groundless,] towards Evening had [more] Calm both within and without; Oh that I may have Wisdom from above - the undertaking in which I am engaged is to me a Consolation & pleasure, and the Word of God is made sweeter by my Afflictions - *(end of page 10)*

17

Went to Calcutta to Mr. T. for money but to no purpose - Was very much dejected all day. Have no relish for anything of the world, yet am swallowed up in its cares. - Towards Evening had a pleasant View of the all sufficiency of God, and the stability of his promises which much relieved my mind - and as I walked home in the Night, was enabled to roll my Soul, and all my Cares in some measure on God; on my coming home I found all much more calm than I expected; for which I bless God - and pray that he may direct us into the patient waiting for Christ - What a mercy it is to have a God, and how miserable must they be who have no knowledge of, or value for the throne of Grace - An Interview with Mohammedans.

18

I find the ardor of my mind after divine things less, and my soul too much swallowed up with the things of this present World - Oh! that I could live entirely to, and for God - at Manicktolla.

19

This day as every Sabbath since we have been in the Country, we went among the Natives, for these three last Lord's Days we have discoursed to a pretty large Congregation at <u>Manicktolla</u>- <u>Bazar</u>, or Market, for we have just the same Business done here on that day as any other - Our Congregation consisted principally of Muhammadans, and has increased every Lord's Day; they are very inquisitive; and we have addressed them upon the subject of the Gospel with the greatest freedom - and in the following manner - A Burial place, with a Consecrated tomb, where offerings are daily made to the spirit of the departed person was near, some enquiries about the reason of their offerings were made, which led on to questions on their part; and then the Gospel & the Koran, insensibly because the subject of Conversation; They alleged the Divine Original of the Koran; we enquired, have you ever seen or read it - The universal Answer was, no - but to day a Man came who pretended to have seen it - We asked him if he knew the beginning of every Chapter, for they all begin with these Words, "In the Name of God Gracious and Merciful"- but he said, no for it was written in *(end of page 11)* Arabic, and no one could understand it - the Question now was then, how can you Obey it? and wherefore are you Muhammadans? To this they could not reply - they said, & so says the Koran, that the Koran was sent to confirm the Words of Scripture, We insisted that the Bible said, Whosoever shall add to - or diminish from the Word of God shall be under the Curse of God, but the Koran was written after the Bible, and pretends to divine Authority - Therefore, if the Gospel be true Mohammed must be accursed, and the Koran of no Authority, and if the Bible be not true the Koran cannot for that you say was to confirm it - They answered, that the Jews, and Christians had corrupted the Bible, which was the reason why God made the revelation by Mohammed - We answered then how could the Koran come to confirm it, if it was corrupted it needed correction, not confirmation - being driven to their last shift, they said Mohammed was the Friend of God, but Esau, by whom they mean Jesus, was the Spirit of God - to which Munshi shrewdly replied, then which would think highest your Friend, or your Soul, or Spirit - all this they bore with great good temper; but what effect it may have time must determine - Many more things were said to recommend the Gospel, & the way of Life by Christ, and as night came on we left them -

20

This is a Day of Seeking Money, had an offer of a Bungalow belonging to the Company at Debhatta - till I can get a place made for myself & Family - so that it has been a day of Mercy, tho to my shame of Spiritual Barrenness -

21

Felt some pleasure in the Morning in Prayer to God, but all the rest of the Day was at an awful distance from God - This Evening I had a very profitable Conversation with Munshi about spiritual Things, and I do hope that he may one day be a very useful, and eminent Man; I am so well able to understand him, and he me that we are determined to begin correcting the Translation of Genesis tomorrow - *(end of page 12)*

22

Began the Correction of Genesis; I find a necessity of explaining many expressions which before I had taken no notice of. For instance, it is said that "God created the Heavens and the Earth", after which it is said "that the Earth was without Form"; This is not very intelligible in English, but in Bengali, is downright nonsense, because every thing must have some form or other, and if it had no form then it must necessarily be void or empty for it could not be filled, having no existence; to this I say that the Chaos or primitive Earth must be a Liquid Mass, there not having been any separation of Land & Water and that the meaning is that it had no settled Form, but was fluctuating like the Waves & Tide in the Sea - It is likewise said that God commandeth the "Earth to produce Grass, Herb yielding Seed, and the Fruit Tree yielding Fruit after its Kind - whose seed is in itself upon the Earth - By Grass is meant I suppose Vegetables in General, and what follows is an enumeration of the two great divisions of Vegetables, viz. Plants and Trees, for all except the English render "Grass". "Tender Herb" the expression whose seed is in itself, relates to the power of propagating their Species, (which is inherent in Vegetables which cannot move from their places,) without the conjunction of Male & Female which is necessary to the propagation of Animals - Otherwise it is not true that their seed is in themselves it being produced by them and some producing none at all; - this expression must relate to all Vegetables, & not to Fruit trees alone and should I think be whose seeds are in themselves in the Plural - but we have no plural in Bengali - therefore all is expressed by the Singular Number - I am full of perplexity about temporal things - but the Word of God is sure; which abundantly promises everything that I can want.

My Wife is within this day or two Relapsed into her affliction, and is much worse than she was before, but in the Mount of the Lord is seen - I wish I had but more of God in my Soul, and felt more submission in my Heart to his Will, this would set me above all things else - I feel happy however in this that I am in my Work, and that is the Work of God; and the more I am employed in it the more I find it a rich reward - *(end of page 13)*

23

This Day I feel what it is to have the testimony of a good Conscience, even in the smallest matters - my temporal troubles remain just as they were, I have a place, but cannot remove my Family to it for want of Money; [Mr. T. has now begun to set his Face another Way; at his motion I went to Calcutta, then to Bandel, at which place all our money was expended; he ordered all the Expences and lived in his own way, to which I acceded tho sore against my Will. He was inclined first, then determined to practice Surgery at Calcutta; I agreed to come & settle as near him as possible, Tho I had previously intended to go to Gowr near Malda, and all this and all, that I might not be first in a Breach of our mutual undertaking; now he is buying, & selling, and living at the Rate of I know not how much, I suppose 250 or 300 Rupees per Month; has 12 Servants, and this day is talking of keeping his Coach - I have remonstrated with him in vain, and I am almost afraid that he intends to throw up the Mission - how all those things can be agreeable to a spiritual Mind I know not - but now all my Friends, are but one.

I rejoice however that he is all sufficient and can supply all my wants, spiritual, and temporal, my Heart bleeds for him, for my Family, for the Society whose steadfastness must be shaken by this report, and for the success of Mission, which must receive a sad Blow from this; But why is my Soul disquieted within me, Things may turn out better than I expect, everything is known to God, and God cares for the Mission - O for Contentment, delight in God, and much of his fear before my Eyes - Bless God I feel peace within, and rejoice in having undertaken the Work, & shall, I feel I shall. If I now only labour alone, but even If I should lose my life in the undertaking - I anxiously desire the time when I shall so far know the Language as to preach in earnest to these poor people.] *(end of page 14)*

24

I wish to feel myself always in the exercise of a spirit of Meekness, but feel it hard work; - (Yesterday my mind was much hurt to see what I thought a degree of selfishness in my Friend which amounted to an almost total neglect of me, my family, and the Mission; Tho I don't think he seriously intends to neglect either; but inadvertently runs into such things as make it impossible to attend to either); this morning went to visit a professor of Religion to whom I was recommended at the Isle of Wight, but to my sorrow found him at Dice from thence went to visit the Rev. Mr. Brown; (he is an evangelical preacher of the Church of England, and received me with cool politeness; I staid near an Hour with him, found him a very sensible Man; but a marked Disgust prevails on both sides between him & Mr. T. [not wholly caused I fear on B's side]- He carried himself as greatly my superior and I left him without his having so much as asked me to take any refreshment tho he knew I had walked five Miles in the Heat of the Sun - To day found my mind more Calm, but the Evening was turbulent and Stormy.)

25

Was employed in buying some necessaries for our removal into the Wilderness; and after that was done, further engaged in correcting Genesis - There are some things that have no name in Bengali - being utterly unknown, as "Whales" - but found no very great difficulties to day - Have reason to bless God for a day of Quietness & Calmness, tho I must mourn over my Barrenness, and the strange stupidity of my Heart. I have abundant cause for Thankfulness, but an unthankful Heart. I feel pleasure in the Work and ways of God, but have a disobedient Soul - When will the Lord take full possession of my mind, and abide there for ever? - *(end of page 15)*

26

Lord's Day - all the Morning I had a most unpleasant time, but at last found much pleasure in reading Edwards on the Justice of God in the Damnation of Sinners, Then went to visit our Congregation of Natives again, they gave very great attention, and all the Mussulmen present (except the keeper of the consecrated place, and one or two fakins) acknowledged that the Offerings made to the Peer, or Soul of the dead Man, whose tomb was consecrated, were made without any Command, either in the Koran or elsewhere - The Person who acted as priest or keeper of the place; was so ashamed, when we told him that all the offerings were made to his Belly, that he went away - confounded with the Laughter of the People - Their inquisitiveness and numbers increase, and one Hindu appeared more than ordinarily anxious to know what was the right Way - I wish that we might see some good fruit of our Labours - and doubt not but we shall soon have some reason to rejoice in the Salvation of God -

27

This Morning went to Baliagut to procure a Boat to carry us over the Lakes, to the Place where we hope to go - (through the Delays of my Companion I have spent another Month and done scarce any thing; except that) I have added to my knowledge of the Language and had opportunity of seeing much more of the Genius and Disposition of the Natives, than I otherwise could have known. This day finished the correction of the first Chapter of Genesis, which Munshi says is rendered into very good Bengali; just as we had finished it a Pundit and another Man from Nuddea came to see me. I shewed it to them, and the Pundit seemed much pleased with the account of the Creation - only they have an imaginary place somewhere beneath the Earth and he thought that should have been mentioned likewise - I said that the Earth was a Planet, & that Heavens and Earth included all the Material Creation - there are several Minutia of Geography, & Chronology, which it is necessary *(end of page 16)* to explain, as they have many superstitious opinions which enter deeply into their System of Idolatry; thus they say that the World is composed of Seven Deeps or Lands, which are thus situated the small Circle - in the Middle is the Earth, the Black part is Bengal the Space round the Earth is Sea, they say 800,000 Miles wide then the Second Deep or Land included between the Circles, and marked Land, then Water 1,600,000 Miles wide, then Land etc. in duplicate proportion - till they have gone through the seven Deeps - I have only marked four of them - but the rest are easily conceived; and all their diversions are supposed to be as follow -

1	Jumbo	Deep	800,000
2	"	"	1,600,000
3	"	"	3,200,000
4	"	"	6,400,000
5	"	"	12,800,000
6	"	"	25,600,000
7	"	"	51,200,000

The Seas are of the same dimensions. Their Chronology is equally ridiculous. They reckon four Yugas, or ages of the World, each of which is terminated by a Deluge or some unusual Calamity, Three of which are already past. Viz. - the Sutty Yuga. Containing 2,688,000 Years. the Tratah 1,344,000, the Dauper 672,000 - and the Kali Yuga or present time, of which 4,896 years are already elapsed, and it is to continue 331,104 Years more - In all the former Yugas there were, they say four Castes of Hindus, but at the Commencement of the Kali Yuga two of them, Viz. the Bice, and Ketra were extinct, and now only two remain, Viz. the Brahman & Sudra; these accounts are so connected with their religious opinions that the Mosaic account of the Creation, and the Biblical Chronology are very new and strange to them - *{apparently someone added "See Dr. Robertson's Historical Disquisition concerning the Knowledge the Ancients had of India. Notes to his Appendix. p. 361}*

28

This Morning at Calcutta - again disappointed about Money - was much dejected and grieved, advised with Munshi, who is my trusty Friend, but could find no settled plan - In the Evening had much relief in reading over Mr. Fuller's Charge to us at Leicester - The Affection there manifested almost overcame my spirits, for I have not been accustomed to Sympathy of Late - O I think again I am not only ready to be offered, so as to suffer any thing - But if I be offered, upon the service & sacrifice of the Faith I Joy & rejoice in it - O what a portion is God, and what a shame that I am not always satisfied with him - *(end of page 17)*

29

This has been a day of Calmness, but the Calm has been rather of the unprofitable kind. I may rather call it a day of Idleness, than any thing else, have spent part of it in my study of Bengali - and yet no communion with God, which only can produce comfortable reflection at night - Had a very pleasant Evening in studying and criticising upon the second Chapter of Genesis - and comparing the different Lections & renderings - There is an obscurity in the Phrase "Created & made", occasioned by departing from the Hebrew, which is "created to make" - that is created the Original matter, in order that he might modify & adorn it, in the manner in which it now is, thus most render it. The 4, 5, & 6 verses appear to be designed to recapitulate the Work of Creation, and to shew that antecedent to the existence of second Causes, God produced everything by his own power - I have rendered it like the English except the 6 Verse, where I have followed, Junius, Tremellius, and many others, in continuing the Negation of second Causes, & have rendered it thus Or vapor ascending from the earth which might water the face of the Ground - the Hebrew will bear this quite as well as But - &ct. - and it seems more consonant to the design of the narration -

30

The Blessings of the Gospel are far greater than we can think unless we discourse with those who never had them - This Evening I had a conversation with the Munshi about his first opinions concerning God - He told me that when he first began to know a few English Words, God & Lord were the first, but for some time he supposed God Almighty, to be a Female, and God's Wife - But his Ideas of Angels were much more consistent than those of our Artists - Seeing a picture in which an Angel was represented, he made this enquiry - Sir, are Angels women or Birds, I see they have got Feathers, therefore they must be Birds; and then I can see them, and catch them. Now we think that they are great Powers which can go any where in an instant without Wings; or any such Helps - these simple enquiries were put to Mr. Udney, as soon as he became acquainted with Mr. T. He is now much hurt at seeing pretended pictures of God, or the Holy Spirit with wings like a Dove, and many of those representations in Cuts with the Bible are to him & others who are still Heathen a very great stumbling Block - *(end of page 18)*

Two Pages back I mentioned the Chronology of the Hindus, and observed that they reckoned four Yugas - in the last of which we now are - but now I understand that these Yugas have been several times repeated like the Days of the Week, and that at the end of Kali Yuga, the Sutty Yuga will begin again &ct. - Thus they reckon the four Yugas make one Dribbyo Yuga and 71 Dribbyo Yugas make one Monoo - 71 Monoo - one Monoostro and 71 Monoostro make two Hours of Birmmha* [*24 Minutes is on Bengal Hour, & 60 Hours a Day] - 15 of which make one day, thirty Days one Month, twelve Months one Year, and every 100 such years of Birmmha there is an entire destruction of all the Material World, which being afterwards renovated goes thro the same round for Sixty such Years more & then is again dissolved, & so ad infinitum - Such is their opinion which if it was only opinion would be scarce deserving confutation, but it is connected with their notions of Transmigration of Souls, and several other superstitious opinions - Calm to day, and felt pleasure in prayer tonight -

31

A Day of Vexation Barrenness and worse than Nothing.

Feb. 1

Spent to day in preparations for our departure on Monday to the intended place of our Residence, was very weary, having walked in the Sun about 15 or 16 Miles - Yet had the satisfaction of discoursing with some Money Changers at Calcutta who could speak English, about the importance, and absolute necessity of Faith in the Lord Jesus Christ - One of them was a very crafty Man and tried much to entangle me with hard Questions, but at last finding himself entangled, he desisted and went to his old occupation of money Changing again - If once God would by his Spirit convince of Sin, a Saviour would be a Blessing indeed to them; but Human Nature is the very same all the world over; and all Conviction fails except it is produced by the effectual working of the Holy Spirit. *(end of page 19)*

2

A day of Barrenness and unprofitableness.

3

Spent in removing our little Furniture &ct. to Baliagut where we were to go on Board our Boats, which we effected by almost Eight at Night - had but little Communion with God to day -

4

Proceeded on our Journey through Salt Rivers & a Large Lake. In the Afternoon saw an Offering made to the Goddess of Learning, viz. of Writing and reading - The Idol was placed under a Shed, and all around her, for I believe it is a Female - were placed large Dishes full of Rice, Fruits &ct. - which the People had Brought. The Brahman was employed in laying the Whole in Order, after which a little was distributed to the attendants, and the Brahman had the rest - the whole was attended with Horrid Music - and the next day the Idol was to be thrown into the River. I felt very much concerned for these poor People but could not speak to them -

5

There not being Water enough for us to go the nearest way we were necessitated to go through the Sundarbans, which is a very large impenetrable Forest only intersected with large Rivers by which our Boats went, these Forests are some Hundreds of Miles in Extent, and entirely uninhabited by Man - they Swarm with Tygers, Leopards, Rhinoceroses, Deer, Buffaloes, &ct.; I thought I heard the Roar of a Tyger in the Night but am uncertain, had a little sweet pleasure in meditation in this place, but no one dares go on shore, so as to venture an Hundred Yards from the Boat -

6

Arrived early in the Morning at Debhatta where the Company have a Bungalow, *{inserted by someone "a very generous or Friendly Gentleman"}* the person whose name is Mr. Short who resides there to superintend the Salt Works immediately sent to me, & invited my whole Family to stay there, till our own House is finished - Here therefore we are at present, and he, tho an utter Stranger to me, (& to all Godliness) insists upon supplying all our wants while here - *(end of page 20)*

7

Had but little pleasure, tho much Leisure, it has been a Day of Lassitudes, and Dullness -

8

Went the Morning to Hashnabad where I expected to have Land, I had the choice of the whole Country; and at last pitched upon a place at Collatullah , which is a fine Soil - and Pleasant Situation, and nearly opposite to the Place where I now am, on the other side of the River - Several Villages are in the Neighborhood, and provisions as Cheap as at any place in Bengal - the River Jubona separates us from Debhatta [which is as large as the Hooghly at Calcutta]

9, 10, 11, 12, 13

Employed at Hashnabad in Building me an House, all these days except the first which was Sabbath my mind is tranquil, but alas not spiritual, too much employed and taken up about necessary things - From that time to the 23 employed in the same work; I met with great kindness from Mr. Short with whom I am (but he is a Stranger to Religion and I cannot, therefore, enjoy that freedom which I could at home -) my Soul is Barren, and absorbed in temporal things - Lord enlarge my Heart.

March 1

After having been employed in building me an House and almost finished it, I received an invitation this day to go up to Malda, to superintend an Indigo manufactory - This appearing to be a remarkable opening in divine providence for our comfortable support I accepted it so that we are still unsettled but I only wait to receive another Letter in order to set off this Long Journey of 250 Miles with all my Family. *(end of page 21)*

2, 3, 4

In this state of uncertainty nothing but suspence and vacancy of Mind is experienced, and tho I have the great pleasure of hoping that the mission may be abundantly forwarded by having a number of the Natives under my immediate inspection, and at the same time my family be well provided for, tho I have no doubt respecting provision even here. Yet a too great part of my time must have been necessarily employed in managing my little farm with my own hands; I shall likewise be joined with my Colleague again, and we shall unitedly engage in our Work; O that my soul was not so barren, and unfruitful in the work and Ways of God.

5

Still I mourn my Barrenness, and the foolish wanderings of my mind, surely I shall never be of any use among the Heathen. I feel so very little of the life of godliness in my own Soul: It seems as if all the sweetness that I have formerly felt was gone, neither am I distressed, but a guilty calm is spread over my soul, and I seem to spend all my time and make no progress towards the desired port either in a publick or private way - I am full of necessities yet am not distressed, I want Wisdom to know how to direct all my concerns, and fortitude, and affectionate concern for the glory of God, and Faith and holiness in all its Branches, then my soul would be like a well managed Garden, but now it is a mere Jungle - *(end of page 22)*

6

This day I feel much remains of my past carelessness and absorption in the affairs of the World, tho somewhat more of an inclination to the things of God than for some time back. I hope my soul like a pendulum, tho it swings to and fro about the necessary things of the World, yet can rest no where but in its Center, God, and I trust I feel that there is an inclination to rest there. O When shall I serve God uninterruptedly and pursue every other thing in a subserviency to his divine Will, and in such a manner as to commune with him in every thing that I do -

7

In the morning had a very miserable unhappy time for some Hours; O What a Body of Death do I carry about, how little can I bear how little patience have I under the contradictions I meet with; and the afflictions I meet how little are they sanctified; Instead of growing in grace I almost conclude myself to be destitute of the Grace of

God at all; How can a Wretch like me ever expect to be of use to the Heathen when I am so carnal myself -

8

Felt much remains of Dullness, and indisposition to the things of God. I see now of the Value of Christian Society. - - When I had that advantage I have often felt that visiting a friend was like throwing Oil upon the fire, or like as Iron sharpeneth Iron, so have the Countenances of my friends stirred me up to an holy activity and diligence in the things of God; Towards Evening however had some more enjoyment, and felt a little drawn forth in prayer to God. *(end of page 23)*

9

This has been one of the most pleasant Sabbaths that I have ever enjoyed since I have been in this Country. Spent most of the Day in Family Exercises, particularly had much enjoyment in reading Edward's Sermon upon, "The manner in which the salvation of the Soul is to be sought" - through the Whole Day enjoyed pleasure & Profit -

10

Felt some Drawings of Soul after God, and prayer has especially been pleasant; the Study of a Language tho a Dull Work, yet is productive of Pleasure to me, because it is my Business, and necessary to my preaching in any useful manner, - the Soul and Spirit of preaching must be wanting unless one has some Command of Language -

11

I begin to find my soul more at home, the multiplicity of other things which I have been forced to attend to, had drawn my mind from God: and employed it too much upon the World - but now I begin to feel again that to live after the Flesh, or to myself is entirely contrary to the spirit of the Gospel, and that no happiness, or usefulness is to be expected unless we live near to God -

12

I am very defective in all Duties; both with respect to the manner; and Matter of them; in Prayer I wander, and am formal; not having that <quiet> lively sense of my Wants which is necessary to wrestling with God; I ask for Blessings, yet seem almost contented to go without obtaining them, I soon tire, Devotion Languishes; and I don't Walk with God, - considering myself always as in his Light. O what a mercy it is to live near to him; and to realize his perfections, and relations to us Constantly - *(end of page 24)*

13

A Day of Sacred Pleasure; the Conversion of the Heathen & the setting up of Christ's Kingdom has been a pleasant theme of Contemplation.

14

Dullness and Peevishness, with a sense of Guilt on my Mind -

15

In this Wilderness O how my Soul wanders, I thirst, but find nothing to Drink - O Lord I beseech thee Deliver my soul -

16

Such another Sabbath I hope I never shall pass - What a Hell it would be to be always with those who fear not God; as is the Case with the Benevolent Man with whom I reside - This is one of the Bengal Holidays, and in the Afternoon a Number of People [smeared over their Heads with Red Powder,] who had been to celebrate the Obitar or incarnation of Krishna, returned and danced & played their Idolatrous tricks before the Door - O how much more Zealous are Idolaters than Christians! I suppose that not less than 10,000 People met at the Temple of Krishna, many of whom had traveled 20 or 30 Miles to Worship - and this is the Case all over the Country - and upon one of these Holidays many of the Rich spend perhaps a Lack or 100,000 Rupees, and they would rather undergo the greatest distress than Labour upon these Days - Tho the most timid people on the Earth at other times, Yet now they are Enthusiastic, Intrepid, and Fearless. *(end of page 25)*

17

Still Low and dejected, preparing for our Journey to Malda, near 300 Miles; this unsettles my mind again and makes me Careful about this present World perhaps too much -

18

Barren in my Soul, O that it was with me as in Months past -

19

Had a little pleasure in Divine things and in the Evening conversed with a Carnal Man about the Things of God - and in vain endeavored to press the importance of Seriousness.

20

A most unhappy Day; Yet much affected with some instances of true Generosity in my Munshi such as I am sure would have done Honour to the most eminent Christian in the World.

21

The Conversion of the Heathens is the Object which above all others I wish to pursue; yet a Long Course of unforseen things and Changing Circumstances have hitherto prevented my making that active Effort which I wish - I however am daily employed in Learning the Language, and as Munshi can understand a Considerable deal of English, we are going over with Mr. Thomas' Translation of Genesis - I find this both a pleasing and profitable employment, - and now begin to see that the Bengali is a Language which is very Copious, and abounds with Beauties. If my Situation at Malda should be tolerable I most certainly will publish the Bible in Numbers. *(end of page 26)*

22

Still in suspence, waiting in Daily Expectation of a Letter from Malda to direct how we may go up, how much pleasure oftentimes in Conversation with Munshi - In this Country there is he informs me something similar to the Scriptural Demoniac - They Call the Spirits of bad Men departed, Bhuta, and say that oftentimes when a Woman walks near the Woods the Bhuta Comes from some tree and possesses her, - upon which she becomes in a manner insane. A man of Learning is employed to expel the Demon, which is performed in the following manner; he repeats by Heart the substance of some Book, and then commands the Bhuta to go out; Upon his refusing, he threatens to Flog him out, and then draws with his Finger the Figure of a Woman upon the Earth, which he beats most Violently, till at last the Bhuta begins to Capitulate, and declares that he will go; and directs the Learned Man to take some very heavy Weight, as a large Jar of Water, or the Like which the Woman is commanded to Lift with her teeth; After much labour she performs this Task, and immediately swoons; Then the Learned Person, by Command of the Bhuta, Calls her three or four Times, and she revives; but if he appoints Ten or twelve Times she dies; he also gives a Sign that when he goes out, such a Tree or some Branches thereof shall Fall, and the Woman immediately recovers *(end of page 27)*

They say that the Bhuta causes the Woman to pronounce his words, in a Whining tone; What this singular thing may be I cannot tell. Munshi says that he has often seen it, and I am determined to investigate it. If true, it is, like the Indian Powowing, a striking Proof of the Power which the Devil exercises even over the Bodies of People in Countries wholly under his Dominion, and must be a Compleat Answer to all the objections which Socinians or others make to the Scripture account of Demoniacs -

23

Lord's Day - Enjoyed much happiness in reading to, and instructing my Family; had much pleasure and a revival of ancient Friendship in my soul by reading dear Mr. Ryland's Circular Letter on Zeal - but sorely feel the Loss of those publick opportunities which I enjoyed in England, hope however to have something more to do for God at Malda -

24

Devoted in some measure to God: but O how little is my Will swallowed up in God's; Long Delay, and Unsettledness have filled me with discouragement; & drank up my Spirit - but I feel some rising Composure in reflecting that all my times are in the Hand of God; This Evening was enabled to contend for the Truth as it is in Jesus (with my Host - O that God would requite his kindness to us by converting his Soul). *(end of page 28)*

25, 26, 27, 28

Days spent in a Mixture of Pleasure and Pain, and every Day in Expectation of being removed from hence - I am loaded with Civility from the kind Mr. Short (but am ashamed to receive the tokens of his friendship -) Was it not that my Wife is so ill to be unable to sustain the fatigue of an incommodious Voyage to Malda, I would set out at any Rate - (but) as it is I cannot till Mr. Thomas sends me a Letter - I rejoice to find and feel that all my times are in the Hand of God; O What must those <persons> undergo in affliction, if their Consciences are at all awake, who have no sense of the infinite Wisdom and Goodness which order all things here below - but eyeing a Covenant God I can say with Exultation, tho the Fig Tree should not blossom, and there be no fruit in the Vine, tho the Labour of the Olive should fail and the Herds be cut off from the Stall, Yet will I glory in God, I will rejoice in the God of my Salvation - - *(end of page 29)*

29

Through mistake spent this Day as the Sabbath, I have however abundant reason to be thankful for the mistake, it has been a time of refreshing indeed to me; O what is there in all this World worth living for but the presence and service of God - I feel a burning desire that all the World may know this God and serve him - O how long will it be till I shall know so much of the Language of the Country as to preach Christ Crucified to them: but bless God I make some progress.

30

To Day had not so much enjoyment as yesterday but it has been a Day of Profit, (tho some accidental circumstances rather tended to discompose us, accounts came that one of the Judges of Appeal, and one of the Salt Agents are coming upon a Visit to the House where we are in consequence of which all is Hurry and Bustle to prepare for them - O how little do carnal men set by the Sabbath).

31

A Day of Hard Labour at Bengali; and I trust some enjoyment in Divine things - this Evening the long expected Letter from Malda arrived at which my Heart was Made glad - the Prospect of reunion with my Colleague and of our being so provided for as to carry on the work of printing the Bible - gladdens my Heart - I am resolved to write to the Society that my Circumstances are such that I do not need future help from them and to devote a sum *(end of page 30)* monthly for the printing *{of}* the Bengali Bible.

Apr 1, 2, 3

These three Days have not all been favourable to the Growth of Grace. The Company of four of the first Gentlemen in the Settlement tho Civil, Genteel, and kind is yet unfriendly to the Work of God within - However this good End is answered, I become more known, and have assurances that even the Officers of Government will help me in the Work which I am engaged in - tho this Cause I am well assured will thrive without any of their Help, however if offered I think it would be criminal to reject any thing that may tend to the advancement of the Work, and the Comfort of my Family - Tho nothing yields me more pleasure than the prospect of Mr. Thomas and I being reunited in the Work (and particularly as he has of his own accord written to me that he knows his conduct at Calcutta was wrong, and he was desperately drinking into the Spirit of the World; to the destruction of Godliness).

4

This Day very much dejected, my own Barrenness and the providential Delays which I meet with, are a weight which depresses My soul, I make so little progress in the Bengali Language, and am so unsettled and so Barren that it seems as if I should never be of any use at all - Yet I think I am too impatient, O that God would make me wholly resigned to his Will in all things. *(end of page 31)*

5

How Wicked is the Heart of Man, and what a Curse must it be to be wholly under its wicked Dominion; then all mercies are repelled; all privileges neglected, and all God's Authority slighted; This awful Spirit so prevails in me that I can scarcely tell whether I have the Grace of God or not, if I have it how very low is the Degree, and if not - then how shall I teach others; I can scarce determine - but be as it may, I am resolved to spend & be spent in the Work of my Lord Jesus Christ.

6

Had some sweetness to day; especially in reading Edward's Sermon, "the Most High a Prayer hearing God" - What a spirit of genuine piety flows thro all that great Man's Works - I hope I have caught a little fresh fire to Day - but how desirable, and important is it that God would constantly fan the heavenly Flame - I need abundance of Grace in order to communicate divine things to others, but to my Comfort God has said "He that believeth on me, <u>out of</u> his Belly shall <u>flow</u> rivers of living Waters", no doubt meaning that Faith is a Communicative principle, & that true believers will as naturally speak of the things of God, as a Fountain cast forth streams of Water, I wish I could speak so as to be understood, I can say a little, but not sufficient to answer the Objectives brought against the Gospel - *(end of page 32)*

7

Bless God I have enjoyed some pleasure in God to Day and <spent the Evening in a long Dispute with my friendly Host, was enabled, through Mercy to be faithful and

speak of the necessity of Faith in Christ in order to salvation - This was called illiberal and uncharitable; as it excluded Unbelievers, and eventually adjudged the Heathens to Eternal Misery. I argued that I was no more uncharitable than the Bible, and that if that was the Case, God would appear Gloriously Just - But my Friend is a Deist - tho not hardy enough to avow it. I can see that he is glad of every thing that he can think of to invalidate the Bible. I feel a pleasure in being Valiant for the truth, and much wish that God would convert his Soul, he is indeed a Kind and Hospitable man.

8

A Day of Business, Hurry, Sorrow, and Dejection; I seem cast out of the Christian World, and unable yet to speak to the heathens to any advantage - and daily disappointment discourages my Heart - I not only have no friend to stir me up, or encourage me in the Things of God but every discouragement arising from my Distance from Mr. Thomas; the infidelity of Europeans - who all say that the Conversion of the Natives is impossible *(end of page 33)* and the stupid superstition of the Native themselves; In England I should not be discouraged by what Infidels say, but here I have not the Blessing of a Christian friend to sympathize with me, nor the Ability to make the trial of preaching the Gospel. All my hope is in, and all my comfort arises from God; without his power no European could possibly be converted, and his power can convert any Indian, and when I reflect that he has stirred me up to the Work, and wrought wonders to prepare the Way I can hope in his promises, and am encouraged & strengthened.

This Day the Horrid Custom of Self tormenting among the Natives begun. A Machine is constructed of Bamboo perhaps twenty feet High from which they precipitate themselves upon Iron spikes, which run into their Breasts, or any other part. I did not know this Horrid thing being transacting till it was over, and therefore had not the opportunity of seeing it - but the servants came and told us, my oldest son also saw it. *(end of page 34)*

9

To Day self tormenting was carried to a greater length than Yesterday - A number of people came near to our Gate with Drums, and Dancing; when presently a Man had two pieces of Bamboo - of twenty feet Long, and each as thick as a Man's finger, these were passed through his sides - and held at each end by two Men; while he danced backwards and forwards in a manner almost frantic, but seemingly insensible to pain - to prevent the violent heat arising from the Rubbing of the Bamboos in the Wound, a man stood to throw water continually upon his sides. This mad practice was continued for an Hour at least, and several others, with long Spits run through their tongues which they were continually drawing up and down, stood dancing by his side, to the sound of their Horrid Music - this was continued through the whole Day.

10

To Day the Cursed mode of Self torturing was varied, a large pole was erected and a Bamboo fixed cross upon the Top, and the Swinging by Hook fixed in the Back was attended to; I went out to see it, and the Man dressed in a blue Cloth like a petty coat was suspended at the Height of twenty feet was swinging rapidly round, presently they stopped turning the *(end of page 35)* Machine, and asked him to come down, which he refused, and insisted upon being whirled round again. I suppose he was thus suspended for half an hour, during which time his looks were perfectly placid and serene, and he rattled a few twigs tied up in a Bunch - He then set his feet upon the top of three Bamboos tied like the Piquet when a Soldier stands Sentry - where the Cord was unloosed, he then descended with the Hooks in his Back and came just before me to shew me how they were fastened. When they were drawn out A man placed his two Knees against the Wounds and holding him over the Breast pushed the wounds with his knees in such a Manner as almost to dislocate the Shoulder Blades - a leaf or two were applied, and the hooks fixed in another, who ascended the Ladder or Picquet, where the Cord was fastened and he underwent the same Operation - Those who torment themselves in any of these manners repeat it annually on these Days, which are the three last Days of their Year, and the only days when these Operations are performed - *(end of page 36)* These tortures are only practised by the lowest Castes of the People; the Brahmans, and Caesto, or Writers never practise it; and they say that Seeb *{Shiva?}* one of their Deities appears to them, Comforts them, and tells them whatsoever they do, or suffer for his sake, will be abundantly recompensed after Death - During these three Days they fast and spend the time in frantically parading the streets and playing upon their Barbarous Music -

11

On this Day the Hindus keep a day of Gladness and feasting, being the first Day of their Year - they, nor their Cattle do any kind of Work, but spend the time in Singing, and Joy - Indeed these Horrid and Idolatrous transactions have made such an impression on my mind that I think cannot be easily eradicated - Who would grudge to spend his life, and his all, to deliver an (otherwise) Amiable People, from the misery and darkness of their present wretched state, and how should we prize that Gospel which has delivered us from hell, and our Country from such dreadful marks of Satan's Cruel Dominion as these. *(end of page 37)*

12

Nothing but Care, Worldliness, and Anxiety to Day - may it be buried in Oblivion-

13

Lord's Day, this has been a Day of real enjoyment to my Soul, and of true profit. I think that if it was not for some opportunities of this nature the Wheel of religion would be entirely Clogged; but these seasons of refreshing now Oil them, and I move on again -

14

Still a time of Enjoyment of God; I feel that it is good to commit my Soul, my Body, and my all into the Hands of God, Then the World appears little, the Promises great; and God an allsufficient Portion.

15

Bless God that his presence is not departed, this Evening during the approach of a Violent Storm of Thunder, I walked alone and had sweet Converse with God in Prayer; O I longed to have all my Fetters knocked off that I might Glorify God without hindrance either Natural or Moral. *(end of page 38)*

16

A Day of Wretchedness, in which my wickedness seemed to be let loose against me. O What a Fountain of Vileness is my Heart - and how desperately wicked is my Nature - Can such a Wretch as I ever expect to be of any use? I think not -

17

Begun with Turbulence and wretchedness of Mind, and so continued - neither could I draw near to God, Great Mountains of Guilt, and Shame blocked up the Way of My Access to God; O Wretched Man that I am - who shall deliver me from the Body of this Death -

18

Tumultuous in the beginning but afterwards More Calm - Yet a Burden of Guilt is not easily removed - nothing short of Infinite Power and Infinite Goodness can remove such a Load as mine. O that I had but a Smiling God, or an Earthly Friend to whom I could unbosom my soul - but My Friend is at a Great Distance; and God Frowns upon my Soul - O may his Countenance be lifted upon me again - *(end of page 39)*

19

O How glorious are the Ways of God. My Soul longeth, and Fainteth for God, for the living God - to see his glory and Beauty as I have seen them in the Sanctuary - When I first left England my hope of the Conversion of the Heathen was very strong, but among so many Obstacles it would entirely die away, unless upheld by God - nothing to exercise it, but many things to obstruct it for now a Year and 19 Days, which is the space since I left my dear Charge at Leicester. Since that I have had hurrying up and down; a five months imprisonment with carnal Men on board the Ship, five more learning the Language; my Munshi not understanding English sufficiently to interpret my preaching - [My Family my accusers, and hinderers,] My Colleague separated from me, Long delays, and few opportunities for Social Worship - no Woods to retire to like Brainerd for fear of Tygers (no less than 20 Men in the department of Debhatta where I am, have been carried away by them this Season from the Salt works) - no Earthly thing to depend upon, or Earthly

Comfort; except *(end of page 40)* Food and Raiment; Well I have God, and his Word is sure; and the Superstitions of the Heathen were a Million times more deeply rooted - and the Examples of Europeans, a Million times Worse than they are; if I were deserted by all, and persecuted by all. Yet my hope, fixed on that sure Word will rise superior to all obstructions, and Triumph over all trials; God's Cause will triumph, and I shall come out of all trials as Gold purified by fire - Was much humbled today by reading Brainerd - O What a Disparity betwixt me and him; he always Constant, I unconstant as the Wind -

20

Began the Day with uncomfortable expectations, and heart breaking views of Wretchedness, Pride, and unmortified Affections within, and Confusing appearance without, yet notwithstanding I enjoyed a very Comfortable Day; I had much pleasure in instructing my Family, and found my soul drawn out in desires for the salvation of my Children. Blessed be God for this Day - *(end of page 41)*

21

Had some holy pleasure in instructing my family to Day; and blessed be God the Translation of the Bible advances, we now go through nearly a Chapter every Day - tho now I find that all which Mr. T. did at Sea is nothing. We go it all over again, and Compare it with the several Versions which I have - I have also hope that in a few Weeks, I shall be able to speak so much of the Language as to begin to preach to the Natives - Munshi says in about a Month I may be able to be understood -

22

Bless God for a Continuance of the Happy frame of Yesterday - I think the Hope of soon acquiring the Language puts fresh life into my Soul, for a long time my mouth has been shut, and my days have been beclouded with Heaviness - but now I begin to be something like a traveller who has been almost beat out in a Violent Storm; and who with all his Clothes about him dripping wet, sees the sky begin to Clear, so I with only the prospect of a more pleasant Season at hand, scarce feel the sorrows of the present - *(end of page 42)*

23

With all the Cares of Life and all its Sorrows, Yet I find that a Life of Communion with God is sufficient to yield Consolation in the midst of all and even to produce a holy Joy in the Soul which shall make it to triumph over all affliction; I have never yet repented of any Sacrifice that I have made for the Gospel, but find that consolation of mind which can come from God alone.

24

Still a Continuance of the same tranquil state of Mind; outwardly the Sky lowrs but within I feel the Soul's calm sunshine and the heart felt joy. Hope more strangely operates as the time of my being able to speak for Christ approaches; and I feel like a long confined Prisoner whose chains are knocked off, in order to his liberation. *(end of page 43)*

25

Blessed be God for Continuation of his mercy to me this Day. I feel a Calm, serious frame of heart, but yet have cause to mourn the want of a Contemplative mind; things come, and go, and seem to make but very little impression upon my heart, O what need I have of a Spirit of importunate intercession with God; I pray for divine Blessings, yet rest too well contented without obtaining them -

26

I spend some pleasant Hours with Munshi almost every Day - have much pleasure to see him turn his Back upon Idolatry; and laugh at the superstitions of the Hindus; I wish sincerely that he had but a little more of the Zeal of the Old Christians; but while I rejoice in his judgement of Divine things; I am grieved at his timorousness; and strong attachment to his Caste, which he looks upon notwithstanding as Chains forged by the Devil, to hold the Hindus in Slavery - had a pleasant Day in my own Soul - *(end of page 44)*

27

Some lowering circumstances served to distress me this Morning, and threatened to spoil all the Comfort of the Whole Day - but blessed be God I found him a Sufficient Friend; and a sufficient Portion, had much pleasure, and Affection in instructing my Family and have seen some such impressions upon my two Eldest Children, as are matter of great encouragement to me; O that they may be followed up by God to good purpose.

28

How much I long for the Arrival of the Europe Ships; surely I shall receive a large packet by them. I want to hear of the Society, of the Ministers, and Churches. I want to see the Circular Letters, Mr. Fuller's Piece- Rippon's Registers - &ct. and to hear how my dear, dear Friends at Leicester go on. Wonder whether they have a Minister, What he is, whether he is beloved or not, whether Judicious, and useful or not; - I want to know the Affairs of Europe, O my Friends, my dear Friends, I long for all the Communion with you that our distance can allow - *(end of page 45)*

29

This has been a time of abundant Mercy to me in every respect. My Soul has been strengthened, and enlightened; I only want an Heart endowed with Gratitude and Love; I want to be filled with a sense of the mercy of Heaven, and to feel my Heart warmed with a hearty regard to him and all his ways, I find great reason to fear lest I should contract an unfeeling carnal form of Godliness without the Power -

30

I have reason to bless God for all the Benefits with which he loads me - O how apt we are to overlook all his goodness, and all his Beauty, and to dwell on those parts of our Experience which are dreary, and discouraging, but I feel that the Light Afflictions, and momentary Sorrows which I endure diminish in their Bulk and lose their Nature while we look not at temporal but at Eternal things; While concerned about temporal things I see all temporal troubles magnify themselves; and on the Contrary when I see the Beauty of Holiness; & the importance of my work; All that I have to meet with in the prosecution of the Work disappears and is scarcely perceptible - *(end of page 46)*

May 1

Still some Rays of Sunshine dart upon my Soul, and I can say with the Apostle Thanks be to God, who comforteth us in all our tribulation. And yet I can derive no comfort from the sources that other people commonly do; [I have none of those helps and encouragements from my family of Friends that many have - they are rather enemies to the work that I have undertaken but tho I find it extremely difficult to know how to act with propriety, and sometimes perhaps act indiscreetly,] yet I find that support in God which I can find no where else, and perhaps these trials are designed to put me upon trusting in and seeking Happiness from the Lord alone - This Evening the Mussulmen were all looking out for the New Moon, which was the time of Mohamed's Birth. All the Last Month, which they call the Moon Ramadan they have fasted all day long, and none of them eat anything till the sun is set - but this Moon Ushers in a time of Gladness and Joy to them - *(end of page 47)*

2

Still I have reason to bless God for serenity and Composure of Soul, but the state in which I am is such as precludes me from Action; and almost discourages me - yet Blessed be God the translation goes on - and I find much pleasure in the prospect of being able to print it soon -

3

My life is attended with very little Variety, I fear that a wretched coldness is growing upon me, and hope that almighty power may prevent it - living at another man's table I have no time or opportunity for fasting and Prayer, which my soul greatly needs -

4

I have had considerable sweetness to day in duty and particularly in reading some part of Witherspoon on Regeneration; I have frequently feared that a Day would end in wretchedness, when the Lord has cleared my skies; and I have felt the Sun of Righteousness arise with healing under his Wings - *(end of page 48)*

5

But little Heart for God, and heavenly things, however we translated a Chapter - and I found some pleasure in that work and in the Evening had a long conversation with two or three Hindus about the things of God. I first shewed them a translation of the ten Commandments, with which they were much delighted: I tried then to make them understand how contrary the second Commandment was to their practice - and as I could tried to tell them of the sinful, helpless state of man - and the willingness of God to save - but my imperfect knowledge of the Language makes me liable to mistake their meaning when they speak - and to be misunderstood by them-

6-7

Went on a visit to Myhattee about 18 or 20 Miles off - was not entirely destitute of spiritual reflection - but tired and wearied with the Journey - having been up part of two Nights - the Wind being contrary to us as we returned - *(end of page 49)*

8

Munshi is employed in preparing Boats to carry us up the River to Malda - the translation stands still - and my Soul is awfully Barren - O what a Wilderness I am without God, may he soon restore to me the light of his Countenance -

9-10, 11

Days of Guilty Vacancy. I never can enjoy peace of Conscience long, if my time is not filled up for God - and I wish to find much less. The second of these days I spent almost wholly with an Oreeha *{Ooriya?}* Bramin - who gave me the Oreeha or Orissa Alphabet.

12

A Sabbath not quite unprofitable, but attended rather with perplexity than any enjoyment. I hope the Sabbath above will more than compensate for the loss of so many below - and I hope not to have many more such as these on Earth - God grant that I may see much more the Beauty of his Ways - *(end of page 50)*

13 -14 -15

Days that have accumulated my Guilt for I have done nothing for God and what is worse have no desire, or scarcely any - O what a Blessing is the Gospel which provides a Saviour, and a Sanctifier-

16

Tempestuous without; but blessed be God Calm and Serene within - O what are all earthly pleasures, or pains if we have God's Presence - and that which is its companion, the testimony of a good Conscience that in simplicity, and Godly Sincerity, we have had our conversation in this World.

17

Feel very much degenerated in my Soul, scarce any heart for God, but a careless indolence possesses my Spirit and makes me unfit for anything - I need much of the presence of God to conquer indolence, to which the Heat of the Country probably contributes; but my own disposition would much nourish it - tho I bless God that I never enjoyed better health. *(end of page 51)*

18

I hope that not many days will be spent like this, Expect our Boats this night and hope we may even go one tide towards Malda.

19

A Sabbath almost fruitless, I think, that I never saw so much of my Ignorance as now - and very distressing circumstances have put my wisdom to the Proof and feel myself to possess very little indeed, but the gracious declaration and promise in James - "If any man lack &ct". is, when considered as the Word of a Faithful God, like Balm to my Soul.

20, 21, 22

Have been days of Delay, and Barrenness to my soul - I think that I have too much impatience under disappointments; Yet I can in general feel a pleasure in thinking that my times are in the hand of God and that whatsoever becomes of me Yet he will be glorified at last.

23

This Morning at three o'clock set out on our journey to Malda, which is about 300 miles - and will take us up about three Weeks. I feel thankful to God for thus providing, and also that now we have a place of our own - tho not an house but a Boat - my Sister stays behind us - *(end of page 52)*

24

On the River Jubona, passed Baddareea and have felt that satisfaction and pleasure, which I have for a long time been a Stranger to But I long for fresh anointing with the Spirit of God.

25

Arrived at Chandareea on the River Isamuty - my Soul somewhat more barren than Yesterday - towards Evening I felt myself rather more drawn towards God, especially when I was surrounded by a large body of the Natives at this Place. I had a little talk with a few of them, but found myself much at a loss for Words - however I find myself begin to improve in the knowledge of the Hindu Language. It is a considerable disadvantage that two Languages are spoken all over the Country, the Brahmans and Caestes or Caests speak Bengali, and the Common People Hindustani - I understand a little of both and hope to be the master of both but in this I need Wisdom from above and in all things else - *(end of page 53)*

26

This day kept Sabbath at Chandareea - had a pleasant Day - in the Morning and Afternoon addressed my family - and in the Evening began my Work of publishing the Word of God to the Heathen, tho imperfect in the knowledge of the Language yet with the help of Munshi I conversed with two Brahmans in the presence of about 200 People about the things of God. I had been to see a Temple in which were the Images of Dukkinroy, the God of the Woods riding on a Tyger, Sheetulla goddess of the Smallpox without an Head, riding on a horse without a Head, Punchanon with large Ears, and Colloray riding on a Horse, in another apartment was Seeb which was only a smooth Post of Wood with two or three Mouldings in it like the Base of a Tuscan Pillar - I therefore discoursed with them upon the Vanity of Idols - the folly and wickedness of Idolatry, and the Nature & Attributes of God, and the Way of Salvation by Christ -

One Brahman was quite confounded, and a number of People were all at once crying out to him, Why do you not Answer him? Why do *(end of page 54)* you not Answer him? He replied I have no Words; Just at this time a very learned Brahman came up who was desired to talk with me - which he did, and so acceded to what I said that he at last said Images had been used of late years but not from the beginning - I enquired what I must do to be saved? He said I must repeat the Name of God a great many times; I replied Would you if your Son had offended you, be so pleased with him, as to forgive him, if he was to repeat the word Father a thousand times? This might please Children or Fools - but God is Wise. He told me that I must get faith. I asked what Faith was - to which he gave me no intelligible reply - but said I must Obey God - I answered what are his Commands - What is his Will - They said, God was a great light - and as no one could see him, he became incarnate, under the three fold Character of Birmmha *{Brahma?}*, Beeshno *{Vishnu?}*, & Seeb *{Shiva?}* and that either of them must be worshipped in order to Life - I told them of the sure Word of the Gospel - and the Way of Life by Christ, and Night coming on, left them. I cannot tell what effect it may have as I may never see them again. *(end of page 55)*

27

Still pursuing our Course up the Isamuty - this Day nothing material occurred, my Soul tranquil, but not so spiritual as I could wish - Peace is little worth unless it arises from seeing him who is invisible - this Day translated a Chapter -

28

Arrived this night at a place which I named Mosquito Creek from the great number of those Insects which infested us - Blessed be God we all enjoy much better Health than we have done - tho I have reason to be thankful that the Climate agrees with me better than England - Could I but see the Cause of God prevail here, I could triumph over all affliction which ever I have had the fear of going through - for indeed I have gone through very little yet - but my Carnality I have daily, nay Constant reason to deplore.

29, 30, 31

Made very little way on account of the Crookedness of the River, we laboured two Days to make about four Miles in a strait Line - I thought that our Course was very much like the Christian Life, sometimes going forward, and often apparently backward, tho the last was absolutely necessary to the prosecution of our Journey - Had some intervals of pleasing reflection on my Journey - *(end of page 56)*

June 1

Blessed be God this has not been a Day totally lost - when I can feel my soul going out after God, what pleasure it Yields and an Hour spent with a near, and enduring sense of the Divine perfection how very pleasant and refreshing it is.

2

In many respects this has been a time of refreshing to me - I thought of trying to talk to some poor people at Sultaurpore this Evening, but just before I was going to begin a fire broke out which consumed three houses and called the attention of the few people who were here till it was too late -

3

Had some serious thoughts this Morning upon the necessity of having the Mind Evangelically employed, I find it is not enough to have it set upon Duty, Sin, Death or Eternity. These are important but as the Gospel is the way of a sinner's deliverance so, Evangelical truth, should and will, when it is well with him, mostly occupy his thoughts, - but alas the Afternoon I felt peevish, and uncomfortable. *(end of page 57)*

4, 5, 6

Deadness and Carnality prevailed these Days - I have no opportunities for retirement and what is worse little Heart to retire - perhaps this is the reason why I excuse myself by saying I have no place.

7

Arrived at Bassetpore, the place where Isamuty River runs out of the Ganges, was busied most part of the Day procuring Sails, making Ropes &ct. for our Boat, to go upon the Ganges. Towards evening went into the River but run upon a Sand Bank & and was forced to Come to under an Island - the River at this place is 8 or 9 Miles wide - but abounds with Shallows, was in a very unpleasant state most part of the Day.

8

Sailed in the Ganges and in the Evening arrived at Bowlea where we lay to for the Sabbath tomorrow, felt thankful that God had preserved us, and wondered how he can regard so mean a Creature as was enabled this Evening to wrestle with God in prayer for many of my dear friends in England - several of my Friends at Leicester lay very near to my Heart - and several Ministers of my most intimate acquaintance

- I seemed to feel much on their account, the Society was an object of my desires likewise, this was a time of refreshing to my soul indeed - *(end of page 58)*

9

I have this Day had more enjoyment of God than for many days past - I trust that the reading of the Bible has been truly useful to my soul, had some affecting views of the Value of Christ & Grace whilst reading part of McLaurin's treatise on Christian piety - felt enlarged in prayer - and thankful for the many mercies which I daily receive from God - but my unprofitableness has been a source of humiliation to me. Kept Sabbath to day near a place called Rampore Bowlea on the banks of the Ganges.

10

Pursued our Journey on the Ganges, twice were stuck fast on some Shallows - which hindered us much, and were the cause of some Anxiety, - but yet had a day of mercy - tho yet a day of negligence & disregard in a great measure of the life of communion with God -

11

This Evening arrived at the entrance of the River Mahanunda, which goes to Malda - had some little enjoyment of God to Day - but travelling with a family is a great hindrance to holy spiritual meditation - *(end of page 59)*

12, 13, 14

Proceeded up the River Mahanunda and arrived this Evening at Boslahaut, about 6 Miles from Malda. Much mercy has followed us all through this Journey and considering the very weak state of my Wife we have been supported beyond expectation - Travelling in general I have always found unfriendly to the Progress of Divine Life in my Soul, but travelling with a Family more particularly so - yet through the mercy of God, I have not been without some seasons of Enjoyment and inward delight in God - tho moved with an awful degree of Coldness, and inattentiveness to that which when attended to has always been productive of the greatest pleasure and satisfaction to my soul.

15

Received a note from Mr. Udney inviting us all to the Factory, to which place we went, and arrived there about 12 o'clock - Found Mr. Udney and his Mother very agreeable people indeed - and had *(end of page 60)* once more the happiness of joining in prayer with those who love God -

16

This Day I preached twice at Malda, where Mr. Thomas met me in the Morning - Had much enjoyment, and tho our Congregation did not exceed Sixteen yet the pleasure that I felt in having my tongue once more loosed I can hardly describe - was enabled to be faithful, and felt a sweet affection for immortal Souls -

17, 18

Had much serious Conversation and sweet pleasure these Days; I feel now as if released from a prison, and enjoying the sweets of Christian fellowship again - O that our Labour may be prosperous, and our Hearts made glad to see the Work of the Lord carried on with Vigour, surely the Lord is now thus making room for us; and removing every difficulty without some gracious design; I must desire a spirit of Activity and Affection. *(end of page 61)*

19

To Day Mr. Udney told me that my Salary was to be 200 Rupees per Month, and Commission upon all the Indigo that is sold; and that next Year he intended to present me with a Share in the Work, so that my situation is very eligible, his manner of conferring these favours upon us (for our situations are alike) was admirable; I always, said he, join the interest of those I employ in places to trust with my own; so that no Obligation lies upon you whatsoever, more than others; - Resolved to write immediately to the Society in England, that they send me no more supplies, as I shall have an ample sufficiency - This gives me great pleasure as I hope they may the sooner be able to send another Mission somewhere, [and I should much recommend Sumatra or some of the Indian Islands, if they send to any part South or East of Bengal, it will be best to send them in a Foreign ship to Bengal, from whence their *(end of page 62)* passage may be taken in a Country Ship to any place, and as we have houses here they may stay with either of us, till an opportunity offers which will save much expence] - This Evening set out with Mr. Thomas for Mudnabati which is to be the place of my residence, and is 32 Miles North of Malda in a Strait line, but near 70 by Water, and is upon the River Tangan -

20, 21

Were employed in Journeying and about the middle of the Night arrived at Mudnabati -

22

Set out again for Malda, and as it was down the stream arrived there in about 15 Hours felt but Barren.

23

Enjoyed a very pleasant Day indeed, preached twice with much affection one time from, "Ye who some time were afar off are brought near by the Blood of Christ" - and in the Evening from "By Grace Ye are saved" - there was much seriousness *(end of page 63)* among us, and I hope the Sabbath has not been in vain -

23

Had some sweet Conversation upon divine things and Affection in praying with dear Christian friends -

24

Employed in sending off my Boat, which I intend to meet to morrow morning - had some pleasure and pain, I trust of the truly Evangelical kind to day -

25-26

Journeyed to Mudnabati, arrived there about two in the Afternoon and spent the day in regulating the Concerns there -

27

Employed in the Works, but had a pleasant Season of Retirement, it is now just One Year and 14 days since I left England - all which time I have been a sojourner and wandering to and fro, at last however God had provided me a Home, may he also give me Piety & Gratitude. *(end of page 64)*

28

I am at present busily employed in arranging all my people and my affairs, having about ninety people under my management, these will furnish a Congregation immediately, and added to the extensive engagements which I must necessarily have with the Natives will open a very wide door for activity, God grant that it may not only be large but effectual. Felt not much spirituality to Day, but had the pleasure of detecting a shocking piece of Oppression practiced by those Natives who managed the affairs of this place before my coming. They had hired labourers for 2 Rupees per Month, - but when the poor people came to be paid they deducted 2 Annas* (*16 Annas make one Rupee) from each man's pay for themselves. I am glad of this detection on two accounts, namely as it affords me an opportunity of doing Justice among the Heathen, and exposing the Wickedness of their leaders, one of these oppressors being a Brahman, and as it so discouraged the poor people from working for us, that we could scarcely procure labourers at any rate, this will serve a little to remove the prejudice of the people against Europeans and prepare a way for the publication of the Gospel - *(end of page 65)*

30

This has been the first Sabbath spent at the place of my intended abode. Spent the Day in reading, and prayer; found some sweet devotedness to God towards Evening; and much concern lest I should become negligent after so great mercies; but if after God has so wonderfully made way for us, I should neglect the very work, for which I came here; the blackest brand of Guilt - infamy must lie upon my soul; found myself desirous of being entirely devoted to God, and disposed of by him just as he pleases; I felt likewise much concern for the success of the Gospel among the Heathens -

July 1, 2, 3

Much engaged in the necessary business of preparing our Works for the approaching season of Indigo making which will Commence in about a Fortnight - Had on the Evening of each of these Days very precious seasons of *(end of page 66)* fervent prayer to God. I have been on these Evenings much drawn out in prayer for my dear Friends at Leicester, and for the Society that it may be prosperous, likewise for the ministers of my acquaintance not only of the Baptist, but other denominations. I was engaged for the Churches in America, & Holland, as well as England - and much concerned for the success of the Gospel among the Hindus - at present I know not of any Success, since I have been here. Many say that the Gospel is the word of truth, but they abound so much in flattery, and encomium which are mere words of course; that little can be said respecting their sincerity - The very common Sins of Lying, and Avarice are so universal also that no European who has not witnessed it, can form any Idea of their various appearances; they will stoop to any thing whatsoever to get a few Cowries, and Lie on every occasion O how desirable is the spread of the Gospel. *(end of page 67)*

4

Rather more flat & dead, perhaps owing to the excessive Heat, for in the Rainy Season, if there is a fine day, that is very Hot indeed. Such has been this Day, and I was necessitated to be out in it from Morning till evening giving necessary directions; felt very much fatigued indeed, and had no spirits left in the Evening - and in prayer was very Barren -

5

Very poorly today from being exposed to Yesterday's heat and obliged to be rather more cautious, felt little Heart for the things of God till Evening, when I was much comforted by reading the fidelity, and constancy of Job in the first two Chapters. Wished much for the same spirit and afterwards was much enlarged in prayer to God. My soul was much drawn out for the success of the Gospel among the Heathen - Had some pleasant spiritual Conversations with Munshi *(end of page 68)* who I hope will lose caste for the Gospel; which with an Hindu of his Caste is a greater sacrifice than Life - his being the Highest except the Brahman. Their strong attachment to Caste may appear by the following incident; As I was coming up here I was in great want of a Servant Boy, at a place which we passed through, a poor Boy of the Shoemaker Caste (which is the very lowest of all, so that no Hindu or even Mussulman of credit will suffer one of them to come into their House; but they are universally despised much more than can be conceived:) came begging to Munshi, and said that he had neither Food, Clothing or Friends, but was an Orphan; Munshi asked him to come as my Servant, and told him that he should have a sufficiency of all necessaries, and if he behaved well, be taken good care of - but for fear of losing Caste he refused; and perhaps this is one of the Strangest Chains with which the Devil ever bound the Children of Men; This is my comfort that God can break it. *(end of page 69)*

6

Very flat and carnal to day; endeavored to attend to something like publick Worship, but was almost alone, I had appointed to attempt the instruction of the Labourers to day, but they had all made some appointment to go to their families, and very few indeed were left, had a little pleasure in reading part of Edwards on Redemption.

7

Busy all Day, but rather more inclined to contemplate spiritual things; this Evening were enabled to plead a little with God for the Heathens, but it was so flat, and destitute of strong crying & Tears that it scarcely deserves the Name of prayer; Had some profitable conversation with Munshi this Evening and indeed he is the only conversible Person in this place, all the Natives here being very ignorant, and speaking a dialect which differs as much from *(end of page 70)* true Bengali as Yorkshire *{which he marked out completely}* Lancashire does from true English - so that I have hard work to understand them, and to make them understand me -

8

To day was calm and placid in the Morning but no Heart for divine things, in the afternoon much engaged in paying wages to near an hundred workmen - in the Evening had some little drawings of Heart after God, but very shockingly lifeless all the Day in the things of God -

9 to **Aug.** 4

Employed in visiting several Factories to learn the process of Indigo making; had some very pleasant Seasons at Malda, where I preached several times, and the people seemed much affected with the Word. One Day as Mr. Thomas & I were Riding out we saw a Basket hung in a Tree in which an infant had been exposed; the skull remained the rest having been devoured by Ants. *(end of page 71)* On the last of these Days I arrived with my Family at Mudnabati the place of my future residence, and the seat of the Mission.

5, 6, 7

Much employed in something of the affairs of the Buildings &ct. having been Absent so long, and several of our managing and principal being sick with Fever, it is indeed an awful time here with us now. Scarce a Day but some are seized with fever, it is I believe owing the abundance of Water, there being Rice Fields all around us, in which they Dam up the Water, so that all the Country hereabouts is about a Foot deep in Water, and as we have Rain tho Moderate to what I expected the Rainy Season to be; Yet the Continual Moisture occasions Fever in such situations where Rice is cultivated: - Yet the Rainy Season is the most pleasant Weather in this Country, - or do I think: yet the Rains are more violent than Summer Rains in England -

Felt at Home & Thankful these Days. O that I may be very useful. I must soon learn the *(end of page 72)* Language tolerably well for I am obliged to Converse with the Natives every day, having no other person here, except my family - On the two last of these Days the Mohammedans were employed in celebrating the Mohamrum the time of lamentation for the Slaughter of Mohamed's family, they were going about with Pipes, Drums &ct. incessantly for two Days & Nights, and on the last Day upwards of a Thousand People of all Ages, came just before our Door, the House being built in the Bank of a Tank part of which is consecrated to a Peer or Spirit of some Saint, who was buried there. They wished much to display the whole Scene to us; tho perhaps half of them came out of Curiosity having never seen a White Woman and many not a White Man before; and it was very Curious to hear them enquiring, one of another which was Saib and which was Bibby Saib, that is which was me, and which my Wife - They brought four or five Ornamented Biers in which the dead Family of Mohamed was supposed to be represented, and after *(end of page 73)* the whole Exhibition was ended they Buried, or drowned them in the Tank; and then dispersed. Their Zeal on these occasions is very great - every thing is sacrificed to their Religion; and every Mussulman Rich or Poor joins in the Ceremony -

8, 9, 10

Nothing particular occurred, the state of my mind Easy but not Spiritual - the Sabbath was tranquil, and Serene.

11, 12, 13, 14, 15

Days much alike, some longings after God, and pleasure in his Word; but much engaged on account of our Works being unfinished, many of the People sick, and the Season far advanced.

16 thru the 24

Nothing worth recording passed, I feel too much sameness to be spiritual - if I was in a more spiritual Frame, the holy War would be carried on in my Soul with greater Vigour, and the fresh discoveries of Sin would cause new hopes, new fear, and new struggles, but when I am at ease, tis *(end of page 74)* like a Calm at Sea, where there is a contrary Current. I not only get no ground but am insensibly carried back: -

The last of these Days was Lord's Day, Spent it in reading to and praying with my family. Towards Evening went out and the Workmen who have built the Works came to me, and said that, as I was to begin making Indigo tomorrow, it was much their Wish that I would make an offering to Kali the Goddess of Destruction, that I might have success in the Work; the Kali is the most Devil-like Figure that can be thought of; She stands upon a Dead Man, her Girdle is strung with small figures of human Skulls, like beads upon a Bracelet, she has four Arms, and her Tongue hangs *(end of page 75)* out of her Mouth below her Chin; and in short a more horrible Figure can scarcely be conceived; I took the opportunity of remonstrating with them upon the wickedness and folly of Idolatry, and set my face as much as possible against their making any offering at all, and told them that I would rather lose my Life than sacrifice to their Idol; that God was much displeased with them for their

Idolatry, and exhorted them to leave it and turn to the true God; but I had the mortification of seeing the next day that they had been offering a Kid, yet I doubt not but I shall soon see some of these people brot *(end of page 76)* from Darkness to the marvellous Light of the Gospel.

25

Had some little spirituality, but much interrupted through the carelessness of our Head man. Had some sweet wrestling and freedom with God in prayer; these seasons are but of short duration, but they are little foretastes of Heaven - O may God continue them long, and frequently thus visit my Soul.

26

I have had much exercise of late on account of the Sickness which prevails in these parts; this part of the Country is full of Rice fields & the vast Quantity of Water necessary *(end of page 77)* to cultivate that kind of Corn makes this Country worse than the English Fens in the Wet Season; the Disorder is an Ague, like that of the Fen: The Natives have suffered much more than my Family, for except the Disorders which we had before we came we have had but little sickness here, but every Servant we have is ill and perhaps forty Workmen. O may the Almighty sanctify these things much to my Soul -

27

Nothing new, my Soul is in general barren and unfruitful; Yet I find a pleasure in drawing near to God; and a peculiar sweetness in His Holy Word. I find it more & more to be a very precious treasure - *(end of page 78)*

28-30

Nothing of any importance except to my shame, a prevalence of Carnality, negligence, and spiritual deadness; no Heart for Private Duties, indeed everything seems to be going to decay in my Soul, and I almost despair of being any use to the Heathen at all -

31

Was somewhat engaged more than of late in the things of God, felt some new devotedness to God, and desired to live entirely to him, and for his Glory; O that I could live always as under his Eye, and feel a sense of his immediate presence, this is Life and all besides this is death to my Soul.

Sept.1 to Oct.11

During this time I have had an heavy and long Affliction; having been taken with a violent Fever, one of the Paroxysms continued for 26 Hours without intermission when providentially Mr. Udney came to visit us, not knowing that I was ill, and brought a Bottle of Bark with him; this was a great providence, as I was growing worse *(end of page 79)* every Day. But the use of this Medicine by the Blessing of

God recovered me; but in about ten days I relapsed again, and the Fever was attended with a violent Vomiting and a Dysentery; and even now I am very ill. Mr. Thomas says with some of the very worst symptoms; On the last of these Days it pleased God to remove by Death my youngest Child but one, a fine engaging Boy of rather more than five years of age: He had been seized with a Fever and was recovering, but relapsed and a violent Dysentery carried him off; On the same day we were obliged to Bury him, which was an exceeding difficult thing; I could induce no person to make a Coffin; tho two Carpenters are constantly employed by us, at the Works; Four Mussulmen, to keep each other *(end of page 80)* in Countenance dug a Grave; but tho we had between two and three Hundred Labourers employed, no man would carry him to the Grave; We sent seven or eight Miles to get a Person to do that office, and I concluded that I and my Wife would do it ourselves, when at last our own Mater (a Servant kept for the purpose of cleaning the necessary, and of the lowest Caste) and a Boy who had lost Caste, were prevailed upon to carry the Corpse; and secure the Grave from the Jackalls, - This was not owing to any disrespect in the Natives towards us, but only to the cursed Caste; The Hindus burn their Dead, or throw them into the Rivers to be devoured by Birds, and Fishes, and the Mussulmen inhume their Dead, but this is only done by their nearest Relations, and so much do they abhor *(end of page 81)* every thing belonging to a Corpse, that the Bamboos on which they carry their Dead to the Water, or the Grave, are never touched, or burnt, but stand in the place and rot; and if they only tread upon a Grave, they are polluted, and never fail to wash after it;

During this affliction my frames were various; at some seasons I enjoyed sweet seasons of self examination, and prayer as I lay upon my bed; many hours together I sweetly spent in contemplating subjects for preaching, and in musing over discourses in Bengali; & when my animal spirits were somewhat raised by the Fever, I found myself able to reason, and discourse in Bengali for some hours together, and Words & Phrases occurred much more readily than *(end of page 82)* when I was in health; When my dear Child was ill, I was enabled to attend upon him Night and Day, (tho very dangerously ill myself;) without much Fatigue; and now I bless God that I feel a sweet resignation to the Will of God; I know that he has wise ends to answer in all that he does, and that what he does is best; and if his great, and Wise designs are accomplished, What does it signify if a poor Worm feels a little inconveniency, and pain, who deserves Hell for his sins.

Oct. 12

This Day Mr. Thomas came to see me and we spent the Sabbath together. We agreed to spend the Tuesday Morning every week, in joint tho' separate Prayer to God, for a Blessing upon the Mission, felt a sweet resignation to the divine Will this Day - *(end of page 83)*

13

This Day every disagreeable Circumstance turned up; Tho the Mussulmen have no Caste, yet they have imperceptibly adopted the Hindu's Notions about a Caste, and look upon themselves as a distinct one, in consequence of this they will neither eat nor drink with any but Mussulmen; In consequence of the four Men above mentioned digging the Grave for my poor Child, the Mundul (that is the principal person in the Village, who rents immediately under the Rajah, and lets Lands, and Houses to the other People in the place) forbid every person in the Village to eat, drink, or smoke tobacco with them and their Families, so that they were supposed to have lost Caste; The poor Men came to me full of distress, and told their Story; Mr. Thomas being with me, we sent for the principal Mussulmen in the neighborhood and enquired *(end of page 84)* whether they thought these men had done anything amiss; and they all said, no. Then we sent two Hirearrahs to call the Mundul who had forbid people to have any intercourse with them; but with secret orders to bring him by force if he refused to come; He soon came however, and then said that they had done no fault, and that he would smoke but not eat with them: As we know it to be a piece of Spite & a trick to get Money we therefore placed two Guards over him, and told him that he must either eat & drink with the Men, before the Men of his own Village, or stay here till we had sent four Men to Dinajpur to the Judge, about the matter. He stuck out however till about dinner time, when being hungry he thought fit to alter his terms; and of his own accord wrote and signed a Paper *(end of page 85)* purporting that the men were innocent and he a guilty person; he then went away and gave them a Dinner, and eat and drank with them in the presence of the people of the Village, and persons whom we had sent to witness to it; Thus ended this troublesome affair, which might also have proved a very expensive one , if it had not ended thus; I feel these things, but blessed be God, I am resigned to his Will, and that makes me easy under all -

14 to the 20th

Very ill and scarce able to crawl about, but supported thro all by the upholding hand of a gracious God - Mr. Udney having for some time past designed to settle me in a more healthy spot, this having proved remarkably unhealthy, had projected a Journey towards Tibet for me and Mr. Thomas. This was designed in part for my Health, and in *(end of page 86)* part to seek for a more eligible spot for new Works; Accordingly I set out this Day (the 20th) in Mr. Udney's Pinnace with my Family up the Tanguan River, but so weak and poorly that I could scarcely hold up my head; I felt however secret drawings of Soul after God, and a desire to be directed by him in all things.

21

Arrived this Evening at Moypauldiggy at Mr. Thomas' Company and Conversation raised my Spirits and I hope the time was profitably spent -

22

At Moypauldiggy, somewhat better, but very weak, had some profitable discourse and spent time in prayer with each other. It is good to enjoy the Communion of

Saints, and its value can scarcely be estimated, unless in a Situation like mine, where I am surrounded with pagans, and Mohammedans, and have no other to converse with - *(end of page 87)*

23

Proceeded on our Journey but very weak; yet was something recovered; my frame far from being spiritual.

24

Still going on our Excursion, this Evening were forced to come to, in the midst of a Jungle and in the Night. I who was the only person awake heard some Animal make a very violent Spring at the Boat; it awoke Mr. Thomas and we immediately concluded that it must be a Tyger; We therefore arose and counted all the Men who to the number of Eight or Ten were sleeping upon the open Deck; but providentially all were safe, but all concluded that it was a Tyger, springing at a Jackall, and that the Jackall to avoid him had jumped to the Boat. We could however discover no marks of any Animal in the sand but Jackalls, yet as they never spring at their Prey it is certain it must be a Tyger, or Leopard, and the People told us that a male & female Tyger had got their Nest with Young near *(end of page 88)* the place where we were, and had killed a Buffalo the Day before; We were however mercifully preserved; indeed the men, and not we were in danger - had but little Communion with God this Day -

25

Still very weak, arrived at Sadamahl this Evening in a very pleasant Country but felt very little spiritual life in my Soul; I have received great favours from the Lord, but to my shame am very little affected therewith -

26

Kept the Sabbath at Sadamahl had a pleasant morning, but very unfeeling and Barren the remaining part of the Day, O what a Wilderness is my Experience. Sometimes when I should most expect Light, Love & the Image of God to abound in me; I feel dead, barren, and dark - and on the Contrary, sometimes light arises when darkness was most expected . *(end of page 89)*

27

This Day arrived at Ranee Gunge where we spent the Evening, and had a little discourse with a Brahman about spiritual things; but I have only deadness and coldness myself. My Soul is like the Heath in the desert which withereth before its beauty appears, and is scarcely profitable for any thing - This Day a Buffalo stood in the River, and as the men dare not pass it, Mr. Thomas shot at it but tho three or four bullets entered his Body, and the Blood ran very copiously he got away -

28

There not being a sufficient Quantity of Water in the River for the Pinnace to go, Mr. Thomas and I left it, and proceeded in a Dinghy, or small boat to Govendagur and intended to have gone to the Mountains which part Bengal from Bhutan or Tibet *(end of page 90)* but we found here a Lieutenant Sloane who is stationed with 70 Seapays at this place to guard the Frontier from the depredations of the Fahirs *{Fakirs}* who sometimes to the numbers of some thousands lay waste a considerable part of the Country; It is but a little time since they attacked a Factory under Mr. Udney's Care but far from his residence, and robbed it of property to a very considerable amount; We spent the Afternoon with this Officer, (but a very unpleasant one it was; I am sure an Eternity with such as he would be a Hell indeed to me). He said that owing to the Jungles of Grass 14 or 15 Feet High which we must pass through it will be impossible for us to get there at this season, and that as the Water was rapidly decreasing we should run a great Hazard of leaving the Pinnace behind us for want of Water. He said that we were about 40 Cose or 70 Miles from the Highest Mountains - *(end of page 91)*

29

Returned to Ranee Gunge and spent the Afternoon there. Mr. Thomas was the greatest part of the Day trying to kill a Buffalo, but tho he had three or four Bullets in his Body and one in his Head, he got away; they are amazing Animals. I believe it was six feet from tip to tip of his Horns, and the largest Ox in England is a small Creature when compared to one of them; There are two Kinds, one much smaller than this; they are very destructive to the Rice Fields; very Sluggish, but when enraged so swift that it is impossible to escape them on a very good Horse - I was in great fear for Mr. Thomas for some Hours, not seeing or hearing anything of him; for as I am no Hunter, I staid at the Boat. He at last however came safe to my great Joy, this Day my soul was somewhat revived, and felt some desires after God. - *(end of page 92)*

30

Came down to Corneigh, a pretty large place, went to look at two temples of Seeb *{Shiva}* which were built by the Rajah, and Ranee or the King and Queen of Dinagepore; they are elevated, and you ascend several steps to go to them. On these Steps Mr. Thomas preached to a pretty large Concourse of people; who heard the Word with great attention.

31

Arrived at Moypauldiggy at Mr. Thomas' House about Nine this Evening. This has been a somewhat more profitable Day than many heretofore. I feel that God is my Portion, and when I feel that I desire no other; O that he could give me grace to live to his Glory, and spend my strength in his service; and If I could but always view his excellency, and all sufficiency, then his work must be delightful and pleasant, and all suffering for his sake easy - *(end of page 93)*

Nov. 1- 2.

Spent these Days at Mr. Thomas' where I preached on Lord's Day, and had some comfortable enjoyment of the things of God. To spend a Sabbath in Society is a precious thing indeed to me, who have so very few of them.

3, 4

Returned to Mudnabati where I arrived early on Tuesday Morning. Feel in some measure humbled before God under a sense of my own unprofitableness, Yet am not without hope that the Lord may soon Work; Munshi has been very ill, for now three Months, with the Fever, so that I could scarcely derive any benefit from him; and as an assistant in Preaching none at all; I am therefore prevented from much discourse with the Natives; for tho I can discourse a little yet not long together, and when they say much, I find it difficult to *(end of page 94)* understand it, for by ignorance of one or two Words, or peculiarities of Construction the thread of the discourse is broken, and rendered unintelligible to me in a great measure - May God give me Wisdom & a Spirit of application till all these Difficulties are overcome -

5

Set out to Malda where I staid till the 10th, had some return of the Fever - but preached twice on the Lord's Day, tho very weak and full of Pain; the Congregation appeared very serious, but I did not perceive that affection either in myself or the Audience that I have seen of some other times; The interval spent at this place was very agreeably filled up; and I trust with profit and pleasure on all sides; Mr. Udney signified his wish for me to remove to Sadamahl as a more healthy place, and to go up immediately and try to get a Pattah *{?}*for Land of the Rajah; he seems desirous to abandon Mudnabati. *(end of page 95)*

11-13

Proceeded to Mudnabati, was very poorly the first day, but afterwards got better and found my Family well; was busied in preparing for my Journey; and in reading a number of English Newspapers, which, considering the very astonishing silence of our Brethren in England, and for which I can find no Cause; was a treat to me; I gather from one of them that Dear Mr. Ryland is gone to Bristol. I wonder who is at Northhampton, and much more who is at Leicester, and how those very dear People do, surely they have not forgot me -

14, 15

Journeyed with my family to Moypauldiggy where I left them, having received an confirmation from Mr. Udney that he intended to improve Mudnabati yet more, and that I must return from Sadamahl as soon as the Pattah was obtained; to superintend those improvements. So now I am all uncertainty and Doubts, and *(end of page 96)* know not which place I am to be at, O I long to be settled, but God does not see proper - Yet I feel a Calm pleasure in waiting the Will of God -

16

Preached at Moypauldiggy had some sweet enjoyment of the things of God, and I trust the day was not unprofitable to any of us, - O may God make it a prelude to a more enlarged Christian Society here -

17

Was detained in fitting up Dinghys to go the rest of the Journey there not being Water for the Pinnace to proceed further, found this a Day of Hurry and Business, and was much fatigued at Night, yet had some desires after God -

18-21

Employed in Journeying to Sadamahl, during which time I was not without some pleasing enjoyment of God, but the hurry of going to and fro, I find to be exceedingly dissipating to the *(end of page 97)* mind and very unfriendly to the more spiritual exercises of godliness.

22

Was much busied in surveying the Country and settling for my Stay in this place. Found my Heart much carried away with the business of the World and had only wretchedness to mourn over.

23

A Solitary Sabbath, in the afternoon tried to preach to the People who were with me, but could not even fix their attention. They seemed shockingly unconcerned, and were all the time going about upon the objects about them; Was grieved with their inattention; yet felt a pleasure that I had addressed them upon the great concerns of another World; besides I know that God can bless that which we are most wretched in delivering, and which is the weakest attempt - *(end of page 98)*

24-30

During these Days I had some sweet seasons of Prayer to, and Wrestling with God; having no one to speak to, and many hours in which no business could be done, I found myself quite retired, and my soul often drawn out; I was enabled to be instant for the Success of my ministry among The Heathen, for the Success of my Colleague; and for all my dear friends in England, who be very near my Heart, especially the Church at Leicester, and the Baptist Society; I was much engaged for many of them by name, and was affected much with what might be their probable situations, both spiritual and temporal; O that these seasons might continue, but they soon decay and alas! I have to mourn the most barren of Souls - *(end of page 99)* I had intended to go and preach to more of the inhabitants of these parts, but had a return of the Fever which prevented me.

Dec. 1- 4

Continued at the same place and with much the same frame of mind, my Fever was also comfortably removed by taking Bark; and on the last of these Days I left Sadamahl without obtaining the object for which I went thither; arrived at a Place called Aslabad and spent the night there.

5

Arrived at Moypauldiggy and found my Family and Mr. Thomas' quite well for which I have reason to be very thankful. Having Business of considerable importance to attend to, I could not stay the Sabbath there. *(end of page 100)*

6

Left Maypol *{Moypauldiggy}* and arrived at Mudnabati. Blessed be God for preserving me during this Journey which cannot be less than 200 Miles by Water, tho not more than 80 by Land. Feel thankful to God for his great Goodness in Providence to me,

7

This morning felt somewhat Barren but in the Evening had much pleasure and freedom in preaching to the Natives at Mudnabati; these were more attentive also than those at Sadamahl - and I doubt not but God has a Work to do here; It has been his general way to begin among the Poor and despised, and to pass by those who imagine themselves to be wise, but here we have only Poor, illiterate people; and scarce any of those who value themselves on account of being the higher Caste - *(end of page 101)*

8-18

Having been so long from home I was busied very much in settling my Books, and in giving directions for several new Works which will be necessary to be made on account of the very great increase of Business for next Year, but tho I mourn want of retirement, yet I feel Happy in being at home, and in my Work - On Lord's Day the 13th preached to the Natives of another Village, who were very attentive and raised my expectations very much. On the Last of these Days set out for Malda with my Family to spend the Christmas with Mr. Udney and other European Friends who are met together there and arrived at Bomangolah in the Evening. *(End of page 102)*

19-20

Journeying to Malda, my mind as full of wretchedness as I can think of but principally from outward Causes, which are like a Shower of the fiery darts of the Enemy; Arrived in the Evening, and was much refreshed and relieved by the conversation of Christian friends -

21

Preached in the Morning from "That by two immutable things in which it was impossible for God to Lye, we might have strong Consolation &ct. - dwelt much on this that it is the Will of God that his saints should have strong Consolation; and in the Evening preached from that in Jude "Now unto him who is able to keep us " - Myself and the whole Congregation were much edified, I hope, and the word seemed to take good Effect - *(end of page 103)*

22 to 31

Spent this time at Malda in very agreeable Society, preached on Christmas Day, and twice on Lord's Day the 28th and I think I may say with truth that the whole of this time was a time of real refreshing to my Soul which had long been in a barren and languid State. O that I could indeed praise the Lord for his goodness towards me. On the last of these Days left Malda to return home and towards night met Mr. Thomas and his family going down to begin the New Year at Malda - I have gone through many Changes this Year but how much has the Goodness of God exceeded my expectations and hopes - *(end of page 104)*

1795

Jan. 1 to 15

This time have had bitters (of a family kind) mingled with my soul. Much cause to complain of want of spirituality, and really have not had time to write my Diary, having between four and five hundred mens Labour to direct - On the Lord's Days I have preached to the Natives in the surrounding Villages, and I hope not without some good effect. The Mussulmen of one Village having appeared much struck with the Word, & promised to cast off their Superstition; Past Lord's Day they continued in the same resolution and were joined in it by several others who had not heard the Word before; Yesterday I was much dejected on *(end of page 105)* finding that one of our Workmen, (a Brick layer) had almost made an Idol of the same kind with that mentioned in my Journal of Feb. 4 - last Year, (Sorosaudi *{Sarasuati?}* the patroness of learning) - and which was to be consecrated on the 4th of Feb. following; I might have used authority and forbad it, but thought this would be persecution; I therefore talked seriously with the Man to Day, & tried to convince him of the sinfulness of such a thing, as well as its foolishness; when he acquiesced in all I said and promised to throw his Work away so that I hope the Idol will be put an end to here; O may God turn them from Idols to himself - *(end of page 106)*

Jan. 16

Had much to struggle with outwardly, and inwardly have great reason to complain that there are not more and stronger struggles. O that I was but more in the Spirit of Christ this would make Sin a Burden to me, and earthly things light, but I am a poor unfeeling, ungrateful Wretch towards God; and much under the deception of living to myself, yet I know that this is diametrically opposite to the Spirit of Christ-

17

In the Morning was in the same wretched state as Yesterday, but in the Afternoon Mr. Thomas came (and appeared more spiritual than for a long time past) I trust his spiritual Conversation was blessed and served to arouse my drowsy Soul in some degree. Had some reviving in Prayer with him; and feel that as Iron sharpenth Iron, so doth the Countenance of a Man his Friend - *(end of page 107)*

18

Bless God for this Day, I trust my Soul has been quickened in it; In the Morning read part of Flavel on Providence which was truly refreshing; In the afternoon Mr. Thomas preached with much Affection to a Company of Hindus, who were met to sacrifice to the Sun; this is a Species of Idolatry in which both Hindus and Mussulmen unite, and is peculiar to this part of the Country. Plantains and Sweetmeats were brought by the Women; and exposed opposite to the Setting Sun; while Singing and Musick, were performed; Just before the Sun set the Women placed Pots of burning Coals on their Heads, (which were so made as not to burn them,) and walked around the offering several times which ended the Sacrifice. Many left the Sacrifice and discoursed all the Way home about *(end of page 108)* the things of God; We formed a plan for setting up two Colleges (Chowparee Bengali) for the education of Twelve Youths in each. I had some Months ago set up a School, but the poverty of the Natives caused them frequently to take their Children to Work - To prevent this we intend to Clothe and feed them, and educate them for Seven Years, in Sanskrit, Persian, &ct. and particularly to introduce the study of the Holy Scriptures, and useful Sciences therein; We intend also to order Types from England, at our own expence, & print the Bible, and other useful things in the Bengal or Hindustani Languages. We have reason indeed to be very thankful to God for his kind providence which enables us to lay out any thing for him, may our Hearts be always ready. *(end of page 109)*

19

A remaining sweetness of Soul, and pleasure in reflecting upon our mutual designs; Mr. Thomas left us this Morning -

20

Blessed be God for a Continuance of Calm sweetness; This being a Season in which Idolatrous Worship is most frequent I have frequent occasion to warn the people against it. To day an Idol (Kali) was made in the neighborhood, had some conversation with some natives on the great wickedness of Idolatry.

21

Much Barrenness but some sweet pleasure in the things of God; had another opportunity of pressing the necessity of obtaining pardon from God for their Idolatry, and other sins, was enabled to be serious and faithful - *(end of page 110)*

22

I have continual reason to complain on account of the Barrenness of my Soul towards God, surely no one who has received such uncommon favours, can be so ungrateful as myself. I have need of more spiritual life, and a more evangelical turn of mind. I want true faith, and in a great degree and I have great need of an aptness, or readiness to teach; indeed I always was very defective in this; and now I need more of this spirit than ever I did in my life; I have often thought, on this very account that I never was fit for the Gospel Ministry, but how much less fit for the Work of a Missionary among the Heathens. O may God give me his Holy Spirit to furnish me for every good Work. *(end of page 111)*

23

Still Barren, O if I did but see and feel any thing, better feel the severest pangs of Spirit on this side of Hell, than live from one Day to another in this most wretched unfeeling state; If I felt the weight of Sin; Shame for it, Resolution against it, or anything else it would be much better than the miserable state that I now am in, "O Lord I beseech thee deliver my Soul".

24

I can only look upon myself as a poor barren Idle Soul. I feel nothing scarce, I scarcely do any thing. I fear the World has laid hold of my Heart; I need a humble spirit and an activity of mind to which now I am almost a total stranger. *(end of page 112)*

25

I bless God for some little revival of Soul and pleasure in the Work of God. This was the Day for the Worship of Sorosaudi *{Sarasvati?}*, the patroness of literature, One was prepared near the place where I live; and in the Morning was enabled to speak feelingly to two or three people about the Sinfulness of Idolatry; and was determined to go and preach to them in the Evening when the Offering would be at height; I accordingly went, and after asking what that thing was; the Brahman who attended the offering said it was God; I said pray did that make Men or Men make that. He confessed that it was made by Men, I then asked him how many Gods there were; he said One; I enquired who made the World, he said Birmmha *{Brahma?}*; I asked whether he was God; he said Yes; then said I there *(end of page 113)* may be a Lack or 100,000 Gods at this rate; He then said that he did according to his faith; and that the Shastra commanded this. I enquired What Shastra? he said the *Bee Accoran*, I said that Shastra is only a Sanskrit Grammar, and commands no such thing; Have you read it? He acknowledged that he had not; then said I, you can have no Faith about the Matter for faith is believing some Words, but this thing cannot speak; and the Shastra you have never read; He then said that it was the Custom of the Country; said I, are all the Customs of this Country Good? He said Yes; I asked whether the Customs of Thieves to Steal and Murder were good? And said I, it is a Common custom in this Country to tell lies, so that you will not find one man in *(end of page 114)* a Thousand but make lying his constant practice, Is this a good Custom? Is Whoredom a good Custom? He was quite stunned with this; but presently said that his ancestors had always done so; I enquired whether there were an Heaven and an Hell. He said Yes; then said I how do you know but they are gone to Hell? He enquired why God sent the Shastras if they were not to be observed. I answered how do you know that God sent the Hindu Shastras, did he send the Mussulmen's Koran also? He answered that God had created both Hindus and Mussulmen, and had given them different Ways to Life. I said then God could neither be wise nor unchangeable to do so, and that all such foolish Worship was unworthy of either God or Men - *(end of page 115)*

I then took an opportunity of pointing out the justice of God, and the Gospel way of Salvation by Christ, and then interested the people to Cast away those fooleries and seek pardon through the Blood of Christ; for said I. You see your Brahman is dumb, he can say nothing; If he can defend his Cause let him speak now, but you can hear that he cannot tell whether this thing is God, or Man, or Woman, or Tyger or Jackall - I felt a sweetness, and a great affection for them in my own Soul, and was enabled to speak from the Heart, and God assisted me much, so that I spoke in Bengali for near Half an Hour without intermission, so as to be understood, and much more than ever before, Blessed be God for *(end of page 116)* this Assistance; O that I may see the good fruit of it and that God may bless it for their Eternal Good; As to the People they care just as much for their Idol, as Carnal Men in England do for Christ, at Christmas, A good Feast, and a Holiday is all in all with them both. I observed before that this Idol is Worshipped on the 4th of Feb but now find that it is regulated by the time of the Moon, like English Easter -

26

Had some longing of Soul for the Conversion of the poor Natives, and an opportunity of discoursing to some of them upon the danger of their state, and the evil of their practices, but was in my own soul barren, and had little Communion with God; consequently but little of the enjoyment of true Godliness - *(end of page 117)*

26

Was employed considerable part of the Day in detecting a Cheat practised by one of the overseers of the Works and am obliged to discharge him. Their dishonest tricks are so common with them that they play them without a blush. O that God would make the Gospel successful among them, this would undoubtedly make them honest men; and I fear nothing else ever will, much shocking barrenness to day.

27

Some little enjoyment in Prayer; I feel it a blessed thing to feel the plague of my own heart, and my spiritual wants in any measure, then it is a pleasing tho a melting and sorrowful enjoyment to pour out the soul to God. O that I had this Spirit of Prayer at all times but alas. I soon loose all that is good - *(end of page 118)*

28

Much engaged in writing having begun to write Europe Letters, but having received none. I feel that Hope deferred makes the Heart sick; however I am so fully satisfied with the firmness of their friendship that I feel a sweet pleasure in writing to them, tho rather of a forlorn kind, and having nothing but myself to write about feel the awkwardness of being an Egotist. I feel a Social spirit tho barred from Society.

29

Such a sameness prevails in my Soul that my diary is scarcely worth writing. I am a poor carnal creature; and this brings to my mind the state of my Soul through the Day, but as it can excite nothing but shame in me, or in others the diabolical pleasure, of rejoicing that others are as bad as themselves, I cannot write it - *(end of page 119)*

30

My great Crime is neglect of God, & a spiritual stupidity; I always am best pleased when I feel most, but live from one day to another without seeing, or feeling, to any considerable degree. I am sure that my deadness and stupidity, want of a spirit to admire God, and honour him is the very reverse to that of Christianity. O may God make me a true Christian -

31

Mercy has brought me through another Month. Many mercies have been received from God and many Evils warded off. Blessed be his holy name; But this day has increased the measure of my ingratitude and neglect. O that I had much Faith, and Grace, and more of the meek and lowly spirit of God. *(end of page 120)*

Feb. 1

Through the Day had not much enjoyment, Yet I bless God for any: my soul is prone to barrenness, and I have every day reason to mourn over the dreadful stupidity of my nature, and the wickedness of my Heart, so that I need daily Cultivation from the hand of God, and from all the means of Grace. Had a little liberty in addressing the Natives but was for some time much dejected, seeing them inattentive, and afterwards putting all the quirking Questions they could think of - I was however enabled to be faithful, and, at last God seemed a little more to fix their attention, and they desired me to set up a Weekly meeting to read the Bible to them and to expound the Word.

2

Had a miserable Day, sorely harrassed from without, and very Cold and dead in my Soul. I could bear all outward trials if I had but more of the spirit of God - *(end of page 121)*

3

This is indeed the Valley of the shadow of Death to me; except that my Soul is much more insensible than John Bunyan's Pilgrim; O what would I give for a kind sympathetic friends much as I had in England, to whom I might open my Heart; but I rejoice that I am here notwithstanding; and God is here, who can not only have compassion, but is able to save to the uttermost.

4

I don't love to be always complaining - yet I always complain. I believe my fault is this - magnifying every trouble and forgetting the multitude of mercies that I am daily loaded with. I have been reading Flavel on Providence lately; but under every new shadow of a Trial, I find myself to be a learner, and even to have made no advances in the necessary Science of improving all Mercies to promote thankfulness, and all Trials to promote Patience. *(end of page 122)*

5

O what a Load is a barren Heart, I feel a little forlorn pleasure in thinking over the time that is past, and drown some of my heaviness by writing to my Friends in England, and, some by going about the various works carrying on here; but the only effectual way is to cast it upon God. This I feel such backwardness to, that the Load is rendered much heavier by the consideration.

6

I sometimes walk in my Garden and try to pray to God, and if I pray at all, it is in the Solitude of a Walk; I thought my soul a little drawn out to day, but soon gross darkness returned; spoke a word or two to a Mohammedan upon the things of God, but I feel as bad as they.

7

O that this day could be consigned to Oblivion, What a mixture of Impatience, carelessness, forgetfulness of God, Pride, and peevishness have I felt this day - God forgive me - *(end of page 123)*

8

I had more enjoyment to day than for many days past; had two pleasing opportunities, and felt my heart encouraged. Went to a Village called Maddabatty to preach to the Natives, but found very few. I felt much for them, but had not the freedom I wished; yet I know God can bless a weak attempt -

9-14

I cannot say anything this week except proclaim my own Shame, I think that it is a Wonder indeed that the goodness of God endureth yet daily -

15

This day had some little Reviving. Preached in the Evening to a pretty large assembly of the Natives, but when I told them of the immortality of the Soul they said they had never heard of that before this day. They told me they wanted instruction and desired me to instruct them upon the Lord's Days - *(end of page 124)*

16

Had some little continuance of Yesterday's frame - I ardently wish for the Conversion of the Heathens, and long for more frequent opportunities of addressing them, but their poverty requires them to Labour from Sunrise to Sunset - I have opportunities of privately instructing them very frequently. O may I never want an Heart.

17

I have to complain of abundance of Pride; which I find it necessary to oppose, (and the more as my Wife is always blaming me for putting myself on a level with the Natives -) I have much to conflict with on this score both without and within. I need the united prayers of all the People of God, And O that I had but the spirit to pray more for myself. *(end of page 125)*

18

I have to bless God for some little pleasure of spirit, but have much of a sinful spirit to deplore, it is astonishing that I am so very little employed in the things belonging to the Kingdom of Heaven. O that God would give me an Heart to glorify him in Body and Soul continually -

19

Have reason to be thankful for any degree of enjoyment of God. My soul is so much swallowed up in its own indolence and stupidity that I have scarcely any enjoyment of divine things or sense of my own necessities, but from day to day the state of my soul is exceeding forlorn but to day I felt rather more inclined to God and Heavenly things, all this light however was only like the peeping out of the Sun for a minute or two in very rainy weather, and soon I felt my gloom return - *(end of page 126)*

20-21

I think I feel some longings of soul after God, but yet my soul feels exceeding solitary, and comfortless, and I want everything in my own apprehensions that belong to Godliness. I have no Zeal, no Love, and no aptitude for Contemplation.

22

A Somewhat lowring morning, read a Sermon of Flavel's on those Words, Now if any man be in Christ he is a new Creature, but felt scarcely anything; In the afternoon I was much cheered by a considerable number of Natives coming for instruction and I endeavored to discourse with them about divine things, I told them that all men were sinners against God, and that God was strictly just, and of purer Eyes than to approve of sin. I endeavored to press this point, and to ask how they could possibly be saved if this was the Case. I tried to Explain to them the nature of Heaven, and Hell, and told *(end of page 127)* them that except our Sins were pardoned we must go to Hell; [They said that would be like the Prisoners in Dinajpur Jail - I said, no, for in Prison only the Body could be afflicted, but in Hell, the Soul; that in a Year or two a prisoner would be released but never freed from Hell, that Death would release them from Prison, but in Hell they would never die;] I then told them how God sent his son, to save Sinners, that he came to save them from Sin, and that he died in Sinner's stead, and that whosoever believed on him would obtain everlasting life, and would become Holy. They said they were all pleased with this; but wished to know what sin and Holiness are. I told them that there were Sins of the Heart, the Tongue, and the Actions, but as a Fountain *(end of page 128)* cast out its Waters, so all sin had its source from the Heart; and that not to think of God, not to wish to do his will, not to regard his Word; and also Pride, Covetousness, Envy, &ct. were great Sins, and that Evil, and abusive Language was very Sinful, that not to be strictly upright in their dealings, was very Sinful; I told them that God was under no obligation to save any Man, and that it was of no use to make Offerings to God to obtain pardon of Sin, for God had no need of Goats, Kids, Sheep, &ct. for all these are his at all times, and that if God forgave them it must be from his own Will; but that he was willing to save for the sake of Jesus Christ. After this part of the 5th Chapter of Matthew was read by Munshi, and explained to them, and they went away, promising to return next Lord's Day - and my Spirits were much revived - *(end of page 129)*

I am encouraged much as this is the beginning of a Congregation, and that they came of their own will and desired to be instructed, they are collected from the Villages where I have preached before, and from some where I have not been: most of them also were men of influence, being Munduls or heads of Villages; their attention was very great, and their Questions serious and pertinent; and had I a greater command of their Language; I might be able to convey much instruction to them, they however understood what was delivered: Another pleasing Circumstance is that they already remember some Religious term as the Name of Jesus Christ, and his Mission with its design, the necessity of Pardon in order to Salvation; They have a Word for Heart as the seat of Affection, viz. (Untokkoran) but here it is not understood, so that when *(end of page 130)* I speak of Sin coming from the Heart I am forced to use the word (Dele) which only signifies the Heart as a part of the Body, and means a Sheep's Heart as well as a Man's. Much Circumlocution is therefore necessary, but God's Cause I doubt not will triumph over all obstacles soon -

23

I felt some encouragement through this Day, arising from the circumstance of the people coming Yesterday for instruction, and was enabled to plead with God for them; I long for their deliverance from their miserable state on two accounts, principally because I see God daily dishonoured, and them drowned in sensuality, ignorance and superstition, and likewise because I think that news of the Conversion of some of them would much encourage the Society, and excite them to double their Efforts in other places for the propagation of the glorious Gospel. *(end of page 131)*

24, 25

I think one of the greatest blessings upon Earth is Christian Society, for if one becomes somewhat dull, Conversation serves to enliven his spirits and to prompt him on in godliness; I have but little to this help, and to my Sorrow often fall, when I have not one at hand to lift me up again. I think my peevishness, fretfulness, and impatience is astonishing. O that the grace of God might but be in me and abound.

26

Rode to Moypal to Day to visit Mr. Thomas, found him well and had some comfortable enjoyment of his Company. We had much conversation, and I hope it has been very profitable, yet I feel distressed with the thought that the Letters to be sent as specimens for types will scarcely be ready. *(end of page 132)*

Feb. & March

This season, it is a considerable work, and requires much care, and attention.

27

Returned home today. On my return had an opportunity of discoursing with some people upon divine things; and of telling them of the danger that they were in, - arrived at home very poorly and much tired.

28

Very busy all day, and engaged in the concerns of the World, Yet not without some desires after God and goodness; What a pleasant life it must be to be quite devoted to him?

March 1

Felt my mind somewhat set upon the things of God, and had some real pleasure in the publick Exercises which were engaged in, in my house this day. I felt a concern for the Gospel, and its spread in other parts, and for the Churches, and ministers *(end of page 133)* of my Acquaintance; was in hopes that my last Week's Congregation would have come today, but was disappointed. I went out however to a Market at about two miles distance called Nalla Gunge, and preached to the people there, who were very attentive, and promised to come for further instruction the day after tomorrow, I hope some good may be done soon -

2-7

This Week I have been uncommonly busy in the Concerns of the World and have had very little leisure for any thing - was not totally without some desires after and Tokens of divine presence. On the 6th at Night was visited by dear Mr. Udney, Mr. Darel, and Mr. Grindly, and on the 7th by Mr. Thomas, had sweet Conversation - *(end of page 134)*

8

To day I preached once and Mr. Thomas once in our House to our Visitors. Hope it was a time of some little refreshing to our Souls - about the Middle of the Night our Visitors left us.

9-10

Much to complain of, such another dead soul I think scarcely exists in the World. I can only compare myself to one banished from all his friends, and Wandering in an irksome Solitude -

11

It is certainly useless to write down any thing of what passes with me, my Days are lost. I go on day after Day in a state of Alienation from God, have no sweet communion with, and scarcely any desires after God, but am a very wretched fruitless Creature indeed - have been much employed and this Evening wrote a Letter to England to my Sisters. *(end of page 135)*

12-14

Much to do in the World, and almost all my time taken up therein, have had a few serious solitary reflections, but want that tenderness of Conscience, and that peace of Conscience which I have experienced in time past; mine is a lonesome life indeed. O that my Soul my be quickened in divine things.

15

A miserable Day. I did not suspect that my Soul was so absorpt in the World as I find it to be. If I try to pray, some thing relative to the compleating of our Works starts up and my thoughts are all Carnal, and Confused. I have been very unhappy, and would not have to manage all the Business of so great a concern again for another person of the World, but it is my own Carnal spirit that is to be blamed. This is the Station which God has in great mercy put me into, and has thus preserved and provided for my family. *(end of page 136)* Munshi was gone to see relation for about a fortnight, but I went out to preach to the Natives, found very few, tried to discourse to them, but my soul was overwhelmed with depression, and I left them after some time. By the Way I tried to pour out my soul in Prayer to God, but was ready to sink under the Burden of my own Soul -

16 to 22

Had very little converse with God, very Barren and fruitless, and much discouraged, on Saturday Mr. Thomas, and his family came to see us, and on the Lord's Day Mr. Thomas and I went to Lulla a Village about two miles off where he preached, and had great Liberty of expression; the people appeared to be much impressed with the Word of God, and I hope it may be of use to them Eventually – *(end of page 137)*

23, 29

Nothing important occurred on Wednesday - Mr. Thomas left us, I trust his visit has been of some use to my Soul; Spiritual Conversation is a great and invaluable Blessing. Preached on Lord's Day to a few People at a Village near my House -

30 to Apr. 5

Had an opportunity or two which I was enabled to embrace of speaking to some Natives upon the Wickedness of the Horrid practice of Swinging &ct. That season is now approaching, and on Lord's Day appointed to preach twice to the Natives; in the morning the Congregation was about five Hundred *(end of page 138)* and after Munshi had read a Chapter in Matthew, I endeavored to preach, and had more enjoyment than for some time past, and the people having attended with great seriousness went away Shouting Alla - that is (O God). In the Evening had about four Hundred, and was enabled to speak to them of the necessity of a Sincere union with Christ. They appeared serious; and, departed shouting as in the Morning, which is a way that the Mussulmen use to invoke the Divine Being. Alla being derived from the Hebrew El and the Arabic and Persian word for God. This the Mussulmen universally use here - *(end of page 139)*

6, 10

Had frequent opportunities of discoursing with the Natives about the Horrid self tormenting mode of Worship which is practised in the 8, 9, & 10th of this Month, as falling on spikes of Iron; Dancing with Threads or Bamboos thrust through their sides, Swinging &ct. This is practised on the three last Days of their Year, but the principal is what they call Chorruh Poojah, that is the Worship of swinging. Poojah *{Puja}* is their Word for Worship, and Poodjah for the Object of Worship; I find that this Worship is only practised by the Huny, or lowest Caste of the Hindus; who are Hunters, Bird Catchers, Tanners, Shoemakers, &ct. - and are esteemed execrable among the other Castes, but great numbers always go to see them. *(end of page 140)* The other Modes of Self tormenting besides swinging are not practised in this Part of the Country, but on the 10th that was attended to in many places; and the Night was spent in Dancing and Mirth; this Day I had a serious conversation with a Man about his Soul -

11-12

On the last of these Days preached twice to the Natives, had a large Assembly in the Morning about 200 and in the Evening about 500. Munshi first read to them a part of the Gospel of Matthew, and I afterwards preached to them, upon the necessity of Repentance and Faith, and of Copying after the Example of Christ - They heard with considerable attention, and I felt some sweet freedom in pressing them to come to Christ. Afterwards had some Meditation on the Effect of the Fear of God on my Soul, and saw plainly that I was restrained from Much Evil *(end of page 141)* thereby, not merely as if I was hindered from Action by bonds put upon me but, by its operation upon my Will, and exciting me to fear doing that which God disapproves of -

13, 19

Passed the week in a tolerably calm manner; had a few opportunities of discoursing about the things of God. On Lord's Day preached twice to a pretty large Concourse of People I suppose five or six Hundred each time. Was very poorly with a Cold; and dejected thinking I could say nothing; but contrary to my expectation, I was enabled to pour out my Soul to God for them and afterwards for God to them. I felt liberty and pleasure much more than *(end of page 14)* I could expect in speaking an hard Language, and with which my Acquaintance must necessarily be slender, tho I believe I spoke more than half an hour so as to be well understood, without any help from Munshi. I have hope that God may at last appear and carry on his Work in the midst of us,

May 9

I have added nothing to these Memoirs since the 19th Apr. Now I observe that for the last three Sabbaths my soul has been much comforted in seeing so large a Congregation, and more especially as many who are not our own Workmen attend from the Parts adjacent, whose attendance must be wholly disinterested. I therefore now rejoice in seeing a *(end of page 143)* regular Congregation of from two to six Hundred people, of all descriptions, Mussulmen, Brahmans and other classes of Hindus, and which I look upon as a favourable token from God - I this day attempted to preach to them more regularly from a Passage of the Word of God, Luke 4.18 "The Spirit of the Lord is upon me, because he hath anointed me to preach the Gospel to the poor, &ct". - in which I endeavored to prove the miserable state of unconverted men, as spiritually poor, as bound by a sinful disposition, and by pernicious Customs, and false expectations of Happiness, from false, and Idolatrous Worship in which I took occasion *(end of page 144)* to observe that both in the Shastras and Koran, there were many good observations and Rules, and which ought to be attended to, but that one thing, they could not inform us of, viz. how God can forgive Sin, consistent with his Justice, and save sinners in a Way in which Justice and Mercy could Harmonize. I told them that their Books were like a Loaf of Bread, in which was a considerable quantity of Good Flour, but also a little very malignant Poison, which made the Whole so poisonous that whoever should eat of it would die, so I observed that *(end of page 145)* their Writings contained much good instruction mixed with deadly poison -

I appealed to them whether any of their Idols could give Rain (a blessing much wanted now) or whether they could do them any service at all; when an old Mussulman answered aloud "No they have no power at all" and in this he included the Mussulman's (Peers) or spirits of their Saints, as well as the Heathen Idols. I observed that the Caste was a strong Chain by which they were bound, and afterwards spoke of the suitableness and Glory of the Gospel which proposed an infinitely great Sacrifice *(end of page 146)* for infinite Guilt, and a free Salvation for poor, and perishing Sinners. In the Afternoon I enlarged upon the same Subject, felt my own soul warmed with the opportunity and hope for Good, - of late God has given me greater Concern for the Salvation of the Heathen, and I have been enabled to make it a more important request at the throne of Grace - Blessed by God have at last received Letters and other Articles from our Friends in England. I rejoice to hear of the Welfare of Zion, Bless God that Leicester people go on well - O may they increase *(end of page 147)* more and more. Letters from dear Brethren Fuller, Morris, Pearce, and Rippon, but why not from others, I am grieved for Carleton Church, Poor Brother West! I am grieved for England. A Residence there with propriety is extremely difficult. Bless God we have no such spies or informers here, we are in Peace, and sit under our Vines and Figtrees -

June 14

I have had very sore trials in my own family from a Quarter which I forbear to mention, have greater need for Faith and Patience than ever I had and I bless God *(end of page 148)* that I have not been altogether without supplies of these Graces from God, tho alas I have much to complain of from within, Mr. Thomas and his family spent one Lord's Day with us May 23. He was much pleased with our Congregation and we concerted means to get all the old Hindu professors together, having it now in our power to furnish them with some employment. We spent Wednesday 26 - in Prayer, and for a convenient place assembled in a Temple of Seeb which was near to our House. Munshi *(end of page 149)* was with us and we all engaged in supplication for the revival of Godliness in our own souls and the prosperity of the Work among the Natives. I am from that day seized with a dysentery which continued near a Week with dreadful Violence - but then I recovered, through abundant Mercy. That day of Prayer was a Good Day to our Souls. We concerted measures for forming a Baptist Church, and tomorrow morning I am going to Moypal for the Purpose of our Organizing *(end of page 150)* the Same - Through divine mercy our Congregation of Natives is very promising; we have rather fewer people now owing to this being their Seeds time, the Rains being just now setting in - I hope for, and expect the Blessing of God among us. Tho it is painful to preach among careless Heathens, yet I feel preaching the Gospel to be the Element of my Soul; had much seriousness to day in addressing them from the Words of Paul, "Come out from among them and be separate, and touch *(end of page 151)* not the unclean thing and I will receive you - " &ct. and I thought the People behaved seriously. The Foundation also goes on, Genesis is finished, and Exodus to the 33rd Chap. I have also for the purpose of exercising myself in the Language begun translating the Gospel of John; which Munshi afterwards Corrects; & Mr. Thomas has begun the Gospel by Luke. O Lord send now Prosperity.

The Letters of William Carey

1793-1833

The Value of Missions

William Carey committed himself and his family to a life of struggle and separation from his homeland. Why would he do such a thing? The answer resonates throughout his correspondence as Carey often refers to the great need for Christian missions due to the spiritual darkness of India and the world. He first expressed these sentiments and the rationale for missions in his *Enquiry*. That commitment never waned and Carey put it into action the rest of his life.

Carey described the idolatry and spiritual dearth of India in his letters. His own dedication to taking the Gospel to India and its neighbors was obvious, but he also encouraged others to remain faithful in the work. He was particularly direct in advising his son, Jabez concerning tenacity to the mission task. William Carey could not condone abandoning the work because of difficulty or discouragement. Carrying the light to those in darkness predominated his sense of Christian duty. Carey rejoiced in the privilege.

The following excerpts from letters reflect Carey's view of the value of missions and his own conviction that Christians must persist in sharing the truth about God in the midst falsehood and ignorance.

The Need for Missions

Carey encountered the people of India and perceived a tremendous spiritual need. He concluded the caste system was one of the most powerful works of Satan that held people in slavery. Carey interpreted many of the Indian religious practices as barbaric and pagan. He grieved over the Hindu and Islamic people regarding their ignorance concerning Christianity. In Carey's mind, the spiritual deprivation was overwhelming and demanded missionary action.

Carey to Sisters, from Bandel, Dec. 4, 1793

> . . . I have great hope of success, but their Superstitions are very numerous and their attachment to their Caste so strong that they would rather die than lose it upon my account. This is one of the strongest Bonds that ever the Devil used to bind the Souls of Men, and dreadfully effectual it is indeed. May God put on his great Power, and attend his Word with great Success . . .

Carey to Society Jan. 11, 1796, Malda

At another Place I preached from Christ being a Blessing in turning everyone from their Iniquities; I observed the superiority of the Gospel to all other writings, and Christ to all pretended saviours, in that point, that believing on Christ was universally accompanied with turning from Iniquity; and that their Worship must be false for they made Images, and offerings to them, and were abundant in their Worship. But said I, there is not a man of you yet turned from his Iniquity.- - There are, said I, among you *Lyars, Thieves, Whoremongers; and men filled with deceit. And as you were last year, so you are this; not any more Holy nor can you ever be so till you throw off your wicked Worship and wicked practices, and embrace the Gospel of our Lord Jesus Christ.

{The following appeared at the bottom of the page.}

*These are all sins for which the Hindus are notorious, and there is not a Company of Ten Men I believe to be fallen in with but you might safely say the above words to - all the good that can with Justice be said in favour of them is they are not so ferocious as many other Heathens . . .

Carey to Fuller, March 23, 1797, Mudnabati

{Carey thanks the Scottish for helping support the mission effort. Then worries out loud.}

Want of success is very discouraging to me in one point of view, as I fear it may operate to the tiring out the patience of our numerous and hearty helpers in England. For their Hopes having been very sanguine, and now meeting with so long a disappointment may at last decline, and their "Hearts be made fickle". *{Carey is assured of God continuing his work. Carey sees two needs.}* ". . . yet I know there are only two real obstacles in any part of the Earth, viz. a want of the Bible and the depravity of the Human Heart. The first of them God has begun to remove; and I trust the last will be removed soon; and when the Spirit is poured down from on high, all superstitions will give way. Be encouraged therefore Brothers, and encourage others, for now the darkness is past in India, and the true Light shineth".Perhaps it may be as Bro. Ryland suggests, general knowledge may first prevail and pave the way for losing past and joining to the Lord. I thank you for your opinion upon, and advice about receiving the natives while they retain their caste; I have since found it to be impracticable, for they would undoubtedly be cast out of society in that case as well as the others. W. Shwartz: people have all lost caste who are joined to his church. I have enough within myself to discourage me for ever; but I know the Work is God's and will therefore continue to go in the strength of the Lord . . .

Carey to Sutcliffe, Mudnabati, Oct. 10, 1798

. . . I hear of a missionary spirit breaking out in America and on the Continent with great pleasure. The Fields are indeed white to Harvest. I think more missionaries should be sent out and it would be a great advantage to send at least one person of tried abilities and prudence. Had this been done at Sierra Leone, in all probability that hopeful prospect had not been so soon obscured. Staying at home is now become sinful in many cases, and will become more and more so. All gifts should be encouraged, and spread far abroad . . .

Carey to Morris, Feb. 25, 1802, Calcutta

I my dear Bro. have been preserved alive tho so many of our Brethren have been taken away; and I have lived to see what they wished to see and earnestly prayed for but were never favoured with the Sight. I have seen the Grace of God richly displayed towards the poor Heathen and fetters riveted by long Custom and implicit Faith, made to fall off from those who have been long bound therewith. Both Europeans and Natives laughed at what they thought to be our enthusiastic Idea of breaking the bonds of the Hindu Castes by preaching the Gospel. When Krishna and Gokul rejected their Caste many wondered at it, but the greatest numbers attempted to carry it off with a high hand and temptingly asked, have any of the Brahmans or Caesto's believed on him. What great thing is it to have a Carpenter and a distiller reject their Caste, &ct. Lately, however, the Lord has taken from them that small consolation and has given to us one Caesto who joined the Church a little time ago. Last Week two more of the same Caste and our Brahman came and voluntarily, even without our preparing it, rejected this Caste. The two Caesto's came from a great distance, I suppose forty Miles. One of them was at our House some time ago and heard the Word. He went home and told his family, viz. his Mother, three Sisters, and a Brother who signified their willingness to unite with him in rejecting Caste and attending the Gospel if after again hearing he should still feel inclined to do so. He came last Week, brought his Brother, and they went to Krishna's house where they ate and drank with him, and afterwards with us. We have had a good deal of talk with the eldest of them . . .

. . . Many are dissatisfied with the Church of Rome; many more know nothing about it and are satisfied with confessing to a priest, and receiving the Sacrament. The great value they set on confession, Baptism, and the Lord's Supper, obliges me to speak very much with them about the Ordinances of the Gospel. There is a protestant Portugese Minister in this place, and Episcopalian, I hope evangelical, but no one (has) been in his Company. He preaches in Portugese - but the dialect of that Language spoken by the natives of Bengal differs so much from Europe Portugese that very few can understand him. [I have spoken with Mr. Udney who is now a member of Council, about the propriety of erecting a place of Worship for the purpose of preaching to them in Bengali. He advises to go on with Caution and has promised to take an opportunity of doing what he can to clear the way with Government which is the only fear we have. I have no doubt of raising Money by Subscription sufficient to do it. My situation in the College has made me better known to Government and indeed the design of the Mission &ct.

I received an order a little time ago privately to make all the enquiry I could into the murders committed by the Hindus under the pretence of Religion and delivered in a report this Week. Mr. Udney told me a little time ago that he was determined to do his utmost to procure the absolution of burning Women with their Husbands, and desired me privately to communicate to him all the intelligence I can get upon that subject. I, of course, encouraged him to do so and told him "Who can tell whether thou art come to the Council for such a time as this. I think that there is such a fermentation raised in Bengal by the little leaven that we may hope to see the whole Mass leavened by degrees. God in carrying on his work, and tho it goes forward, yet no one can say who is the instrument. The printing and dispensing small Tracts, seems to be more useful than any thing else, tho all means contribute to the carrying on of the Work.

. . . The openly avowed Sentiments of many here, are Deism - and you may expect their practices to correspond with their principles. In this I assure you that you will not be disappointed. All fashionable vice are openly practiced; and from the profaneness of the multitudes you would be tempted to suppose that they received their education under a Hackney Coachman, or a Wopping Waterman. There are however a few who sigh and cry for the Abominations which are practiced. May the God of all Grace greatly increase their Numbers.

Carey to Sisters, Aug. 9, 1808, Calcutta

This part of the World is, as it respects divine things, a vast uncultivated wilderness. We see thousands and thousands of people wherever we go and no extent of charity can make us say of one of them “That is a Christian”. I am often discouraged when I see the ignorance, superstition, and vice with which this country abounds; the vast numbers who have not heard of the word of life, the obstacles of various kinds, external and internal, to the conversion of the Heathen, the fewness of the Labourers, the imperfections that are among them, the comparatively little success which has hitherto attended the gospel and many other considerations which perpetually occur to my mind.

I do not know that I have been of any use to any one, but my mind has been constantly more or less burdened with various painful things. When I first came into the Country, I had to learn a difficult language before I could hope to be of any use, and I had nothing to help me in it. I recollect that after I had preached, or rather thought I had, for two years, a man one day came to me and declared that he could not understand me, and this long after my flattering teachers declared that every one could understand me. I feel the impression which that poor man’s remark made on me to this Day. I laboured long and saw no fruit. Afterwards the Lord wrought and several Hindus and others were baptised. Some of these are an honour to the Gospel, and some have died in the Lord with triumph on their tongues, but many others have pierced us through with sorrows. God has endured several of our native Brethren with ministerial gifts and they have been called to the ministry. Yet still our solicitude continues. Brethren and Sisters have come from England. We rejoice to see them, but a multitude of cares which none but myself, and my two elder Brethren know, press upon our hearts from this quarter. Besides all this the care of several weak infant churches, widely separated, and like tender plants, which are easily crushed by every foot, presses upon us, and sometimes nearly drinks up my spirit.

I, however, must not complain. I ought rather to rejoice that, to me who am less than the least of all saints is this grace [favour] given that I should preach among the Gentiles the unsearchable riches of Christ.

Carey to Ryland, Aug. 16, 1809

The state of the world occupies my thoughts more and more, I mean as it relates to the spread of the Gospel. The harvest truly is great, and labourers scarcely bear any proportion thereto. I was forcibly struck this morning with reading our Lord's reply to the disciples, John IV, when he told them that he had meat to eat which the world knew not of, and that his meat was to do the will of his Father and to finish his work. He said, "Say ye not there are yet four months and then cometh Harvest". He by this plainly intended to call their attention to the conduct of men when harvest was approaching, for that being the season upon which all the hopes of men had for temporal supplies, they provide men and measures in time for securing it. Afterwards directing their attention to that which occupied his own as to be his meat and drink, he said, lift up your eyes and look upon the fields (of souls to be gathered in) for they are ready to harvest.

After so many centuries have elapsed, and so many fields full of this harvest have been lost for want of labourers to gather it in, shall we not at last reflect seriously on our duty. Hindustan requires then a thousand ministers of the Gospel, at the lowest calculation, China as many, and you may easily calculate for the rest of the work. I trust that many will be eventually raised up here: but be that as it may, the demands for missionaries are pressing to a degree seldom realised. England has done much, but not the hundreth part of what she is bound to do. In so great a want of missionaries, ought not every church to turn its attention chiefly to the raising up and maintaining of spiritual gifts with the express design of sending them abroad? Should not this be a specific matter of prayer and is there not need to labour hard to infuse this spirit into the churches.

17th August. A mission to Siam would be comparatively easy of Introduction and support on account of its vicinity to Prince of Wales' Island, from which vessels can often go in a few hours. A mission to Pegu, and another to Arakan would not be difficult of introduction, they being both within the Burman dominion. Missions to Assam and Nepal should be speedily tried. Bro. Robinson is going to Bhutan, but sister R. is very poorly, and his fears are so high about personal safety, that my hopes from him are greatly lowered thereby. I do not know anything about the facility with which Missions could be introduced into Cochin China, Cambodia, and Laos, but were the trial made I believe difficulties would remove. It is also very desirable that the Burman Mission should be strengthened. There is full liberty of conscience, and several stations might be occupied, even the borders of China might be visited from that country, if _____ entrance into the heart of the Country could not be _____.

The Mission Society, I hear from Dr. Taylor are about to send LEARNED men to the Burman Empire (So says Mr. Boyne). I have not mentioned Sumatra, Java, the Moluccas, the Philippines, or Japan, but all these countries must be supplied with missionaries. This is a very imperfect sketch of the wants of Asia, only without including the Mohammedan countries, but Africa, and South America call as loudly for help, and the greatest part of Europe must also be helped from the Protestant churches, being nearly as destitute of real godliness as any heathen country on the earth. What a pressing call thus is there for labourers in the spiritual harvest, and what need that the attention of all the churches in England and America should be drawn to this very object. I have filled my paper with these reflections because they were uppermost in my mind. The Lord is prospering his cause here. Last night at our Church Meeting one person was received, and three more proposed for communion. Krishna labours indefatigably in Calcutta, doors open for him, and he has more invitations to make known the word to private families than he can attend to. Bro. Mardon is at Goamalti, where his labours are blessed, he is a good man. Sister Mardon is ill with a liver complaint, and is not at Calcutta. Bro. Chamberlain is at Cutwa. He has pleasing encouragement among the soldiers, and their wives at Berhampore. My son William is settled at Sadamahl, Bro. Fernandez at Dinajpur, Bro. Carapiet in Jessore, and John Peter intends, with his family to go to Orissa as soon as the rains are over.

Carey to Sutcliffe, June 1813

Englishmen will not be tolerated if they are sent out without the consent of C. of D. (Council of Directors) and though the Lord has graciously raised up a goodly number of valuable men among us, yet they bear scarcely any proportion to the vastness of the field which lies before us. Had we a sufficient number of proper men, and did not an iron hand paralyzing our efforts there is not a town of any conveyance in British India where the Gospel might not be introduced with hope of success. We have discouragements also from other quarters, but the Cause is God's and does prevail.

COMMITMENT TO MISSIONS

Carey to Father, Moulton, Oct. 13, 1787 or 88

Duty forces me to write, but what can I write to you? News I might send, but my natural aversions to writing; prompts one to pass by that as a too trivial concern to employ my pen about that which will be of infinitely more concern to us. Namely the Concerns of our Eternal Souls. I would advert too. But oh me! I am myself a source of conflicting passions. I long to be different from my present self, - am Dissatisfied with my self and feel a most amazing degree of Indolence, Guilt, and Confusion, in my mind but, I have no resolution even to make an Effort to Examining my heart and recollect my ways. I am unworthy to live or act on the Earth, but so inadequate to the Great work of the Ministry that I wonder why God has not confounded me before his People, before now. And Oh! how dreadful will it be, if after having preached the Gospel to others, I myself should be a Cast away. Oh! how important are the concerns of Eternity. How dreadfully do I trifle away time and Do nothing for God, and yet my Relentless soul doesn't truly grieve nor do I rush to the Light of God or man for my Barely being a Disgrace to the Human Species.

My Dear Father can undoubtedly sympathize with me under these feelings, and will certainly make it a Point to pray for me. Oh, how important are religious things, to die without Christ is to be forever! ever! lost. How important is time. One moment gone is gone eternally, the Opportunity to honour God, or Benefit our

Fellow mortals, irrecoverable past. Then if on reflection we are angry with ourselves for prodigality of time, tis all in Vain. Guilt fastens on the Conscience. Work is cut out for future repentance if we should ever have a heart for that. But I cannot help trembling under a sense, that God would be just in giving me up the next moment to a hard and impenitent state, when I have foolishly let one moment go without doing something good for God or man. God of mercies hold me up and then I shall be safe. Don't suffer me to spend time needlessly in Worldly amusements, Vain Pleasures, Needless solicitude - Eating, Sleep or Company either Good or Bad. May I always live Close to thee, delight in thy Perfections. Depend on thy Magnanimity and Bounty and keep the strictest watch on every fugitive thought by watching narrowly all the motions of my Breast.

Pardon this Soliloquy. I know that there are sublime and exalted pleasures in real religion but only they that walk with God are admitted to intimate intercourse with him. Christianity is Glorious but its Glories are innate and the real Christian only feels them. I at a distance from God my chief Good - both labour and languish and pine.

Carey to Ryland, Bandel, Dec. 26, 1793

I cannot say anything of success more that I did in my last - nor quite so much - Cassinut Mookorjee is gone from me, for employment; Tho I have some reason to hope that his convictions will, and must remain - but he is now at least 200 Miles from home. I am, notwithstanding the little success we have had, far from being discouraged; and should I never succeed, yet I am resolved in the strength of the Lord Jesus to live and Die persisting in this work, - and never to give it up but with my Liberty or Life. The worth of Souls, the pleasure of the Work itself, and above all the increase of the redeemer's Kingdom are with me motives sufficient, and more than sufficient to determine me to die in the Work, that I have undertaken.

Carey to Fuller, March 23, 1797, Mudnabati

I have thot it my duty to consider the Mission as far superior to private friendship, and as that to which many things which otherwise private friendship would require, must and ought to give way.

Carey to Father, Calcutta, July 11, 1805

. . . On a review of what we do we often wonder how it is that persons who are under such strong obligation should feel so little love to , and do so little for the Saviour who has done so much for us. I often feel depressed on my own account, I hope you will never cease to pray earnestly for me that I may be upheld to the end of my course . . .

Carey to William, Apr. 27, 1813

Divine Providence is at this moment opening so many new places for dispensing the word that we cannot supply them half. I rejoice much in these openings of Providence, but the consequence is that if every Brother could divide himself into two, and occupy two stations instead of one it would be his duty so to do.

Carey to Jabez, Sept. 13, 1819

. . . I hope you have before this made a beginning with a school or schools. If not pray begin one, at least without delay. We can only raise funds for the schools in Rajputana by some report of their commencement. Do also write to Bro. Marshman as Secretary to our schools, a short report of what you have done or are doing. The time to make our report is fast approaching; and we therefore wait with considerable expectation for your report that it may be incorporated in our general report.

Pray My Dear Jabez, do not let anything else divert your mind from the important object in which you are engaged. To do good is the greatest honour of Man, and to persevere in doing good in the midst of discouragement is what will give you more happiness and ensure you greater respect than a crown would do. For my own part I consider every, even the lowest part, in the Church of Our Lord Jesus Christ, to be higher honour than the greatest earthly dignities.

You are placed in a situation bearing some resemblance to that in which I was when I first came to this country, viz. you stand almost alone in the midst of a large population. You must expect difficulties, you will meet with discouragements, but the work in which you are engaged is the work of God. He first opened the way. He has removed difficulties which formerly blocked up all access to those extensive Regions and I doubt not but he will at last crown your persevering efforts with his blessing.

Carey to Jabez, Apr. 2, 1823

. . . I believe you know and feel that we should all feel much happiness in seeing you; yet the opinion of myself and Jonathan - for I have consulted no one else - is that you ought not to leave your station now. Your station is of vast importance as one from which the light of the Gospel will in due time spread on every side. I have reason to fear that there is no member of the Government who feels the interest in it that Lord Hastings did and a new Governor General is soon expected. What his sentiments on this head may be no one can say and it must be some time before he can be even acquainted with the existence of your Schools and the circumstances under which they originated. Under all these considerations I think your leaving the station at the present time might issue in the breaking up of the schools altogether and with them, the prospect of introducing the Gospel with success into the central parts of India. I should think Mrs. Mills quite capable of taking charge of little William to Calcutta and have no doubt but she will do it with pleasure. William will be here in the midst of those who will do every thing for him with the utmost pleasure and every desirable end will be answered by this arrangement. You are certainly the sole director of your own affairs, nor do I wish to interfere in them, but as an affectionate Father I give you my advice, which is also dictated in a great measure by the interest I feel in the Redeemer's Kingdom, of which I consider the settlement in Ajmere an important part.

Carey to Jabez, Jan. 31, 1825

. . . I am sorry to hear from Jonathan and Lucy that Eliza has written to you to leave your station and come down here. She mentioned it to Anna, and I believe to Lucy or Dolly, but not to me or your Mother. In the first, place I think you to be in a situation evidently opened for you by Divine Providence and though you have not all the liberty of preaching the Gospel you could wish, yet no one can prevent private conversations of the most serious nature, and perhaps your liberty is as great or greater than mine was when I first arrived in the country. Your settlement in these parts is recognized by Government, but I was considered an interloper, and had not authority whatever to exist in the country. God can bless your labours, though they are contracted, and if necessary, he can open the door to the utmost width.

In the second place, Providence has opened no other door for you, and I think it would be wrong to leave a place, evidently prepared for you by God, to go you know not whither, and without any call to another situation. What the Society would do if your were to apply to it for an allowance I cannot tell; but I should think every conscientious person would disapprove the step.

Thirdly, I never heard that you were dissatisfied with your present situation, consequently cannot judge of the grounds of your dissatisfaction, if it exists. If there is not dissatisfaction but that of Eliza, I must say I think that should not weigh against the evident leadings of Providence, and the more so as I fear, no change of situation would make a change for the better in that respect. I am, however, happy to say that Eliza's present appearance is plain and becoming, and inconceivably more consistent than the tawdry appearance she made when here before. She has applied to Jonathan to advance her money, but he has lately lost a large sum of money by the failure of a merchant in Calcutta, and could not advance any without great inconvenience. I am in the same situation, viz. unable to advance money having given my last Rupee, I believe, for my accounts are not yet made up to assist my poor Relations in England, and my greatest distress now is, that I fear I must discontinue the help I have hitherto afforded them. I was greatly distressed while my former Wife lived, lest, in case of my death, she should be left destitute. My present Wife had property of her own, which I settled on and, therefore, I have not now that source of distress.

Carey to Jabez, Apr. 16, 1826

I received your - date unknown - and since that one dated 16th March informing me of Eliza's return to Ajmere. I am glad to hear of her return, and also that the children are safe and well, still more rejoiced shall I be if your hopes respecting a change in her mind may be realized. The very distressing accounts in your last letter but one, respecting the obstructions laid in the way of preaching the Gospel by the violence of her temper filled me with distress and led to earnest prayer on your behalf. Your last letter, however, contained a formal relinquishment of the work of God and must therefore be considered as a step chosen by yourself and not forced on you by external circumstances. So far as relates to men you are certainly at full liberty to relinquish any line of life and to adopt another but surely you cannot suppose that any of our determinations can set us free from the obligations we owe to God. The Scripture says explicitly "Ye are not your own, for ye are bought with a price, therefore Glorify God in your body and spirit which are God's". The whole parable of the Talents is founded upon the same truth, viz. that we and all we have belong to God and that he expects us to improve all our opportunities and advantages for the promotion of His cause. Again "Ye - or we - are workers together with God. Ye are God's husbandry. Ye are God's Building". It therefore appears plain to me that none of us can throw off our obligations to the service of God, and that even the engaging in his service is not a merely optional thing, but that every person is under an indispensable obligation to serve God in promoting his work to the utmost of his ability and opportunity. God does not require the employment of greater abilities than he bestows but he does require the employment and improvement of what he gives, whether it be five, two or one talent and we can no more withdraw our abilities, however slender, from his service with impunity than he who had but one talent could safely hide his in the earth or wrap it in a napkin.

MOTIVATION AND ENCOURAGEMENT FOR MISSIONS

Even though the need for a mission effort stood clear in Carey's mind, he regularly reminded and encouraged others about the urgency of the work. He worried the Society in England would become discouraged about the lack of visible success and wrote to them with information designed to bolster their resolve to missions. He praised his English colleagues for their vision and courage in organizing for and executing missions.

Carey to Father, Moulton, Jan. 12, 1788

. . . Dear Father, to negotiate between God & men is a Weighty important Work. Indeed, let me have a Share in your Private address to the Great Eternal and never let You, or I Cease to act for God in our Spheres, with indefatigable industry, till we can't find a Soul that's Destitute of Christ in all the World. The thot of a Fellow Creature Perishing for Ever should rouse all our Activity and engage all our Powers. The God we serve deserves all our Hearts and Souls. Tis ever Sordid and Bane to care for none but ourselves. Tis our Divine Jehovah that is Dishonoured by Sin. The Enemy of God Prevails & Reigns with imperious Rage, and Souls are Perishing. The matter is desperate. It Calls for us to live and Act alone for God.

Carey to Sisters, Mudnabati, March 11, 1795

. . . Many changes have taken place with me since I left England, but I find that all have been conducive to my Good, and I trust will be found so to the promotion of the knowledge of the Gospel of our Lord Jesus Christ. Tho I have abundant Cause to complain of my leanness from Day to Day; and the exceedingly ungrateful returns that I make to God for all his very great goodness, and bounty towards me; I am surrounded with favours, nay they are poured in upon me. Yet I find the rebellion of my Heart against God to be so great as to neglect nay forget him, and live in that neglect day after Day without feeling my soul smitten with compunction. I trust that I am not forgotten in the prayers of my friends and perhaps it is in answer to their requests that the spark of love to God is not quite extinguished.

The inestimable blessing of Christian Society is enjoyed but scantily here, to what it is in England; for tho we have very valuable Christian friends, yet they live 20 or 30 miles distant from us; and as traveling is very difficult here there being no High Roads, or Inns, to call at, and in the Rains no way of traveling but by water, we have the pleasure of seeing each other but seldom. Tho when we do it makes our meetings much more sweet and agreeable that they might be if we met oftener. We have in the Neighborhood about fifteen or sixteen serious persons or those I have good hopes of all Europeans. With the Natives I have very large concerns. Almost all the Farmers for near 20 miles round cultivating Indigo for us, and the Labouring people working here to the number of about 500, so that I have considerable opportunity of publishing the Gospel to them. I have so much knowledge of the Language as to be able to preach to them for about half an hour, so as to be understood but am not able to vary my subjects much. I tell them of the evil, and universality of Sin, the misery of a natural State, the Justice of God, the incarnation of Christ and his sufferings in our stead, and of the necessity of Conversion, Holiness, and Faith in order to Salvation. They hear with attention in general, and some come to me for instruction in the things of God. I hope in time I may have to rejoice over some who are truly converted go God.

Carey to Society, Dec. 28, 1796, Hooghly River

Addressed: To the Baptist Society for sending the Gospel to Heathen

{Carey does not have a success report but does want to encourage the work of the Society.}

. . . I want now to attempt to encourage our beloved Friends, not by relating our own Zeal, activity or success; we can only say that upon the whole we have not forgot our errand, and tho we have very great reason to bemoan our own unfitness for the great Work, yet we have been doing something. But I wish to encourage you by the recollection of what God has wrought. When the society was first established many were the doubts whether it would not be crushed in its infancy, but is has now stood a considerable time and its success tho not equal to its wishes, is not however so small as to be imperceptible. Many Thousands have heard the Word of the Gospel from our mouth; and the name of Christ begins to be known in several parts of the Country. Seven Persons we hope are indeed Converted in this Country - and you have been enabled to send two Missionaries to Africa and one more to us who is safely arrived. Perhaps two more proper spots to make a larger stand, for the spread of the Gospel could scarcely have been chosen. Sierra Leone is a central situation in Africa, and Bengal in Asia - from which Missionaries may go forth to very, very distant parts. I, therefore, sincerely wish you to fix your attention to the strengthening these two Missions by all the means in your Power

Carey to Society Dec. 9, 1797 to Fountain as well

One of our own Poets had said, when speaking of the Principle which prompts us thus to address you,

"The Fellowship of kindred Minds
Is like to that above".

Experience proves the truth of this Observation & the Consideration of it rejoices our Hearts. Could the same be said of our Communion we should feel an Additional Delight, but this will not, cannot be compleat till in a better World than this we all meet together".

. . . Amongst all the similes made use of in the Scriptures to represent a Minister's Work, that of Husbandry seems the best adapted to comfort our Minds and inspire our Hopes. In that occupation of Life it is frequently seen that "one soweth and another reapeth". Yea, it seldom happens that he who casteth the seed gathereth in the Harvest. In this Wilderness Brethren, your Missionaries have been labouring for four Years: A Wilderness where nothing hath yet grown but the most rank and poisonous weeds. Breaking the Uncultivated ground, Rooting up its native productions, and Sowing the good seed, hath been their constant employ. Though no fruit yet appears, they must not desist from their Labours. "The Husbandman waiteth for the precious fruit of the earth, and hath long Patience for it, until he receive the former and the latter Rain". So when the Holy Spirit shall be poured from on high this Wilderness shall become a fruitful field. A great Harvest was gathered in by the Apostles of our Lord; but it was observed to them, that they "reaped that whereon they bestowed no Labour".

. . . With the Moravians none are yet to be compared either for Zeal - Labour - Perseverance - or success; but after them You were the first to engage in the God-like work of Missions. Your Zeal, worthy Brethren, hath provoked that of many others, to whose noble efforts we devotedly wish success. But as you have sent to this distant part of the World, where before, Christ had not been named, but by his enemies, we earnestly entreat you to follow up what you have begun. Embrace presenting prospects. Enter the Doors opening by your God and Saviour. I think how many and great are the Asiatic Nations here laying contiguous to each other; All of them are morally dark as the World itself naturally was . . .

. . . What could three Ministers do even in England, supposing it now as dark and rude as when Caesar first discovered it?

JOY IN THE WORK OF MISSIONS

Carey to Ryland, Bandel, Dec. 26, 1793

. . . I never in my life found more satisfaction in any undertaking than in this in which I am now engaged. And tho I have lost much in point of social intercourse, yet I find a sweetness in reflecting upon the cause in which I am embarked which more than compensates for every loss that I can sustain. The pleasure of being able to preach the Gospel I enjoyed greatly while in England which I cannot now enjoy on account of my ignorance of the language tho I can speak a few phrases and understand several things relating to the common business of Life . . .

Carey to Society, Dec. 28, 1796, Hooghly River

. . . I have nothing more to add but my warm wishes for the prosperity of the Society, and its establishment on the most permanent Basis. I rejoice much in the mission to Africa. Pray convey my warm Love to Brethren Grigg and Rodway, and tell them that they are often remembered by us in our solemn meetings for Prayer; especially on the first Monday of the month when we meet constantly unless something unavoidable detain us from each other. I hope the Labours of those dear Souls may be far more successful than our own have been and that they may be supported to labour constantly for God.

Carey to Fuller, July 17, 1799, Mudnabati

All these letters have given us much pleasure particularly of our being soon joined by other Missionaries . . . The success of the Gospel, and among other things, the hitherto inextinguishable missionary flame in England and all the Western World give us no little encouragement, and animate our hearts. I wish we could warm yours with good tidings in return.

Life on the Mission Field

"Culture shock" is a common phrase used in discussions about missions, but imagine what a missionary in 1793 India faced? Certainly, Carey understood "culture shock" and wrote often about his encounter with India and its cultural oddities—at least odd in the eyes of an Englishman. His descriptions and opinions concerning his new home express both admiration and repulsion. He accepted some aspects of life in India and sought diligently to change others.

Much of Carey's life on the field consisted of his daily work as a missionary. Some of the most interesting letters are those which report his activities. Carey busied himself in mission work, leaving hardly a moment for leisure. Most of his time focused on the job of translation. He worked with Pundits and other missionaries to produce and perfect translations of the Bible into several languages. He declared frequently his commitment to providing the people with the best text of Scripture possible, feeling that all future interpretation and theological understanding would grow out of the accuracy of the translation.

Life on the field as a missionary consisted of successes and failures. Early on, little success occurred but the later letters are sprinkled with names of people and movements touched by God's power. Life centers around relationships that are often both pleasant and difficult. Carey's relationships with the other missionaries and the problems associated therein became a prominent correspondence theme. Life for the missionary was also punctuated with death, disease, tragedy and opposition. In spite of the tribulations, Carey resolved to stay and make India his new country and missions his lifelong work.

India

Carey was fascinated with the natural phenomena found in plants and animals in India. He studied the cities and people to discover lifestyle and character. Occasionally, he made some rather stereotypical statements about groups of natives. He also held strong opinions of opposition toward the customs dictated by caste and religion. Practices such as suttee *{sati}* (the ritual of a Hindu wife burning herself at her husband's funeral) and the sacrificial system that Carey confronted caused him to crusade against their continuance. Following are accounts of Carey's encounter with India.

Carey to Ryland, Bandel, Dec. 26, 1793

Jan. 2, 94 - On account of Mr. T's embarrassed circumstances he is obliged to practice Surgery at Calcutta where there is a prospect of a large and effectual door for the Gospel likely to be opened. Several Brahmans and Pundits have been very pressing with us to settle here and preach to them. Accordingly Mr. T. was at Calcutta and I at an house belonging to a Black man, who generously offered it to me for nothing, till I am otherwise settled. I am about renting a small quantity of land of a native about ten miles east of the city so that we may have an opportunity for preaching the Gospel all over the most prosperous part of Bengal - the City of Calcutta is very large; Munshi guesses the inhabitants to be ten or twelve Lack of people, or 1,000,000 or 1,200,000. This must exceed the truth, tho I have no doubt but there may be 200,000 black people in it besides the Europeans - among whom also there is a probability of our preaching, as several have wished for it.

Since I have been here My Family has been very heavily afflicted with the Bloody Flux. My Wife and two eldest children have been very ill, and it is still a great doubt whether my eldest son will recover of not. Many might attribute this to the climate, I believe it might arise from cold - but I am more convinced that all my times are in the hand of God - and that as all is under his direction, so all things shall work together for good to them who love God. I had fully intended to devote my eldest son to the study of Sanskrit, my second, Persian - and my third Chinese. I shall have opportunity for this, and if God should hereafter bless them with his grace this may fit them for a Mission to any part of Persia, India, or China. The difficulty of preaching to Heathens is I presume much less than has been imagined, I think from what I have seen that there would be very little danger of hurt, in either Heathen or Mohammedan Countries and if this country is any specimen at all, I think the encouragement to be very great. I hope the Society may be strengthened, and encouraged, - and that we may soon be able to encourage them by good accounts of us.

Carey to Fuller Jan. 30 1795

I have frequent opportunities of preaching to Europeans here; and of Social Converse with Valuable Men; and I am able to preach a little in Bengali or rather I mix Bengali and Hindustani together but can be understood tolerably well; much better than I can understand them. My situation obliges me to travel much, and I have had opportunities of preaching near [100] one hundred Miles further up the Country. I was a little time ago within sight of the Mountains which part Bengal from Tibet; and almost out of the Company's Dominions: So that not only in my own neighborhood, is the Word preached, but I have opportunities of publishing [the Word] it to the more distant inhabitants of the country and where no European has ever been before.

I cannot help hoping that God will soon work for his own glory, in the Conversion of some of the People. They hear with great attention, and some have declared their resolution to part with all their Superstitions, and seek the true God. Poor Souls - they have need of the Gospel indeed! Their Superstitions are so numerous, and all their thoughts of God so very light, that they only consider him as a sort of Plaything. Avarice and servility are so [joined in, I think] united in almost every individual, that Cheating, Juggling, and Lying, are esteemed no sins with them: and the best among them, tho they speak even so great a falsehood, yet it is not considered as an evil, unless you first charge them to speak the Truth. If they Cheat you ever so much, when you charge them with it, they cooly answer, "It is the Custom of the Country".

This may serve to show you how difficult it is to convince them of Sin for tho their Shastras abound in expressions of the evil of the Heart, and the necessity of an entire Change. Yet not one in a Thousand has ever seen or heard even them. Nay, I have found many Brahmans so Ignorant that they have never seen their own Shastras; and many who are esteemed Learned don't know the difference between the Sanskrit Grammar, and a Religious Book. [An instance of this occurred] Thurs Last Lord's Day. I had occasion to go and preach to a Company of people who were worshiping Saroseade *{Sarasvati}*, the Patroness of Literature. [The Brahman who attended the ceremonies told me plainly that the Image was God.] [tho] The general opinion of the most learned is, that the Idols are only images, having no power in them, but that it is well pleasing to God to worship them, in honour of persons they represent, who they say were eminent for Virtue or Good to Man: [he said] The Brahman, however, who attended this ceremony told me plainly that the Image was God. When I asked him by what authority [command] he did this he answered that the Shastra commanded it. I enquired what Shastra. He said, the *Bee Accoran*, which I knew to be only a Grammar. I was much drawn out in Love to their Souls, and was enabled to discourse with them, and warn them against the devices of their teachers for a considerable time, and felt [a very considerable] more than usual Liberty in speaking, and but little Want of Words.

Carey to Richard Brewin, March 12, 1795

I would perhaps appear an intrusive Egotist if I were to detail the leadings of Providence with respect to myself and family. I therefore shall only say that our passage was safe.

. . . The caste is the great obstacle to improvement and knowledge for whatsoever employment the Fathers followed that is the employment of their children from generation to generation, nor can they get out of it to any other on which account very few can read or write, that thing being the employment of the Brahmans and Caste and very few others knowing any thing of it.

Carey to Ryland, Mudnabati, April 1, 1799

As I was returning from Calcutta I saw the Sahamoron, or a Woman burning herself with the corpse of her husband, for the first time in my life. We were near the village of Noya Serai, or as Rennel calls it in his chart of the Hooghly River, Niaserai. Being Evening we got out of the Boat to walk, when we saw a number of people assembled on the River Side. I asked them what they were met for. They told me to burn the body of a dead man. I inquired if his Wife would die with him, they answered yes, and pointed to the Woman. She was standing by the pile which was made of large Billets of Wood, about 2 feet high, 4 feet long, and two wide, on the top of which lay the dead Body of her husband. Her nearest relations stood by her, and near her was a small basket of sweetmeats, called Kivy. I asked them if this was the woman's choice, or if she were brought to it by an improper influence? They answered that it was perfectly voluntary. I talked till reasoning was of no use, and then began to explain with all my might against what they were doing, telling them that it was a shocking Murder. They told me it was a great act of Holiness; and added in a very surly manner that if I did not like to see it, I might go further off and desired me to go. I told them that I would not go - that I was determined to stay and see the Murder, and that I should certainly bear witness of it at the tribunal of God. I exhorted the woman not to throw away her life - to fear nothing for no evil would follow her refusing to burn. But she in the most calm manner mounted the Pile, and danced on it with her hands extended as if in the utmost tranquility of spirit.

Previous to her mounting the Pile the relation whose office it was to set fire to the Pile, led her six times round the Pile, at two intervals, that is thrice at each circumambulation. As she went round she scattered the sweetmeats above mentioned among the People, who picked it up and eat it as a very holy thing. This being ended and she having mounted the Pile and danced as above mentioned (N.B. the dancing only appeared to have been to shew us her contempt of death, and prove to us that her dying was voluntary) she lay down by the corpse and put one arm under its neck and the other over it. When a quantity of dry Cocoa Leaves, and other substances were heaped over them to a considerable height, and then Ghee - melted preserved butter - poured on the top. Two Bamboos were then put over them and held fast down, and fire put to the Pile blazed which immediately very fiercely owing to the dry and combustible materials of which it was composed. No sooner was the fire kindled than all the people set up a great shout, "Hurree Bol, Hurree Bol" - which is a common shout of joy, and invocation of Hurree the wife of Hur or Seeb *{Shiva?}*. It was impossible to have heard the Woman had she groaned, or even cried aloud on account of the mad noise of the people, and it was impossible for her to stir, or struggle, on account of the Bamboo which were held down on them like the levers of a press. We made much objection to their using these Bamboos and insisted that it was using force to prevent the woman getting up when the fire burnt her. But they declared that it was only done to keep the pile from falling down. We could not bear to see more but left them exclaiming loudly against the Murder and full horror at what we had seen.

Carey to Father, Serampore, Oct. 6, 1800

. . . We now live at Serampore near Calcutta which is a Danish Settlement, and here we enjoy the protection of the Governor, Col. Bie who is a most friendly man and may be called the father of the Settlement. In this place we all live together in one happy Family having purchased a House and premises for the Mission sufficiently large to accommodate us all. This part of the Country is very populous indeed, and wholly given to Idolatry. It is not possible to describe the stupidity of the Worship or the strength of their attachment to the customs and practices of their forefathers. We preach to them, converse and dispute with them; visit them at their Houses, and are now printing the word of God in their Language. The Gospel of Matthew has been dispersed, and also several other pieces, calculated to strike their Hearts and engage them to think of their immortal Souls. At present, however, very small fruit appears, tho perhaps we sometimes overlook what would be esteemed very great effects, was it not that by their appearing so gradually they don't strike us much . . .

. . . I wish you to be quite easy about the dangers which you suppose we may be exposed to. I don't think our personal danger is greater; perhaps not so great as that of many preachers of the Gospel in England. We oppose the Brahmans to the utmost of our Power and take opportunities to persuade them against the worship of Idols even before the face of the idols themselves but the Hindus tho sunk in the grossest vice are yet not ferocious.

Carey to Fuller, Jan. 21, 1802

Several religious murders were lately detected at Langur Island, which is just at the mouth of the holy Ganges. In consequence of which I as Teacher of the Bengali language received an order from the vice President through the medium of Mr. Buchanan to make every enquiry which I can into the number, nature, and reasons of those Murders, and to make as full a report as I can of the whole to the government. You may be sure that I shall do it with great pleasure for I think that burning of women, burying them live with their husbands as is the case of many Yagiis *{Yagas?}*, exposing of infants, sacrificing children of Ganges, and voluntary death in the River, ought not to be permitted, whatever religious motives may be pretended because they are all crimes against the state.

Carey to Ryland, Jan. 20, 1807

. . . Rev. Buchanan is now returning from his tour to the south. He has visited all the most noted places of idolatry, all the Missionaries and Christian congregations in the south and the Jews at Cochin and its environs. He went to Ceylon to see the state of the Christians there, and has visited the Syrian churches at Malabar, where he has met with some most interesting circumstances. These Christians have resided there ever since the fourth century, if not before that. They some of them, had never seen a printed Bible, and did not know that there were any Christians in the world besides themselves, except the Roman Catholics: from whom they have met with much persecution, by whom they were subjugated to the Roman Church for about eighty years, and whom they compleatly abhor. Dr. B. found many very ancient Mss. of the Syrian Scriptures, and other ancient books, and has engaged them to set up Christian Schools in every village, and to encourage the translation, and circulation of the S. Scrip in the Malayala *{Malayan?}* language. I hope I will publish an account of his tour. It will be one of the most interesting accounts ever published. At a meeting for prayer, held in a cidevant heathen temple, belonging to our friend Rev. D. Brown, for the purpose of discussing Brethren Mardon and Chater from thence to their work at Rangoon, Mr. Brown read a letter from Dr. Buchanan for more than 20 pp. giving a most interesting account of his interview with these Syrian Christians.

Carey to Ryland, Apr. 27, 1808

. . . You have puzzled yourself about Bro. Marshman's consistency by confounding two things which we think totally distinct, viz. Human Sacrifices, and the burning of Women with their husbands. - We do not reckon the latter under the denomination of sacrifices. Human sacrifices are such as are immolated to some god: and are seldom offered. Women very frequently burn themselves with their husbands, but in this case they are not offered to any god. They burn themselves to attend their husbands in the next state of existence and as a proof of their constancy. I have no opinion of Dr. Buchanan's scheme for a religious establishment here, nor could I from memory point out what is exceptionable in his memoir: All his representations must be taken with some grains of allowance. The report of the burning of Women, and some others, however, were made by me. I, at his expence, made the enquiries, and furnished the reports, and believe they are rather below the truth than above it. I have since I have been here through different mediums presented three petitions or representations to Government for the purpose of having the burning of Women and other modes of murder abolished; and have succeeded in the case of infanticide, and voluntary drowning in the river. Laws were made to prevent these, which have been successful. Lord Minto told Bro. M. and me that a district in Goozerat had lately agreed to abolish infanticide.

Carey to Ryland, Oct. 24, 1810

About a month ago I received a Letter from my Son Felix of which the following extract will give you pleasure. "The present Viceroy is uncommonly kind to strangers of every description, but more especially to me. He has been once to see us, and wishes us to call on him as often as we can find it convenient. He is of a very free and affable disposition. The other day I went to him to intercede in behalf of a poor sufferer who was crucified and condemned to die in that situation. After I had pleaded for about half an hour he granted my request though he had denied several other people among whom was the Ceylon Priest. I took the poor man down after he had been nailed up for more than six hours, brought him home, and dressed his wounds and now he is nearly cured. This man will now, by law, belong to me as long as he lives, and I hope may not only be useful as a servant, but a real Christian".

. . . I have just been asking Bro. Chater, who is now here with Sister Chater, whose health is in a very weak state, about he crucifixion of this poor man, and the procuring of his deliverance. He confirms all I have mentioned above except two things in which I suppose I was mistaken. I have stated that Felix was returning from visiting his patients, but I find it was as he was going to visit them that he saw the poor man. I have also said that the Viceroy had in a moment of confidence given Felix leave to enter his private apartments: this is not correct, I find that Felix was in the habit of visiting a female relation of the Viceroy who was ill, and, therefore, as a medical man had access to all the private apartments. The Viceroy had given orders that no one should be admitted.

I understand that the punishment of crucifixion is not performed on separate crosses elevated to a considerable height as in pictures of the Crucifixion of Christ, but several parts are set up which are connected by rails near the top, to which the hands of the criminal are nailed: and by a rail at bottom even with the ground to which the feet are nailed in a horizontal position. The crucifixion of this man took place about the 10th of August. The man was nailed up about three in the afternoon and taken down between nine and ten at night. Bro. Chater says he believes that Felix was the only person in the place who could have succeeded, and that it has gained him much renowned among the Burmans. The family was much alarmed for his safety and knew nothing of the transaction till he arrived at home with a number of officers and others with the poor man. I understand that he was able to sit up the next day, and expressed a high sense of gratitude. In about a fortnight he was able to stand.

Carey to Sutcliffe, Calcutta, Mar. 20, 1811

Bro. Robinson and Bro. & Sister Cornish had arrived at Bro. Robinson's old habitation on the border of the Bhutan dominions; when the third night after their arrival their house was assaulted about midnight by a gang of fifty or Sixty robbers, armed with spears, They murdered three of their Servants, and it was owing to a most kind providence that they escaped. The two Brethren, with Mrs. Cornish and a young Child escaped through a window, and providentially went over a ditch out of the premises where there was no road. To this circumstance they were indebted, under God, for their lives; for every road to the house was guarded by armed men. They remained in the field all night, and in the morning found that the house had been plundered of every thing, and that the thieves had destroyed what they could not take away. They left the House and traveled to Dinajpur, where their wants were relieved by Bro. Fernandez and Mrs. Derazios family. Bro. Cornish has since that left that Mission and returned to Serampore. Indeed the two brethren did not - perfectly move in unison. They were not formed for each other. I am glad, however, to say that Bro. Robinson perseveres in his undertaking and, having provided himself with a tent, is going immediately to concert matters with the Bhutan governor.

Carey to Sisters, Aug. 18, 1828, Calcutta

. . . A few months ago, viz. April and May, the heat was so intense and debilitating that I had almost made up my mind to return to England if Government would allow me a Pension. I quite dreaded such another season. But since I have reconsidered the matter and feel resolved to end my days in India. I am here in the midst of a sphere of some usefulness, and among Friends whom I love, and also love me, and Medical men whom I have consulted think it very doubtful whether England would suit my constitution so well as India. All my old Friends in England are dead and England looks to me like a vast blank.

Carey to Sisters, Dec. 17, 1829, Serampore

On the 4th of this month a regulation was passed by The Governor General in Council to forbid the burning or burying alive of Hindu Widows with their husbands. This is a matter of utmost importance and calls for our loudest thanks.

DAILY WORK

Undoubtedly the most fascinating information Carey records in his correspondence describes his regular work as a missionary. He even details a week's routine for Ryland and his Father. Although Carey reckoned his greatest and most important work to be that of translation, he was ever busy at other tasks like preaching, teaching, organizing, encouraging, and leading the mission project. No one accused William Carey of being indolent or unmotivated.

Carey to Society, Aug. 13, 1795, Mudnabati

An Opportunity now presents itself, for me to write you a few words of my Welfare, and State; and by this Opportunity I send my Journal by which you will see a little of the manner of my Life; [Some things in it, as Mr. Thomas' engaging in Business &ct. at Calcutta, I desire to have forever suppressed, and buried in Oblivion; as I am convinced that it was only occasioned by temporary Circumstances; and from that time to this] the utmost Harmony and affection has prevailed between us. I think the whole of it can only present a melancholy picture of Sameness, and be tedious as a twice told tale.

I trust we have not been altogether Idle tho I know not as yet of any Success that has attended our Labours. Munshi, and Mohund Chund are now with me; but I don't see that disinterested Zeal which is so ornamental to a Christian in either of them; Yet they have good knowledge of the things of God considering their disadvantages; with their help we have divine Worship twice on the Lord's Day in Bengali; which is thus conducted. First, Munshi reads a Chapter in Bengali, then we Sing; afterwards I pray, and preach to them in that Language. Partly from Local Circumstances, and partly from paucity of Words, my Preaching is very different to what it was in England; but the Guilt and depravity of Mankind and the Redemption by Christ, with the presence of God's Mercy; are the themes I most insist upon . . .

. . . One great Difficulty in speaking to the Bengal people arises from the extreme Ignorance of the Common people, who are not able to understand one of their own Countryman who speaks the Language well without considerable difficulty. They have a confined Dialect, composed of a very few Words which they work about and make them mean almost everything and their poverty of Word, to express religious Ideas is amazing, all their Conversation being about things earthly. Tis for otherwise, however, with them who speak the Language well; the Language is extremely rich and Copious; and the publishing of the Bible must make it more known to the Common People - . . .

. . . I have only to add that I suppose you will have great difficulty in reading my Diary; the Damp Air of the Rainy Season had extracted all the size out of the Paper, and I was Short of that article so could not replace. I have discontinued it for some time, but now new occurrence has taken place since I wrote my last Journal. I intend now immediately to resume it and send you regular accounts thereof.-

Carey to Sisters, Mudnabatti, Apr. 10, 1796

I know not what to say about the Mission. I feel as a Farmer does about his crop; sometimes I think the seed is springing, and then I hope; a little time blasts all and my hopes are gone like a Cloud. Twas only weeds that appeared; or if a little Corn spring up, it quickly died, being either choked with Weeds, or parched up by the sun of Persecution. Yet, I still hope in God and will go forth in his strength and make mention of his Righteousness, even of him only.

I preach every day to the Natives, and twice on the Lord's Day constantly, besides other itinerant labours, and I try to speak of Jesus Christ and him crucified, and of him alone, but my soul is often much dejected to see no fruit. This morning I preached to a number from "to know the Love of God which passeth knowledge". I was much affected myself, filled with grief and anguish of Heart, because I knew they were going to Idolatrous and Mohammedan feasts immediately after, this being the first day of the Hindu Year; and the new Moon Ramadan of the Mohammedans. They are going I suppose to their Abominations at this moment, but I hope to preach to them again in the evening. I spoke of the Love of God in bearing with his Enemies, in supporting and providing for them, in sending his Son to die for them, in sending the Gospel to them, and in saving many of them from eternal Wrath.

Carey to Fuller, Nov. 16, 1796, Mudnabati

{Carey is replying to several letters he finally received from Fuller and others. He was asked by Fuller to give an account of Mr. Thomas and does so.}

Thomas is a man who is either hot or cold in religion and the cold runs longer. He cannot take any correction but always "misconstrues" it as a "reflection upon his conduct". He was not in debt in India when he arrived but owed in Europe of not less than 2,000 pounds. He is now in debt to almost every one who would give him credit, either little or much and what will be the consequences I dread . . . Indeed, I do not think he could live upon any income . . .

Mr. Thomas is a man of great closet Piety and has lately preached much among the Natives. I have great hope of some People there, and am not without hope of one here. Mr. T. is very compassionate to the poor, and in instructing those who are enquiring he is indefatigable; he has excellent ability for that work; being perhaps one of the most affectionate and close exhorters to genuine Godliness, and a close walk with God that can be thought of. The Natives who appear under Concern here are all Mussulmen. I went out one Monday morning when a Man named Soohman very earnestly desired to know "what he must do to be saved", two more made the same inquiry; adding We heard you yesterday, when you, having shared the Danger we were in of going to Hell, enquired "Whither will you flee from his Spirit -

whither will flee from his presence". We knew we were unacquainted with the way of Life, and our [Saints long since died] cannot help us; for if the Master be angry what can the Servant do? You have told us of Jesus Christ: but who is he, how shall we be saved? I talked much with them almost everyday. But two whose names were Tuphanee and Jungloo soon ceased their enquiries. Soohman still gives me hope tho it is three months since the enquiry began; . . .

Carey to Ryland, Mudnabati, April 1, 1799

On the way down we stopped at a large town called Kulna, for the Sabbath - I tried to collect a Congregation there but in vain, yet in the course of the Day, I had several publick disputations and one which gave me great pleasure. I sat under a tree near a large temple of Jagganath, and after disputes with several persons, a young Brahman came and accosted me thus. Sir, if you will not be offended I will sit down and prove all that you have said to be false. I desired him to sit down and try which he did, and after about two hours close reasoning on both sides, in which he used all sophistry he was master of, and that was not a little; he found himself impounded. He had declared at first that God was Light and in him was no Darkness at all, but he was now forced to say roundly that God was possessed of sinful inclinations like Man or to give up his Cause. I seeing his difficulty thus addressed him before the Multitude. Brahman, You know that you have used every crooked argument in your power to support your Cause, notwithstanding which you are involved in an inextricable difficulty. Why will you adhere to so bad a Cause? I then spoke to him of the Way of Life by Christ, and the Harmony of the Gospel plan (and) prayed with them. After Prayer he told me, Sir, Never in my Life had I a Day of such Pleasure. I left my Country (he was a Native of Orissa) and friends to come here and study the Shastras, but I am convinced that the Way of the Shastras is not the true way. When you prayed I felt my Heart pray with you. - This open free young man we left, and he perhaps may never hear the Word of Life more . . .

Carey to Father, Nov. 23, 1801, Serampore

. . . Delivering two Lectures in the Sanskrit and two on the Bengali Language in a Week, Preaching to the natives, and my turn to Europeans, visiting our little Flock, and attending to my share of domestic concerns occupy my time so much that I am sometimes forced a little to transgress the just Bounds of propriety, and infringe upon the Hours of Sleep. I say this that no one may wonder at my not writing more often than I do, and I think that it will be a sufficient apology . . .

We all live in a common Family, and together with our Scholars (for we have a School for Young Ladies & another for Gentlemen) we make between thirty and forty at Table every Day - It is impossible perhaps that greater harmony should subsist in this imperfect state than does exist among us . . .

Carey to Father, Dec. 1, 1802

{Carey gives his father an example of a week of his work.}

. . . On Tuesday at three o'clock in the afternoon I leave Serampore for Calcutta and arrive there about six. I have a House and table in the College, and as soon as I arrive my labour begins, viz. preparing my Grammar, and Dictionary for the press. At eight in the evening we have a meeting for Prayer with a few persons in Town. On Wednesday, I deliver lectures on the Bengali and Sanskrit languages which begin between nine and ten in the morning and last till about three in the afternoon. The morning before Lecture is little enough for my private reading, &ct. At three o'clock I dine, and then to those labours till church time. For we have a Lecture at Church at eight o'clock on Wednesday evenings by Bros. Brown or Buchanan, both of whom are evangelical clergymen. After Church time I sometimes write Letters, sometimes other things. On Thursday after private reading &ct. I often go out to Breakfast with some religious friend, and at ten o'clock I am surrounded by the Pundits; some of them servants of the College, and some expecting to get places. With them I examine all that I write in the time of their absence. This lasts till dinner time.

After dinner I preach at the House of a Portugese man to a few of that Nation, and I hope not altogether without affect. On the Evening I attend the Philosophical and Chymical Lecture at College which is delivered by Dr. Dinwiddie. Friday is my day for Lecturing in the languages again, which last till three or four when dinner is on the table. The Buggy is waiting at the door before dinner is over and I arrive at Serampore which is a distance of 14 miles for tea. Immediately after Tea is family worship, and then a meeting for relating the state of our Minds with our Hindu Christians. We have a fine large garden; I spend half an hour on Saturday morning, then Family prayer. Afterwards Breakfast and every one to his work. Mine is that of preparing the copy of the Bible for the press, correcting proof sheets &ct., which can scarcely be done in the day. An Hour before night we go out to preach or converse with the Natives. On Saturday night settle our temporal concerns, Lord's Day morning preach in the street in Bengali, at eleven in English to a few persons in our own houses and in the evening go to some neighboring village to preach. After which we have preaching in Bengali in our own Family. Monday is spent as Saturday. On Monday evening I deliver a Lecture on Geography, Astronomy or Natural History to the Scholars. Tuesday Morning we have a meeting of prayer for the success of the Gospel. The day till three o'clock is spent as Monday. At three I set off again for Calcutta. This is our ordinary course besides journeys to preach, and visits from Natives for the purpose of hearing the Gospel, or at least pretendedly so. Thus you see that we have no time for Idleness . . . Thus I have given you a hearty sketch of my ordinary occupation for a Week that you may form some Idea of what we are doing.

Carey to Ryland, Dec. 13, 1804

. . . Some time ago a Class in the Mahratta - prop. Maharashtra languages was set up in the college, and placed under me: so that I have now this language to teach. I have in consequence been obliged to study that Language, and have begun to print a Grammar of it.

I shall probably send you by this conveyance, or soon after, a copy of the College disputations for 1802 and 1803. At the latter I was chosen moderator in the Bengali and Sanskrit, and was obliged to deliver a publick speech before the Governor General, and all the first officers of Government and principal people of the Settlement, in each of those languages. My speech in Sanskrit is printed amongst the disputations. It is much enlarged. The address to the Governor General in the original speech was very short. Mr. Buchanan, to whom I gave it for correction, added to it (the whole of the flattery is his) and sent it to Lord Wellesley for his inspection without saying anything to me till it was returned, with a Letter of the highest approbation from his Lordship, written and signed with his own hand. Mr. B.'s design was to bring our mission forward upon that publick occasion, and he was very anxious about the event till Lord W.'s letter came.

Carey to Ryland, June 12, 1806

My Dear Bro.

I am extremely loth to let this opportunity pass without dropping you a line, and yet scarcely can find time to write to any one. I give you a short view of my engagements for the present day which is a specimen of the spending one half of the week. I rose this day at a quarter before six, read a chapter in the Hebrew Bible, and spent the time till seven on private addresses to God, and then attended family prayer with the servants in Bengali. While tea was pouring out I read a little in Persian with a Munshi who was waiting when I left my bedroom - read also before breakfast a portion of the Scriptures in Hindustani. The moment breakfast was over set down to the translation of the *Ramayana* from Sanskrit with a Pundit, continued this translation till ten o'clock, at which time I went to College, and attended the duties there till between one and two o'clock. When I returned home I examined a proof sheet of the Bengali translation of Jeremiah, which took me till dinner time. I always, when in town, dine at Mr. Rolts which is near. After dinner translated with the assistance of the chief pundit of the College, greatest part of the 8th chapter of Matthew, into Sanskrit. This employed me till six o'clock, after six set down with a Telugu pundit (who is translating from the Sanskrit into the language of his country) to learn that language.

Mr. Thomas (son of Rev. Tho. Thomas of London) called in the evening; I began to collect a few previous thoughts into the form of a Sermon, at Seven o'clock, and preached in English at half past seven. About forty persons present, among them one of the Puisne Judges of the Sudder Dewany Adaulut. After the sermon I attacked him and got a subscription from him of 500 Rupees (63 pounds. 10 schillings) towards erecting our new place of worship. He is an exceeding friendly man, bears a sort of general good will to religion, and the congregation gone by nine o'clock. I then sat down and translated the 11th of Ezekiel into Bengali. (I have thrown away my former translation and am retranslating the Chapter in the Greek testament, and commending myself to God.) I have never more time in a day than this, though the exercises vary.

On Tuesday evening I come down from Serampore and sit down to the *Ramayana* till eight o'clock, when a few friends meet for prayer and Conference. Wednesday evening at five o'clock I preach in Bengali, and at eight in the evening go to hear Mr. Brown at Church. This is Thursday. On Friday evening return to Serampore. We have then a Conference with our native Brethren, after which Bro. Marshman and I revise the *Ramayana* till eleven o'clock or past. At six o'clock the next morning we begin the same business and continue at it till near eight. Then Breakfast and family prayers. Revisal of proof sheets and translations occupy the rest of the day till family prayer in the evening. After tea, family consultations and other temporal concerns of the Mission employ us till midnight. Lord's Day. Exercises are various. Monday, *Ramayana* till Breakfast. After breakfast proof sheets & translations till night. After tea, a lecture on some science till nine, then *Ramayana* till eleven. Tuesday, at six *Ramayana* till seven - At seven social prayer for the Gospel in Hindustan. At eight breakfast. Then the same course as on Monday till four o'clock. Then to Calcutta. Thus I spend my time. All our Brethren are in various ways fully employed.

Carey to J. D. Moxon, Jan. 3, 1816

. . . To this may be added that my time is closely occupied from early in the morning till ten at Night without interruption in the labours of translating the Scriptures and superintending the press, viz. correcting the proof sheets. I am frequently so worn out that I am tempted rather to indulge myself with an hours relaxation than to sit down to write a Letter.

DIFFICULTIES WITH THE GOVERNMENT

The complex arrangement between the British East India Company and the British government presented the Baptist missionaries in India with some very trying problems. A legal cloud hovered over them regarding their right to be in the country without being directly connected to the company. Some missionaries were indeed sent back to England upon arrival in India. More than once the government issued decrees demanding censure rights to missionary publications and forbidding the open evangelization of the natives, fearing riot and rebellion. Carey and his associates remained faithful, refusing to bend to the will of government as opposed to the will of God.

Carey to Fuller, Aug. 26, 1806, Calcutta

. . . message to communicate to me from Sir G. Barlow to express his wish that we would not interfere with the prejudices of the natives by preaching, dispensing books or pamphlets, or any other mode of instruction nor permit converted natives to go into the country to preach. I told him I thought it very hard that a privilege should be denied to a body of Protestants well known to government which had been always allowed to Roman Catholics. I told him also that we would conform to the wishes of government as much as we conscientiously could do; and that my business was not with Sir. G. Barlow himself.

This morning I went to see Mr. Udney and told him all the whole affair asking his advice. He told me that he had not heard a syllable of the matter, but supposed it to have been occasioned by a circumstance which lately took place on the coast. A native regiment there mutinied and one night murdered all their officers. It is likely that this arose from an attempt made to oblige them to wear a piece of leather as a cap or in the turban. They suspecting it to have been manufactured from cow hides opposed it.. Men who hate the Word of God will say anything, and many are weak enough to believe what they say . . . I told him *{Mr. Udney}* that we were exactly in the situation that the apostles were in when they were commanded not to preach any more in his name and that we must reply as they did, "whether it be right in the sight of God . . . judge ye". He advised me to be as cool as possible saying . . . it would in all likelihood blow over . . .

Carey to Ryland, Nov. 11, 1806

I wrote a little time ago in a mournful strain to give an account of the obstruction in our work which we met with from Government. The arrival of our Brethren Chater & Robinson has caused us great joy, and has been attended with some difficulty. The G.G. in Council passed an order for them to return by the same ship, and the Captain was informed that a clearance would be refused him unless he took them back. Our Friend (Rev. Mr. Brown) interested himself much on our account and Mr. Udney promised me to do his utmost to prevent ultimate evil consequence: we represented to Government that the Capt. cleared out from Rotterdam for Serampore, and that his clearing out from England for Serampore was no more than a necessary step to accomplish the first intended voyage: that Brethren C. And R. were then at Serampore and had joined the Mission under our direction and the protection of the King of Denmark. This produced an enquiry whether we lived at Serampore because it was our choice as a suitable residence, or because we were actually under the protection of the Danish Government. This enquiry was directed to Rev. Mr. Brown, who referred them to the Governor of Serampore for an answer. His answer was very full and explicit, stating that on our first coming to reside at Serampore the late Governor of that Settlement represented the matter to the Court of Copenhagen, stating that our conduct was such as he highly approved, and that our residence might be useful to the Settlement: to which an answer had been sent by the Court of Denmark, approving of our settling there and requiring him to extend his protection to the Mission; that in consequence of this high authority he had taken the Brethren Chater and Robinson under the protection of his Danish Majesty, and that the Missionaries were not to be considered persons in debt who were barely protected, but as persons under the patronage of the Danish Government.

We thought this would have ended the business, but when the Capt. applied for a clearance he was treated rather cavalierly by the Justice of Peace, and informed that the former sentence had been confirmed. A little time afterwards, however, he was sent for to the Police office and after he had represented that we had resolved not to oppose Government but send back our brethren if all fair means proved ineffectual, and that though it might be made a serious affair both with America and Denmark if he and we were determined to be obstinate. Yet we considered the peace and good understanding of nations to be a matter of such importance that both he and we would give up anything rather than occasion anything disagreeable. Just at that time Mr. Brown entered the office. When the Magistrate called them both aside and gave him the necessary papers for his departure; I suppose that he is by this time out of the river. This was, and is, matter of praise to us all. A Letter from the Police of Calcutta, however, was sent to our Brethren informing them that the Sentence respecting them was confirmed, and desiring them to inform the Magistrate on what ship they intend to return to Europe. To this they cannot reply without acknowledging the Jurisdiction of the English court at Serampore, a step which must be highly offensive to the Danish Government; We have, therefore, chosen to make no reply and wait consequences.

All these distressing circumstances have made us think of extending the Mission in another direction; The Burman Empire lies contiguous to Bengal on the East, and is an independent Empire. We have, therefore, thought of beginning a Mission to that Country (Ava) and have fixed upon Rangoon (the sea Port) as the place to make a beginning. Brethren Chater and Mardon are considered as the fittest persons to make the first attempt. We, therefore, proposed it to them and they cheerfully agreed threreto: I hear that a Ship is to sail thither soon, and we hope to send them in her. They will go, at first without their wives, and, having gained proper information, return, take their wives with them and sit down to the work there. There is a constant intercourse between the port of Calcutta and Rangoon, and by a publick Act of the Emperor (see Syme's Embassy) British Subjects have full liberty of ingress and egress to and from any part of the Empire. Rangoon is about ten days sail from Calcutta, and all their wants may be supplied from us: This is indeed a part of the original plan detailed in our publick letter lately sent to you.

Carey to Ryland, Jan. 20, 1807

. . . We are going on silently with our work to as great an extent as we can: and, perhaps our exertions are not much less than they would have been if we had had perfect liberty. It is true we feel ourselves to be in an uncomfortable predicament, but have not heard anything lately which is calculated to abridge our efforts. On the contrary we have received some recent favours from Government which call for our thankfulness.

I have no doubt but these distressing circumstances will turn out eventually for the furtherance of the Gospel. Our thoughts were previously fixed upon the extension of the Gospel in Hindustani, and the idea of sending it to other countries was somewhat remote: but considering our way as hedged up in these parts we resolved lately upon a mission to the Burman empire, or the Kingdom of Ava. Brethren Mardon and Chater accepted gladly a call to that country, and on Saturday morning last sailed for Rangoon in the Brig *Prawn.* I expect that they will arrive there in about ten days from their leaving Calcutta. O Lord send now Prosperity. We have our eyes upon Siam, Malacca, Cambodia, and Cochin China, as soon as we have a supply of Brethren to send thither. A Burman came to me today to engage himself as a teacher of the Burman language. We have engaged to translate the Bible into that language among others, and shall even have occasion for it if the Lord should open a way for our brethren in that country.

Carey to Sutcliffe, Sept. 16, 1807

. . . On that day I recd. a note from the chief Secretary to C-t *{court}* requesting me to go to the Government House. I, therefore, went immediately, and in the Chief Secretary's office had a conversation with the Chief Secretary, and the Secretary of Gt *{government}*. The latter informed me that a Persian pamphlet published at our press had excited the attention of G-t, and enquired if I knew anything of it. I had not heard of it, and therefore said, no. He then produced the pamphlet, and read me the translation of an appendix to it, in which were some epithets applied to Mohamed which it was feared would excite commotion amongst the Mussulmen. After a long conversation I came away and wrote an account of what had occurred to Serampore: In reply I was informed that a letter from G. Genl. in Council had been sent to the G. of Serampore requesting the Suppression of the pamphlet. This appendix was originally written in Bengali by Bro. Ward, and printed at the end of Pearce's address to the Lascars. It was extracted from the preliminary discourse of Sale's Koran, giving a short account of the life of Mohamed, to which was added a few reasons why we could not believe the Koran to be the work of God.

About three months ago Bro. W.. Gave it to Hedut-ulla who had left Mussulmanism and been baptised, that he might translate it into Persian. He foolishly added the epithet Tyrant to Mohamed's name whenever it occurred, and made several alterations in the reasons given why we do not believe the Koran to be of divine origin. Bro. W. not suspecting this had printed it, and a few copies had been dispersed in the neighborhood of Calcutta, one of these fell into the hands of a Munshi belonging to the Sec. to Gov., he shewed it to his master who, being a great alarmist, shewed it to G-t. We replied to the Danish Government and cheerfully gave up the pamphlet, acknowledging our fault in not examining the copy, and he made the report to the Eng. Govt.

Last Friday, the day in which the Danish Governor's letter was sent, I recd. an official letter dated several days prior to that day, requiring me to communicate its contents to the Society of Missionaries at Serampore. In this we are required to remove the press to Calcutta: and not to print anything which has a tendency to convert the native, also to cease from preaching at a house in Calcutta, at which we are charged with uttering inflammatory expressions. A charge utterly unfounded and absolutely incapable of proof, as no person belonging to Government ever attended there. It is a house belonging to an Armenian, who appropriated it to the purpose of preaching, for the benefit of a few Armenians, and Portugese Protestants, who cannot understand English sufficiently to receive benefit from preaching in it, and are therefore now destitute of religious instruction. I yesterday simply replied to G-t that agreeably to their request I had communicated the contents of the Letter.

Being under the protection of the Danish flag, we thought it our duty to shew this letter to the Governor of Serampore, especially as he had been officially applied to before - he desired us not to reply to it till he received a reply to his official communication.

We are preparing a memoir in which we intend to give a brief history of the Mission and its success: to shew the improbability of disturbance being excited by attempts to convert the natives, To shew that it is consonant to the spirit of the Charter, which requires the "Chaplain to learn the Portugese and Hindu language for the purpose of instructing the Gentoos &ct. in the "Christian religion" and to embrace some other points. It is designed that I shall request a private audience with Lord Minto, and then present it. I have no doubt but our troubles will tend to the furtherance of the Gospel: but to what extent they may be carried it is impossible to say. We mean to inform his Lordship that we are prepared to suffer in this cause, rather than to give up our work: but we hope to do all in the most respectful manner we can.

Such a Letter was never written by an Christian Government before. Roman Catholics have persecuted other Christians under the name of Heretics, but since the days of Heathen Rome: no Christian Government, however corrupt has, that I know, prohibited attempts to spread Christianity among the Heathens.

We hope to send you the whole of this corresponding by this Ship, and a copy of the intended memoir: It will be your duty to stir in England. I think a respectful application to H.M. in Parliament, backed with respectful addresses signed by as many names as could be procured, (which I suppose might amount to near a Million if pains were taken to procure them) would be likely to do the business and get us full liberty to preach the Gospel. You will judge what is best. We are all in mourning - trembling for the Ark, and trust are willing and ready to suffer for the cause.

I do not know that anything ever affected me so sensibly as the present affair - my mind is full of tumultuous cogitations: I trust the Lord will appear for us.

I forgot to mention that Religion is proscribed also in the Fort. We have two members there, who with a few others frequently met for prayer, and Mr. Edmond sometimes went down and gave an exhortation: A room was till lately allowed them by the commanding officer for that purpose.

One evening an Irishman who had obtained leave to attend, instead of joining them took the opportunity of secretly conveying spirituous liquors into the fort. One of our Brethren discovered and gave information of it. In consequence Sir. E. Bayley stopped all religious meetings and a proclamation is posted up forbidding all unlicenced preachers from entering the Fort.

Idolatry is supported at a vast expence by the British Government and Christianity suppressed - I tremble for my country, for the Lord is a God of Judgement.

Carey to Ryland, Oct. 7, 1807

. . . We have lately very serious alarms from G-T, have been forbidden to preach to the natives, to do anything with a design to their conversion, and have been ordered to remove the press to Calcutta, that it may be under the inspection of G-T. The Danish Governor told us that he would not suffer the press to be taken out of the settlement, and that if the English proceeded to use force, he would strike the flag and surrender himself as a prisoner of war. We are under great obligations to him for his steady and manly defence of us. - We, however, thought it duty to do all we could to prevent things from going to extremities, Bro. Marshman and I therefore requested a private audience with Lord Minto, which was granted. We conversed with him about twenty minutes upon our affairs and begged leave to present a memorial on the subject of the Mission. This was presented last week - and I hope the matter will end here. It arose from a Persian pamphlet addressed to the Mussulmen, but as the whole of the correspondence will go to England by this conveyance, I shall not enlarge. It has been a time of sore trial: I trust that we found that "God was our strength, a very present help". I dare not boast, but I hope that I and all of us are ready to suffer if called to it.

Carey to Fuller, Calcutta, Oct. 1807

We shall send copies of what we intend to print, to the Gov. of Serampore who will transmit them to the British Governor . . . I believe that the final audience which Bro. Marshman and I had with him, in which we freely stated our situation and views; and the Memoir which was thereupon presented to him, had a considerable effect, and that his sentiment was much more favourable towards us. These measures had a great affect also on the opposite party whose crests fell considerably on the occasion. I, however, consider all this help as coming from God, and as remarkably displayed on the present occasions. We intend to keep a day of thanksgiving for this deliverance as soon as I return to Serampore. As the circumstance of our dispensing pamphlets in the Company's dominion is recognized in their letter of revocation, we shall find no delicacy in distributing them; and as we wish to avoid every thing inflammatory, and have a genuine desire to promote the tranquility of the country. I have no doubt but we shall be permitted to finish nearly all our works - Our pamphlet work will not be greatly interrupted by this inconvenience; and I have reason to hope that the obstacles which yet remain will be gradually taken away. Perhaps our situation is even now better than it was before. There are, however, many in this Country who would rejoice to see Christianity wholly expelled from this country, and particularly to see any harassment thrown in our way. We, therefore, have our security but in God. I this evening preached from Isa. 51 ch. 1, 2, 3 vers. - I think I feel a trust in God as it respects the concourse of his Church. The example of his preserving and increasing Abraham; who was <u>alone</u> when called and . . .

Carey to Fuller, April 20, 1808

Half a dozen things press on me at this moment and each declares itself to be an indispensable duty. At the same time my conscience joins with every one of them; as however I can do but one thing at a time, I shall lay all the other aside to write to you. . . . I bless God that we are still here and still doing something in the work of God. - We can scarcely say that we are tolerated, however, we go on and make known all we do, when there is an occasion for it.- I have reason to think that the opposition we have met with has arisen more from political panick than from a wish to hinder us in our undertakings. These panicks, however, sometimes occasion still greater panicks in us, and if the Lord had not been on our side would have never *{held}* us up before now.

Carey to Sutcliffe, March 8, 1809, Calcutta

. . . I ought just to mention a circumstance of which Bro. Fuller has written in a letter to Bro. Ward, received last night. I mean about the Pamphlet entitled the rising of knowledge. It is, no doubt, a weak piece, and full of abuse. All that I can say in our defence is, that it was a piece written by Ram Ram Basu, a Heathen, against the Brahmans; and printed by us when we had a great scarcity of such things and no ability to write them. It never was supposed that it contained Gospel sentiments, and comparatively very few copies of it have been distributed. However, neither that nor any things much heavier, would stir up the Brahmans to do more than turn like the sluggard of Solomon on his bed. I have no opinion of it and a very low one of some others written by ourselves, which contain no abuse (I only wrote one, *{it}* was intended as a short compendium of the Christian System). I, therefore, never considered the prohibition of Govt. respecting the distribution of these pamphlets as likely to be attended with much evil. Though I must confess they did tend to keep up, and even to produce a spirit of enquiry among the Hindus, and I am sorry that any restraints are laid on the means which we might use; for though, as in this case, we might inadvertently, or for want of something better (for that was the case when the Pamphlet was printed) publish some foolish things, yet I trust the great body of our exertions have been more substantial. We are fallible creatures, and see need to correct ourselves every hour; I hope also that we are willing to be corrected by others, and that no more such useless things will be done or suffered by in.

Carey to Ryland, Apr. 14, 1813

My dear Bro. Ryland,

Before this reaches you, it is probable that you will have heard the resolution of G-t respecting our Brethren Johns, Lawson, and Robinson, and will perhaps have even seen Bro. Johns who was by that cruel order sent home on the *Castlereach*. Government have agreed that Bro. Lawson shall stay till the pleasure of the Court of Directors is known, to whom a reference will be made. Bro. Robinson was gone down to the river and was on board a Ship bound to Java, when the order was issued, he, therefore, got out without hearing of it, but I understand it will be sent thither after him. - JEHOVAH reigneth.

Since Bro. Johns' departure I have tried to ascertain the cause of the severity in G-t. I had a long conversation with H.T. Colebrooke Esq., who has been out of Council but a few months, upon the matter. I cannot learn that G-t has any specific dislike to us, but find that ever since the year 1807 the orders of the Court of Directors to send home all Europeans not in the service of H.M. or the Company, and who come out without leave of the Directors, have been so peremptory and express, that Govt. cannot now overlook any circumstance which brings such persons to notice. Notwithstanding the general way in which the C. of D. have worded their orders, I cannot help putting several circumstances together, which make me fear that our mission was the cause of the enforcement of that general law, which forbids Europeans to remain in India without the leave of the Court of Directors.

Whether Twining's pamphlet excited alarm, or was only an echo of the minds of a number of men hostile to religion I cannot say, but, if I recollect dates aright, the orders of the C. of D. came as soon as possible after that pamphlet was published, and as it would have been too bare-faced to have given a specific order to send home Missionaries, they founded their orders on an unjust and wicked clause in the Charter, and so enforced it that it should effectually operate on missionaries.

I hope the friends of Religion will persevere in the use of all peaceful and lawful means to prevail on the legislators to expunge that clause, or so to modify it that Ministers of the Gospel may have leave to preach, form or visit churches, and perform the various duties of their office without molestation, and that they may have a right to settle in and travel over any part of India for that purpose. Nothing can be more just than this wish, and nothing would be more politic than for it to be granted, for every one converted from among the Heathen is from that time a staunch friend of the English Govt. Our necks have, however, been more or less under the yoke ever since that Year, and preaching the Gospel standing in much the same political light as committing an act of felony. Witness what has been done to Mr. Thompson, the five American Brethren, and our three Brethren. Mr. Thomason, the Clergyman, likewise has hard work to stand his ground.

I trust, however, that it is too late to eradicate the Gospel from Bengal. The number of these born in the country who preach the Word is now very considerable. Fifteen of this description preach constantly, and seven or eight more occasionally exhort their countrymen: besides our European Brethren. The Gospel is stationed at eighteen or twenty places belonging to our mission alone, and at several of them are churches. The Bible is either translated or under translation into twenty four of the languages of the East. Eighteen of which we are employed about, besides printing most of the others. Thirteen out of these eighteen are now in the press, including a third edition of the Bengali N. T. Indeed so great is the demand for bibles that though we have eight presses constantly at work, I fear we shall not have a Bengali N.T. to sell or give away for the next twelve months. The old edition being entirely out of print. We shall be in almost the same predicament with the Hindustani. We are going to set up two more Presses, which we can get made in Calcutta, and are going to send another to Rangoon. In short though the publishing of the word of God is a political crime, there has never been a time when it was so successful. "Not by might nor by power, but by my Spirit saith the Lord". Through divine mercy we are all well, and live in peace and love. A small cloud which threatened at the time Bro. Johns left us is mercifully blown over, and we are now in the utmost harmony. I will, if possible, write to my nephew Eustace by these ships, but I am so pressed for time that I can never promise to write a letter. The Lord has so blessed us that we are now printing in more languages than we could do before the fire took place.

Carey to Jabez, Sept. 17, 1816

. . . You, My Dear Jabez, appear, like Bro. Robinson, to have a great fear of the Dutch. I do not know how they may act here, but in Europe there is no nation where liberty of conscience is admitted to so great an extent as in Holland. I think you will be put out of your offices but I cannot suppose the Dutch will do more than that, and if they do that, rest assured the Society will support you in your work. Should you be put out of every capacity of doing good, which, however, can scarcely be the case if you are permitted to reside on the Island, I approve much of Bencoolen as a place for you future labours, unless you should rather choose the Island of Borneo. I mention this because it is not improbable that the English may send a resident thither after a time. I mention this from conversation I had some months ago on this subject with Lord Moira, who told me that there is a large body of Chinese in that Island. I do not recollect whether ten or a hundred thousand who have cast off the authority of the Sultan and applied to the late Lieut Gov. of Java requesting that an English resident may be sent to govern them and offering to be at the whole expence of his salary and government. He informed me that Mr . . . Hall had it in charge to make a proper enquiry into the Circumstance and proposed that J. Marshman should accompany him, saying that a resident would have it in his power to do much for him. He also mentioned you as a fit person to go if I chose it rather than for John to go. I declined it then telling His Lordship that you were in a very useful situation at Amboyna and on his enquiry, informed him of both your offices at which he expressed great satisfaction.

The Borneo business may come to nothing but if it should succeed it will be a glorious opening for the Gospel in that large Island. Sumatra, however, is much larger than any one man can occupy and I shall be happy for you to be settled there. All my hopes as it respects the usefulness of my children now centres in William and you, for Felix is become an awful profligate and Jonathan's religion, to say the least of it, is doubtful. One year of heartbreaking circumstances like what I have experienced in the present one will doubtless quite overset me. Indeed I shall never recover the wound I have received but expect it will gray my hairs with sorrow to the grave.

DEATH, DISEASE, AND DANGER

In nineteenth-century India, one would expect a very hard life considering the climate, mosquitoes, medical care, travel dangers, and cultural issues. According to Carey's correspondence, that assessment stands correct. Cholera, the plague, malaria, and numerous intestinal ailments afflicted the inhabitants. As a result of this and other dangers, Carey and his friends faced death and its resulting grief often. The work slowed from time to time due to these difficulties. Carey speaks frankly about the tribulations associated with life in India.

Carey to Father, Aug. 8, 1794, Mudnabati

For my own part India agrees with my Health much better than England, and tho I could not bear the Sunshine in England. Yet the hottest weather in this Country agrees with me the best. My Wife has had a long illness with the Flux but is now almost well - and Felix is now ill of the same disorder, William has had very good Health except a few Ague. Little Peter is a fine Boy, and Jabez who was but six weeks old when we left England, now runs about briskly; thus Mercy and Goodness have followed me all my Days, and still my Cup runs over.

Carey to Ryland, Dec. 13, 1804

. . . On the 13th of November it pleased the Lord to remove Sister Chamberlain from us to the world above. She was delivered of a daughter (I believe on the 9th) and was as well as could reasonably be expected for two days after her delivery. On the third day she was seized with a convulsive affection attended with considerable delirium which terminated in her death in two more days. The child is alive and likely to do well. Bro. and Sister Chamberlain settled in a subordinate station at Cutwa about 20-30 miles north of Nuddea *{Nadia?}*, where they had been for several months past. Her lying in was not expected so soon by a month at least, and Bro. Marshman went up to bring her down to Serampore that she might have the assistance of the family at that time. He arrived the night before her death, and instead of bringing her, brought her distressed partner, and motherless child. The loss to Bro. C. is seemingly irreparable, but he feels the importance of resignation to the divine will. Sister C. had many lucid intervals, and then expressed a firm confidence in, and strong desire after the Lord Jesus. She died like a Christian.

Carey to Ryland, July 17, 1806

. . . Bro. Biss has had an hepatic affection but is recovering. Mr. Ephraim Burford, a grandson of the late Rev. Mr. Burford of Goodman Field (lately Capt. here) has had an attack of the same disorder, he is also recovering. I suspect that I have an incipient attack of the same disorder (an intduration) but, in the spleen. I have begun a course of Mercury, and as the disease is but just perceptible, hope it will soon give way to it. Otherwise, we are all in good health & spirits, and live in love. I account the translations of S. Script. the great business of my life.

Carey to Sutcliffe, May 4, 1808

. . . The work of God among the Heathen has for some time past been at a stand, or nearly so, we have now and then baptised one or two, but we have lost more by death and other ways than have been added to us. (I mean of Hindus) some of our native Brethren have left this world triumphing in Christ. - This was eminently the case lately with our aged Brother Rughoo-natha, and with Futtika; I expect that Bro. Marshman or Ward will send particulars of their deaths.

Carey to Fuller, May 5, 1813

{As Carey recounts the anniversary of the church in Mudnabati, he speaks of the afflictions and sufferings of mission work in a foreign country, but also how it can survive.}

Eleven were received into the Church, and admitted to the Lord's table last Lord's day and the number (that has been) baptised since the union of the organized church with those then arrived is more than five hundred. Yet so many have been removed by death, so many have been visited by afflictions, such visitations by fire, and by the violence of men have befallen us, as to show us how easily the Lord could cut us all off, and blast all our hopes. We are a bush that has been burned with fire for several years and yet the bush is not consumed. Perhaps last year was a year of greatest afflictions that the mission has ever suffered and yet so merciful has been the Lord to us that we have comparatively felt less of the pressure of afflictions than on many former occasions.

Carey to Ryland, May 30, 1816

. . . You must be deaf or very discriminating, in your hearing Sister Ward's accounts. She is a good, weak woman with prejudices for or against individuals as strong as the stormy wind, and for which she can give no reason.

You see I have written to you in the freest manner, perhaps no part of this letter is fit to be published - but it may be useful to you in guiding your judgment. Through Divine mercy we are all well. My dear Wife is better than she has been for some years. Sister Marshman is this day pronounced well of the Liver by two medical men, Dr. Wallich and Dr. Robinson (Son to Dear Mr. R. of Liecester) - Rum, Abstemiousness &ct. I never drink anything but Water except a little before I go to bed, I then drink a glass of Rum or Brandy or a glass of Wine. Wine does not agree with Bro. Ward, and Bro. Marshman drinks very little. I think you would think our living rather profuse than parsimonious. Bro. Moore I fear is in no danger of injuring himself by abstemiousness or self-denial. And you may rest quite easy about us. Our table is well supplied and the first people in the settlement occasionally come to it.

Carey to Ryland, Dec. 30, 1816

I am still under the operation of Mercury for a Dysentery. My mouth is very sore, but I trust the disease is almost removed, it now occasions me but little pain or inconvenience. I have, at least fourteen years labour still on my hands, How long it may please the Lord to continue me I cannot tell, but His Will be done. Bro. Yates has made very good progress in the study of Sanskrit, Bengali, and Hindu and will, I doubt not, in a reasonable time be able to take my work himself. My wife joins me in love to Mrs. R.

Carey to Jabez, Feb. 3, 1817

. . . In my last I informed you that I was just recovering from a dangerous fever. Soon after that I was taken with a bowel complaint which has kept me under a course of medicine nearly till the present time. Through mercy I am now so nearly recovered as scarcely to feel the . . . of the disease. I was, however, very near losing my life about ten days ago by jumping from the buggy. I was returning from Dum Dum . . . when the belly band of the harness broke and the stops of the shafts were drawn out of the saddle slings which fell on the ground, in which condition the horse, who was spirited, continued to (drag) . . . which would have been highly dangerous to me. I, therefore, jumped out of the buggy but in so doing sprained my foot very badly and fell down and cut my face much. Through the mercy of God I am now nearly recovered from the bruises though I am very lame. In the midst of life we are in death. Oh, that we may be always ready to meet our Lord and may have our loins girt and our lights burning that when our Lord comes we . . . to him immediately.

. . . What need have we to work while it is day. The night of death will soon come when none of us can work. I look with deep regret on my past life and am ashamed to see what a loiterer I have been.

Carey to Sister, Oct. 28, 1817

. . . I have this day received a most distressing account of the death of one of our most active native preachers, Mr. de Bruyn, who was murdered by a young man to whom he had been a father. It appears that de Bruyn reproved him for something he saw wrong when the other in a fit of rage snatched up a knife and stabbed him. I am the more distressed as the murderer was accounted a pious man and had been of great use among the Mugs, whose language he spoke fluently. William, who was there last year, spoke very highly of him; and all thought well of him. We have sustained, therefore, a double loss for de Bruyn is dead and Bandey will be hanged. And we have not a man who can speak that language, or one who will leave all and go to that country. Yet there is a large Church raised there in a new country. I could wish to go myself and learn the language and watch over them in the Lord, but that would be attended with leaving the most important situation in the world. O! that Felix were faithful. O! that God would raise up fit men for his work. Most who come from England have no wish to go among the heathen. A life of ease and gentility in Calcutta among Europeans is thought preferable. I am greatly afflicted with this event. May the Lord appear and provide for his own cause.

Carey to Sisters, April 1818

. . . but so great is the call for the Word of God, that we are obliged to give parts away before the whole can be printed. Add to this that I am now left alone in this most important work. Bro. Yates who was chosen to assist me therein has deserted it and has settled in Calcutta as a Schoolmaster . . . A dreadful disease (Cholera morbid) has raged for a long time in Bengal and the neighboring provinces for the last six months. At one time the numbers who died in Calcutta amounted to from 600 to 1,000 persons a Week, besides those carried off in the Country, who are very numerous. My Wife had a severe attack of it, about a month ago; or rather three attacks within four or five days. I suppose I did not give her less than a thousand drops of Laudanum within that time. Opium being now found to be the most efficacious remedy for it; Indeed owing to the kind attention of the Europeans, and the establishment of a great number of native physicians, with proper medicines, and directions how to use them. I suppose two thirds of those who are attacked by it now recover. My Wife is still very weak, and her stomach is so unstable that she can scarcely take nourishment enough to support life. A Physician is now trying what a salivation will do; to which may God grant a blessing.

Carey to Jabez, Dec. 16, 1819

. . . I am disappointed that Govt. has not allowed us free postage to Ajmere, I twice mentioned it to Lord Hastings, and he gave me hopes that it would be done, I believe it has fallen through.

. . . I have felt much for you under your afflictions and rejoice to find that William is better. Be not discouraged on account of the apparent unhealthiness of the place. Many places have been supposed to be so when first settled, which have afterwards been found to be very salubrious. The Season has been a very unhealthy one all over India, I never knew so great a number of Deaths as has taken place this year, since I have been in India, if I except the ravages made last year by the Cholera Morbus.

If Duty lead us to any place, however unhealthy it may be, we may safely trust the Lord, at whose command we go, to take care of our bodies and it is certain that under his protection we are safe. I have always thought your call to Ajmere . . . as clear as I ever knew a call in Providence to be. I trust the Lord will set your heart wholly on your work there, and give you that success which will cause you to rejoice in his goodness.

Carey to Ryland, May 7, 1823

. . . The death of my Son Felix has thrown a great additional load upon me which no one else can take, and has made it absolutely necessary that I should attend thereto.

Dear Bro. Ward was removed from us after about thirty six hours of illness, on Friday March 7. He preached on Wednesday evening, breakfasted with us on Thursday morning when he complained to Sister Ward of being unwell. About two I was called, when he told me he thought it was an attack of the Cholera Herbus. Medical aid was obtained in a few minutes, and an English Physician was also called from Barrackpore: In short every medical help was afforded that could be given, and very considerable hope was entertained of his recovery. My wife was with him the greatest part of the night, and early in the morning I called to see him and found him in a fine sleep: I went to Calcutta to attend on my collegiate duties, and returning abut half an hour before he breathed his last. I found that his pulse sunk about eleven o'clock, and that he had not spoken all day except to give the reply yes or no to any question put to him. There were, therefore, some of those intimations of his feelings on the approach of death which we should have rejoiced to hear. Bro. Ward however, was ready to depart. Our junior Brethren, several of the Independent Brethren, and a very large concourse of people both European and natives attended his funeral, and the next Sabbath but one, I preached a Sermon on the occasion in Calcutta to the most crowded assembly I ever saw in India. The next Sabbath Bro. Marshman, by the desire of the Independent Minister, Mr. J. Hill preached another sermon on the occasion at the Independent Chapel, to an equally crowded assembly. Few men were more beloved than Bro. Ward. His death leaves a void which it will be difficult to fill up. Our consolation is "The Lord Liveth" and "He is able to do exceeding abundantly above all we can ask or think".

Carey to Sisters, Sept. 5, 1823, Calcutta

. . . Through divine mercy I enjoy tolerably good health, and spirits; My labour is, however, rather too heavy, and I must, some against my will, reduce gradually the number of versions of the Scripture in which I am engaged. Two reasons induce me to do this, the first that above mentioned, *{he mentioned above an illness - Bilious or liver attack}* and the second the almost certainty that funds for printing them all cannot be furnished.

. . . I am now in my 63rd year and must soon expect to feel the weight of age; at present I feel little of it, except a dullness of hearing, and seeing, the latter of which is mercifully remedied by spectacles: I am as happy in my situation as a man can be. My Wife is an affectionate and kind woman, and contributes much to my happiness . . .

Carey to Jabez, Jan. 26, 1824

You have I believe repeatedly heard of me though I have not written to you since I got my hurt, four months ago. I slipped down owing to landing from the boat at night in a slippery place and was unable to rise. This was followed by a fever which brought me to the gates of death, scarcely any one, I believe, expected me to live. I am, however, through mercy recovered from my illness though still unable to walk without crutches. The most I have done has been to walk the length of my bed-room and back again, which I one night did to shew your Mother what I could do.

During this long illness I have experienced very much of the divine mercy both to body and soul. The constant and unremitting care of your Mother and her excellent nursing took off much of the weight of the disease, and the affectionate conduct of all my friends added to the certainty that all of them who knew the throne of Grace pleaded hard with God for my recovery were very consoling to my mind. The medical Gentlemen took a lively interest in my case, and Lord Amherst sent his private Physician, Dr. Abel to report thereon. While the fever was coming to it's height an abscess, I believe on the liver, though some of the medical Gentlemen thought it was on the lungs, was formed and burst, and was brought away by expectoration. I frequently thought the quantity of matter and the rapidity of it's coming up by the lungs would have suffocated me.

. . . We have had unprecedented floods. The house in which I lived is standing but the foundations having begun to crack, I removed from it and am living on the College premises, in a house intended for one of the professors. There is now no road left by the side of my house, and all the people go through our premises. There was three or four feet of water in our garden for more than a week and the desolation all over the country was dreadful. The scourge is now past but I fear no one lays it properly to heart. Most Europeans and all the natives appear as insensible as ever.

. . . s little girl is very ill, it is feared she cannot recover . . . also has been very ill, their afflictions are many and great . . . have now for nearly a month attended on my duties at College. I go down in the carriage, and am lifted by two bearers out of my Palankeen *{Palangin}*but I bless God that he has enabled me to attend on these duties again. I have also preached once in the two last . . .

Carey to Sisters, Feb. 6, 1824, Calcutta

{Writing to his sisters about an accident where he fell and hurt his hip, Carey gives some very interesting insight into the medical care.}

. . . They all concluded that the Bone was not dislocated, which a few days after when I got a pair of crutches, and by the help of them could stand and measure my feet together, was confirmed. The medical Gentleman who came over from Barrackpore though he lived in Calcutta, took charge of me. A hundred and ten leaches were applied to my thigh, and for a fortnight my health continued good, though the torture I felt in the limb was such as prevented my getting any sleep . . .

Carey to Jabez, Aug. 3, 1824

. . . I was through mercy so far restored as to walk with ease and comfort, tho I limp considerably. Within the last week I have been troubled with excoriations between the toes, and my lame foot or rather the foot of my lame leg is now so violently inflamed that I can scarcely set it to the ground and am going to commence a course of medicine for it. I hope this inflammation may be recovered in a day or two. In every other respect my health is good.

Calcutta and Serampore now present the most gloomy and distressing scene imaginable. A fever, which however, has not been known to be mortal, prevails so that it is supposed full three fourths of the inhabitants, both Europeans and Natives have been or are now ill. Some publick offices are shut up. Bro. Lawson's family and School, with the exception of Mrs. L. have been ill. Several children in Sister Marshman's school are now ill as is she herself. Your Mother, Charlotte and Bro. Marshman have been ill with it. It is a sore chastisement, and a loud call to turn to God, lest a greater chastisement be sent.

Carey to Sisters, Oct. 27, 1824, Serampore

. . . I walk as much as I can, and occasionally run, when in danger of being caught by a shower. I go to Calcutta as usual two or three times every week; and sit about ten hours a day at my desk. I have no doubt but the exercise I use contributes much to my health, and cheerfulness.

Carey to Ryland, June 7, 1825

. . . On the 17th of August next, I shall be 64 years of age: and though I feel the enervating influence of the climate, and have lost something of my bodily activity, I labour as closely, and perhaps more so than I have ever done before. My Bengali Dictionary is finished at press. I intend to send you a copy of it by the first opportunity, which I request you accept as a token of my unshaken friendship to you. I am now obliged, in my own defence, to abridge it, and to do it as quickly as possible, to prevent another from forestalling me, and running away with the profits.

. . . It is still uncertain whether Brother Judson, and Price are living. There was a report in the News paper that they were on their way to meet Sir Archibald Campbell, with proposals of peace from the Burman King, but no foundation for the report can be traced out. Living or dead, they are secure.

Carey to Sisters, Aug. 20, 1825

The Cholera Morbus, that awful scourge, is very fatal at Calcutta, and its environs, two or three hundred deaths are reported daily at the Police office, and those are only among the Hindus, so that the total must be a third more than that. The troops in Arazen are so sickly that when one Regiment was called over at Parade there was only one man to give an answer, and he was taken ill in the course of the day. A great number of officers and Men have died. There are many pious soldiers there, and several officers. I believe the commanding officer, General Morrison, a pious man, Col. McInnes is decidedly so, and several others whom I could mention. The Soldiers have erected a place of Worship there, where the true God was never worshiped before.

Carey to Jabez, Oct. 27, 1827

. . . I am through great mercy, now in good health, but about a month ago was seized with a total suppression of Urine; which was occasioned , I believe, by getting my feet wet in going to the Ghaut while it rained violently. I was for about a fortnight unable to make a drop of urine naturally. I went to Calcutta and put myself under Dr. Nicholson, who is eminent for his knowledge of all that class of diseases. The urine was drawn off by a Catheter twice or thrice a day for a fortnight. Indeed he taught me how to perform the operation for myself, and ordered me to do it till the bladder would compleatly empty itself; which he said had not been the case for the last ten or twelve years, owing to an enlargement of the prostate gland, which is situated at the top of the bladder. I still occasionally draw off what remains after a natural evacuation. The pain I suffered while in Calcutta was very great. Indeed I had no command over myself, but could only call upon God for patience and support. That support he graciously bestowed, and in about a fortnight the natural evacuations returned.

Carey to Sisters, Feb. 21, 1831, Serampore

. . . Since my last, God has removed our old tried Friend Fernandez to Glory. So far as I can ascertain he was the first fruits of the Mission to this country. Mr. Powell who came out with us, and had been brought up under the Gospel in London, set out in Religion about the same time, but I do not recollect which of them was first. Bro. Fernandez was the instrument of collecting the greatest native Church in Bengal. I think there were about 80 members, and their families amounted, according to a letter received from one of them since his death to about two hundred persons, all of whom bear the Christian name, and are continually under the means of Grace.

I consider it a great mercy that we had a tried, and faithful Brother to put into our late Brother's place; During Bro. Fernandez's life time we had, our eye on Bro. Sinylee, and he had consented to go; so that we sent him, and another young man from the College, named Bareira, to supply that place. - Our late Bro. came to Serampore very ill, and the first thing he said to me was. "Bro. Carey I have come to lay myself down with you". He lived but a few days after his arrival, with his mind in a truly happy state, set on the things which are above. He has left one fourth of his property to his son, who is in England, and three fourths for the support of the interest in Dinajpur.

Carey to Sisters, Dec. 6, 1832

. . . My Wife and I are well, except that I am greatly reduced in strength and spirits, a walk to the further end of my Garden quite fatigues me, and I am only able to preach once a Lord's Day. God has preserved me to see an edition of the Bengali Bible in one Volume, through the press. That was a work upon which my heart was much set, and so great is the demand for it that another edition will be required before it can be brought through the Press.

Carey to Sisters, Apr. 3, 1833

With respect to myself, I cannot say much that is favourable; Now I am so well that I hope to preach this evening, but the last attack which I had about six weeks ago was very severe; and was attended by a swelling of the left leg from the toes to the hip that it appeared as the skin must burst. I was confined to my bed for several days, and even now lay up my leg while sitting.

Carey to Sisters, Sept. 25, 1833

At that time the Medical Gentleman who attended me recommended and indeed almost insisted upon my drinking Edinburgh Ale, and I, of course complied, and have drank a bottle a day ever since. Whether it is to be attributed to the Ale I cannot say, but from that time I began to recover, and am now able to sit and to lie on my couch without the greatest pain. I have a little vehicle like a child's cart on which I placed a chair and am drawn slowly about our grounds when the weather suits, and am able now and then to read a proof Sheet of the Scriptures. I am too weak to walk more than just the area of the house, nor can I stand even a few minutes without support.

SUCCESSES AND FAILURES

Carey to Society, Jan. 12, 1796

Dear Brethren,

Since my last I have waited with anxious expectation to receive letters from you; [but Europe Letters are tardy in arriving, and those from the Society peculiarly so - This I hope will not always be the case; but on the contrary, I could wish them to be much more frequent than any others.-] I am, however, certain that the tie with which we are united cannot be broken by length of time, distance of place, or any of the common intervening incidents of Life; but that we shall continue to love one another in all situations whether prosperous or Diverse.

I can with pleasure inform you of our Bodily Welfare, and that of our children; and further that a Baptist Church is formed in this distant Quarter of the Globe. Our members are but four in Number, viz. Mr. Thomas from England, Mr. Long had been Baptised by Mr. Thomas when he was in India before; and on the 1st of November this Year I baptised Mr. Powell. At this place we were solemnly united that Day as a Church of Christ; and the Lord's Supper has since been twice administered among us . . .

. . . With respect to the Heathen I wish I could write more favourably than I can - - Our lives, however, are not quite spent in Idleness, nor our Labours quite without effect. I am just returned from a tour through about half the district in which my Business lies, and the whole of which consists of about two Hundred Villages. In this tour I took a Boat for my Lodging, and the convenience of Cooking my Victuals; but performed the Journey on foot walking from twelve to twenty miles a Day, and preaching, or rather conversing, from place to place about the things of God. This plan I intend to pursue statedly the whole of the dry season; tho often traveling less journies. I have not yet seen much fruit of my Labours . . .

Carey to Sisters, Mudnabati, Apr. 10, 1796

I know not what to say about the Mission. I feel as a Farmer does about his crop; sometimes I think the seed is springing, and then I hope; a little time blasts all and my hopes are gone like a Cloud. Twas only weeds that appeared; or if a little Corn spring up, it quickly died, being either choked with Weeds, or parched up by the sun of Persecution. Yet I still hope in God and will go forth in his strength and make mention of his Righteousness, even of him only.

Carey to Fuller, June 17, 1796, Mudnabati

{Carey has had to dismiss his Munshi (servant) who had been accused of infidelity. He committed adultery with a widow resulting in a pregnancy and abortion.}

The discouragement arising from this circumstance is not small as he is certainly a man of the very best natural abilities that I have ever found among the Natives; and being well acquainted with the Phraseology of Scripture was peculiarly fitted to assist in the Translation - but I have no hope of him. The Translation is going on, tho more slowly than when he was here, however, almost all the Pentateuch and New Testament are now Translated; I have a young Pundit with me now who I hope will prove useful, tho I yet see nothing promising with respect to the great point of all.

You very encouragingly tell us not to faint if we see no fruits yet. I hope and trust we shall not and hope you will also be kept from discouragement on our accounts. I feel very much lest the friends of Religion should faint at our want of Success, and by the doubts yet which I find have been plentiful on account of our engaging in Business. I fear some such discouragement has already taken place. I hardly think it worth while to notice the slander that we are become slave owners - but observe that there are no slaves allowed in this country.

. . . and I certainly expected more success than has attended us at present.

Mr. T. and I are Men and Fallible, but we can only desire the Work of Preaching the Word of Life to the Hindus, with our lives - and are thro Grace determined to hold on tho our discouragements were a thousand times greater than they are - we have the same ground of Hope with our Brethren in England, viz. The Promise, Power, and Faithfulness of God; for unless his Mercy break the Heart of Stone within England, India, or Africa, nothing will be done effectually; and he can as easily convert a superstitious Brahman as an Englishman.

Carey to Ryland, Mudnabati, Nov. 26, 1796

. . . I am very much obliged indeed by the friendly communications you have made to me, and feel very much interested in them. Nothing respecting the Churches of England can be uninteresting to me –

. . . An awakening took place here and at Moypal, at the same time; Three began to inquire here, but two turned back. One holds on and now appears to be concerned in a more lively manner than at first, tho the work has stood about three months. Five or Six appeared under Concern at Moypal, three hold on well and give us much pleasure. They have a daily meeting for prayer one among another, and their Conversation is very pleasing and becoming the Gospel: One appears to be a man of very good natural abilities and may become a Preacher, they are learning to read and write . . .

Carey to Ryland, Mudnabati, July 6, 1797

You will naturally inquire, have any been converted to the Lord Jesus Christ this year? And those mentioned last year, how do they walk? I answer no instances of recent conversions appear - Nor have I all the expectation I had last year from those I then mentioned - Yardee, and two others, however, still give us much pleasure, I doubt of Sookmu *{Soohman?}*he does not go back, nor does he go forwards. Parbotee is with Mr. Thomas. I see little promising in him. He appears to be ashamed of the name of Christ, tho he attends the word at Moypal. Mohun Chund is at his own house. I supported him at Mudnabati till I could no longer afford it, and when I ceased he went home. He since sent to borrow money, but as I fear he never had anything in view of interest in his profession of Christianity, I refused, as did Bro. Thomas also. Ram Ram Basu has turned out a compleat villain and has been guilty of embezzling a sum of money committed to his care by another Master - and we have been obliged to exclude Mr. Long from our Communion for dishonest practices. Yet people hear with more seriousness than heretofore, and my hopes are not lessened. I have composed a few Hymns in Bengali, and Mr. Thomas also, I have also translated three, viz. "Salvation, O the joyful sound" Watts, "Jesus and can it ever be" and "O'er the gloomy hills of darkness". Rip. Sel. translating Hymns, however, is much more difficult than composing new ones. Bro. Fountain takes great pains to instruct them in Singing, and I hope it will not be useless.

Carey to Sisters, Mudnabati, Jan. 10, 1798

. . . To say that none are converted among the Natives would be wrong, and it would be as wrong to say positively that any are. Yet there are hopeful appearances on several and I think much more enquiry than I ever was witness too before. The People are very fond of Singing Hymns, and I have been forced to commence as Poet, to furnish them with Hymns to sing. We have sometimes Harmony that cheers my Heart, tho it must be disgusting to the ears of an Englishman.

Carey to Fuller, July 17, 1799, Mudnabati

Tho we have had no success among the Heathens, or Mohammedans this year, yet we have reason to rejoice in the conversion of Mr. Cunningham, Register of the Court and Assistant to the Judge at Dinajpur. I look upon this as the greatest event that has occurred since our coming to this country. He has a Soul far above the common size. His coolness and consistency are very great and his understanding commands respect from all.

Carey to Sisters, Mudnabati, Nov. 30, 1799

. . . The past year has been a year of Labour, Disappointment, and perplexity. My mind has been almost absorpt in temporal concerns of the Mission and but little fruit has appeared to encourage our Labours in the Gospel. Among the Europeans, however, God has given us some success. I think I can speak with confidence of a young Gentleman of the first abilities who was deistically inclined before we came to these parts and indeed till last year. He gives good evidence of a Work of grace in his Heart, and indeed several of the Gentlemen at Dinajpur are much altered for the better in their conduct. Among the Natives things rather go backward, than forward. Yet I indulge a hope that we have not laboured altogether in vain, and we are quitting this part of the country with the best wishes of the inhabitants.

Carey to Fuller, Feb. 5, 1800, Serampore

Every day is so productive of something new in our situation that what we wrote ten days ago as a representation of our circumstances would not be so now. We are all of us, however, alive and in tolerable good health and excepting the very afflicting circumstances of Br. Grant's death have enjoyed a very good share of the Blessing of health.

The last year has been a most remarkable one for changes in our circumstances; some afflicting and the greatest part encouraging and I trust the whole will eventually turn out for the benefit of the Mission. Our removal from Mudnabati to this place is among the most remarkable of those providences which have occurred, and was at first so afflicting to my mind, that I scarcely ever remember to have felt more on any occasion whatever. It was, however, so clearly the leading of divine Providence that no one of us can entertain the shadow of doubt respecting it. I was, and am still much distressed on account of the heavy expences . . . At this place we are settled out of the Company's dominion, and under the government of a Power, very friendly to us, and our designs; here is a more populous neighborhood, we can work our Press without fear; and pursue our work with security. People also hear us with considerable attention, and in considerable numbers so that we are not discouraged but trust that our Lord will appear at length and set up himself over this part of the Earth.

I have been much distressed because of the great Expence to which we shall necessarily subject our dear Brethren in England, especially as it will so far exceed their Calculation. Yet I really think it to be impossible to pay more attention to economy than we do, for all our Brethren, and Sisters are of one Heart in this respect.

Carey to Fuller, Aug. 4, 1801

Yet as you will have learned before God has done much, very much for us - While I am writing I hear some of our Hindu Friends in the Hall joining in a song of Praise to our Lord Jesus Christ. Since the date of my last to you we have baptised . . . five others . . . and my eldest son and it gives us pleasure to say that hitherto every one of them walk as it becomes the Christian calling. I have no doubt of the conversion of my second son, and very little respecting that of Mr. Fernandez's son who is with us for education.

Carey to Ryland, June 29-30, 1802

I expect that the news of the death of Bro. Brunsdon and Thomas, and also that of Mr. Short has reached you before now, as we wrote the accounts thereof immediately after the events had taken place. We who remain live in the closest harmony. Bro. Ward was married to Sister Fountain a little time ago, but I cannot recollect the date. Sister Brunsdon is expected to be married in about a month to Mr. Rolt of Calcutta, a very pious man - in very good circumstances - Sister Grant and her children are well. Bro. and Sister Marshman are sometimes poorly, especially the last. I believe they both are so anxiously attentive to the work of the Mission as to injure their Health. They are great Ornaments to the Cause in which they are engaged. I alone am unfit to be called a Missionary - and often doubt whether I am a Christian. Our Church now consists of twenty four members, four of whom were received last night, and are to be baptised on next Lord's Day - we baptised a Lady, <u>Miss Rumohr</u>, a daughter of the Countess of <u>Alfeldt</u> at <u>Schleswig</u> about three weeks ago. She is the first European Female who has ever been baptised in this country - came here about two years ago for her health, and found healing for her Soul - as well as much benefit for her body. One of the four who gave an account of himself last night to the Church is the first Mussulman who has given himself up to God - his name is <u>Peeru</u>.

The other three are Hindus; One an old man whose name is Bhurut, the other a Man of the Caesto or Writer tribe whose name is Pitambar Mitra and his wife whose name is Dropodee. They all gave an account of themselves such as would have gratified any Gospel Church in Europe.

Carey to Ryland, August 31, 1802

My two sons walk so as to afford me much pleasure. William has not yet been received into the Church but we have now a Church of 25 members, viz. 13 Natives and 12 Europeans - and we have great hopes of several more. We have many things to exercise our Faith and Patience among them, principally arising from the uncultivated state of their minds (The natives I mean) but we have also much to rejoice in, both as it respects their conduct and their acquisition of evangelical knowledge - and even when we have viewed them on the worst side - we can truly say that they are the excellent of Bengal.

A most encouraging circumstance turned up lately which has much strengthened our hands, viz. About six months ago three Mussulmen came from a distant part to hear the Gospel and desired much that one of us should pay them a visit - which we promised to do in the rainy season when the progress by water would be open. About six weeks ago one of the them, deputed by the others came again to conduct any of us who could go. Bro. Marshman was the only one who could undertake so long a journey and a better could not have been chosen to go. He, therefore, went and took with him Pitambar Mitra and Bhurut - The place where they live is in the district of Jessore near the river Isamuty. Bro. M. on arriving found about 200 persons who have several years rejected Caste. They were convinced of the folly and wickedness of both the Hindu and Mussulman faith but confessed that they were ignorant of what was right and hearing of us they were very desirous to know the Gospel. Bro. Marshman's reception among them exceeded all expectation; Many were ready gathered together to hear the Word when he arrived, having had previous notice, and they heard with a kind of pleasure and eagerness seldom seen in this country. They desired us to write to them and visit them and promised to visit us when they can.

In short, a very hopeful prospect presents itself there and we hope that a Church may in a little time be formed in those parts. Bro. M. in returning home got intelligence of another body of Dissenters - whom he determined to visit. He did so and found that at another about a days journey nearer home than the one he had visited. There are at least two thousand persons who have publickly renounced their Caste. They received him with great pleasure, and were desirous of seeing him again. We have since written a Letter to the first people and intend to send it off by Bhurut. The whole account of this very interesting journey will be sent by Bro. Marshman who kept a journal of all the proceedings. We are wishing for more help that we might be more entirely employed in the prosecution of this great object.

Carey to Ryland, Dec. 13, 1804

. . . Some of our young friends grow both in gifts and Gospel knowledge, and, I trust in grace, Krishna, and Krishna Prasad, preach at Calcutta, on the Lord's Day: the latter of these is a truly valuable Character.

Notwithstanding what I have said, the Church never appeared in a more promising state than now. The increase of Gospel knowledge is as great as can be expected, and greater than ever before, and there is a greater substantialness of Character than at any former period in many of our young friends. Opposition is as great as ever, but enquirers are coming from various quarters notwithstanding.

Carey to Ryland, Nov. 11, 1806

. . . We have had some additions to the church, indeed we have reason to bless God that few ordinance days have been without one or more baptised: Some we have been obliged to exclude but in general we have cause for great thankfulness. Several of our Native Brethren regularly itinerate to preach the Gospel. We usually sent a Brother of good abilities attended by another of less gifts, as a helper or companion. Krishna, Krishna-Das, Sebuk-ram *{Sadukshah?}*, and Deep Chund, are regularly engaged in publishing the word. Ram-mohun, Ram Ratan, Kanay, Roop, Neeloo, Bhagvut, Manik, and Ram Prasad frequently itinerate, and Setta-ram, Koovera, Kangalee, and others live in the Country and proclaim Christ as the Saviour of Sinners.

Carey to Ryland, Jan. 20, 1807

. . . Some time ago we received a letter from our friend Mr. Creighton, near Malda, giving an encouraging account of the state of things among the natives there, and enquiring whether our Native Brethren who had been sent thither some little time before, were authorised to baptise: As they had not been regularly called to the ministry, we sent our Bro. Krishna to administer that ordinance if he found proper subjects, attended by my son William, who will labour in the work with him, or others, for some months in those parts.

Carey to Sutcliffe, Jun. 2, 1807, Calcutta

. . . A few weeks ago our Brethren who reside in Jessore and the adjacent parts formed themselves into a separate church. The whole business was conducted in Serampore. Our Bro. Krishna has administered the Lord's Supper once to them since, and our Br. Ram Mohan is going to them this week for that purpose. The People of Cutura are a distinct church as the ordinances are regularly administered there by Bro. Chamberlain. There are therefore, four Churches in Bengal, viz. that at Serampore, that at Dinajpur, that at Cutura, and that at Jessore . . .

Carey to Ryland, March 1809

. . . I have written something more largely to Bro. Sutcliffe respecting the state of the Mission here. Upon the whole I think it is far from being in a discouraging state. The Gospel is now as it were, established in nine places in Bengal, including

Munihuri where Bro. Moore is, which in on the border adjoining Hindustan proper. The churches, it is true are small and feeble, but are now all furnished with Pastors or regular ministers. Bro. Mardon has had some increase. At Serampore a Young Mug (the first of that nation) stands proposed to the Church. - That nation inhabits the mountains of Arakan, but a great number of them some years ago settled in the Company's territories, driven thither by the tyranny of the Burman Government.

At Calcutta the prospect is highly encouraging. The new Chapel was opened there on New Year's Day last. The congregation is from one to near two hundred. Last night at Week day Lecture, there were about 130 present. Last Lord's Day I baptised four persons there, and two more stand proposed for baptism.

I expect, and hope that in time the interest may prove of the greatest benefit to India. I think 44 members sat down last Sabbath to the Lord's Table. The word appears to be made useful to a class of people who may be ultimately the instruments of disseminating truth all over Hindustan. I mean the native Portugese, and the Armenians.

Carey to Sutcliffe, March 8, 1809, Calcutta

. . . Last Lord's day I baptised four persons there in the Baptistry, and two more stand proposed for next ordinance day . . . A Mussulman of some consequence who attended the Baptism last Lord's day, came and drank tea with me to night, and seems to be inquisitive. I think 44 members joined in communion on last Lord's Day, besides those who communicated at Serampore.

Carey to Ryland, Oct. 13, 1809

. . . We are now in peace with all men, so far as I know. I have reason to believe that the late efforts of the enemies of the Mission have contributed rather to our enlargement, and that there are now in India, a greater number of friends to it than there was some time ago. The late disturbances at Madras, may shew Sir. G. Barlow where the real danger lies, and call off his attention from imaginary danger.

Brother Chamberlain has lately baptised twenty four of the soldiers in one of the European Regiments, who have formed themselves into a church: While he was here, he received accounts of seven or eight more who are desirous of Baptism. These men are at Berhampore, a military station about 40 miles north of Cutwa. They have been convinced of the importance of believer's baptism by the mere reading of the word of God. Some of them would have been gladly baptised more than twelve months ago, but we were afraid some wrong construction might have been put upon it, and therefore advised Bro. C. not to baptise them. They, therefore, waited until neither his conscience nor theirs would permit them to wait longer: and at last the ordinance was administered at the different times without any notice being taken of it by three officers.

Carey to Sutcliffe, May 11, 1810, Calcutta

. . . Last Lord's Day was the anniversary of our uniting as a Church at Serampore, and one of the days which we annually observe as a Day of thanksgiving. I had occasion in preaching, then, to take a survey of what the Lord has done for us. When the Church was united (formed I cannot say for we were a little Church before) our whole number was eleven persons, the number of persons in full communion in all the Churches now amounts to about twenty times that number. The number of ministers of the Gospel then, was thirteen including our brethren, just come out, W. Forsyth, two clergymen, and the German missionaries on the coast. It now amounts to about forty. The printing of the Bengali Bible appeared then a work beyond which our hopes could not be carried, but the Lord has now enabled us not only to finish that, but to see our way through several other versions.

Carey to Ward, Jan. 20, 1820, Serampore

. . . I wish you however to know that we have lived in utmost harmony ever since you left us. We consult upon everything . . . and I believe are of one heart and soul. Brother Carapeit was ruined by the kindness of friends at . . . When he returned to us he had so much of the spirit of a tradesman that we could do nothing with him. I addressed a very serious letter to him upon his mercenary spirit, and we parted. After that the Calcutta Brethren employed him for about two months, but finding him as we had found him, they dismissed him, and last Tuesday he embarked for Egypt on a trading speculation. I hope the Lord will bring him at last to a right mind.

We have an enquirer in Calcutta of a singular character. He had resided at Ihalles Ghasit for four years, having engaged in a vow of perpetual violence . . . which he had kept all that time. After that a tract, I believe from Mr. Townley, found its way to him, which opened his mouth. When I first saw him he had as many superstitious ideas as I ever knew a man have, but he appears to trust wholly in Christ, and has now nearly parted with all his nostrums. When he first walked up from Calcutta with John Peter, several principal persons came down from their houses and fascinated themselves at his feet; but they soon discovered their mistake. He wore a number of Malos made of snakes bones, all of which, with every other external appearances of Superstition he has cast off and I think, is truly a partaker of the Grace of God.

Carey to Jabez, Oct. 12, 1820

. . . I hope you will not be discouraged at your Schools not filling faster at Ajmere. Everything must have a beginning and we have reason to hope that a work to which divine providence most evidently led the way and which has been upheld by him till now will be finally successful. Be not weary in well doing for in due season you shall reap if you faint not; our labours may be weak but they shall not be in vain for the Lord has his eye upon his own work and will in his good time give success far exceeding our calculations.

Carey to Ryland, July 4, 1822

. . . In yours you enquire about some native Christians applying to the Bishop. The matter was this, about ten persons who had been excluded the church for a course of evil conduct, persuaded four or five others to join them in an application to the Bishop for support. The Archdeacon the next day wrote to me about it, and we immediately by letter informed the Bishop of their real character, who replied saying that on account of the information we had given him should give them nothing, and that the most he should have given them, even if he had had no information would have been about a Rupee. Those who were in communion were suspended for the steps they had taken, but subsequently restored. The junior Brethren made a great fuss about it, as it was just at the time of the greatest irritations between them and us, and I suppose they reported it to England. The matter was not worth repeating in the next village.

Carey to Sisters, Sept. 1822, Serampore

The cause of Our Lord Jesus Christ gains ground in this country, though when we compare its success here with what has taken place at Tahiti and the other Islands of the Pacific ocean we must call ours a Day of small things, but when we compare the present state of India with its past state; we must say "The Lord has done great things for us whereof we are glad".

Carey to Sisters, Feb. 20, 1826, Serampore

I have plenty of work and, what is best of all, I see the cause of God prosper in a variety of ways. Some little party collisions still exists, yet the cause of our Redeemer prospers more or less among all them who love him. Preaching is made a blessing. Schools are attended by blessings. I now hear little girls read and understand, better than three fourths of those called Pundits could, a few years ago. Some, principally Socinians, or such as join them in running down all serious religion, assent with unblushing boldness that no good has been done by missions; I as boldly assent that incalculable good has been done by them, and I have no doubt but the good will continue and increase till India is filled with the knowledge of God and His Gospel.

RELATIONSHIPS WITH OTHER MISSIONARIES

Relationships on the mission field produce some of the greatest blessings and challenges a missionary encounters. Carey drew great strength from those missionaries who were committed to the mission goals. Other relationships caused him some of the deepest heartache he experienced. Carey speaks of these relationships in his letters and shares some of the emotional response that resulted from them.

Carey to Ryland, Dec. 26, 1793

. . . but he *{Mr. Thomas}* is much more fitted to spend his life at sea than upon land - he certainly is not an economist and his absence of mind is so extraordinary as to appear often like inattention, when pursuing anything, let it be of ever so trivial a nature, he is so completely absorbed in it as to disregard everything else tho ever so important or necessary, and if once he forms a low opinion of anyone his prejudices run so high as to suspect everything that is done or said by that person. I say this to account for the differences between him and Mr.Grant. Poor Ram Basu is likewise now in this uncomfortable situation; but the utmost harmony subsists between me and him. - Notwithstanding poor Munshi's fall I entertain a very high opinion of him as a converted man - and a very sensible and intelligent person, tho the superstition of the Caste, and much more its great inconveniences if once lost, work upon his mind more strongly than could be wished, but not more than anyone who considers the state of Human Nature might expect.

Carey to Fuller, Mudnabati, April 23, 1796

. . . I wish I could see more of his hand with us in the way of conversion; but we at present lament a barren Land -

I have, however, one consolation more than I had, to see my dear Colleague stirred up to the Work of God. He had not since his coming to the Country till since Christmas last, been zealous, but always discouraged, and discouraging; but he has been remarkably stirred up to preach, and translate, since that time, and I hope it is a token for good towards us. *{Obviously a reference to Mr. Thomas.}*

Carey to Fuller, June 22, 1797

When we *{Thomas and Carey}* arrived in the Country we intended to have lived together and I committed the management of the joint family to him. The consequence was, as you will observe from my Journal of the time, that in two months from our landing, ours was all spent and he then told me that my share of the goods was gone and consequently I was entirely destitute. At that time he engaged in his profession of a Surgeon, and I lived in a Home rent free, without sufficiency for my family. In a little time he furnished me with 150 Rupees with which I went to Hashnabad. Afterwards when I came to Mudnabati I considered myself about 300 Rupees in his debt and sent him half of it by the Post as we both acted in the fullest confidence. I neglected to keep an account with him till after this period, the consequence of which was that, last June he being in Want for the first time informed me that I was deeply in his debt and had three years interest to pay him for a large sum laid out on my account soon after our landing. This was followed when to my amazement I found that Principal and Interest in 12 months amounted to more than 1,000 Rupees . . . Thus you see I have discouragements. Mr. Long we have been obliged to exclude from our church for dishonesty. Mr. Thomas is gone far away, and my domestic troubles are sometimes almost too heavy for me. I am distressed, yet supported and I trust not totally dead in the things of God; I do a little, and I wish to do more, but the whole weight lies on me. Bro. Fountain is diligent, has good preaching abilities, and is a great encouragement to me, tho he cannot speak the Languages so as to be understood in preaching. Mr. Powell is a good man and given me great pleasure, but he is not professedly a Missionary and it is doubtful to me whether he has the abilities to speak in publick. He is, however, very useful in other respects, and is now going to undertake the making of our Printing Press. The prospect among the Natives is more encouraging. Our school prospers, and I trust there is some revival among the religious Europeans in this Neighborhood.

Carey to Sutcliffe, Mudnabati, Oct.10, 1798

. . . Yourself and all our Brethren both in and out of the Ministry, are often the subjects of conversation between Mr. Fountain and myself for not having much of that soul enlivening conversation with the Saints which you enjoy so cheaply in England. We often supply its place by talking over our former friendships, and enjoying the pleasure of calling to mind the delightful seasons which we have enjoyed formerly. Nor do we infrequently desire most earnestly to see some more of our acquaintances join our standard, and participate with us in the work of the Mission.

We are not, however, without some agreeable conversation, and acquaintances, tho obliged to travel for it. At Malda and its vicinity are several whom I fear not to reckon among the number of true Christians. [About one day's journey further, on the west side of the Ganges, at a Place called Tenasing is another Gentleman, a Mr. Hasted, the Husband of Mr. Powell's Sister who accompanied Mr. Thomas to India. He is a man of good understanding, and I doubt not, a real Christian. I have the pleasure of corresponding with him. At Dinjapur which is about 30 miles to the North of this place we have increasing evidence of a genuine piety. I trust God has changed the heart of our good friend Mr. Ignatius Fernandez . . .

Carey to Ryland, Mudnabati, April 1, 1799

I went to Calcutta in company with Mr. Fernandez, a gentleman whom I have often mentioned in my letters, and concerning whom I entertain great hopes - He lays himself out much to induce people to attend the preaching of the Word. At Calcutta I saw much dissipation, but yet I think less than formerly. Lord Mornington has set his Face against Sports, Gaming, Horse Racing, and Working on the Lord's Day, in consequence of which these infamous practices are less common than formerly. I found a Mr. Forsyth at Calcutta who says that he came to the Cape in a Ship belonging to Mr. Hardcastle, and I understand that he has some connection with the London Missionary Society. He, however, has brought no letters to anyone, and Mr. Hardcastle in a letter which I received from him makes no mention of him. He appears to be a Man of great seriousness, and I was much pleased with him, and invited him to this place, but since that I received a letter from a very respectable quarter, cautioning me against forming an hasty connection with a person, concerning whom I know so little. I hope well of him, and think well of him, but wish he had come recommended or at least mentioned by somebody. As it is , I am in a delicate situation, for I desire to shew the most unreserved friendship to him - but existing circumstances make it improper so to do.

I saw Bro. Thomas several Times. He has a small House at Chandernagore where he resides with his Family - He had written to me that he was going to Baptise a Brahman at Nuddea *{Nadia?}*, but when I arrived I found the grounds for such hopes were but slight. I shall mention to you what I am sure you will make no bad use of, viz. that when I got there, I found that Bro. Thomas had anticipated the sale of our Goods, and had taken up Money from Tullet and Co., to an amount somewhat greater than his share came to - - With this money he had paid no debt what I heard of, but had laid it out in Clothes, most of which lay then at a Commission Warehouse for sale.- - He wanted me to draw on the Society for his next year's Allowance, which I refused to do. In consequence of which he poured out a torrent of vulgar abuse upon me and I left the House - - The whole was in the hearing of Mr. Fernandez and two others, and together with some other circumstances wrought to his prejudice in their eyes. He, however, followed me and desired me to go back and be reconciled. I went back, we prayed together, and I am sure that I heartily forgive him; but it would be imprudent to commit myself to him or to form that close and unreserved connection with him, which I formerly did. Indeed I fear that his affairs must turn out dishonourable to the Mission at last. His debts cannot be less than a Thousand Pounds, and are constantly accumulating, none are paid off, and at every place where his concerns were known at Calcutta, I had the distress to hear very disagreeable accounts of his Affairs. He is not suited at the Society appointing me treasurer - and I advised him to write them about it - I am truly sorry for him, and more so for poor Mrs. Thomas, who has manifested an exemplary spirit through the whole.

On my way I visited Rev. Mr. Buchanan at Barrackpore. I was induced to do this from the very pleasing account Mr. Newton had written me of him - but tho I have no occasion to suppose him not to be a good, and eminent Man, yet I saw nothing very pleasing in him. He is Chaplain at a Military Station, and except he goes to Calcutta never preaches. I asked him why he did not: and he pleaded that he had not congregation. I asked him if he made no attempt among the Natives, he said that he could not do that while he held a Military Station, and He at first began to examine me as if he had been by Suffragon - asked what had become of that chap Thomas! And a number of officious questions but afterwards was more agreeable, and asked me to call and dine with him on my return. In short, tho he acted the Gentleman, I saw little of the Christian and Mr. Forsyth who was with me was so disgusted, as scarcely to admit him to have any right to the name.

Carey to Ryland, Calcutta, June 23, 1803

The news of four new Missionaries coming to join us would a few months ago have been very glad tidings to us indeed, but when I communicated the contents to Brothers Ward and Marshman they felt much as I had done before, a very serious concern for the consequences.- - I scarcely know how to open the matter to you, but this circumstance lays an obligation upon me which I cannot dispense with; I am loth, and much grieved to say anything unlovely about my Brethren, but am forced to do it. The fact is that Bro. Chamberlain has manifested so much of a spirit of discontent with our measures, and has such a degree of obstinate adhesion to his own opinion in everything, (tho it is absolutely impossible for him to know enough of circumstances yet to enable to form a proper judgment of any thing) that it is difficult to know how to deal with him, and the morose criminating way in which he constantly acts makes us dread the thought of a majority of inexperienced persons among us.

Bro. Ward, Bro. Marshman and myself have always felt the utmost confidence in each other: and I am sure that they have both of them devoted all their strength, knowledge, and exertions to the service of the Mission. I am what I am but we have scarcely known an attempt to carry our own private opinion against the voice of the majority, and if we could not see propriety of every measure have always accounted it a sacred duty to acquiesce. Indeed I do not believe that a difference of opinion has subsisted among us for twenty four hours upon any measure which we have debated: we, I hope, desire to spend and be spent in this work, and God has I think greatly blessed his interest, (principally through then instrumentality of our native brethren, or providential interposition). I am as sure as my judgment of things will enable me to be, that if we had listened to any of those things in which Bro. C. has differed from us, we should have burst. While there is but one or two persons of such a dogmatical turn they can do but little hurt, except that they clog our operations and grieve our minds, but a majority would be able in one hour to undo what we have been doing for some Years.

I think that I can say that we do not wish to be Lords over our Brethren, but we should be greatly distressed to see the whole work overthrown in a few days by any hasty step. While Candidates are with you on a trial they feel their situation, when they come to us and are upon the most perfect equality they also feel one part of their situation, and unless they are such as can practically devote all to the work the part which they see is their own importance, and not the great responsibility which lies upon them. No person can in a few months be able to form a proper judgment of the vast body of complicated affairs which we have to manage: and unless possessed of much more penetration than I am, cannot in several years have that knowledge of the feelings, habits, and prejudices of the natives as to be able to form an infallible judgment of things. Young men with but little knowledge of men and things and little experience in the manner of acting in difficult circumstances, if they are not humble and teachable will too frequently run to the other extreme, and become opinionative, precipitate, or obstinate. I fear this ruined the Sierra Leone Mission, and has been hurtful to that in Otoheite & its vicinity.

On hearing the contents of yours, Brethren Ward and Marshman were for immediately writing a Letter to the Society stating our feelings; but as the intelligence came in a private letter to me, I could not agree to make that a foundation for a publick letter: and likewise thought that every desirable end might be answered by immediately replying to yours. Our Brethren, therefore, desired me to state the above as fears which are common to all three of us.- - I am sure that the wisdom of the Society will do what can be done to obviate the inconvenience above mentioned. I have thought of two or three things which might contribute to it which will just mention 1. As Missionaries just arrived from Europe must be deficient in experience and knowledge for the first Year or two, might it not be advisable for them to have a vote which should amount to only half one of theirs who have been longer in the work - and to remain in some measure under the direction of the older Missionaries till their Tempers were known, and their judgments somewhat matured? 2. It will be desirable to form subordinate stations for the Mission Query. Might it not be proper to give the elder Missionaries a power to detach others of their Brethren to such situations (for instance Dinajpur, Benares, Luknow, or the East) where they would distribute pamphlets, Testaments, &ct. and when able preach? A native Brother might accompany them. If these are not advisable would it not be proper. 3ly *{thirdly}* To send only two at a time, and wait to hear from us before a greater number were ventured on? You will probably be able to think of some other means. Missionaries are necessary and, provided our harmony be maintained, we cannot have too many: but Human Nature is Human nature even in the best of men.

I hope you will not think that there is any ill blood between Bro. Chamberlain & us, there is not. We are unhappy to see him so unhappy and have in private talked very affectionately to him about it, but he does not soon lose an unlovely impression . . .

Carey to Ryland: Date unknown (June 23, 1803-Dec. 13, 1804)

The last letter which I wrote was upon a very disagreeable subject. I have since that frequently wished that I had not written, and have also feared that I may have said something too severe; Though I am sorry to say that nothing has yet turned up to alter my general opinion of Br. C. Sister Chamberlain was delivered of a Son about six weeks, who is called John Sutcliffe Chamberlain. I am much afraid that she is going into a consumption, She is an excellent Woman, May the Lord preserve her.

Carey to Ryland, Nov. 11, 1806

. . . About three weeks ago a school boy came to me on Lord's day morning and told me that an Israelite was in the school. I went and found a Jew reading the Hebrew Bible with great fluency. He was born at Hebron, left Judea 14 years ago, ten of which he resided in Persia, and four in Kabul. He was going from Kabul to Surat with Shawle when a Sikh chief plundered him of everything. He came into the English dominions where he met with Mr. Gladwin who gave him a Hebrew Psalter. He is going to Jerusalem in an Arab ship. He says that the Jews are not oppressed by the Turks, but that the Persians use them very ill. He confirms Sir Wm. Jones' account of the Afghans, among he lived in Kabul. I had much talk with him. He repeatedly acknowledged to me that Jesus Christ was the true Messiah, that his nation knew him not, and therefore rejected him, on which account the wrath of God has been on them every since. He expects him to come again and restore the Jews to their own land. After seeing and conversing with some of our Native Brethren he exclaimed: "Now I see the glory of the Messiah's Kingdom, and its power in turning these idolaters from their idolatry". He is a very interesting person, last week he introduced to me another Jew born at Babylon, a good Hebrew scholar, who would be a valuable help in our translations, but I fear our funds will not allow us to employ him. We treated the first Jew, Isaac ben Mordecai, with all the attention we could, O that he might carry a favourable impression of the Gospel with him. I must conclude. Pray for us - We live in Love . . .

Carey to Fuller, April 20, 1808

{It appears a competitive spirit arose between the missionaries and the Bible Society. They tried to cooperate but had trouble over the dispensing of the monies. Several of the letters in 1808-09 give examples of the problems. This letter gives a long discussion of the relationship.}

We have no objection to their printing their translation of Madras, we even offered to Des Grangen to print it for them at Serampore; and never mentioned once to them any objection to their doing it any where. Why then is that charge brought against us? On the other hand we know that their good friend at Madras (Dr. Henn.) intends soon to return to Europe and we know that the Company's Press there will then go into other hands. We also know that we had communicated our having undertaken the Telugu, before they had a mission begun there. (See Evangelical. - May.) We had in fact begun it before they were there if I recollect right. - As for it being the work of a wicked Brahman - Des Grangen was here long enough to know that we never print any translation till every word has been revised, and re-revised. We have employed all the help we can obtain, Brahman, Mussulmen, and others to assist us, and in some instances to write out rough copies; but I have never yet suffered a single word, or a single mode of construction to pass without examining it, and seeing through it. I read every proof sheet twice or thrice myself, and correct every letter with my own hand. Bro. Marshman and Bro. Ward read every sheet. Three of the translations, viz the Bengalese, Hindustani, and Sanskrit I translated with my own hand, the two past immediately from the Greek, (the Old Test. not being begun) and the Hebrew Bible lies by me while I translate the Bengalese. I constantly avail myself of the help of most learned natives, and should think it criminal not to do so, but I do not commit my judgement to anyone. - Bro. Marshman does the same with the Chinese, and all that he engages in, and so does Bro. Ward.

The idea that a translation made by a Brahman will be unintelligible to the mind of the people is founded in ignorance. Would you if you were translating the Bible into English despise grammatical language, and the assistance of learned men, and use the dialect and orthography of country clowns and if you did would it be better understood than the present translation, which was the work of a learned man? If ever we finish the Telugu we shall first see through every word; but I do not expect any first attempt to be perfect. I, therefore, wish they would finish what they have done so we may avail ourselves of their labours, and they themselves of our, and between both a good version may be at last produced. This would be much better than the man's honor of "I was the translator of the Bible into Telugu-" The same remark will apply to Chinese, and other languages.- If the end be published, I am not anxious about who gets the glory.

I feel my ground in all the languages derived from Sanskrit, but I perhaps may not have a compleatly understood some passages. Others may here after be better expressed; and some mistakes may have escaped observation. Indeed I have never yet thought any thing perfect which I have done.

Carey to Ryland, March 15, 1809

. . . I with pleasure also see a reconciliation effected between us and Mr. Brown. This took place some time ago in the following manner. According to the wish of the Bible Society we engaged in the corresponding Committee last August. There was a disagreeable reserve on both sides at the first meeting, at our second meeting last January, in consequence of an idea started by Mr. Thomason, some very illiberal expressions were uttered by Mr. Brown. I felt unhappy at this, and as Mr. Thomason had first introduced the subject, I took an opportunity to call on him a few days afterwards, and talk the matter over with him. He declared himself to be quite friendly to our undertakings and hostile to the ambitious scheme which had occasioned the rupture between us and Mr. Brown & Buchanan, and said that he had not intention to introduce anything disagreeable when he introduced the subject above mentioned. We had much conversation in which I informed him of the particulars of our disagreeable difference: he lamented the whole and we parted.

Mr. Brown had exceeded his powers as secretary, in conveying the resolution of our first meeting, and we concluded it to be necessary to write to him about it: but as __________ very sensible on that delicate point, the thought occurred to me to persuade Mr. Thomason to become the mediator of peace between us, and to undertake the rectification of the false step Mr. B. had taken. I mentioned it to Bro. Marshman who was then in Calcutta, and he immediately sent to Mr. Thomason and made the proposal. He gladly accepted it, and a few days afterwards Mr. B. called on me, and made every concession one could wish for, and promised to write to the Bible Society to remedy the step he had improperly taken. We then agreed mutually to bury all the past and to act in unison in the common cause. We are now going to institute a *Bibliotheca Biblia* in Calcutta, for the purpose of disposing of Bibles at a moderate price to persons of all nations who visit the port, and for those who wish to purchase them to give away: and have written to the Bible Society for a large supply in the English, French, and Portugese languages, and some Dutch, German, and Danish ones, to which we hope to add Bibles in several oriental languages, the design of it is to give an extended circulation to one word of God in all parts of India.

Carey to Fuller, Oct. 25, 1809

The state of the society is greatly altered of late years. When I came first there was no friend to whom I could go or at whose home I could stay ten days but a missionary now comes into the bosom of a good number of warm hearted friends, who are with each other to shew them kindness. This, in most instances, operates as a poison, and begets a dislike to that life of seclusion, deprivation, and self-denial which a missionary should embrace. It begets a spirit of expence and excess and of self-indulgences. So we have found it, and so we see it.

Carey to Ryland, Dec. 10, 1811

We have baptised 61 persons in Calcutta this year, I expect six more will be baptised before its close. My youngest son Jonathan is proposed to the Church. The Lord has in respect to my Children been very gracious. One of them Jabez, however, still remains unchanged: and lies a heavy weight upon my mind, not because of any open profligacy or disobedience, but because he is unconverted. Bro. Chater has relinquished the Burman Mission through fear of the dangers of a civil war which rages there, but at bottom, through a dislike his wife has of a country where European food and Society are not easily obtained. I hope he will soon choose another station. He wished to cover his defection by retaining the name of a Missionary to that country, and living at Calcutta to superintend the printing of the Burman Scriptures, but as the copy must be prepared there, and no alterations made here that would be perfectly unnecessary for Bro. Chater's knowledge of the Language is not greater than Felix's, and his helps in this country much inferior to his at Rangoon. All, therefore, that is necessary is to print exactly by the Mss, and we can compare with that. Felix is now there alone, but will I hope be preserved firm in his work.

Carey to Sutcliffe, Aug. 5, 1812, Calcutta

The whole bustle about learned men in India, Learned translation &ct..,was a mere phantom raised to create a noise, and to take vengeance upon us for not yielding the translation, and even the property of the Mission itself into the hands of Dr. Buchanan to whom Mr. Brown was entirely devoted. - The only translations we could even have given up to others were the Persian, the Hindustani, the Chinese, and the Telugu for no one pretended to know the other languages.

Carey to Ryland, Apr. 12, 1817, Calcutta

. . . I tremble for this self seeking. The same spirit was carried by Griffiths to Ceylon where the most lamentable, and scandalous breach between him and Chater has taken place. I think they are both entirely wrong. Chater is bloated with self importance, and Griffiths supposed he had an absolute authority in Chater's house, and over all his property. This led to altercation, disputes, angry letters, and at last the exposure of the Baptist Cause to the utmost contempt of all, and all this about an old horse and a young one, and to whom these said animals did respectively belong.

Carey to Ryland, Sept. 1817

. . . That spirit of preferring personal considerations to the general cause of the Mission, which has so much prevailed among our Younger Brethren, had well nigh threatened the whole work here with ruin and had done more mischief than all the opposition from without, we have ever met with. The Church at Calcutta was very near being brought into a state of ruin a little time ago by this spirit, and at this moment we are in the most disagreeable circumstances with respect to the Benevolent Institutions that can be imagined. I will just relate the out lines.

We had some little time ago occasion to elect two Deacons and fixed upon Capt. Kemp, and Bro. Penny. I was perhaps more active in this step than any one else. Capt. Kemp is a strong defender of mixed communion as is Bro. Yates, who has resided in Calcutta to supply the place of my Nephew who was obliged to go up the country for his Health. Yates has always been dissatisfied with no one knows what ever since he came among us, and has if I am not mistaken carried on an opposition in the most cold-blooded manner imaginable. No sooner were these two men chosen Deacons than they made an attempt to introduce mixed Communion, without, however, so much as mentioning the matter to me, though, I dined at Mr. Penny's table constantly twice a week. This step would have separated three of the Pastors from the Church if it had been carried, viz. myself, Bro Marshman, and Bro. Lawson; and what was still more extraordinary Bro. Marshman whose turn it was to attend the Church meeting was required personally to bring forward this motion which would have excluded him from the Church. He remonstrated and succeeded in getting them to withdraw the motion till an adjourned meeting.

Carey to Ryland, Serampore, Apr.11, 1818

{In April 1818 the younger brethren led by Eustace and Yates formed their own society in Calcutta separate from Carey, Marshman, and Ward. These younger missionaries had some problems with Marshman concerning mission funds and his family and criticized him heavily. Carey defended him. This was the beginning of a long standing feud between the groups.}

. . . Last Week, however, a circumstance occurred which is it possible still more unlovely. I mean the formation of a Mission Society Auxiliary to the present one, from which the three older pastors of the Church are excluded. Eustace mentioned it to me a few Days before, and asked me if it met my approbation, I answered yes; for I heartily approve of forming a society for that purpose; I could not, however, suppose what happened, that we were to have no share in it.

. . . A Society was formed in the Church, over which we are Pastors, by the two younger Pastors and Bro. Y. without consulting the elder Pastors, nay absolutely excluding them . . . but the thing is supremely unlovely, and will not pass unnoticed by either the Church party or the Independents.

Carey to Ryland, Oct. 4, 1818, Serampore

You know, I suppose, long before this that Brothers Adam and Pearce have left us and joined the Calcutta Faction. I leave it to them to account for what they have done. With the latter I used all the arguments in my power; but not with the other because he left us before I knew that he was at all dissatisfied.

. . . It appears (though I only conjecture this) that they have set up a counter-Baptist Mission which is intended to be more pure than the old one, and to answer higher purposes. They, so far as I am acquainted with their object, intend to throw their funds together for Missionary purposes, and I am sure labour to do good. They laboured much, I believe, with Bro. Pearce on his arrival to induce him to settle with them as Printer, and this he has since done, an account of which I must give you before I finish.

. . . I do not recollect any thing in my whole life which has given me so much distress as this Schism in the Mission has done. Many sleepless nights have I spent examining what we had done to give occasion for it; but can discover nothing on which I can fix; The Mission is, however, rent in twain, and exhibits the scandalous appearance of a body, half of which is divided against the other half, and doing everything possible to wound their feelings. We could easily vindicate ourselves, but that vindication would be our and their disgrace. We have, therefore, resolved to say nothing for ourselves, but leave the matter in the Hand of God. I hope my penning out these my distresses into the bosom of an old, and much beloved Friend, will not be accounted a deviation from this resolution.

The division of the Mission, distressing as it is, is a much smaller evil than that crippling every effort to spread the Gospel which results from it.

Carey to Ryland, March 30, 1819, Calcutta

. . . As it respects the Brethren in Calcutta, I hope the spirit which has so long prevailed begin to subside. Eustace has lately been twice to see me, and Bro. Pearce once. I am determined to do all I can for peace; and to overcome evil with good to the utmost of my power. I think respecting the Schism as I have always done, as a very wrong and most unnecessary thing. There is no doubt much on both sides to be forgiven; but the worst evil has been the weakening the cause they came to strengthen, and exposing it to contempt. They are labouring among the natives in and about Calcutta, but for that a wide circle is totally neglected . . . "Only by Pride cometh contentions". There has been much pride, and still, I fear, much exists, on both sides. I think, however nothing has been said or done which ought not to be immediately forgiven on both sides, and that there has been no misunderstanding but what Christians ought to use their utmost endeavors to remove by trying to understand each other.

Carey to Carapeit, July 2, 1819

I yesterday saw with much pain your Letter to Mr. J. Marshman which I was surprised at after what I had last Tuesday spoken to out of the fullness and distress of my heart on your account. I am greatly distressed to see you thus higgling *{haggling}* For money in an affair of such great importance as that of publishing the Gospel of our Lord Jesus Christ. Compare, Dear Brother, the sentiments of the Apostle Paul with your own. Paul said "Unto me who am less than the least of all the saints is this grace given, and this favour bestowed, that I should preach among the Gentiles the unsearchable riches of Christ", and again "neither count I my life dear unto myself so that I might finish my course with joy and the ministry which I have received from the Lord Jesus, to testify the Gospel of the grace of God". You, My Dear Bro. say "I will go to Chittagong if you will give me 150 Rupees a month, and allow me half my time, viz. six months in the year to study Latin and English language, if this be not agreed to I will not go". And when you agreed to go for 100 Rupees a month for four to six months, you demand the whole pay in advance, or else refuse to stir.

My dear Bro. You are accountable to our Lord Jesus Christ himself for putting a price upon preaching his gospel, and not to us. He put you into the Ministry, and undoubtedly expects that you should serve him therein with your Spirit.

I have long been in great distress of Soul about the poor destitute Church at Chittagong; but I can do no more. God does not need your labours. He can raise up ministers for the wants of his Church, and I trust will do so.

We last night, seriously weighed the contents of your Letter, and came to the following resolutions, which I am desired to mention to you.

1. We are exceedingly sorry to see the mercenary spirit of Bro. Carapeit especially as we are fully convinced that the offer we have made him of 100 Rupees a month, at a distance from Calcutta is very liberal.

2. As there is no particular necessity for more Preachers in Calcutta, we will not allow Bro. Carapeit an increase of Salary for the two months he has been there, and from the 1st of August no salary will be allowed him for staying there.

3. We will allow Bro. Carapeit 100 Rupees a month at Chittagong, which he may draw there when due [we having made arrangements for that purpose] as he may have any part of it paid to any person in Calcutta when he may appoint, only giving us notice of it that we make further arrangements funding it.

4. No further advance will be made to Bro. Carapeit than what he has already received.

Now, My Dear Bro. You are quite at Liberty to go to Chittagong or not, as you please, but the above are our unalterable resolutions, unless you can shew very different reasons for desiring further advance of money, than you yet (have) done. If you go we will pray that God may be with you and bless you. If you refuse to go, you had better pay back the advances you have received to me, next Tuesday and in the mean time discharge your boat that there may be no further expence on it . . .

We sympathize with you in the afflictions of your Child, but pray consider, that it is God who has laid this affliction upon you. We feel for you under it and whether you are separate from us, or continue with us in the Work of the Lord, shall love you, pray for you, and seek your good.

Carey to Jabez, Aug. 15, 1820

. . . I am sure it will give you pleasure to learn that our long continued dispute with the younger brethren in Calcutta is now settled. We met together for that purpose about three weeks ago and after each side giving up some trifling ideas and expressions came to a reconciliation, which I pray God may be lasting. Nothing I ever met with in my life, and I have met with many distressing things, ever preyed so much upon my Spirits as this difference has. I am sure that in all disputes many very wrong things must take place on both sides for which both parties ought to be humbled before God and one another.

Carey to Ryland, Oct. 23, 1820

It will afford you pleasure to learn that a termination has been put to the disputes between us and our younger Brethren. In consequence of the Letter sent by the Society recommending a meeting to accommodate our differences, they wrote us a letter proposing a meeting to which we agreed. I forget the dates, but that is no matter. We met at the time appointed, opened our meeting in prayer, and then proceeded to business. We required as a preliminary step that they should relinquish their claims to the legacy left to the Serampore Missionaries by the last Mr. Bryant to which they agreed. We also requested that we might not be called on to approve the steps they had taken in forming a separate interest, and erecting another Chapel in Calcutta, and left them at full liberty to approve or disapprove of anything we had done. There was a good deal of altercation upon various subjects, the greater part of which I have forgot. They were certainly under a strange mistake respecting the Serampore property, which they supposed had been purchased with the Society's money and subsequently alienated by us from the society and appropriated to ourselves; to that mistaken idea they seemed determined to adhere with a pertinacity bordering on obstinacy. We assured them that the premises were bought by us with money which we borrowed upon our own responsibility and afterwards paid; and that as the most sure way of securing the premises for the use of the Mission, we vested the property in the Society, and made ourselves trustees for it . . . that we had never felt a moments vacillation of thought about the right of property, but that all our dispute with the Society was about the right to manage our internal concerns, and dispose of our income for the cause of God in the way we ourselves thought fit.

They intimated that we ought to carry all our means to the Society's account and pay it into their funds, and said that they did so, and sent their accounts regularly to the Society. I told them they had a right to do as they pleased with themselves and their earnings, but that Liberty was my birth right which I would not sell, even to my Brother. I told them that we had never sent an account of our income and expenditures to the Society since the different stations of the Mission had been made independent of each other, and that no such thing had been ever required; that, however, our all was devoted to the object which the Society existed, and I thought the Society ought to be satisfied if the objects for which it was formed were promoted; without endeavoring to reduce their Brethren to a state bordering on slavery. I believe our ideas were at last mutually understood, and we parted, agreeing to forgive, on both sides, all unkind expressions or actions to which the state of irritation which had previously existed had given rise . . .

Carey to Jabez, May 15, 1821

. . . I am sorry to say that Mr. Adams, who some months ago separated from the younger brethren in some disagreement with which I am unacquainted, appears likely to embrace the sentiments of the Arians. In a letter of his which I saw, he speaks of his doubts about the proper divinity of Christ, and of his seeing fewer difficulties on the scheme he has adopted. He says also that Mr. Yates has the same doubts. The latter, however, has not himself declared any such thing. They have opened their new Chapel and the Independents theirs. These things seem a little to lessen our Congregation, but I do not apprehend that it will be felt long. Mr. Adams has long given up preaching both in English and Bengali and appears to be quite at enmity with our other Brethren. I think Divine Providence generally returns improper conduct upon the heads of those who are guilty of it, and I think their conduct towards us was highly unjust. I have, however, cordially forgiven them and am now truly sorry to see their divisions.

Carey to Dyer, Dec. 24, 1824

Are many gratifying circumstances attending the present state of things here, in the cordial harmony and reciprocal affection which subsists among the ministers of different denominations. We visit each other, love each other, and pray for each other, and I am certain rejoice in each other's success, and sympathize with each other in all circumstances of discouragement and distress. We love the Brethren.

Carey to Jabez, March 2, 1831

{Continued problems with the younger brethren.}

. . . I am truly sorry to witness the unlovely spirit manifested by the Circular Road brethren against Serampore. They carry it so far as to leave the Interest in the Lall Bazar out of their publick reports, notwithstanding, Bro. Robinson is a missionary belonging to the Society and supported by them and has been successful in his labours, and all this is owing to his being suspected of entertaining friendly sentiments for Brethren at Serampore. They have always pretended to have a high regard for me, but since Mr. Yates return have engaged in making a rival translation of the N. Testament. As this, viz. the Translation of the Scriptures, has been the chief business of my life and I have done the best I could to make the translation compleat and correct, I feel this unfriendly attempt, or rather the spirit which has dictated it very much. They have published a prospectus in England with a specimen. The specimen is at least twenty years behind the Serampore translation, but it is very distressing to see Brethren wasting their time without any occasion to so little purpose, while the direct hostility to me is a matter of serious regret.

OPPOSITION

Carey to Sutcliffe, Calcutta, Mar.17,1802

. . . I have been much astonished lately at the malignity of some of the infidel opposers of the Gospel, to see how ready they are to pick every flaw they can in the inspired writings, and even to distort the sense to make it appear inconsistent; while these very persons will labour to reconcile the grossest contradictions in the writings which the Hindus account sacred, and will stoop to the meanest artifices to apologize for the numerous glaring lies and horrid violations of all decorum and decency which abound in almost every page. But it seems that anything will do with some people except the Word of God. These men ridicule the figurative language of Scriptures, but will run allegory itself mad to support the merit of the most worthless books that were ever published. I should think it time past to translate any of them and only a sense of duty excites me to read them. An idea, however, of the advantage that the friends of religion may obtain by having these mysterious sacred nothings exposed to publick view which have maintained their celebrity so long merely by being kept from the inspection of any but interested Brahmans, has induced me, among other things to write the Sanskrit Grammar and to begin a Dictionary of that Language. I sincerely pity the poor people who are held by their claims of implicit faith in the grossest lies, and can scarcely help to despise the wretched infidel who applauds and tries to vindicate them. I have long wanted to get a Copy of the *Vedas*, and am more in hopes of getting all which are extant. A Brahman this morning offered to procure them for me for the sake of Money, and I believe I shall succeed. If so I shall be strongly tempted to publish them with a Translation, pro bono publick.

Carey to Fuller, Feb.13, 1807

India swarms with Deists, and Deists are in my opinion the most intolerant of mankind. Their great desire is to exterminate true religion from the earth. I consider the alarms which have been spread through India as the fabrication of those men who took occasion from the concurrence of two or three circumstances, viz. the massacre at Vellore, and rebellious disposition of the inhabitants in some parts of Mysore, and the publick advertisement for subscriptions to destroy the expence of Oriental translations to represent the introduction of Christianity among the natives as dangerous. The effects of their attempts have been greater under the Madras govt than here.

Carey to Sisters, Feb. 21, 1831, Serampore

It is scarcely advisable to trouble you with things relating to myself, but you must have heard of the attack made on the translations of the Bible by Mr. Morton, a Clergyman, and of the triumphant manner it has been replied by Mr. Greenfield. Mr. Greenfield's defence of me was quite gratuitous and I feel it with much gratitude. Besides that, a complaint was made by the Independent ministers of Calcutta to the Bible Society, because I had translated the word *baptizo* which occasioned a letter from Mr. Hughes at Battersea to me, to which I think I replied in a manner which will not soon be answered. Since that, chiefly by the intrigues of the same persons the Bible Society at Calcutta appointed a committee to make a new Translation; and I was waited upon by two of them to request me to unite with them. I told them that I had done the best I could in translating the Scriptures, and that I, therefore, was not prepared to pass a sentence of condemnation on all I had been doing for the last thirty years or more; and moreover that I could never join in a translation in which *baptizo* was not translated. This put an end to any further application to me; and now I understand the undertaking is likely to be relinquished through contentions of the Labourers. Since that our Junior Brethren have advertized to print a new and improved edition of the New Testament, a prospectus and specimen of which they have published in the Baptist Magazines, and the Society's reports.

Mission Strategy

Anyone who has ever lived on the mission field and labored to plant churches in a foreign setting recognizes the need for a plan or strategy to be successful. The genius and creativity of Carey and his associates becomes apparent as we study their mission program. Carey wrote frequently about ideas pertaining to missionary qualifications, the structure of the mission, language missions, translation and publication, incarnational missions (the concept of fitting in with the native population in order to reach them more effectively), indigenous missions (planting Indian churches rather than transplanted English ones), education, and cooperation with other missionaries and the government.

This section of the letters will be lengthy due to the focus of the collection, which allows Carey to speak to us on missions. The tried methods and dreams of Carey encourage missions in all ages. Consequently, many of the strategies Carey and his colleagues worked out under great stress are still utilized today in various forms. Who can imagine missions today without emphasizing vernacular Scripture or striving to develop a native church with native leadership? The Indian mission offers us a laboratory for observing strategy in action.

Laying a proper foundation for the work was critical for Carey. He believed that the Bible in the language of the people was that foundation and success in India might even be required to wait until the word of God was disseminated. Several conversions came not from direct contact with the natives, but rather from an encounter with the Bible.

Included in this section are examples of Carey's presentation of the Gospel to Hindus, Brahmans, Mohammedans, and the common people of India. Early on, Carey traveled the rural areas and gathered congregations wherever possible. He argued in favor of Christ over the idolatry and superstition he detected in India. The effectiveness of his approach could be debated but his sincerity and conviction cannot. The presentations of Carey give us an insight into his theology and perception of the target audience in India.

ADVICE TO A YOUNG MISSIONARY

Carey to Jabez, Jan. 24, 1814

Dear Jabez,

You are now engaging in a most important undertaking in which not only you and Eliza have my prayers for your success but those of all who love our Lord Jesus Christ and know of your engagement. I know a few hints for your future conduct from a parent who loves you very tenderly will be acceptable and shall, therefore, give you them, assured that they will not be given in vain.

1. Pay the utmost attention at all times to the state of your own mind both towards God and man. Cultivate an intimate acquaintance with your own heart, labour to obtain a deep sense of your depravity and to trust always in Christ. Be pure in heart and meditate much on the pure and holy character of God. Live a life of prayer and devotedness to God. Cherish every amiable and right disposition towards man. Be mild, gentle and unassuming yet firm and manly. As soon as you perceive any wrong in your spirit or behaviour set about correcting it and never suppose yourself so perfect as to need no correction.

2. You are now a married man. Be not satisfied with conducting yourself towards your wife with propriety. Let love to her be the spring of your conduct towards her. Esteem her highly and so act that she may be induced thereby to esteem you highly. The first impressions of love arising from form or beauty will soon wear off but the esteem arising from excellency of disposition and substance of character will endure and increase. Her honour is now yours and she cannot be insulted without you being degraded.

I hope as soon as you get on board and are settled in your cabin you will begin and end each day in uniting together to pray and praise God. Let religion always have a place in your house. If the Lord bless you with children bring them up in the fear of God and be always an example to others of the power of Godliness. This advice I also give to Eliza and if followed you will be happy.

3. Behave affably and genteelly to all but not cringingly or unsteadily towards any. Feel that you are a man and always act with that dignified sincerity and truth which will command the esteem of all. Seek not the society of worldly men but when called to be with them act and converse with dignity and propriety. To do this, labour to gain a good acquaintance with history, geography, man and things. A gentleman is the next best character after a Christian and the latter includes the former. Money never makes a gentleman much less a fine appearance but an enlarged understanding joined to engaging manners.

4. On your arrival at Amboyna your first business must be to wait on Mr. Martin. You should first send a note to inform him of your arrival and know when it will suit him to receive you. Ask his advice upon every occasion of importance and communicate freely to him all the steps you take.

5. As soon as you are settled begin your work. Get a Malay who can speak a little English and with him make a tour of the Islands and visit every school. Encourage all you see worthy of encouragement and correct with mildness yet with firmness. Keep a journal of the transactions of the schools and enter one under a

distinct head therein. Take account of the number of scholars, the names of the schoolmasters, compare the progress at stated periods and in short consider this the work which the Lord has given you to do.

6. Do not, however, consider yourself as a mere superintendent of schools, consider yourself as the spiritual instructor of the people and devote yourself to their good. God has committed the spiritual interests of the Islands, 20,000 men or more to you - a vast charge - but he can enable you to be fruitful to the trust. Revise the catechisms, tracts and school books used among them and labour to introduce among them sound doctrine and genuine piety. Pray with them as soon as you can and labour after a gift to preach to them. I expect you will have much to do with them respecting baptisms. They all think infant sprinkling right and will apply to you to baptise their children. You must say little till you know something of the Language and then prove to them from Scripture what is the right mode of Baptism and who are the proper persons to be baptised. Form them into Gospel churches when you meet with a few who truly fear God and as soon as you see any fit to preach to others call them to the ministry and settle them with the churches. You must baptise and administer the Lord's Supper according to your own discretion when there is proper occasion for it. Avoid indolence and love of ease and never attempt to act the part of the great and gay in this world.

7. Labour incessantly to become a perfect master of the Malay language. In order to do this associate with the natives, walk about with them, ask the name of everything you see and note it down. Visit their houses especially when any of them are sick. Every night arrange the words you get in alphabetical order. Try to talk as soon as you get a few words and be as soon as possible one of them. A course of kind and attentive conduct will gain their esteem and confidence and give you an opportunity of doing much good.

8. You will soon learn from Mr. Martin the situation and disposition of the Alfoors - an original inhabitant - and will see what can be done for them. Do not unnecessarily expose your life but incessantly contrive some way of giving them the word of life.

9. I come now to things of inferior importance but which I hope you will not neglect. I wish you to learn correctly the number, size and geography of the Islands, the number and description of the inhabitants, their customs and manners and everything not relative to them and regularly communicate these to me.

10. I wish you to pay the minutest attention to the natural productions of the Islands and regularly to send me all you can - fishes and large animals excepted - but these you must describe. You know how to send birds and insects. Send as many birds of every description alive as you possibly can, and also small quadrupeds, monkeys &ct. and always send a new supply by every ship. Shells, including crabs and tortoises &ct. corals, stones of every description may be put in a box but each should have a label with the Malay or country name, the place where found &ct. Rough stones broken from the rock are preferable to such as are worn or washed round by the sea. Beetles, lizards, frogs and insects may be put into a small keg of rum to Arakan and will come safely.

. . . Your great work, My Dear Jabez, is that of a Christian minister. You would have solemnly set apart thereto, if you could have stayed long enough to have permitted it. The success of your labours does not depend upon outward ceremony nor does your right to preach the Gospel or administer the ordinances of the Gospel depend on any such thing but only on the divine call expressed in the word of God. The church has, however, in their intentions and wishes borne a testimony to the grace given to you and will not cease to pray for you that you may be successful. May you be kept from all temptation, supported under every trial, made victorious in every conflict and may our hearts be mutually gladdened with accounts from each other of the triumphs of divine grace. God has conferred a great favour on you in permitting to you this ministry. Take heed to it, therefore, in the Lord that thou fulfil it. We shall often meet at the throne of Grace. Write to me by every opportunity and tell Eliza to write to your Mother.

THE MISSIONARY

Critical to success in any endeavor is the quality of personnel assigned the job. Carey recognized this from the start and informed the Society of preferred missionary characteristics. The task required people of good morals and able to endure the rigors of life in India. A humble nature, which does not seek ease or selfish goals, ranked also close to the top of the Carey's list of missionary qualities. In addition, Carey describes the kind of wife fit for missions.

Carey to Ryland, Bandel, Dec. 26, 1793

The plan laid down in my little piece, I still approve of and think the very best that can be followed. A Missionary must be one of the companions, and equals of the people to whom he is sent and many dangers and temptations will be in his way. One or two pieces of advice I may venture to give. The first is to be exceedingly cautious lest the voyage prove a great snare - all the discourse is about High Life, and every circumstance will contribute to unfit the mind for the Work, and prejudice the soul against the people to whom he goes and in a Country like this the grandeur, the Customs, and prejudices of the Europeans are exceeding dangerous. They are very kind and hospitable, but even to visit them, if a man keeps not table of his own would more than ten times exceed the allowance of a Mission - and all their discourse is about the vices of the Natives, so that a Missionary must see thousands of People treating him with greatest kindness, but whom he must be entirely different from, in his life, his appearance and everything - or it is impossible for him to stand; their profuse way of living being so contrary to his Character, and so much above his ability. This is a snare to dear Mr. T which will be felt by us both in some measure.

It will be very important to missionaries to be men of calmness and evenness of temper, and rather inclined to suffer hardships than to court the favour of Men and such who will be indefatigably employed in the Work set before them, an inconstancy of mind being quite injurious to that Work.

Carey to Society, Dec. 28 1796, Hooghly River

Let the number of Missionaries be increased as much as the finances of the Society will admit of and let the Missionaries be either married or single as they may be procured. There are many advantages attending Families engaging in the work provided proper rules are adhered to , and the Missionaries' Wives are as much impressed with the missionary spirit as they themselves are, and are people of prudence, and not afraid of hardship, but if they are otherwise, they will prove a far greater Burden than you can well conceive of as many things will occur that will feed a discontented mind as full as it can well be.

Let the missionaries be men possessed of Gifts such as are not despicable; but perhaps the gift of utterance or rather eloquence may be accounted at present one of the best; a readiness to communicate knowledge to others; inward Godliness, meekness, and Zeal, are the principal, but headlong rashness either in speaking, judging, or acting if it predominates should determine the Society to reject such. If they are acquainted with any trades, especially of the more necessary kind; and particularly the business of Husbandry it will be a great advantage; and one if acquainted with the management of and direction of Children for the purposes of a Schoolmaster would be necessary.

Carey to Fuller, March 23, 1797, Mudnabati

The failure of the African Mission is a very distressing circumstance, and shows the importance of being very careful what men are sent on a Mission. [Bless God we are all as cold as a stone in a political sense except Bro. Fountain, and I believe he is cooling.]

Carey to Fuller, Oct. 4, 1809

I understand by a letter from Dr. Taylor that the London Missionary Society have sent out two persons to the Burman empire and that they are at the Cape of Good Hope waiting for a passage to India. I am very sorry they should have acted so unlovely a part as to try to enter into other men's labours. I wish you send out men to begin new Missions in the countries around. I now think of Nepal, Tibet, Assam, Annahan *{Annam?}*, Pegu, Siam, Cambodia, Laos, Malaysia , and Cochin China. I trust that men will by degrees be raised up here who will carry the gospel in one way or another all over India. Bro. Robinson has been designed for Bantam & Tibet now nearly two years but I am quite discouraged at his delays. I believe he is strongly inclined to stay at Calcutta, where his abilities as an English preacher are (he thinks) acceptable, but the truth is, Bro. R. fears dangers and his imagination creates a thousand dangers where not one exists. Brothers Marshman & Ward are quite discouraged at his excuses and delays, and have nearly given over all hopes of him. The truth is he might have engaged in the work two years ago, had it not been for his fears. Our brothers say, his covetousness also, but I hope that is not the cause. He and his wife have lately been heavily afflicted; and I have still doubts whether her's will not terminate in a consumption. As to Bro. Moore, I have no hope that he ever will do anything, he knows nothing yet of the language, nor ever tries to acquire it. Indolence and a thirst for European society are his bane. In other respects his conduct is consistent, but as to the Mission he is nothing but the name of a Missionary.

Carey to Fuller, Aug. 2, 1811

There are two or three circumstances in the Mission which occasion us pain. I mean an anti-missionary Spirit which operates on a love of ease, an anxiety for European Society, and other things of the same nature which (enervate) the soul of a missionary and unfit him for his work . . ."

{It appears there was a problem with a Brother Robinson who was in Serampore and wanted to stay there while there was much work to be done elsewhere. Carey seems to be having trouble with the large number of missionaries unwilling to go where the need is. They tried to get Robinson to go to Java but he did not want to. Carey felt too many missionaries were in Bengal.}

I confess that I think it a great waste of strength to send two Europeans together to any visitation in Bengal, especially as . . ., one can scarcely go in any direction far, without finding a European.

Brother M. is a man whose whole heart is in the work of the Mission, and who may be considered as the soul and life of it. He is very sanguine, especially tenacious of any idea which (impresses) him as right or important. His labours are excessive. His body scarcely susceptible to fatigue, his religious feelings strong, his jealously for God great, his regard to the feelings of others very little when the cause of God is in question . . . In short his diligence reproaches the indolence of some . . .

Carey to Sutcliffe, Aug. 18, 1812

. . . We have suffered much from the strong propensity of Missionaries Wives (and Missionaries too) to stay about Calcutta. They go, tis true with their Husbands, but still their longing after the leeks and Onions of Calcutta makes them unhappy when in the country, and that discontent hurts their health, and too frequently operates in a way unfriendly to missionary work upon their husbands. Dangers and inconveniences are found where they never existed, and where they do exist are unreasonably magnified. Missionaries must go into the country, Indigo manufacturers do. Military officers do, and it is probable that a military officer, not to mention a private suffers more real privation, and encounters more dangers than a missionary will in his whole life. Through this cause I fear Bro. Chater will relinquish the Burman Mission. His mind is set on a mission to Pulo Prenang. It is an important place, and I doubt not but he will be faithful, diligent, and useful there, but three years spent on the Burman Mission are thrown away."

Carey to Jabez, March 31, 1814

. . . Felix left us last Lord's Day. We were forced to purchase a small vessel to carry him back. I hope, however, it will sell for as much as it cost. I fear the honours Felix has received from the Burman government have not been beneficial to his soul. If I am not mistaken a spirit for feeling complacency in worldly respectability has gained too much upon him. I have conversed with him upon the subject and I hope what I have said will not be in vain. Our hearts are very deceitful and often promise us pleasure and respectability from those things which are hostile to both. Felix is certainly not so much esteemed since his visit as he was before it. It is a very distressing thing to be forced to apologise for those you love.

Carey to Jabez, undated but arrived in Amboyna Sept. 10, 1814

. . . I have nothing particularly to add to the advice I gave you when you left us. I trust you will see the vast importance of devoting yourself entirely to the cause of our Lord. Labour to the utmost by kindness and constant attention to their good to obtain affection . . . Above all things labour to acquire a good knowledge . . . language and to instruct them in the great thing . . . Gospel. Seek also to gain a correct and intimate acquaintance with evangelical truth. Study the word of God and watch incessantly over your own mind. Backsliding in divine things comes on us by insensible steps but has the most fatal effect on our souls.

Carey to Ryland, May 30, 1816

. . . I am exceedingly sorry that you have resolved to send Miss Wilson to Serampore. I think it should be a settled rule with the Society, not to send out unmarried ladies, whether young or old, unless written to for that purpose. Sister Chaffin is an excellent woman, but she cannot possibly be of any use to the Mission, and is consequently only supported by its expence. This must also be the case with Miss Wilson. It is utterly in vain to expect that any one will or can be associated with Bro. or Sister Marshman in the management of the school. Bro. Marshman's eldest daughter is grown up and is quite able to give all the help needful there. Phoebe Grant also is full able to do the same. Now, when a woman comes out and finds nothing which she can do, and sees that she is merely supported, she will and must be unhappy.

. . . I hope you will be very explicit with all the Brethren who come out in talking with them and telling them that they must not expect to settle at Serampore. The want of this formerly occasioned us much trouble. This, indeed, was the original cause of all the difficulty we had with Bro. Johns and Lawson. We only need a certain at Calcutta and Serampore. Others must go to other situations. I wish also you could warn them against such sentiments of personal Segregation. My Nephew and Bro. Yates brought out a superabundance of this, had we acted on these principles we should long ago "have gone every one to his own". That, and a spirit of condemning in the most unqualified manner every thing done by the elder Brethren, was very distressing. Poor Bro. Marshman who is naturally a little tortuous, but than whom a more excellent and holy man does not exist in the Mission, had a most abundant part of this unqualified and unmerited condemnation. We yielded to their singularities, but came to a decided resolution to give up the entire management of the pecuniary concerns of the Mission to the Society. We are now all happy and I think are useful.

Mr. and Mrs. Hough from America to Rangoon are now within: I believe they will very soon go thither. We think of his taking a Printing Press compleat, with him, as he is a Printer. Mrs. White, a widow lady, accompanied them with an intention of setting up a school at Rangoon, a thing in the present state of Society absolutely impossible. They did not well agree on the passage, providentially Bro. Rowe was here in expectation of a partner from England, but instead of the lady received a letter informing him that she was married. He is, therefore, on the point of marriage with Mrs. White, who appears to be an excellent woman.

I enclose a Letter to you from Mr. Bruckner, one of the Missionaries sent to Java by The Missionary Society, and by every account the best of them. He is become a Baptist, and has for Conscience Sake given up his Chaplaincy in the Dutch church unless they will dispense with his sprinkling infants, and receiving persons indiscriminately to the Lord's Table. He has written to Dr. Boyne informing him of his change of sentiments, I hope you will feel no delicacy about receiving and employing him as a Missionary on your Establishment.

STRUCTURE OF THE MISSION

Structure exists to promote the goal. Carey desired a mission structure that would best ensure the effective spread of the Gospel in India and the neighboring countries. He initially envisioned a central mission station with sub-stations that would report to and draw support from the main base. A careful study of the letters in this section reveals some evolution in Carey's notions of structure as circumstance and personnel changed. This might be interpreted as flexibility or perhaps just utilitarianism on Carey's part.

Carey to Fuller, Nov. 16, 1796, from Mudnabati

I must now just tell you my thoughts about the Mission. Bro. Fountain is safely arrived and gives us pleasure but our affairs as a Mission are in a delicate situation. [I have written what I think of Bro. T's affairs]. This place I expect given up. Mr. M. has not mentioned anything - but I have written to him all that I think about it, however, the experiences obtained here I look upon as the very thing which will tend to support the Mission. I now know all the methods of Agriculture that are used here. I know the tricks of the natives, and the nature of the lowest rate of housekeeping in this Country, having had a monthly allowance I have made all those experiments on those heads which could not have been made without ruin had I not had those resources and I will now propose to you what I would recommend to the Society - you will find it similar to what the Moravians do. Seven or eight Families can be maintained for nearly the same expences as one, if this method is pursued. I then earnestly entreat the Society to set their faces this way and send out more Missionaries. We ought to be seven or eight Families together - and it is absolutely necessary for the Wives of Missionaries to be as hearty in the Work as their Husbands. Our Families should be considered as nurseries for the Mission, and among us should be a person capable of teaching School, so as to educate our

Children. I recommend all living together in a number of little Straw Houses forming a Line or Square, and of having nothing of our own but all the general stock. One or two should be elected Stewards to provide over all the management which should with respect to eating, drinking, working, Worship, Learning, Preaching excursions yet be reduced to fixed Rules. Should the above mentioned Natives join us all should be considered equal and all come under the same regulations.

Carey to Ryland from Mudnabati, Nov. 26, 1796

From what I have written to Bro. Fuller (and which I wish you to see; tho I beg that the facts relating to Mr. T. or to Mr. U. may not be made known -) you will see that we are not in a very delicate situation. More Missionaries I think absolutely necessary to the support of the Interest; and should the Plan which I have proposed, and which must resemble that of the Moravians be judged eligible, it will then be absolutely necessary to pay the strictest attention to Missionaries and Missionaries Wives, being quite hearty in coming into the necessary regulations for the ordering of such a Family. I propose that all should have separate houses, but one common table, and one common stock - and be under the direction of a steward. This is the more necessary as should any natives join us, they would become outcasts immediately, and must consequently be supported by us. But if the Stock is common so would the labour in that case, and of Consequence every addition of members to our Society would be an addition to our Stability, by superceding the necessary number of Servants, Labourers, &ct., which are the great sink of money here. The Missionaries on the coast are to this day obliged to support those who join them, as I saw in a Letter from a Son of one of the Missionaries to Mr. Thomas. And a Community at least in the beginning of the Work here seems to me as necessary as in the Primitive Church. Should there be any danger from John Company, we might fix our residence out of the limit of their Dominions, and make our Intineration from thence, but I don't see much danger. Sir John Shore is esteemed a person of Genuine Piety; he is certainly very friendly to the Gospel.

I advise that no Missionary stay in Calcutta even one day if it can be avoided, but that they apply to the office for letting Boats, take the smallest that will be convenient; get a servant who can speak English from the office for hiring Servants and proceed without delay to join us. They will be continually losers by the Theft and Frauds of their Servants till they arrive tho in no danger of injury.

. . . The Ways, Customs, and religious opinions of the natives I may send at some future time; perhaps I may send some extracts translated from the Shastras - The *Bhagvad Gita*, - *Ramayana* - and *Institutes of Menu* are translated into English – I have read some of the Shastras, they are the most like Homer's *Illiad* of anything I can think of both in manner and matters.

Carey to Society, Dec. 28, 1796, Hooghly River

To avoid expence which would otherwise be very great, all the Missionaries should live together on a small Farm which would be just enough to support them with grain and Cattle. The profits of this would not be so much an object, as the example of Industry which it would set to the natives, and our own Children. It would also tend to fix the minds of the natives, who would scarcely ever join us if we are always wandering to and fro, and they would in losing Caste be wholly maintained out of the general stock which would be amply compensated by their share in the Labours of the Farm. And they would sooner be induced to unite with us on such a Plan, than upon any other; and the more persons either European or native are together so much the cheaper will they live; besides the advantages of Christian Society, daily Worship; a Common School; proper Rules for appropriation of time, regular preaching excursions; all Learning of Languages etc. being in one place, a publick Library; and the accumulation of everyone's knowledge set into one aggregate &ct. I have written to Bro. Fuller a calculation of expences which would become less and less in proportion as our Company was enlarged, and the experience already gained by us in the Country, would not a little contribute towards lessening expences especially as every thing must be brought under stated rules; and regular Books of Accounts kept.

As this Country will easily command all Asia, the Indian Islands not excepted, Query whether it would not be better to have all the Missionaries educated in the various Languages here, under all these advantages of one Society, and to make their excursions under fixed regulations; than to be divided into small solitary parties - at least till God had so blessed us as to raise up Churches in other parts where it would be proper for missionaries to reside near them; and watch over them and by this method it would not be difficult to publish the Gospel in every part of India by Eight or ten Persons in the space of Twelve Months . . .

. . . I am afraid of frightening the Society with the appearance of Large expences, or I should speak something about printing the New Testament which is (about twenty Chapters of the Acts of the Apostles excepted) all translated and will be ready for printing long before means to print it can arrive from Europe. I am now going down to Calcutta, and intend to make all enquiries about the expence of printing here; but it strikes me that a Press, new Types, and a Missionary Printer if all are sent from England, will yet save at least a Thousand Pounds in printing Ten Thousand Copies - but this I intend to ascertain in a Letter by the last Ships to some one in the Connection [I believe Mr. Fuller] - and a Press here would [if the other scheme aforementioned be put in practice] be an invaluable blessing to us; and it should consist of Bengal, Arabic, and English Letters - or the last might be omitted; as it should be convenient to the Society.

Carey to Ryland: Date unknown (June 23, 1803-Dec. 13, 1804)

. . . Another plan (I write this to you, but as the plan may never be carried into effect, it will be better not to say anything about it except to a few. If much talked of also it might excite the jealously of the Court of Directors tho without reason) - has also lately occupied our attention. It appears that our business is to provide materials for spreading the Gospel - and to apply those materials - Translations, Pamphlets &ct. are the materials. To apply them we have thought of setting up a number of subordinate stations, in each of which a Brother shall be fixed. It will be necessary &

useful to carry on some worldly business. Let him be furnished with a sum of money from us to begin, and purchase Cloth, or whatever other article the part produces in greatest perfection; the whole to belong to the Mission, and no part ever to be private trade, or private property. The gains may probably support the station: Every Brother in such a station to have one or two native Brethren with him; and to do all he can to preach, and spread Bibles, Pamphlets &ct., and to set up, and encourage schools where the reading of the Scriptures shall be introduced. At least four Brethren shall always reside at Serampore which must be like the Heart, while the other stations are the Members. Each one must constantly send a Monthly account of both Spirituals and Temporals to Serampore, and the Brethren at Serampore who must have a power of control over the stations must send a Monthly account likewise to each Station, with advice &ct. as shall be necessary.

A Plan of this sort appears to be more formidable than it is in reality. To find proper persons will be the greatest difficulty, but as it will prevent much of that abrasion which may arise from a great number of persons living in one house, so it will give several Brethren an opportunity of being useful whose tempers may not be formed to live in a common family, and at the same time connect them as much to the Body, as if they all lived together. We have judged that about 2,000 Rupees will do to begin at each place, and it is probable that God will enable us to find money, (especially as assisted in the translation & printing by our Brethren in England), as fast as you will be able to find men.

This plan may be extended through circular surface of 1,000 miles Radius and a constant communication kept up between the whole, and in some particular cases it may extend even further. We are also to hope that God may raise up some Missionaries in this Country who may be more fitted for the work than any from England can be.

At present we have not concluded on anything, but when Bro. Ward comes down we hope to do so, and I think one station may be fixed on immediately, which Bro. Chamberlain may occupy. A late favourable providence will I hope enable us to begin, viz. the College have subscribed for 100 Copies of Sanskrit Grammar, which will be 6,400 Rupees or 800 pounds Sterling. The Motion was very generously made by H. Colebrooke Esq. who is engaged in a similar work and seconded by Mssrs Brown & Buchanan, indeed it met with no opposition. It will scarcely be printed off under 12 Months more but it is probable that the greatest part of the Money will be advanced.

Carey to Fuller, Dec. 10, 1805

We have long desired to spread the Gospel by fixing Brethren in collateral stations and this appears to be more desirable now than it ever was. God has given us several native Brethren who have good gifts for making known the Gospel. They must be employed, but it is desirable that they, for the present, should be under the eye of a European Brother. We, therefore, wish to fix Brethren in twelve or fourteen stations as soon as we have them. These Brethren to be surrounded with native Brethren at proper distance as radius diverging from a centre. Two obstacles have hitherto stood in the way, if we had had the men, namely want of money to support them, and the difficulty of getting permission from the government.

Carey to Ryland, July 17, 1806

. . . We have for a long time intended to extend the Mission by subordinate stations, the difficulty of obtaining permission from Government has prevented us from doing it hitherto, for though inclined to shew us every favour they have not the formal power of doing it. I told Mr. Udney that we must send without their consent if we could not obtain it, we have, therefore, now resolved to send my son Felix and Brother Rowe to settle at Benares: We should have chosen Patna, but Mr. Martyn, an evangelical clergyman, whose heart is much set on preaching to the Heathen hopes to be appointed to that place. We, therefore, thought it best to wait till we see how he may be disposed of, before we send thither, as his labour will save us the expence of supporting a station where he may be fixed; should he not go to Patna we can send one thither afterwards. Bro. Mardon will go to Orissa, and settle in the neighborhood of the great Moloch, Jagganath. Bro. Biss is this day gone to settle at or near Dinajpur, accompanied by Bro. Moore and Dr. Taylor, who will proceed to Benares to look for a proper spot on which to settle a mission there. Dr. Taylor intended to have gone overland to Surat, and had provided boats &ct. for the journey, but the danger of the journey was represented to be so great that we persuaded him to relinquish and go by the first Bombay ship, to which he has consented, and is gone on this excursion in the meantime. He has been labouring very hard at the Hindustani and Mahratta Languages and has made great progress. Bro. Mardon is now gone to Malda with two native Brethren. Krishna was there a little time ago, Our friends Creighton, Ellerton & Grant were highly gratified with his preaching. I hope good will arise from it. Two native brethren, viz. Deep Chandra and Kuntha are gone to their own village in Jessore, and the Lord has opened a door for them to preach the Gospel there.

. . . It is our ultimate design to settle four more stations in Bengal, and about ten more in Hindustan, also to extend our attempts to Kurnata, and the eastern part of the Mahratta empire (the western part will probably be supplied from the Surat Mission) also to Nepal, Bhutan, Tibet, Assam, the western half of China, the Burman Empire, and Cochin China. All these places lie within a circle which we can reach, if we have Men and Money; and should a first attempt to enter any of these places be found impracticable, no loss would be sustained, as the brother could immediately occupy another station. It would be madness to suppose that so extensive a plan can be immediately filled up, but no time must be lost. An open door is before us. A Bible or part of a Bible will be ready for all these countries by the time that men can be found to carry it. - - The Lord is raising up native brethren to accompany the Missionaries (an invaluable advantage) and I trust will in time open the hearts of his people here to assist in the work. I hope you will do your utmost to send out men: This will also be the way to get money to support them. I may just observe that if the Missionaries are well instructed in the principles of general Grammar, it will save much time, and if they have habits of study it will save much more.

Carey to Fuller, Oct. 25, 1809

{Speaking of Rangoon, Burma, and the sending of two missionaries from the London Society.}

I am very sorry to hear that the London Society have sent two missionaries to that country, it is an unlovely step, and when one considers the need there was for them in other countries an improper one. The Apostle Paul did not boast of another man's line of things made ready for his hand.

I shall always advise the sending of missionaries as soon as possible to the place where they are to settle, and I believe it will at present be advisable to send all who may be sent out to us to the surrounding countries to begin new Missions, and not keep them in Bengal. One ought to go immediately to join Bro. Robinson in Buntam and I shall recommend the sending one of them who are now ready to come out and the other two to one of the other countries where there is no beginning yet made either, Siam, Pegu, Annaham *{Annam}*, Assamlan, and Nepal for each of which two missionaries are wanted.

I think you should not delay sending them out for fear of government. They need not report themselves as Missionaries to the Tokea, but as persons going to settle in any of these countries, and only waiting for a proper conveyance thither. I fear the two brethren lately arrived from America for Vizagapatam will meet with some unpleasant obstructions from the Madras government through Bro. Deprgrongen having made an application by means of a Military gentleman friend for leave for them to settle there. . . . I have no idea that an application to this government to get them to recommend to the Court of Directors, the sending of missionaries, would be attended with any success. The Board of Directors are their masters, and the only end that I can see likely to be answered thereby would be the creating of endless delays. The way by America is now open, and, I think you should make use of it and trust the results to God. It would perhaps, be a good way for you to let the Missionaries know that they are not to stay in Bengal, but to go to some of the surrounding countries, this would prevent them thinking harshly of us for proposing another country to them.

Carey to Ryland, Apr. 12, 1817, Calcutta

I think it should be an invariable rule with the society to recommend separate establishments and households for all Missionaries who come out. If they afterwards come together voluntarily, all will be well; but there are few who can be put into the same household with safety. At Serampore we love one another and live in peace. Bro. Randall is a man who heartily unites with us, and Bro. Penny would do the same, but he must live at Calcutta where the Benevolent Institution is.

Carey to Dyer, July 15, 1819, Serampore

. . . From this statement you will see that I disapprove as much of the conduct of our Calcutta Brethren as it is possible for me to disapprove of any human actions. The evil they have done is I fear irreparable. And certainly the whole might have been prevented by a little conversation with either of us, and a hundreth part of that self denial which I found necessary to exercise for the first four years of the mission would (have) prevented this awful rupture . . . I certainly think a monstrous waste of strength, and money for four Missionary brethren, besides Pearce and Penny to be crowded together in Calcutta where there are besides them four Paedo Baptists, and four Evangelical Clergymen, besides four native Brethren and where we also preach.

My plan respecting spreading the Gospel has for several years past been to fix European Brethren at the distance of 100 or 130 miles from each other . . .

I have now only to recommend to the Society to send out all Missionaries hereafter, so that they may be independent of each other, and to appoint them to the stations they are to occupy naming, however, optional stations for them if any thing should make it impossible to occupy those first intended, and to fix their monthly or yearly income, including in all cases either a sum to erect a house, or an increased allowance for the rent of one. [In most cases, however, the latter will be scarcely practicable]. I consider this as the only means of preventing Missionaries from crowding together in a few large places, to the neglect of all the country around.

Carey to Jabez, Jan. 16, 1830

. . . Our commercial firm, viz. Carey, Marshman and John Marshman expired the 31st of December last and will not be renewed, indeed we have managed our business separately for the last twelve months, though our notes &ct., were in the name of the Three. I am no richer than I was before, but manage my affairs independently. While at the same time we are united in the management of the Mission to which we each contribute a specific sum, and the remainder is supplied by subscriptions in England, independently of the Society, with which we have no connection.

Nothing has filled my last years with so much distress as the division in the Mission first brought about by the Junior Brethren and still maintained with an implacable hostility. This, however, I cannot remedy and must, therefore, cast it like all my other troubles on the Lord. I rejoice to say that the cause of our Redeemer is getting ground, and I trust will prevail more and more.

INCARNATIONAL MISSIONS

Carey believed firmly in the concept of incarnational missions, meaning a missionary must fit well into the culture and relate effectively to the native population. Many of the new missionaries to India tended to huddle around the more Europeanized area of Calcutta leaving the rest of the country without an evangelical message. Carey insisted that missionaries live in a manner and in a place that would allow them the most impact for the Gospel. He opposed bigotry against the Indians and the desire to remain comfortable surrounded by Europeans.

Carey to Ryland, Bandel, Dec. 26, 1793

I have read a considerable part of the *Mahabharata,* and epic Poem, written in most beautiful Language; and much upon a par with Homer. And was it like his Iliad only considered as a great effort of human genius, I should think it one of the first productions in the world, but alas! It is the ground of Faith to Millions of sinful sons of men; and as such must be held in the utmost abhorrence. - - Yet I find a curious piece of Chronology in it, viz. that, Saul, king of the Jews was contemporary with Joodheshteer; being mentioned in this poem as being a Guest with that King - and called Saul the Great. This serves to confound their Chronology also, for from a list of the Kings of Hindustan, which I have procured, and in which every kings reign is noted to a day - Joodheshteer's Reign is carried to the distance of 2,854 years before Christ; which was before the Flood. I will send you this account enclosed.

Carey to Ryland from Mudnabati, July 6, 1797

{Carey spent time trying to learn and understand the culture.}

Some things are as much against that opinion - as the astonishing antiquity which they assign to themselves; and the total difference between the Sanskrit language and the Hebrew; for tho about half the words in common use are evidently derived from Hebrew, yet it is remarkable that very few Sanskrit words have any affinity thereto. I am forming a Sanskrit dictionary in which I mean to include all words in common use also. Should I live to finish it, I should also try to collate the Sanskrit with the Hebrew roots, where there is any similarity in them. One of the first things which strikes us with regard to the Hindus, is their Castes. The word Jati or Caste signifies a genus, or Kind; and is originally applied to distinguish between the different Geni of Animals; it being inapplicable to inanimate beings, except figuratively. Thus the Sanskrit grammar *Bee Accoran*, "Jati" signifies a species or kind which may be distinguished by its outward appearance from every other kind. - -It will, however, be enquired, what distinguishes different Men, who all wear poitous, as Brahman, Kyetra ?, Dybyggya ?, &ct. I answer any animated being which has not three genders is a Jati, thus Brahman makes the feminine Brahmee, but has no neuter. It will be further inquired whether Bhogaban ?, viz. God is a Caste - Because we can say Bhogaban ?, Bhogabanee ? - to this the answer is - whatever may be distinguished at first blush is a Jati, but God is indescribable and therefore is not a Jati. The first and last of these definitions agree - but a second appears to be only a subterfuge.

Carey to Jabez, May 5, 1819

. . . Pray write your sentiments about the Country and (the) people, the languages spoken, and the difficulties in your way, consider, I am your Father my hopes are in great measure fixed on you as it respects all that part of the Country and indeed as it respects maintaining the spirit of the Mission in our family.

Carey to Jabez, June 12, 1819

. . . We think you will not, at present, however, have occasion for Benches & Tables; I suppose the natives of those parts sit on the ground as in Bengal. This is the best posture for them. You should hereafter find it necessary to introduce them partially, write fully upon the subject, we must endeavor in every instance to do the most good at the least expence, and if in any instance the native method is cheaper than the European, and equally answers the purpose, it must be adopted . . .

You some time ago requested my opinion of the plan now about to be adopted by the London Missionary Society, of instructing Missionaries in the Languages of the countries to which they are to be sent, before they leave England. I should not like to condemn a plan which is sanctioned by so many men of experience and sound judgement, but I really am unable to see its advantages. The languages must be acquired. Are the facilities for acquiring them in England equal to those obtainable where they are spoken? Or can they be made so? Is there anything in England which can be substituted for the advantages of daily, familiar intercourse with the natives of a country? And will not the highest acquisitions obtainable in Europe amount to a mechanical collection of words applicable to scarcely any practicable use where the languages are spoken? I suppose that all things also being equal, a longer time will be required in England; to which may be added that sometimes the language of a country is mistaken and another substituted for it, as was formerly the case in India, where Hindustani, or *Lingua franca*, was supposed to be the current language of the Hindustanis, and was studied to the neglect of the languages spoken in the various provinces. A System now abandoned in the College of Fort William.

Presenting the Gospel to the Indians

How does one present the message of truth to those who are steeped in falsehood and darkness? In a way, William Carey became something of a master at this. He developed a clear understanding of the Indian culture and religions and used that information to argue the Christian case. Carey also possessed a unique logic, which he utilized in discussions with the holy men and common people. His presentation approach did not resemble any of the memorized evangelism plans common today, but rather would be described as dialogue and argumentation.

Carey to Ryland, Dec. 26, 1793, Bandel

We have regular Worship now every day, I preach once a day, and twice on the Lord's Day to the Natives and have very frequent opportunities of conversing with them upon the Word of God. I find it easy to confound their Arguments - but their Hearts still remain the same. I frequently when speaking of the Death of Christ for Sinners; have occasion to speak in this manner. Suppose your Shastras to be true, What security is there in them for a Sinner's escape from eternal Wrath? What provision for sanctifying his Soul; You talk of 9 Incarnations past and one to come - but what were they for? The utmost was to kill a tyrant, or a Giant, or to restore the Earth when drowned in the deluge, but what has this to do with your Salvation, or deliverance from Sin; respecting the Debtahs or Demigods which are innumerable, I often say after this manner, suppose these things exist, yet you acknowledge them all to be inferior to God; yet you fear them more than him - but why if they are pleased what will it avail if he is angry - and if he is for you what can they do against you? The Fears, Quarrels, Lusts &ct. of the Debtahs also as recorded in their Shastras are an Argument against them which I find it important to use - but my great Weapon is, and shall be Jesus Christ and him Crucified. But I must leave off my Congregation is now assembled at 7 o'clock in the Morning and the Post is just going. My sincerest Love to all the Ministers and Congregations of the Lord Jesus especially your friends of whom I rejoice to hear; I intend to write to some others by this opportunity.

Carey to Society, March 18, 1795, Mudnabati

. . . I am not able to send to you the tidings that I desired namely of the Conversion of the Natives; yet it may give you some pleasure to hear that we are employed more actively in our work than we have been heretofore. My Mouth was shut, on account of not knowing the Language; but of late I have begun to preach, or rather converse with them statedly every Lord's Day; and have met with greater encouragement than I expected; being yet unable to vary my subjects much, and having need frequently to pause, and sometimes to stop, and ask what is a proper Word to express myself by. Yet for about half an hour at a time I can be tolerably well understood. I have generally aimed at convincing them, that they are sinners, & that God is just & will not allow of iniquity, and have enquired; If this be so What will become of you? They universally allow that the good will go to heaven, and the wicked to Hell; but their ideas are so confused, that they have no settled notions of either. There is a pretty large congregation in this neighborhood, many of whom have told me, that they never heard before that the Soul would survive the Body; and seemed much struck when I told them that their Souls would live after Death. They believe the Doctrine of the Transmigration of the Soul through all different species of Animals, and that after this it will again Animate an human Body; after which, if Righteous it will go to Heaven, if not it must go through a Second Course of Transmigration, and this is their Hell.

One Lord's Day twenty six persons came to my house for instruction in the things of God. [and after I had told them that Hell was the place for Sinners], one of them said; I suppose Sir we shall be used there, as we should in Dinajpur Jails. I said no, in prison only the Body can be affected, but in Hell the Soul; a person may escape from Prison, but not from Hell; and death puts an end to imprisonment, but in Hell they shall never die; There God's Wrath will be poured upon them for ever, and they must dwell in endless Fire. I have also constantly inquired whether any of their Books can tell how God can be just and the justifier of a Sinner. And this leads me to speak to them of the appointment of Christ to be the Saviour of Sinners, of the substitution of him in the Sinners stead; the necessity of Faith in him and of Holiness of Life. So some have enquired what is sin and What is holiness? In answer to this I have endeavored to enumerate some of those Evils to which they are most addicted, and then to prove that the Heart is the Fountain of all. I have tried to convince them that all their Worship, and Offerings make no part of Holiness, but are on the Contrary very great Sins. No one can think, however, how little they think of the Evil of Lying, Cheating and the like; and what low thoughts they have of God, and Religion . . .

Carey to Society, Jan. 12, 1796

. . . With respect to the Heathen I wish I could write more favourably than I can - Our lives, however, are not quite spent in Idleness, nor our Labours quite without effect. I am just returned from a tour through about half the district in which my Business lies, and the whole of which consists of about two Hundred Villages. In this tour I took a Boat for my Lodging, and the convenience of Cooking my Victuals; but performed the Journey on foot walking from twelve to twenty miles a Day, and preaching, or rather conversing, from place to place about the things of God. This plan I intend to pursue statedly the whole of the dry season; tho often traveling less journies. I have not yet seen much fruit of my Labours . . .

Carey to Ryland, Aug. 17, 1800

I am very irregular in keeping a Journal which you must excuse: for in the printing I have to look over the Copy, and correct the Press, which is a Work about Ten times as great as it would be in England because printing, Writing, Spelling, &ct. in Bengali is a new thing and we have to fix the Orthography in a manner: Brethren Ward, and Brunsdon and my son Felix are the Compositors, and we have two sets of Press Men. They, therefore, pursue me as hounds pursue a deer, and I am obliged to work very hard to get Copy ready, & the Press corrected for them: I rejoice in this, and only mention it to excuse my not writing largely to my friends, or keeping a regular Journal. - I will, however, just give you a short account of Last Lord's Day, & today (Friday). - - - On Lord's Day I rose about Six, and with Bro. Marshman went to preach in the highways, we had a middling Congregation of Bengalis and one Greek, to whom I endeavoured to point out Christ as the Way of Life. We then distributed a few copies of an Address composed by Ram Basu: on our going a little further, we saw a Man to whom we had given a pamphlet with about a dozen persons around him reading it to them - this did good to our hearts. We then went to visit a weaver whose name is Kharat - This man desired to see us some months ago, and desired a Friend to inform us, since that we have regularly visited him once a Week, except, once, when I was ill. I see no signs of his being under concern, but he is very inquisitive, and we wish to follow up what appears an opening in providence. After this I preached in English unexpectedly from Acts 4.12 - "Neither is there Salvation &ct."

In the evening I went to a neighbouring Village called Chatterah where I preached to a middling assembly in the street. Bro. Ward accompanied me: just as I was finishing, all the people ran away. I enquired the reason, they informed me that a Man was dead, and his Wife *{was}* going to be burnt with him. We immediately went to the place, where the Corpse lay, and the Woman sat by it on some steps, which go down to the River: I began to talk to the Brahmans about the wickedness and inhumanity of such a practice. - They said that all the Brahmans had tried to dissuade her from it but in vain: I spoke to her, and entreated her to desist, but to no purpose, she gave no answer but sat calling out "Gunga, Gunga". She was a fine looking young person, they said only thirteen, or fourteen Years old. I proved from their Shastras that no evil could attach itself to her (even on their principles) if she even mounted the Pile, and yet desisted from fear.

At last when I saw all was determined, I told them that I had heard that the Governor General had threatened to have the first man hanged who was proved to have kindled one of these fires. That I would be a witness against them &ct. (N.B. I had heard such a report tho I think it was without foundation.) It was then high Water, and the Ceremony could not be performed till the Ebb was nearly run out. We, therefore, came home and as it is our Custom to instruct the Servants, and any who come, on a Lord's Day Evening, Bro. Thomas who was here, delivered a discourse from "No man can serve two Masters &ct." Bro. Ward went out before the Worship was concluded, and I and Bro. Marshman as soon as it was over, to see the dreadful burning, but it was over, and the fire half burnt out. -

. . . We went on to Baddhee Garee, and when we had entered the town I accosted a man, who pointed me to another who stood by, who he said, was a learned Brahman, or Pundit. After a few words I saw that he was desirous to get away: which gave rise to a conversation something like the following. - Why do you wish to go away? Brahman. Because I want to perform the Sundhya or Evening Devotions. W.C. What will be the advantage of performing the Sundhya? Brahman. By that all the sins that I have committed in the day will be blotted out. W.C. I am a Sinner, I have committed Sins today, will my Sins be blotted out by performing the Sundhya? Brahman. No, everyone will be saved by attending to the Religion of his Country. W.C. You know that there is but one God, and that he is of one mind. How then can he appoint one way for you, and another for me? Brah. The fruit of both is the same. W.C. You see there a Sozeana Tree (*Guilandina Moreninga*) and there a Mango Tree, now you may as well convince me that the fruit of these two trees is the same - You call me a Mleech - very well, I suppose you think my fruit like Ahoonda (*Axlepias Gigantea*) You are a Brahman, I suppose yours to be like Dhootoora (*Datura Metel*) which will infallibly intoxicate the man who eats it. Yet you see the Fruit is not the same.

On this he manifested a strong desire to be gone, but the people laughed at him, and called on him to answer. I then put this question. You are a Sinner, I, and all present are Sinners, how shall we get our sins pardoned, and blotted out? ..This small disputation had collected a considerable number of people, to whom I then turned and preached Christ as the only Saviour. While I was addressing the poor People, the Brahman slunk away, and I continued to address those present till Rain prevented our continuing longer. Bro. M. and I then returned and by the way had some Conversation about the way in which he was induced to engage in this work, which was very interesting.

. . . In the Morning Bro. Ward, myself, and my eldest son went out to a place where two roads cross each other, where I had frequently preached before, when we got there I saw three Men sitting , and asked one of them, What News? And what they were talking about? He said they were talking about their Work: I asked what was their work: they answered they were thatchers. I told him that they laboured very hard for a scanty meal, but that I was come to tell them of the Bread of Life, which they might get for nothing: that their labour was in vain, for they would hunger again & again, and labour again & again. That they were in a wretched state, but God did not delight in their Misery, but invited them to lay hold of happiness. One Man (for a good number soon collected) observed that we must serve God. I said true, but how will you serve him without knowing his will. He said, we might worship the Debtahs. I answered, suppose I have a boat to go to Calcutta, and order the man to take me there. If instead of going to Calcutta he went to Nuddea *{Nadia?}*, it is plain that he would labour as hard or harder than if he had gone to Calcutta. Yet he would not serve me, but do just the contrary to my Will. So you may labour to worship idols, and labour harder than many do to worship God, yet all would be disgusting to him and contrary to his will.

I had much of this kind of discourse with them for near an hour. We then went to visit our Friend Bharat, found him reading in Matthew's Gospel. He appears to read here and there a bit in a detached manner, he asked several questions about several parts of the *Mahabharata.* I told him that though I often used it as a weapon to fight against the Hindus, yet I only did it to reason with them on their own principles, but that I did not believe a word of it to be true. He inquired where I thought Brahmans came from (this was the second time the question had been put to me this morning) I answered that God had created men - but when Man sinned the devil became the Lord of this World, and he made Brahmans: and then Brahmans made Shastras for their own Emolument which I proved by several passages from the *Mahabharata.* It was late and we came home to breakfast, afterwards Bro. Marshman preached from the parable of the Sower . . .

Carey to Fuller, Nov. 1800

{Carey had a conversation with three Hindus about the gospel.}

You will laugh but I am totally unable to recollect so much of the conversation as to write any thing connected about it, so must leave it, as this is the case with so many disputes, conversations, and conferences held with the Hindus. They appear important while they last and I trust are really so but sometimes the sameness of one to another, renders them unimportant when written in English. Often the apparently little quibbles, tho really important in our situation don't appear sufficiently so to send to England. We know nothing of the disputes which you in Europe are engaged in; ours bear a nearer resemblance to those of the Protestants with the Papists at the Reformation but a nearer still to those of the old Fathers, with the Heathen, and Gnosticks, such as you will find in Justin Martyr, and Irenaeus.

{Carey and Bro. Brunsdon went to the villages about 3 or 4 miles from town and encountered an old Brahman. Carey had asked if anyone knew how sins could be pardoned. The people referred him to an old Brahman who was wise. He replied that "profound meditation and acts of Holiness would answer the purpose." Carey shared the Gospel. Here is a sample of the great missionary in action.}

You and I, and all of us are Sinners, and we are in a helpless state but I have good things to tell you. God in the riches of his Mercy became incarnate, in the form of Man. He lived more than thirty years on the earth without Sin and was employed in doing good. He gave sight to the Blind, healed the Sick, the lame, the Deaf and the Dumb - and after all died in the stead of Sinners. We deserved the wrath of God, but he endured it. We could make no sufficient atonement for our guilt but he compleatly made an end of Sin and now he has sent us to tell you that the Work is done and to call you to faith in, and dependence on the Lord Jesus Christ. Therefore, leave your vain customs, and false gods, and lay hold of eternal Life through him. After much discourse of this sort we presented him with a copy of Matthew's Gospel and three more to three other persons. He promised to read and make himself well acquainted with its Contents and then to converse more about it. It was now dark. I, therefore, prayed with them and we returned home.

Nov. 2. This has been a good Day on the whole. In the morning I went out, and after several efforts to collect a few People together, I got a greater number than I expected. It is the time of the Rhau ?, or celebrating the play of Krishna with the gopinis or female cowkeepers of when he is recorded to have had 16,000 concubines. The people had been up all night at this play and worship. I asked them what would be the fruit of this Worship. They said it was to appear hereafter, on which I tried much to impress their minds with this, that believing on Christ insures a present reward, as well as a future one.

The People are so moveable, some going, and others coming that often the Congregation is quite changed before we have done. I think it desirable that all should hear of the incarnation, and death of Xt (Christ) and the reasons thereof, but as that account am often obliged to repeat those circumstances several times even at one standing that all may hear the Gospel.

{Mr. Thomas and Carey went to Calcutta and visited Mr. Wilcox.}

There were a great number of Merchants, Sailors, &ct. perhaps thirty or more at his house. I entered into a conversation with one of them, a Man of great wealth and respectability . The others listened after a few preliminary questions and answers, I insensibly got into a preaching mood, and discoursed with them upon the Way of the Life by Christ, and the insufficiency of all other Ways. They objected to the Death of Christ saying that God could not die. I told them twas true God as the divine nature could not die, but God incarnate could and that he was incarnate for that very purpose, "made lower than the Angels for the suffering of Death". They acquiesced and wondered. The great Man to whom I principally directed myself at first told me that he had that day or the day before received a Gospel by Matthew. We have dispersed near 500 copies of Matthew's which are read by many. Yesterday at the House or rather as I was leaving the house of a Friend in Calcutta I met with

Rev. Buchanan. Tis three years since I saw him but he remembered me and we had a very pleasant conversation.

Last Lord's day we had perhaps the most mixed congregation that you ever heard of. It consisted of English, Danes, Norwegians, Germans, Americans, Armenians, a Greek, and a Malabar whom I addressed from How every one that Thinketh Isa. 55, 1, 2 - We preach in the Evening of the Lord's Day in our own House. This was originally designed for the instruction of the servants - several there, however, attend, and among them a good number of Portugese have lately come to hear.

Carey to Ryland, Jan. 30, 1801, Serampore

It is with great pleasure I inform you (tho by a Letter sent overland a few days ago you will have intimation of it) that our God has at length begun to smile upon our Labour. Within the Last Month we have baptised four Persons, viz. my eldest son Felix. Mr. Fernandez, and two Hindus, a Man called Krishna, and a Woman whose name is Jeymooni. Two more are given up to the Church, viz. a Man named Gokul and a Woman whose name is Rasoo *{Rasamayi?}*, but some things have prevented their hitherto. I have a pleasing hope of the Woman, who by the bye is Krishna's wife, but the Man has something enthusiastic in his character - I mean Gokul. For Krishna walks so as to give us all great satisfaction - and by his affectionate simple Conversation with others is likely to be of much use - There are four more concerning whom we have some hopes, all of whom have heard the Word from him - viz. his eldest daughter, a girl of about 13 years old, another Woman whose name is Unno and concerning whom my hopes are sanguine - the others are two men, the name of one is Bheem, the other Sunder Das *{Syam Das?}*, but of these two I cannot say much at present.

A Week ago yesterday I went as usual to a neighboring Village where Bro. Marshman and myself generally go once a Week. A Person the week before had told me that a Brahman of some Consequence who had for some time entertained many doubts about his own religion wished to know something more about the Gospel, and I then had promised to visit him. In consequence of this a person stood in the street to meet me: I went with him and was soon joined by four or five more. We went forward to another village and at last entered into a Temple, not dedicated to any one idol but designed for the worship of all. Here we sat, and a number of very respectable persons, principally Brahmans soon came, and among them the enquirer. I conversed with them for a long time, and they freely confessed that the Idols were a lie, and Deceit and that they paid no regard to any of them. They, however, said the same about Sin and Holiness. I found that they were a sort of Hindu Infidels yet was much pleased with the openness of their minds. One of them enquired if God had a Body or no, I answered, God was a Spirit - he replied how then could God speak his Word, without organs of speech he could not speak, and organs of Speech must suppose a material substance. I answered that God is all sufficient, that the Creator of all things could create a voice when needful for his own purposes: without the least difficulty. I told them of Christ and his undertaking, and having stayed till it was late and dark left them and returned home -

Yesterday I went again to the same place; where I found several met in readiness to hear the Word. They asked why I was so late, said that I must have but little bye for their souls to come when it wanted but an Hour or Two of night. That my mind was not like that of Christ, who I had said laid down his life for sinners: but that I could not afford half a day to talk with them. We sat down between twenty and thirty, and I conversed with them till the stars appeared. I believe them to be all very wicked persons: but they may be wrought on by the Grace of God. The distributing of Matthew's Gospel is the thing that has excited enquiries of different kinds in many -

Things have taken a new turn as it respects the temper of people in general: Formerly what we said made no impression, the People heard like stocks: now the most violent opposition is heard on every side, and the Boys in the street when we pass along call out "Jesus Christ" - as if they thought we should be ashamed to hear the name repeated. Tis true we are grieved at their opposition and hardness of heart, but we also hope that the "Fire is now already kindled for which our Redeemer expressed his strong desire" - I have received several letters from Rev. W. Geriche which I will get copied for you and send soon. I shall however conclude this with an extract of a Letter of a gentleman at Rangpur whose name is Lang. He is a hopeful enquirer, to whom I trust dear Cunnignham has been useful - but a little time ago he was a thoughtless deist.

Carey to Morris, Feb. 25, 1802 Calcutta

We have it in contemplation to erect the place of Worship which I have mentioned in Pag. 4 - Bro. M. and I had a great deal of conversation today with Mr. Brown upon the subject, he thinks that Government will not do anything to hinder it, and as to their protecting us in our preaching in it we must commit that to the Lord. You ought not yet to publish anything about this, as it would be highly improper to say much about it, till we see our way somewhat more clearly.

. . . Our course of action is much altered, We have neither time nor occasion to go out to preach so much as formerly. Our Printing Press sends out Missionaries (Pamphlets, New Testaments, &ct.) and the People who come to us for instruction are often as many as we can attend to. I have appointed a regular time to instruct the Portugese enquirers in this Town, at the house of one of them - a Mr. Pereiro. We have also begun a weekly meeting for Prayer at the House of an European, whose Heart the Lord has lately opened - a Mr. Bolt. In short, I believe that God is surely tho slowly bringing this Country to himself.

Carey to Sutcliffe, Aug. 18, 1812

. . . There are a few circumstances in the mission which I have not particularly mentioned to Mr. Fuller or Dr. Ryland which I shall mention to you. The first respects the labours of our native brethren, which will give you pleasure, though we have in two instances occasion for grief. There are two native preachers of the name of Krishna, and the other with John Peter at Balasore. The first one of them, the first Hindu who was baptised is settled in Calcutta, labours at Calcutta with great success. Krishna is now a steady, zealous and well informed, and I may add, eloquent minister of the Gospel, and preaches on average twelve or fourteen times every week in Calcutta and its environs. Seluk-nam, another honourable minister of the Gospel is also employed in and about Calcutta, and preaches nearly as quite as often. Calcutta is a large city, three miles long, and one broad, very populous, and the environs are crowded with people, settled in large villages, resembling (for populations not elegance) the environs of Birmingham. The fort is about a mile south of the town, the publick jail, and the general Hospital nearly the same distance. We preach in English at the Jail every Lord's Day, the jailer being one of our Deacons, and did preach in the fort till a military order stopped us. Our Brethren Krishna and Seluk-nam, however, preach once or twice a week in the fort, in the Jail, in the House of Corrections, at Alli-poora a village south of the Jail, at ten or twelve houses in different parts of Calcutta, at a large factory north of Calcutta where some hundreds of men are employed, and at other places. Some of their congregations are small, and others are larger.

In several instances Roman Catholics having heard the word have invited them to their houses, collected their neighbors, and they or some of their neighbors have received it with gladness. The numbers of enquirers constantly coming forward, awakened by their instrumentality among this poor and benighted people fills me with joy. I do not know that I am of much use myself, but I see a work which fills my soul with thankfulness. Not having time to visit people I appropriate every Thursday evening to receiving the visits of enquirers; seldom fewer than twenty come; and the simple confessions of their sinful state, the unvarnished declarations of their former ignorance, the expressions of trust in Christ and of gratitude to him, with the account of their spiritual conflict, often attended with tears which almost check their utterance presents a scene which you can scarcely entertain an adequate idea. At the same time meetings for prayer and mutual edification are held every night in the week, and some nights (for convenience) at several places at the same time; so that the sacred leaven spreads its influence through the masses.

Carey to Burls, Feb. 22, 1814 from Calcutta

{Addressing false accusations and reveals some mission strategy.}

Every syllable of what Prendergast asserts as contained in the extract from the *Times* in your Letter is false. I never preached in Calcutta streets in my life. I have preached very few sermons if any in Calcutta to the Natives; indeed I have not time to do it. I never mounted either a Hogshead Pipe, or Tun, in my Life to preach, and I believe I may say of all my Brethren both Europeans and Natives that they never preached in the Streets of Calcutta. We have no need to do so. We have a good Place of Worship, and our Native Brethren have more open for them to preach in, than they can supply.

. . . I observe, however, that I should perhaps have acted more like a Missionary, if I had often preached in Calcutta Streets, and if I had asserted that they would go to Hell if they did not leave Idolatry, I suppose it would have been no more true.

Often I blame myself for doing so little, and the only excuse I can make is that the translation leaves us not Time, unless I excuse myself by maintaining my native disinclination to do. I speak of what is of first importance.

TRANSLATION AND PUBLICATION

Carey to Fuller, Nov. 16, 1796, from Mudnabati

I have a Pundit who has with me examined and corrected all the Epistles to the 2nd Peter, we go through a chapter every day. The Natives who can read and write understand it perfectly - and as it is corrected by a Learned Native the style and Syntax cannot be very bad. I intend to go through it again and as critically as I can compare it with the Greek Testament but wish to have a Greek Concordance sent by the very next conveyance. I expect the New Testament will be compleat before you receive this . . . I was in hope of printing it at my own expence, but the unfavourable situation of the Works for the production of Indigo has kept me incapable of doing that.

Carey to Ryland from Mudnabati, July 6, 1797

I have been thus particular because I considered the importance of having the translation as just as possible. If an individual draws wrong conclusions, or false doctrines from Scripture, they may be refuted or corrected by recurring to the Words of Scripture itself. And even a wrong translation in a country like England could not be productive of lasting mischief; because the Hebrew Scriptures may be consulted, and the error detected, but here a mistake would be like poison at the fountain head which would contaminate all the streams in proportion as the error was more or less pernicious. And even should the Gospel prevail, of which I think there is more prospect than at any former period, yet it would spread a mistake which would probably degenerate into a prejudice among the common people, before Learning could be expected to have made such a progress as to be sufficient to correct it.

Carey to Society, Dec. 9, 1797

. . . The New Testament is all translated, as also the five Books of Moses, and half the Psalms. Your Advice and Assistance will now be required in order to their being printed. We cannot but think that great advantage would result from having a Printing Press of our own, thereby, we could print not the Scriptures only, but many other useful things which might diffuse knowledge and science among these Illiterate Indians. These things Brethren we trust you will consider . . .

Carey to Sutcliffe, Mudnabati, Jan. 16, 1798

. . . I am fully convinced of what you say respecting the propriety of keeping two journals: but owing to my numerous avocations which engross all my time, I have long since dropped the practice of keeping any journal at all. When you consider my situation you will believe that I have enough upon my hands; and yet am scarcely perceived among the millions of Bengal. Translating the Scripture, and correcting former translations, occupy all my candle-light, and often all my afternoons. This you will readily conceive when you consider the difficulty of translating into a foreign language, and the labour of collating my translation with various other versions, and also having to transcribe the whole with my own hand in the Bengali character, which is an arduous task, notwithstanding I write it nearly as fast as I do English. Besides my ordinary labours I am learning the Sanskrit language; which, with only the helps to be procured here, is perhaps the hardest language in the world.

I rejoice much at the missionary spirit which has lately gone forth: surely it is a prelude to the universal spread of the Gospel! Your account of the German Moravian Brethren's affectionate regard towards me is very pleasing. I am not much moved by what men in general say of me; yet I cannot be insensible to the regards of men eminent for godliness.

Carey to Ryland, Aug. 17, 1800

I know that it will gratify you to know these things, therefore, have written them. The Printing of the Bible is, however, the Work which most occupies our time now, and which I look upon as the introduction of a new Era into India. We thought first that the New Testament would be the most important part of the Word of God, that is, if we had it in our power only to give an Old or New Testament to the Heathen, it would be most desirable to give a New. - 2nd There are many people who would scarce read four volumes, who would read one with attention. 3rd That printing would go on as uninterruptedly if we printed the New Testament first, as if we began with the Old Testament.

These considerations added to that of our Friends in England expecting the New Testament first, have induced me to begin with that part, and to print 2,000 Copies of the new, and 1,000 of the Old. _ Matthew being the first compleat account of the Life and Death of our Lord - we printed 500 Copies extraordinary of that Gospel, that we may be able the sooner to put a compleat Book of the Scriptures into the Hands of the Heathen. Matthew, Mark, and part of Luke are now printed off - and I am happy to say that Matthew, and I have opened a Book in which I insert, the Name, and place of abode of every person to whom a Book is given. The design of this is, that when we go to any part we may be able to know whether the Word of Life has been sent thither or not. We send by the first conveyance a few Copies of Matthew, just to convince our dear Friends that we are not altogether idle.

I intended to send you a list of the difficulties which have occurred in the translation, but I doubt whether I shall have time to arrange them now: because the packet which is on the point of Sailing may go at an hours notice, and I may not safely delay. I shall, however, send them as soon as I can. Bro. Marshman is a great help to me in many of these difficult passages: and the valuable assortment of Books which they brought out leaves me without excuse if I don't get all the information possible on these points. I have but a slight knowledge of ancient Languages and like most people who know but little, am often tenacious of my own opinion - and I often fear that this may be an injury to the work. We have printed several small pieces in Bengali which have had a large circulation, and the Brahmans are almost as much afraid of us as of a Pestilence.

Carey to Fuller, Nov. 1800

I have met with many difficulties in the translating. Indeed I begun to write a series of questions upon the hard places but really have not time to continue it. The introduction to the Epistle to the Romans is particularly difficult to put into intelligible sentences. The words Carnal, Spiritual - the phrases "after the flesh" &ct. are so foreign to any idea in the Bengal language that tho I have laboured much, I have scarcely been able to express the precise ideas, but I hope the defects of that sort will be found to be much fewer than I feared some time ago.

Carey to Ryland, Serampore, March 7, 1801

It will be necessary for the binder of the New Testament to be very careful that he does not displace the loose leaves in Matthew and Mark. I had used a word for cross which was improper. The Bengal language has no word which means - cross - and the word used means a sort of picquet. After we had begun to print it was thought proper to use the Portugese word "cruz" - that being well understood in the neighborhood of Calcutta. We, therefore, reprinted all the leaves in which the word occurred. Except a few typographical errors, which I have since discovered notwithstanding the closest attention to the proof. I believe there is now no one of consequence sufficient to affect the sense. The uncertain state of Bengal orthography has made it impossible to fix the true spelling of some words - and the Pundit has altered his opinion too frequently respecting the spelling of several. After all, however, I do not hesitate to say that even in that respect it is far more correct than any of their manuscripts.

Carey to Fuller Jan. 21, 1802

Our Lord has been gracious to us in our Missionary work. We have now three men - Krishna, Gokul, and Pitambar and four women, Rasoo *{Rasamayi?}*, Jeymooni, Jhamal, and Unna who are members with us in full communion - all Hindus. *{He tells how Pitambar was saved. A tract written by Ward was distributed and one ended up in his village.}* . . . It appears that he had been long seeking rest and had found none. But when he saw this small tract, which mentioned that "one had come from a distant country to seek the eternal happiness of the Hindus, and that there was free salvation in Christ for the vilest Sinner," he immediately exclaimed, this is the true way! This is what I want! Seeing that the papers were printed at Serampore he immediately came there about thirty miles in search of us, heard the Word of God, went back to inform his family, immediately returned and tho of the Writer caste which is high - rejected Caste, gave a most satisfactory account of the work of God on his Soul to the Church, was received and Baptised the first Lord's Day in Jan. and walks as becomes the Gospel. He is near 50 years of age by his looks and a very intelligent man. This morning another Man came about 35 miles brought by what he had seen in the above mentioned tracts. He appears to have been unhappy about his Soul for a long time - says that he has repeated that name of some idol for several years but has received no good. He says I think God is very angry with me, which is the cause why I get no place to rest my foot upon; an expression to denote "nothing which I can depend".

The wide dispersion of the New Testament and the little tracts has spread a ray or two of Light far and near, so that we frequently have people come from great distances for a Testament. This is succeeded with disputations among themselves all of which increase the Light more and more.

Carey to Brother, Aug. 18, 1802, Calcutta

{In addition to the translation of Bible and Grammar, Carey produced other works.}

. . . I am also writing a theological work in the Bengali Language designed to shew that the Hindus are going in a wrong Way, or rather that a renovation is necessary in their Disposition, Custom, and Sacred Writings. This will occupy near two Hundred pages in Octavo. My Heart is much set upon the finishing of these Works so that I am constantly employed upon them from Morning to Night, and indeed till near Midnight.

. . . I should never have begun the Grammatical Works, and the Dictionaries, had it not been for my situation in the College - This in a manner made it a work of necessity; and my being placed in a situation in which I could command every help in these studies made it appear criminal for me (to) let the opportunity pass without doing what was in my power to lay open to the World Those Writings which have been the least of Infidels - and the enemies of real religion - It has been their custom to appeal to the Writings of the Hindus, and their extravagant Chronology to subvert the authority of the scripture of truth and to cut up Christianity by the roots. I believe nothing more is necessary to drive them from this Hold, than to open the Way to the Knowledge of Hindu literature, and to put their Writings into the hands of the publick without any Comment or observations upon them.

I have great hopes of several Portugese People who were formerly Roman Catholics - They now appear not only to have broke off from that communion, but to have embraced Christ for their Saviour; and there are several Europeans who may be esteemed the fruits of the Mission. A Society is just formed for the purpose of publishing and distributing small evangelical pamphlets wherever there may be an opening. I hope it will be attended with the divine Blessing. There is much need to stand up against Infidelity and profligacy in this Country, I hope their attempts may be useful.

Carey to Ryland, August 31, 1802

. . . It is next to impossible to get all our Friends to spell Indian names alike, they are so numerous, and we frequently write them without even reflecting that they are Indian. The Language is universally called the Bengali Language by Europeans. The arguing upon a proper substitute for the short or inherent Vowel, viz. the Vowel naturally inherent in every Consonant erects the difference and the pronunciation of that Vowel in Bengali, Sanskrit, and Hindustani is different. Perhaps the short U in BUT is the best general substitute. I have used AW in my Bengali Grammar, which, however, must be pronounced short. Mr. Forster uses O and Mr. Halbed an italic O, which I think misleads most learners. Mr. Gilchrist in his Hindustani Works uses U short, I do the same in my Sanskrit Grammar which is now in the Press, and will be about 600 pages Quatro . . . I am much encouraged in the work by those who wish that Language to be laid open - and have perhaps paid an undue degree of attention to it. We have published several literary works in the Bengali Language which are nearly sold off and have now five works in the Press, 100 Copies of each of which are bespoke for the College as Class books.- - These things are a great assistance to me. The Earth helpeth the Woman.

A little time ago a few persons formed themselves into a Society to publish little tracts in the English Language, to distribute wherever an opening may present. Our first work will be Dodderige's sermon on the "Care of the Soul". The expences are defrayed by a voluntary subscription, and we mean to give the scheme a fair trial. There are thousands of persons in higher life who are either utterly careless about religion or Deists but we have access to many of them, and the putting a small neat piece into their hands may be useful. There are also thousands of Portugese who understand English, but are plunged in all manner of vice, and are grossly ignorant. These call for our attention. I suppose many may be given away among the European soldiers - and some among the Armenians. We have a wide field. There are some very excellent Christians here, tho very few in proportion to the great number of inhabitants. I suppose that we could give away a thousand New Testaments in a little time among the above classes of people if we had them. I dare say that 100 Arabic Bibles might be given away to advantage tho I am not acquainted with many Mussulmen of education but there are some in the College and many in Calcutta.

If the Pentateuch and Gospels could be printed in Persian from Walton's Polyglot Bible, I should hope for good from dispersing of them in various parts of India, and it could be sent to Persia. I have sometimes thought of printing them, but have not yet proposed it to our Brethren. Indeed our hands are completely full - Tho we have six Native compositors besides Bro. Ward, Felix, and William. The small tracts which we have distributed are of several sorts - all close addressed to the Conscience and many Thousands of them, perhaps not less than 20,000 have been distributed and still people are eager to obtain them in many places.

I have some time past contriving the plan of a Work which I intend to write in Bengali. The design is to prove that the Gospel is a most necessary blessing to them; on account of the TOTAL DEPRAVITY OF THEIR HEARTS, THE ENTIRE CORRUPTION OF THEIR CUSTOMS, and the INSUFFICIENCY and CONTRADICTION of the Books by them accounted SACRED. I intend that it shall be about two hundred pages. May the Lord assist me in it. Another circumstance, tho not immediately connected with the Gospel will yet give you pleasure.

One of the first persons in point of prosperity in Bengal - a grandson of the late Gunga Govind Sing - has been several times to see me, and I have closely pressed the importance of a Saviour upon him. He accounts himself inconvertible but has a strong desire to get a knowledge of the Sciences, particularly Astronomy. I have persuaded him to get some of our best books on Science translated into the Bengali Language, have offered him all my assistance to correct his copy, and put him in the way to get subscribers to the Work among the rich Natives. He went from me today very full of this scheme. I advise him to begin with Bonnycastle's *Astronomy*, should he do it I shall esteem this to be the dawn of Science in this dark quarter of the World.

Carey to Sisters, Aug. 24, 1803, Calcutta

We have nearly distributed the first Edition of the New Testament, and have begun to print a second edition; This and the great numbers of small Pamphlets which we have distributed have been means of shaking the false faith of some, exciting very alarming fears in others, and we trust producing genuine conviction for sin in a few. If only one Soul be converted by these means it is a most ample recompence both to us and all our friends.

Carey to Fuller, Feb. 27, 1804 from Calcutta

I have been just writing a letter to the Society informing them of our having engaged in a translation of the Scriptures into the Hindustan, Persian, Maharashtra, and Dothal languages, and of our intentions to engage in more. Perhaps so many advantages for translating the Bible into all the languages of the east will never meet in any one institution again, viz. a possibility of obtaining learned natives of all these countries, a sufficiency of worldly good things with a moderate degree of annual assistance from England to carry on through it, a Printing office; a good library of critical writings, an habit of translating, and dispositions to do it. We shall, however, need about 1,000 pounds sterling a year for some years to enable us to print them, and with this it may be done in about 15 years if the Lord preserve our lives and health.

Carey to Sutcliffe, Jan. 1 1806, Calcutta

. . . I think the past year has been on several accounts the most successful one of the Mission, since its commencement. We have disagreeable things in sufficient number to keep us from security, and to humble us, nor is the success of the Gospel, at all, proportioned to the vast multitude of souls in this country. Yet we have increased and been blessed. Twenty seven natives and three Europeans have been this year added to us by baptism. We have less irregularity, and fewer defections to mourn than in any preceding year, though some instances of both have occurred. We have some growing, useful gifts among our native brethren, and I am mistaken if there be not an increase of true piety among them.

My whole time is occupied in translating and preparing copy for the press, correcting proof Sheets, &ct. When I came to correct Bro. Fountain's translation of the historical Books of Scripture I found that it was impossible to make anything of it. I am, therefore, re-translating them. My own translation of the Prophets, Isaiah excepted, was not much better. I am, therefore, writing the whole of that out again.

Besides this we are engaged in several translations into other Languages. We are now strenuously supported by our Friends Mr. Brown, and Buchanan, in the work of translations. The latter has been for a long time past engaged in translating into the Chinese. He has not transferred that to us, but bears the expence himself. A young Armenian, born in China, who speaks and writes both the current, and Mandarin language is engaged to assist us at 300 Rupees per Month.

In consequence of a letter from the Bible Society, Mr. Udney is very warmly engaged with the two above mentioned and ourselves in forwarding translations, and we are about to issue proposals for a subscription to carry them on. I expect the plan will be successful, being so strongly supported. It is sent up the country to the Governor General for his approbation, which if obtained, will greatly favour its success. At any rate it is intended to persevere. The Languages into which translations are proposed to be made are the Sanskrit, Bengali, Hindustani, Mahratta, Orissa, Telugu, Hinnata, Gujarati, Persian, Bhutan, Tibetan, Assamee, Chinese, Burman, and Malay. Of these the first four are more or less known by me, and the next five easily attainable. The other six will be attained by proper labour, and some of the Family will study them. But so much use can be made of natives as will greatly facilitate the work, and I should not despair of seeing the New Testament printed in all those Languages in five years more, if we have proper support.

Carey to Father, Feb. 18, 1807, Calcutta

At present I am employed in a great and most important work, and the only thing which makes twenty more years of life desirable, I mean the translation of the Holy Scriptures into the languages of the East. We have received much pecuniary assistance in this from England, Scotland, America, and India and are now labouring at it with all our powers. Translations have begun, and several of them carried on to a considerable length in eleven distinct languages, and the printing of six of them is more or less advanced. To these a twelfth will be added in a few days, if nothing prevent. When it is considered that all these languages are as distinct from each other as English, French, Italian, &ct. and that each language is written in a character differing from the others; that I have to learn not only to read these languages, but to judge of the construction of sentences, and the force of words in all of them, except one (the Chinese) which Bro. Marshman has exclusively undertaken. You will think twenty years few enough for the completion of the plan.

Carey to Sutcliffe, Sept. 16, 1807

My Dearest Bro. Sutcliffe,

It is with great difficulty that I can allow myself time to write to my dearest friends, I consider the work of translating the Scriptures into the Oriental languages an undertaking of so much importance that I count all my time lost which is not spent upon that, or studies conducive thereto: such as translations of Sanskrit books, and study of languages. The fourth volume of the Bengali Bible is finished to the end of Micah. The Sanskrit to the 4th of Acts. The Orissa to the 15th of Luke, The Hindustani, Mahratta, and Gujarati are in the press and nearly the whole of

Matthew printed in the two first of them. The printing of the Persian is stopped for a little time, to admit of the corrections or rather new translations of our friend Nathaniel Sabot, an Arabian of Mohammedan family, who has embraced Christianity - and I trust is partaker of the Grace of God in truth. I believe he will go from us to reside in a distant part of Hindustan with our dear friend Rev. C. Martyn, but will pursue the same object. He was christened by Dr. Kerr of Madras, and I except we shall baptise him, for he has been much disquieted of late about baptism. In addition to the translations carrying on by us we have just received Mss copies of the Gospels translated into Malayalam (the language spoken in Travancore and the adjoining countries). It is translated from the Syriac under the directions of the Bishop of the Syrian churches in those parts and sent to us to be printed.

Carey to Father, May 4, 1808, Calcutta

. . . There is not a sentence, or a word, in these six versions which I do not compare with several versions; I translate the New Testament immediately from the Greek, and every sentence of the Old Testament is constantly compared with the Hebrew.

Carey to Ryland, March 15, 1809

. . . Govt. has given its publick consent to Bro. Lee's settling at Vizagapatam, so that I think you need not hesitate any more about sending out the Brethren who have been so long waiting for an opportunity, especially as we wish them, with very few exceptions to go to the neighboring countries for the purpose of beginning missions there. One person of good information, and a tolerable share of acquaintance with the original languages of the Scriptures, and of a spirit of subordination, should as soon as possible be fixed on for Serampore. It will require seven years to fit such a person to occupy the place of either of us in the business of translations, and in the management of the affairs of the Mission. The affliction with which I was last year visited has led me to consider myself as one who ought to stand ready to leave this world at an hour's notice: and though my health is now as well as ever it was, yet I am afraid to look forward to a very extended period of life: my sight likewise is so much impaired that I expect to be unable to see to read, even with glasses of the greatest magnifying power, for many years to come. The Lord has graciously favoured me with a sight of more than I once expected.

When I first entered on the translation of the Scriptures into the Bengali language, I thought that, if I should ever see it compleated, I could say with Simeon, "Lord now lettest thy servant depart in peace according to thy Word", but he has preserved me to see not only that version finished, but has given me opportunity of making many corrections in succeeding editions of various parts of it and also has preserved me to see one half of the whole Bible printed in the languages of Orissa, the Whole N.Test. and half the Pentateuch in Sanskrit, nearly the whole New Testament printed and the whole Bible, except the Pentateuch translated into Hindustani, half the New Testament printed and the poetical books translated into Mahratta. [He goes on to include translations into Kurnata, Telugu, Sikh's language,

Chinese, Burman,] . . . Nay, it is possible that, without my life being extended to any uncommon length, I may live to see the Bible compleated, and printed in these languages and perhaps begun in several others.

Carey to Father, May 3, 1810, Calcutta

. . . The translation of the Scriptures into several of the Oriental languages is a work which lies near my heart and in which I employ all the time I possibly can. Through the mercy of God the Bengali translation is wholly printed off. I am now busy translating it into Sanskrit. The New Testament was printed in that language last year and I hope the Pentateuch will be published by the end of the present year. I finished the book of Numbers this morning and began Deuteronomy. We are now printing the Bible in Sanskrit, Hindustani, Orissa, Chinese, Mahratta, and the language of the Sikhs besides a second edition of the Pentateuch in Bengali and hope ere long to begin printing in the Telugu and Kanarese languages for which we are casting types.

Carey to Ryland, Dec. 10, 1811

I am, however, more in my element in the translation of the word of God than in any other employment, and now begin to entertain an idea that I may yet live to see this work, compleated in most of the languages in which it has begun. The progress may appear slow to you, and sometimes does so to me: yet it must be considered that the difficulties are great. I have to learn all three languages myself, so as to be able to read them, and judge of the justness of every sentence: and however these languages may have an affinity with each other through their common parent the Sanskrit, yet they differ as much from each other as the modern languages of Europe, derived from the same source, do from each other, and some of them differ so widely as Spanish and German do. There is likewise another great disadvantage in the acquiring these languages arising from the want of books, there being no books in any of them beyond a few legends translated from the Sanskrit into miserable rhyme, nearly on par with Sternhold and Hopkin's metrical version of the Psalms, and of course utterly unfit to be consulted as models of prose style. I trust, however, the Lord will enable us to surmount these difficulties, and that, at least, intelligible versions, if nothing more, will be obtained.

The number of versions now carrying on or finished in India, is twenty. Of these Tamil, Cingalese N. Test, and the Malay have been made several years ago by missionaries in the countries where those languages are respectively spoken. The Malayan, the Persian, the Arabic, and the Arabica-Hindustani, are carrying on by other translators. The Chinese by Bro. Marshman, and the Burman by my Son. All the rest go through my hand: and I consider myself as responsible for their correctness, though learned men of these different countries are employed to write out the rough copies, and to assist at every step with their knowledge, and counsel. This intercourse with these learned men, all of whom are good Sanskrit scholars though of different nations greatly facilitates the accomplishment of the work, and contributes a little to its perfection.

The necessity which lies upon me, of acquiring so many languages, obliges me to study and write out the grammar of each of them, and to attend closely to all their irregularities, and peculiarities: I have, therefore, published Grammars of three of them, the Sanskrit, the Bengali, and the Mahratta: I intend also to publish Grammar of most of the others, and have now in the press a Grammar of the Telugu language and another of that of the Sikhs, and have begun one of the Orissa language. To these I intend in time to add those of the Kurnata, the Kashmiri, and Nepal, and perhaps the Assam languages. I am now printing a dictionary of the Bengali which will be pretty large, for I have now got to the 256 page [4to] and am not nearly through the first letter. That letter, however, begins more words than any two others. I am contemplating, and indeed have been long collecting materials for a universal Dictionary of the Oriental languages derived from the Sanskrit, of which that language is to be the ground work: and to give the corresponding Greek and Hebrew words. I wish much to do this for the sake of assisting biblical students to correct the translations of the Bible in the Oriental languages after we are dead, but which can scarcely be done without something of this kind, and perhaps another person may not in the space of a century have the advantages for a work of this nature that I now have. I, therefore, think it would be criminal of me to neglect the little that I am able to do while I live.

Carey to Sutcliffe, Feb. 5, 1812,

. . . I have of late been much impressed with the vast importance of laying a foundation for Biblical criticism in the East, by preparing grammars of the different Languages into which we have translated the Bible, or may translate it. Without some such step all who follow us will without the advantages which I now possess, have to wade through the same labour that I have, in order to stand merely upon the same ground that I now do. If, however, elementary books are provided, the labour will be greatly shortened, and a person will be able in a short time to acquire that which has cost me years of study and toil. I have, therefore, resolved to add to the three Grammars I have already published, grammars of the Telugu, Kurnata, Orissa, Punjabi or the language of the Sikhs, Hashmirian, Gujarati, Nepal, and Assam Languages. Two of these are now in the press, and I hope to have two or three more of them out by the end of the year. I also think this a necessary step to furnish an answer to the question which has been more than once repeated. "How can these people translate into so great a number of languages?" Few people know what may be done till they try and persevere in what they undertake.

I also have another scheme in my head, for the purpose of securing the object of a gradual perfection of the translations. This is an universal Dictionary of Oriental Languages derived from Sanskrit. [I do not mean that this should, however, comprise all the Languages from the Mediterranean to China, which are all usually thrown together under the general appellation of Oriental Languages. I mean to take the Sanskrit as] the ground work, to give the different acceptations of each word with examples of this application, in the manner of Johnston, and then to give the synonyms in the different Languages derived from Sanskrit, with the Hebrew and

Greek terms answering thereto, and perhaps the Arabic, always putting the word derived from the Sanskrit term first, and then those derived from other sources. I intend always to give the terminology of the Sanskrit term so that the etymology of those deduced therefrom in the cognate languages will be evident. This work will be great, and it is doubtful whether I shall live to compleat it, but I mean to begin to arrange the materials which I have been for some years collecting for this purpose, as soon as my Bengali Dictionary now in the Press is finished.

Carey to Fuller, March 25, 1813

Five natives of high caste have lately been baptised who have been brought to a knowledge of the truth without any communication with us. They met with Bibles, and other tracts; and God (wrought) by them. These men had begun to sanctify the Sabbath and meet for Christian worship before we knew them. They have boldly. . .

Carey to C. Stuart, M.D., Nov. 30, 1813

The translations of the Word of God occupy the greatest part of my time, and when you know the number of versions now actually under translation at Serampore is twenty, besides the Bengali, which is finished, you will account for my times being closely occupied. Two excepted, all these versions go through my hands, and I am obliged to acquire such a knowledge of the languages as not merely to read them, but to judge of their style and composition. For I do not allow a sentence to be printed till I fairly see through it. After all my necessary ignorance will undoubtedly occasion many mistakes, though I hope the mistakes will be few and of small importance.

Carey to Sister, July 20, 1814

Could you see me driving on from morning till late at night every Day you would be thankful for my Health. I am sometimes weary, but I rejoice in the daily approaching prospect of giving the Bible to the various nations of the East. The call for the Bible is so great that all our exertions, with Ten Presses constantly at Work, cannot supply the demand. . .

Carey to Burls, Aug. 19, 1818, Serampore

{The British and Foreign Bible Society in cooperation with the mission pledged 500 pounds for the printing of translation work. However, the conditions were that the translations be checked by competent judges to determine how good they were. Carey and Marshman had just completed a Pashto N T and Konkani and announced the Telugu as printed. The difficulty of cooperation is found in this situation. Mr. Thomason suggested the following and we have Carey's response.}

He, therefore, proposed to send the Konkani to Dr. Taylor at Bombay to be submitted by him to some native or natives there, and to give the Pashto to a General in Calcutta to be examined by an Afghan in his service, or rather under his control. You will easily see that we could not deem this a fair trial of the merits of the translations, and as the opinions of these persons would have been a final approbation or condemnation of what had cost us so much labour and expence, we could not think the opinion of a native who would not perhaps read an entire Chapter, a competent Tribunal to decide upon a work, which had costs us years of anxious care, and close study. Every word of which I had read, revised, corrected, and taken all the pains with, that I was able. Dr. Taylor, I believe does not understand Konkani and I know the other Gentleman does not understand Pashto. The whole must, therefore, have been suspended upon the report of a single Native, or perhaps two in each instance. We, therefore, requested leave to withdraw our claims as the Tribunal was incompetent.

. . . You are now aware perhaps that there is a very disagreeable Spirit of rivalry and envy in this Country. Mr. Thomason does not like that the Translations should go through the hands of the Dissenters, especially Baptists. He has, therefore, tried every little art to publish counter-translations. Mr Ellerton, a man I have highly respected for many years, has made a translation of the Gospels into Bengali, which scarcely differs from ours, and to show our approbation of it, we printed an Edition of it. He used the same Word for Baptism in that we had done, and in a letter to Bro. Ward, stated his reasons for wishing to retain it. Mr Thomason, however, has published another Edition of it at Calcutta, retaining the Greek Term *Baptizo*. We have of course taken no notice of this, but I mention this to show you that there is a disagreeable Spirit of rivalry in this Country. [We cannot, therefore, expect fair play.]

The Mission Society also has shown the same Spirit. Some Years ago Mr. Burls wrote to me modestly wishing us to give up the Chinese Translation, and his argument for it was, that Their missionaries were Men of good learning. I replied that I thought Bro. Marshman was not altogether destitute of learning, and I thought also that he had honesty enough to be faithful to the original. I, therefore, recommended that their Missionaries should do what they could, and assured him that we would do all we could in the work of translation and that if from the whole a good version was produced at last, all would be well. I recommended to Mr. Hardcastle their fixing a Mission at Vizagapatam and to Bros. Crain and Des Grangen to engage in translating the Scriptures into Telugu, which they did. We had, however, begun translating into that language more than a year before Them. Several illiberal squibs of this Translation were published by that Society, or some of that Party, but We have persevered. I should not, however, choose to suspend the approbation or condemnation of our Telugu version on the judgement of one of their Missionaries. I did, however, two years ago give to Mr. Campbell of the Civil Service of Madras, who as well as myself has published a grammar of the Telugu language, all that was printed of the NT requesting Him to criticize upon it and send me his remarks. He did the same to me by his Grammar. He, however, has not yet sent me any list of Faults.

We do the very best we can in every language and then publish the Translation which is from the moment open to every ones animadversion. We publickly count, nay even solicit, observations on what is published, and in subsequent Editions avail ourselves of those observations, whither good natured or ill natured, our object being the perfection of the Translations. We have the fullest opportunity of knowing whether those already finished are correct and wherein their defects consist, as Natives from every part of India are continually translating from them into their vernacular tongues. Where they translate wrong, I always suspect the version from which they translated, and of course re-examine the passage, and I believe more faults have been detected by this than all other methods put together.

I may also observe that as Mr. Harrington is obliged to have this Country for England, and as the Calcutta Aux. Soc. has evidenced its principles of Action so as to distribute the Bible among the Natives in their own language, and, moreover, as they do not like the acting with dissenters, to whom half the sums voted are secured by the parent Society, and who have also an equal right to vote respecting the application of the remaining half. They wish to dissolve the Cor. Committee altogether. We should not oppose this, if the sums granted to us by the Bible Society can be sent to us direct. I assure you that in this Case, in which all dangers of Control over us will be removed, we shall be happy to draw, as near, as possible to the Bible Society. I mean as near as can be done consistently with the connection We stand in with our own Society, which we shall be always proud to maintain.

There is, however, now no danger (of) Mssrs. Brown and Buchanan, who laboured to bring us into Bondage are I trust gone to Heaven. If the C.C. be dissolved Mr. T. will have no place for interference and no one else wishes to do it. We, therefore, can see nothing to fear in as close a connection with the Bible Society as any one can desire. Our independence we will never surrender. We will think for ourselves and act for Ourselves, labour to do all the good we can, especially in translating, publishing, and perfecting versions of the NT. We shall be glad, however, to receive pecuniary aid from B.S. or any other quarter. We will faithfully apply and freely [gladly] acknowledge it. You will make whatever use you please of all this information because it will put you in possession of facts, which You may employ to advantage with the B & F Bible Society.

Carey to ? Feb. 7, 1819 from Calcutta

The number of churches in our denomination is now considerable amounting to near twenty besides situations occupied by ministers who now amount to more than sixty, including those raised up among the natives. In Calcutta, our Brethren have erected three or four places of worship which the word is preached twice or thrice weekly. The people now hear the word of God without showing reluctance or making opposition, and the general knowledge of the gospel gains ground continually . . . When we first engaged in this work the languages of India were not supposed to amount to more than fourteen or fifteen. We are now actually printing the Bible in more than forty languages, all of which differ from each other so much as the languages of Europe which have a common origin, and are so unintelligible to those of other provinces as Italian and Portugese to a Spaniard. It would be the height of folly to say that any of our translations are perfect; yet I have reason to believe that they are in general intelligible to the people of the respective countries. In several instances we have satisfactory proof of this; having with us men from every part of India who are employed in making a rough translation from the versions already printed into their own languages. These being all afterwards read and corrected by myself with the help of these men, all their mistakes are easily detected.

Carey to Ryland, March 30, 1819, Calcutta

. . . It is not to be supposed that the Bible Society at Bombay, or the American Missionaries will use our translations unless as the ground work of those which they have respectively begun. The rivalry of parties, and the desire of being numbered among the translators of Scripture has both there and elsewhere a very great influence. Good will, however, ultimately arise from these things, and if among us all a correct translation into any language is compleated, the great object will be accomplished. We do the best we can, and I trust shall rejoice to see our mistakes rectified, and our inaccuracies corrected. But men are greatly needed . . .

EDUCATION AS MISSION METHOD

Early in his work William Carey realized the importance of education in disseminating the light into India. The need for science, math, and literacy coincided with the need for salvation. Carey, Ward, and Marshman started or encouraged several schools for girls and boys. They solicited subscriptions to support them and depended on the income from tuition to maintain mission work. For more advanced study, Serampore College was established. This strategy enhanced the possibility of an indigenous Indian church.

Carey to Fuller, June 22, 1797

We have also about a month ago set up a school again; the former having been discontinued from Ram Basu's defection. We have now thirteen scholars; and others doubtlessly will soon come in. They write part of the Scripture for their Exercises and learn common arithmetic. I mean to introduce other branches of useful knowledge of which the Hindus are yet ignorant. A Gentleman in Dinajpur whose name is Fernandez, born at Macao in China of Portugese or Italian [Parents] extraction, I am not [sure] certain which, has heard us preach, since which time he has shewn great regard to us, and is now erecting a Brick House at Dinajpur for the Preaching of the Gospel to either Natives, or English; entirely at his own expence. He writes that it will be finished in about a Month; when he intends to have it opened with Prayer and Preaching. This is the more remarkable as he was intended to be a Popish Priest himself, but he says being shocked at the worship of Images, he began to examine and the more he examined the more he was inclined to protestant principles and so gradually relinquished the Church of Rome.

Carey to Fuller, Nov. 1800

{Carey encloses some letters from a Mr. Geriche, one of the missionaries.}

I was much encouraged by this man and thought indeed I have long thought whether it would not be desirable for us to set up a School to teach the Natives English. I doubt not but a thousand scholars would come. I don't say this because I think it an object to teach them the English tongue but query is not the universal inclination of the Bengalis to learn English, a favourable circumstance which may be improved to valuable ends. I only stick at this expression.

Bro. Marshman visits the Bengali's school every day. The superintendence of it belongs to him and he is very diligent in his attentions to it. We have an intention as soon as we are able to set up a school to teach the Natives English. The design of this is to turn the almost universal desire of those people to acquire English to some profitable account. The plan is not yet matured, nor will our circumstances permit it at present.

Carey to Ryland, June 29-30, 1802

We have a school which is supported by the subscriptions of the Christian friends in Bengal. It is designed for the education of the Children of such who lose caste for the Gospel, and consists of three Classes under three superintendents - The first is for teaching Bengali reading and writing and is under the tuition of our friend Pitambar Singh. The second is for teaching English, and Writing and Arithmetic. This is under the management of a Portugese Man whose name is Ferguson, none are admitted in this who have any Caste. The third and highest, is for teaching the Science, for disputing against Hinduism, and explaining the principles of Christianity. Short Catechisms, and abstracts of Christian Doctrines are drawn up and printed for this Class, who are properly Catechumens, or people apparently enquiring after Salvation, also such children who have no Caste, who are able to comprehend the things taught them. This is under the superintendence of Thomal, a Brahman of whom we have considerable hopes, tho he has not yet rejected his Caste. Yesterday was set apart to examine the progress of the Caste Class: and I must say that the knowledge which they had acquired in a little time, very far surpassed my expectations.

Carey to Ryland, August 31, 1802

A school which we set up some time ago will I think give you pleasure. The design is to instruct the children of those who lose Caste for the Gospel, in useful science, and the Christian religion. It, however, embraces more objects than we at first thought of. The expence is defrayed by the voluntary subscriptions of Europeans. We purchased a piece of ground last week to erect a School House upon and have much encouragement in the undertaking.

. . . Many people would gladly buy the Evangelical and Missionary Magazines here if our friends would but send them. We, however, get but one

Copy each which is lent from one end of Bengal to the other. All religious publications of note will sell well here, and it is desirable to inundate the Country with religious Books if possible . . .

Carey to Ryland, Oct. 24, 1810

. . . A few weeks ago I called upon one of the Judges to take a breakfast with him, and going rather abruptly upstairs as I had been accustomed to do, I found the family just going to engage in morning worship. I was of course asked to engage in prayer, which I did: I afterwards told him that I had scarcely witnessed anything since I had been in Calcutta which gave me more pleasure than what I had that morning witnessed. The change in this family was an effect of Mr. Thomason's ministry. This morning I called on him again, when I had a very pleasing conversation with him, his wife and wife's sister upon the subject of setting up a charity school for Portugese girls. We had begun one last January for boys, and now more than seventy boys are instructed in it gratis. This laid the foundation for a conversation upon the best manner of constituting and managing such a school. My heart was filled with thankfulness to see the Zeal of the ladies in this undertaking, and I have little doubt of its being soon set on fact. About ten days ago I had a conversation with one of the Judges of the Supreme Court, Sir. John Royds, upon religious subjects. Indeed there is now scarcely a place where you can pay a visit without having an opportunity to saying something about religion.

Carey to Jabez, March 31, 1814

. . . I trust you will as soon as settled, set in earnest about your work. Make out a list of the different schools in the Islands, visit them closely, try all you can to improve them, especially by introducing the plan of Lancaster into them. Take every opportunity of various affectionate conversation with the masters . . . and recommend to them spiritual and evangelical religion. Let nothing short of a radical change of heart satisfy you with respect to any of them. Conduct yourself in an amiable and affectionate manner towards them. You must never expect them to pay attention to what you say unless you are beloved by them.

Carey to Jabez, April 15, 1814

I think the Lord is now making use of three powerful engines to spread blessings over the face of the world. Missions, Bible Societies and the Lancastrian plan of Education. I rejoice to see you engaged in the promotion of these important objects. You will have much to conflict with, but persevere in your work. Consider the management of the Malay schools and the giving of religious instruction to the Malays as a charge committed to you by God; often reflect upon your responsibility, and as often upon that sufficiency of Grace which is treasured up in Christ for your help in every time of need, and devote yourself entirely to the promotion of the object in which you are employed.

Carey to Jabez, Jan. 12, 1815

. . . Pay the utmost attention to the Schools. I consider Schools as one of the most effectual means of spreading the light of the Gospel through the world. Treat the rising generation with kindness and attention and you will see the advantage of so doing hereafter.

Carey to Brother, Dec. 17, 1817

There is a wonderful spirit of doing good now raised up in all ranks of Europeans in India, especially as it relates to setting up Schools for the instruction of the natives. There is also a Society lately formed for translating and publishing School Books in the country Languages. We have about 100 Schools in which at least 7,000 Children are instructed. I am a member of the School Book Society, and am pretty much employed in its most active undertakings.

Carey to Ryland, Oct. 4, 1818, Serampore

{In conversations with the Marquis of Hastings about setting up more schools, the idea of a college is put forth.}

He also told us of his hearty concomitance with our wishes in establishing a College at Serampore, a draft of which we had sent to him. He promised a handsome subscription (1,000 Rupees) and gave us leave to put his name at the head of it. By this Providence a tract of Country larger than Great Britain is put into our hands, in which several of those Languages are spoken in which we are preparing translations of the Scripture. Had we Funds and Men, five or six hundred Schools might be immediately organized and Men of God if we had them might be instrumental in doing more good than can be calculated.

Carey to Jabez, May 5, 1819

By this time I trust you have safely arrived at Ajmere; you have been followed by my prayers and will I trust always have a share in them to the end of my life.

I advise you immediately to begin with your work, and open one or two schools as soon as possible. I would also recommend to you to make a survey of the City and get intelligence of the number of schools therein and the state of instruction. If by some little assistance given to them an improved system can be introduced among them a great point will be gained. I hope you will do your utmost to raise up and qualify schoolmasters, who may be employed in the other parts of Rajputana by degrees and that thus the great and noble plan contemplated by His Lordship may be realised . . .

Carey to Jabez, Nov. 16, 1819

. . . I am greatly pleased that you have begun a school and trust it will be in the commencement of a widely extended circle of schools in those countries which so little time ago were only dens of robbers. Do pray my dear Jabez, bend all your attention to the promotion of this very important object. You can scarcely imagine how many eyes are upon you, some earnestly desiring and praying for your success and others perhaps secretly wishing the miscarriage of the plan in which you are engaged. I hope you will be enabled to fix your whole soul on your work and consider it as the work of God, engage in it as such and as such persevere in it to the end. "Let us not be weary of well doing for in due season we shall reap if we faint not." You must expect discouragements and perhaps opposition, but I entreat you seek the Lord under all circumstances and account nothing dear to you that you may finish your course with joy and the ministry which is committed to you.

. . . Your ministry embraces two things. The establishment of schools and the spread of the Gospel. The first of these if it can be secured will I trust be an effectual introduction to the other. I hope, however, you will not neglect any opportunity that offers of making known the Gospel of our Dear Redeemer. Success must depend on God but the Cause in which you are engaged is that for which our Redeemer shed his blood and to which he, therefore, will never be indifferent.

Carey to Jabez, July 16, 1822

. . . Last week I received a letter from Lord Hastings informing me that intelligence had been just received from Rajputana that your Schools had suffered from your having attempted to introduce the Holy Scriptures into them, and requesting me to write to you not to repeat the attempt. It had been circulated among the natives that this was only a prelude to introducing Christianity among them and then getting these children to Calcutta for sinister purposes.

I suppose this is nothing more than what you informed me of some months ago and I in reply said this to His Lordship, and told him that I believed you were too cautious to repeat an attempt which was likely to be injurious to the Schools. He said he would take away all necessity for it by sending you immediately a supply of the works published by the School Book Society.

I have no doubt but my letters contributed to your taking that step. As, however, Government is extremely cautious upon this head I advise you scrupulously to avoid any attempt to introduce the Scriptures into the schools. You will, if you watch for them, find many other opportunities of doing good, and of promoting the knowledge of the Gospel in private conversation, and many other ways which are, and must be, perfectly unexceptionable. The same caution is preserved in the Schools about Chinsura under the superintendence of Mr. Pearson, who yet is a most valuable man and a minister of the Gospel. By the bye, he is to be baptised at Serampore tomorrow.

Carey to Jabez, July 4, 1823

. . . I wish you not to try imprudently to introduce the Bible into your Schools, but there can be no objection to your conversing with, and recommending the Gospel to the natives of the town and neighborhood. Success depends on God, but it is our business to use the means put into our hands, and I believe no one ever did that for a considerable length of time without some success.

Carey to Jabez, Jan. 4, 1825

. . . Schools for the education of native female children are prevailing more and more in these parts. I attended the examination of Mr. and Mrs. Wilson's schools in Calcutta a fortnight ago, the sight was truly gratifying. Other schools are not behind them. We have a pleasing number at Serampore and its neighbourhood. Lucy, Dolly, Charlotte - my Wife's daughter by her first husband - and Rachel Marshman superintend the Schools, and a pleasant work it is for them. I trust the cause of God is on the increase, yet I want to see more evident downpourings of the Holy Spirit upon us.

Carey to Jabez, Feb. 16, 1827

Bro. Marshman's last letters were from Copenhagen, whither he went to obtain a Charter of incorporation for Serampore College. There was every prospect of his succeeding in that application.

Carey to Jabez, May 19, 1827

. . . Eustace says nothing about his own or Mary's health or about his future intentions. We have received very good news from Bro. Marshman. He has obtained from the King of Denmark a Charter for Serampore College by which it is invested with all the privileges of the Colleges at Copenhagen, Kiel, or anywhere else within the Danish dominions.

Indigenous Missions

Establishing a church on foreign soil that is led by natives and fits the native culture occupies a key focus for modern missions. William Carey affirmed the same goal and was quick, in spite of criticism, to train and use native preachers. He developed a plan for sending the native preachers out with European trained missionaries for the purpose of mentoring them through on the job training. Convinced that these Indian ministers could be more effective, Carey never wavered from this strategy.

Carey to Society, Dec. 28, 1796, Hooghly River

This also is a situation so central that had we sufficient Men and proper means the Gospel might with ease, and small expence be sent from hence through all Hindustan, Persia, Bhutan, Assam, and what are generally called the Rajmahal Hills - on the west of the Ganges, and was a proper plan adapted all the Educations necessary for this extensive design might be obtained in one situation in this Country, and a connection with the Mission here invariably, and regularly maintained.

The importance of a proper and practicable plan of Education for not only the children of Natives, but also of Missionaries, some of whom it is to be hoped, might in time be converted by the Grace of God, and become missionaries themselves, or be otherwise serviceable in the Mission, is obvious not to mention the almost necessity of Females well Qualified to communicate the Gospel of Christ in a situation where superstition secludes all the women of respectability from hearing the Word; and the advantage which would arise, from considerable numbers being embarked in such a cause; to our own souls, when the numbers engaged would all add to the impetus of each particular Soul.

Independent of what I have mentioned above; the necessity of having a succession of proper persons to succeed in the Work in case of our Death, or any other occurrence in providence which might prevent our being able to occupy longer and the importance of the numbers of immortal Souls to whom we have access require a strengthening of our Cause and in order to that I propose something like the following scheme.

Carey to Fuller, Aug. 4, 1801

We in some measure feel the importance of working whole of a Day and indeed myself excepted there is no one indolent among us. It appears to us all we ought to make the most of the gifts of our Hindu Friend and we are thinking how to employ our Friend Krishna so as to make him useful in the Lord's Vineyard. It is our design to take him out short journeys with us by which his gifts for conversation and Prayer with his countrymen may be exercised. He has a good capacity and perhaps something above the common sense. I have frequently thought upon several facts which appear to me very striking and thoroughly incline my mind to make all possible use of the gifts found in the church at least prove that we should no more neglect those gifts which are found in the Church than those found in ourselves.

The facts I allude to are the following. The Churches in Wales go very much upon the plan of encouraging all promising gifts. The consequence is that Wales is not only supplied with a gospel ministry from herself, but furnishes a number of Ministers for England which bear a considerable proportion to the whole of those employed in that country. - while England scarcely ever sends a minister to Wales. Scotland goes upon the plan of having none but learned Ministers- the consequence is that Scotland sometimes receives Ministers from England but seldom furnishes any, no doubt but thousands of useful gifts are quite neglected there.

In the Methodist societies especially those of Mr. Wesley's profession almost every thing like a gift is encouraged, and perhaps some who ought to be silent. There may be many weak men among those ministers through this step, but there are also a very great number of truly useful men, whom God has greatly blessed, and perhaps the prosperity of that Body is to be attributed to this sending out such a number of men as a justified means.

On the coast from Madras to Palmcottalon are reckoned about 40,000 Christians, and yet the cause is in danger of dropping through for want of Labourers. It would be highly uncharitable to suppose all these men to be nominal Christians especially when we remember that Ziegenbald, Schwartz, and Geriche and others were and are men of genuine piety and evangelical sentiment. How then is it that men are not found in some tolerable position who are proper for the ministry without having constant supplies from Europe. I suppose it to be wholly owing to this, that the Germans and Danes think it unlawful to employ any one in the ministry except he have gone through the formalities of a collegiate education. We hope to profit by such reflections and such facts as these and to make all the use we can of the gifts which God may give us in the church.

It has been the custom with the Moravians to give new Names to those who were converted from the Heathens. We had some consultations about it. I opposed it because I thought there was no connection between baptism and giving names but principally because it does appear to have been the primitive practice to change the names of those who believed for among the primitive Christians we have Sylvanus, Olympus, Hermes, Nereus, Fortunatus and others which are evidently Heathen names. Our Brethren convinced in the opinion that it is unnecessary and, therefore, we have not proposed it. This we should recommend to them not to name any more children with Heathenistic names.

Carey to Ryland, August 1, 1805

. . . I wish I could conquer that habitual aversion to letter writing which I feel and have always felt, but I almost despair. A sensible awkwardness at constructing sentences makes epistolatory correspondence peculiarly difficult to me.

. . . The state of the Mission, the Church, and the family will be detailed by others of our Brethren: In general I may say they are prosperous. The whole number who have been baptised or received by Letter, by us, is 74, of whom eight are dead and twelve worse than dead, three or four of the others are doubtful Characters, Twenty-five of these members are Europeans of whom eight have been baptised here, and the rest are our Brethren and Sisters who have come from England. The others are native. Among our native Brethren there are some with very respectable gifts, who often preach to their countrymen. We are thinking much of scattering them over the country that they may be more extensively useful, but we need more European Brethren to superintend them. And I fear that we are not able to bear much more expence than what we at present do - We think of two Brethren labouring in Calcutta, as this is so near Serampore we can superintend them without difficulties. A brother must soon go to Jessore and settle there. We have several members in one neighborhood who must be embodied into a separate Church, soon, they being about 80 miles distant from us. I believe Bro. Biss will go to Dinajpur. Bro. Fernandez writes that he has hopes of two persons at Sadamahal. Probably Bro. Mardon will go to Jessore, he is now at Cutwa with Bro. Chamberlain who is labouring with hope of success, and I hope that in a little time a church may be formed there. Two members are gone into that neighborhood.

Fewer than six brethren can scarcely manage the home department, two of these we wish to be always itinerating in a circle of an hundred Miles radius. We want to fix two stations immediately in Hindustan, one somewhat towards Lucknow or Delhi, and the other about Patna. And another in Orissa near Jagganath. The East of Bengal will then be unoccupied and must be thought of, so that we have need of both men and money. I lay every station at 100 rupees a month, including house and everything. We wish so to station our Native Brethren that they shall occupy several stations which the European Brother, who is to itinerate in a circle from his station, may frequently visit. This will be necessary in the infant state of things while our Native brethren must necessarily have but a limited stock of knowledge or experience.

Carey to Fuller, Nov. 18, 1806, Calcutta

In this troublesome time some Armenians and Portugese have come forward to encourage preaching among the Hindus, and are fitting up a place for that purpose in Calcutta. Our brothers preach in the School of an Armenian while the place is fitting up. This is matter of great encouragement. It is the Lord's doing, and marvelous in our eyes. About a dozen of our Native brethren are constantly employed in itinerant preaching. They go two and two together, viz. one gifted for preaching, reading, &ct., and another of inferior gifts as his companion. I trust that fruit will come from this.

Carey to Ryland, Jan. 22, 1808

. . . You have frequently enquired about the Armenians, I have the pleasure now to say that one of them has proposed to join our Church. His name is - - Carapeit. He is a young man of an inquisitive mind and good genius. He is anxiously desirous of traveling through the Armenian Churches all the way from hence to Jerusalem to tell them of the Gospel, when he shall be thought sufficiently grounded therein. I heard another of them, John Peter, deliver a good discourse in the Bengali Language a few weeks ago. I have little doubt of the conversions of these two persons, and trust that this is but the beginning of a harvest among them. I hear of one or two more who begin to enquire, but the great body of the Armenians are fierce in opposition to them.

Carey to Fuller, March 27, 1809

We endeavor to remedy this inconvenience as much as we can by settling stations in different parts of the country. I trust they will all succeed at Part. All our native brethren who have ministerial gifts are now employed, and stationed out, one or two excepted, concerning whose consistency of conduct we doubt. I wish we had two or three hundred more such men as our first brother Krishna. Indeed both the Krishna's give us much pleasure.

{Concerning the work in Calcutta.}

Next Lord's Day I expect to baptise two more; I trust there are not fewer than ten others enquiring after the way of Salvation. I trust the Lord will raise up in this church as sufficient here of spiritual gifts, to convey the knowledge of the truth through this, and perhaps some of the neighboring countries. The native Portugese, and persons born in the country from the illegitimate connections of Europeans with native women, will, if converted, be the fittest for this work of any other, and the Europeans among us will I trust contribute to give substance to the ideas of these people. Yet a succession of brethren for Serampore to fill up our places when we are removed by death will be necessary.

Carey to Fuller, Oct. 25, 1809

Last Wednesday the Church at Calcutta solemnly called out two Armenian brethren, John Peter and Carapeit Aratoon to the work of the ministry. Bro. Carapeit the next Lord's Day baptised four Persians who had the day before been received into the Church at Changuehkee in Jessore of which a majority of the Members were at Serampore. Few things as deeply impress my mind than this pleasing sight. It was the first time I had seen anyone besides ourselves administer the Ordinance of Baptism, for though Bro. Fennaday had administered it, none of us had seen it. Bro. Carapeit set off for Jessore yesterday. Bro. J. Peter will go to Donesso as soon as we can hire a sloop to carry him down and as no ship goes there we must hire a sloop on purpose.

Bro. Moano will set off next week. I believe from Bankapore near Patna where there is a prospect of getting a school, and a congregation of Europeans. In this land he may be useful and I hope will, and though I have no hope that he will ever preach to the natives yet he may keep one or two native brothers near him who may be very useful there.

Carey to Fuller Jan. 20, 1811

I think there is a now a church of about fifteen persons in that country. (Parifia) Some of them, being in the army, have been lately removed from Balasore to Cuttack, the chief town in Parifia; I have seen some letters from one or two of them to Bro. J. Peter in which they appear to be employed in the work of the Lord, making known [and to] as well as they are able the gospel to the heathen. Being natives of the country, they are able to do that with great advantage.

Carey to Pearce, January 15, 1812, Calcutta

The concerns of the Mission are very great, so great indeed that I am often astonished at their magnitude, and not infrequently calculate upon it future operations and probable effects for years to come. The confessed difficulties in the way of the universal spread of the gospel thro the east discourage me, and the want of labourers who shall with a disinterested regard to the cause of our Lord Jesus Christ, devote themselves to the work of publishing his holy word, is sometimes with so much weight upon my spirit as to overwhelm it. I see plainly that Europeans can only be employed to introduce the gospel into new countries, for the expence of employing them so as to occupy a fiftieth part of the country for which ministers are wanted, would be so great that no funds could support it. If we could calculate upon every European missionary being as full of zeal, love, and every other grace as is to be expected in only a very few, yet it would upon an average require three years for each person to acquire the language in any country, so as to preach in it intelligibly, and a much longer time to do it fluently, during all which time he must be supported;

which cannot be done in this country for less than 100 pounds a year, so that every missionary costs the publick at least six hundred pounds before he is effectual, [including his voyage and preparatory expences] and afterwards must be supported at the same expence. All, however, are not effectual, and it would be folly to expect they should, some want daily strength, some want zeal, and others want other qualifications equally important so that when all deductions are made it will be at least 1,000 pounds for every effective missionary before he is fitted for his work, and after that his maintenance as above.

I am, therefore, fully of opinion that persons born in this and other countries to which missionaries are sent, must be employed to as great an extent as possible. These, however, are far below Europeans in religious knowledge, in energy of mind, and in many other very important requirements and that we account them our glory and joy. Yet we find much to struggle with in the many obvious disqualifications which are found in them. I do not say what I have said about European brethren to deprecate their value nor to prevent their coming out. Very great members are wanting and must be found somewhere before the gospel be sent into all parts of the east . . . Yet two is the smallest number that ought to be sent to any country. The Harvest truly is great, but he labourers are very few. On the other hand I am much encouraged by many things which I see. The success which has attended our feeble labours. Printing types cast for almost every character used in the East. The Bible translated or under translation into fourteen languages . . . The Auxiliary Bible Society at Calcutta which has already in the press four versions besides these above mentioned. The prayers of God's people and the dispensations of providence all conspire to prove that the day of mercy is hastening forward notwithstanding all the gloomy circumstances which present themselves to view.

Carey to Fuller, May 5, 1813

Some of our native Brethren are good preachers, but they want judgment and facitude. We, therefore, try to mix them, as to produce the greatest possible advantage from the mutual help that they afford each other.

Carey to Ryland, May 30, 1816

I understand a prejudice against our native Brethren has been spread abroad. From Sister Ward's letter I understood Capt. Kemp has imbibed it. My Nephew, who talks too freely about people's characters and actions from very imperfect information, has prejudiced Capt. H. Our Native Brethren, I mean those employed in preaching the Gospel, are our real strength: I do not say they have no faults, but I say that nearly all that is done among the Heathen is done by them. I bless God for them, and glory in the Grace given to them. Our younger Brethren are not quite free from envy and detraction.

COOPERATION ON THE MISSION FIELD

Ecumenism on the mission field normally exists to a greater degree than at home. Perhaps this cooperative inclination rises from the overwhelming need. As the missionaries survey the tremendous task to be accomplished, they quickly realize the necessity for working together. Another reason for this mutuality might be the desire for Christian fellowship which exists in scarce quantity in a foreign country where Christianity is less prominent. Whatever the reasons, Carey readily cooperated with others involved in the same task of missions.

Carey to Fuller, June 17, 1796 from Mudnabati

I am obliged to finish as the Post is going but must say that the pleasure afforded by [the two missionaries being sent to Africa is very great; and much heightened by] the account of the other Denominations of Christians uniting in a Society to send the Word of Life to the South Seas is very great. Surely God is on his Way; if success does not immediately attend every effort don't be discouraged - God will surely appear, and Build up Zion.

Carey to Professor Bently, Jan. 8, 1807

Our highly esteemed Mr. Brown preached the Gospel in Calcutta and there were a very few who feared God there and in one or two more parts of the country, but these scarcely knew one another, and nothing like the communion of saints was seen. Things are now widely different. There are now in Bengal and the provinces dependent on this presidency, six Evangelical Clergymen, Chaplains in the Company's service, and one at Madras, all united in the bond of love and striving for the faith of the Gospel. In our Society there are ten missionaries and two who, though not missionaries, labor in the work and, belonging to the London Society, eight or nine, including those at Ceylon, besides Danish Missionaries on the coast making all together a number of about thirty ministers of different persuasions, but united in a manner which has scarcely a parallel in Europe. To these may be added, at least, six native brethren who are constantly employed in the work of preaching the Gospel in our connection, and the Catechists and teachers on the coasts, the number of which is unknown to me.

Carey to Fuller, Aug. 11, 1807

{Cooperation with the Bible society became stressful when Mr. Brown and Buchanan...}

. . . sent us an unaccountable proposal for instituting a College at Serampore, to be called the British Propaganda. We were not asked whether we would have any hand in it [not consulted about it], but it was to be exacted on the ruin of our mission. All the property whereof was to go to this new institution, and the whole to be under the direction of a Minister of the Church of England. These proposals were sent to us by Mr. Brown for us to sign. This was of course precipitously refused, and gave rise to a correspondence, which I suppose Bro. Marshman will send you. Dr. Brown said nothing but is I find now trying to set up some thing else which is to be called The Christian Institution and I believe the money which may be (given) in our name by the address which you so much condemn will be appropriated by him to this new institution, which is to run away with all the applause which the world may better on the translation of the Scriptures. Well, let them have the applause, if we can but finish the work. Dr. B. has very disingenuously sent copies of all that we have done to the Bible Society to influence them to send money to support this new puff which is avowedly set off for the carrying on of translations. And in which he will expend as much on one language as we do on six . . . but I feel very much at our names *{employed and}* doing any thing to collect money of which we have not the disposal.

We do not think ourselves at liberty to appoint our own Children to be missionaries, however well they may be fitted for it. The most we think ourselves authorised to do is to recommend them to the Society after we have made a proper trial of them. I believe the evangelical episcopalian had an intention of trying to get one of Lady H. (Huntington) connections if other means failed; and that they have now a good fund to maintain a minister for the Mission Church, but this is entirely a different place from what we are erecting. We shall no doubt be the principal preachers in the new Chapel, though it will be open to evangelical ministers of other denominations, just as your places of worship are. Govt. have given us permission to erect it and the greatest part of the roof is now on it. We have now more than twenty members in and very near Calcutta, so that a place of worship there was very desirable.

Carey to Jabez, Oct. 6, 1815

. . . I hear there is a Dutch minister sent out from the London Society for Amboyna. He had arrived at Java a good while ago from which I conclude he is now with you. I hope you will live on the most friendly terms with him and strive together to promote the cause or our Lord Jesus.

Carey to Sisters, Jan. 31, 1816, Serampore

The number of Mission stations is very considerable, I think there are not fewer than sixty who labour in the Gospel, connected with us, and a good number belonging to the London Society, the Church Mission Society, and the Methodists. There are also a good number of pious men spread all over India, and not a few of them in very high situations.

Carey to Ryland, Dec. 30, 1816

. . . So far as I see the two Brethren from the M. Society are men of the right stamp; we live in great harmony with them. They have obtained the Free Mason's Lodge to preach in and have a decent congregation. If there is any party spirit here it is among the Church Clergy, for the people have it not. I think our good friend Mr. Thomason has a world of envy in him, he keeps it in as much as he can, but it now and then appears. He, however, has all the trouble of it, for we have never hinted it to him or any one else. Good Mr. Currie I fear is not quite clear of it, and I fear others may feel it. They are not comfortable, the Bishop lays his leaden fingers on all their endeavors, and they are smarting, good, churchmen.

. . . Bro. Bruckner now labours at Samarang, and will, I trust be a truly useful man. I wrote you long ago an account of his Baptism, his relinquishment of his situation in the Dutch Church, and of his connection with The Missionary Society. I also sent you a letter from him to you requesting to be received and employed as a Missionary by our Society, to which I hope they have agreed. Things in general wear a promising appearance through the whole Mission, and notwithstanding all our causes for humiliation we have many, very many for rejoicing, and still more for hope.

Carey to Sisters, Feb. 16, 1822

{In speaking about Eustace's work Carey tells of his illness and how he expects him to come and visit. Some information about cooperation is revealed here.}

He is at Chinsura, about twenty miles from us, among our Independent Brothers, who are excellent men, and half Baptists; I have a great esteem for them. I rejoice to say that all our contentions are at an end, and that I believe we all, viz. Senior and Junior Baptists, Independents, Churchmen, and General Baptists love one another with a pure heart fervently.

Carey to Sisters, May 1822

The independent Brethren and those of the Church of England are also very successful. We are all united in the Work of God, and bear good will to each other. From distant parts of the country we frequently receive accounts which are highly encouraging, and upon the whole, I think the prospect is as fair as I have ever known it. The two General Baptist Brethren are settled at Cuttack in Orissa and from a letter I yesterday received from one of them I think their prospects are hopeful. Three Independent brethren arrived a short time ago, further we are on the best terms.

Carey to Ryland, July 4, 1822

I received your most welcome letter of <u>no date</u> a few days ago. I was afraid that some thing I had said in former letters had offended you and put a stop to a correspondence which was always highly prized by me: a letter, therefore, from you, and especially without any allusion to our past unhappy circumstance was exceedingly grateful.

. . . At the present time I believe we are all here in perfect peace with each other. Poor Adam has declared himself an Arian, but I understand he and Ram Mohan Ruya have disagreed: and that he has entirely left off preaching, and is now an Usher to a School in Calcutta. The most perfect harmony now subsists, so far as I know between us, the junior brethren, the independents, and the Episcopalians, and I believe a divine blessing attends all our labours. I expect to receive two persons into the church today, and I believe there is scarcely a month in which there are not additions to more than one church. A great number of excellent pamphlets printed by one or another in the Bengali and some other languages which contribute not a little to the edification of believers, and to the stirring of a spirit of enquiry in a people whose most prominent feature is apathy. There has also been a great change in the circumstances of the natives themselves. There are now three Newspapers printed in the Bengali Language, and one in Persian: In these many things connected with heathenism as well as Christianity are discussed by the natives themselves, and facts brought to light respecting the blackness of idolatry, which might otherwise have been sought for in vain.

That spirit of establishing and maintaining Schools, especially Charity Schools, which now prevails and is much increasing among the natives, some of the chief men for wealth and respectability among them, coming forth and voluntarily taking an active part in the institutions, is to me a matter of great encouragement. They now unite with Europeans, and Europeans with them in promoting benevolent undertakings, without servility on their part or domination on ours. God is doing great things for India, and for all the World. About fifty years ago, one of the Sovereigns of Europe was employed in writing fourteen volumes of learned poems on Christianity: Voltaire in all his multifarious, much read publications constantly made Christianity the butt of his ridicule and sarcasm. The Encyclopedist attacked Christianity in a more grave manner: Gibbon and Hume did the same: and a host of novelists, writers for the Theatre and pamphleteers followed in the rear: if not actually saying, as the Abbe Burnal asserts, *ecrazes l'infame,* at least acting fully up to the spirit of that charged upon them by that writer. - Now Sovereigns on their Thrones declare themselves on the side of Religion, and encourage Bible Societies and other associations to do good, while all ranks from the noble to the Slave unite to promote the same object. Who that loves God and Man, can behold the present state of things without thanking God?

Be assured, My Dear Brother, I sincerely sympathise with you in all your trials as far as I know them. I generally appropriate two mornings in the Week to pray for all my friends by name, especially all employed in Missionary work: You, on these occasions, are frequently remembered by me. If I am not deceived, with generous affection, and indeed you are almost the only one left of my Brethren in the Ministry with whom I have enjoyed sweet communion in England.

COOPERATION WITH THE GOVERNMENT

Cooperation extended beyond other missionaries and included working with the government when necessary to accomplish the goals. The government along with the British East India Company controlled the colony with rigor. In order to carry on the work of missions, Carey and the other missionaries endeavored not to appear obstinate regarding the rules and made themselves available to help government objectives when possible. In Serampore, Danish rule generally presented a more tolerable circumstance and the missionaries took advantage of that freedom and protection.

Carey to Fuller, Nov. 16, 1796, Mudnabati

Numbers have absolutely refused to regard the Regulations at all, but I think we should study peaceableness and obedience to the Laws . . . yet we have always been denominated Indigo workers hitherto;

Be very careful that the Missionaries be charged to say nothing about Politiks on their first arrival, during their stay in Calcutta, and for the first three months is all the danger; afterwards Political Fire will go out for want of Fuel.

Carey to Fuller, March 23, 1797, Mudnabati

. . . yet it is a point of conscience with me, to be submissive to the powers that are, for the time being; so that let my opinions about the best mode of Government be what they might, yet the Bible teaches me to act as a peaceful subject under that govt. which is established where providence has placed, or even may place my lot, provided that govt. does not interfere in religious matters, or attempt to constrain my conscience in that case, I think it my duty to peaceably to obey God rather than Men; and abide by all Consequences.

Carey to Fuller, July 17, 1799, Mudnabati

The visit which you propose for us to make to the Governor General, Lord Mornington, tho proposed in the utmost simplicity of your heart yet excited a little sensibility in us. I wish I could make you understand a little about legal settlements &ct. &ct., but you must first drop your English ideas and get Indian ones. No such thing as a legal settlement in the English sense can ever be made here. Because a general Law has prohibited Europeans settling in this Country. This general Law cannot be reviewed unless by the English. All Europeans, therefore, only reside by convenience and some are permitted to stay in the Country for a term of Years; the Company having covenanted to protect such persons, while they observe the Laws. Once a year the Magistrate of every District has orders to make a return to Government of all persons (Europeans) in his District with their Employment, and whether they have executed Covenants or no.

Was a person on this occasion to return his Name as a Missionary it would be putting Government to the proof and obliging them to come to a point on the subject whether Missionaries should be allowed to settle in the Country, as such, or no, and there cannot be much doubt but it would be negatived. But when a person returns his name as a Manufacturer no suspicion can arise, if his conduct be good in other respects - and it would be more proper for new persons to appear as assistants to those in covenant with Government than otherwise.

I would not, however, have you suppose that we are obliged to conceal ourselves, or our Work. No such thing. We preach before Magistrates and Judges, and was I to be in the company of Lord Mornington I should not hesitate to declare myself a Missionary to the Heathen, tho I would not on any account return myself as such to the Governor General in Council.

You should also know that Europeans are not permitted to purchase or occupy more than 50 biggahs of Land, or about 20 acres, so that all Business is carried on by purchasing the produce of the Soil of the Natives and whoever engages in any Business must acquaint the Board of Trade therewith so that such a settlement as you propose for us to make, is impossible. I am, however, doing what will approximate as near to it as circumstances admit, if the Society approves of the Plan.

Carey to Ryland , Aug. 17, 1800

The Mission is settled at this place in a very desirable manner under the protection of the Danish Governor. Col. Olie Bie, a Gentleman to whom we are under the greatest obligations, and whose kind and affable conduct makes him beloved by all - - He attends the English preaching - and encourages others so to do, calls on us frequently in the most friendly manner, and has assured us that whatever he can do to serve us at any time, he will cheerfully do. I think if our beloved Society in England were to write him a letter it would be a gratification to him. We at his desire have written to the Court of Copenhagen informing them of our wish to settle here, and asking their protection.

It gives me much pleasure to inform you of the very friendly and Christian behaviour of Rev. D. Brown of Calcutta to us, it has much exceeded my expectation, and is a real gratification to me to be able to say so. Mr. Forsyth the Missionary from the London Society, is also a very warm and true friend, much beloved by us all, he is a man of the right stamp and the more he is known the more he will be beloved. He has been a friend and saved us to the utmost of his power: It would gratify us if the Society, or any one of our Brethren would send him a friendly Letter. Mr. Udney is also very friendly, and has shewed his good will in more instances than one.

Carey to Fuller Dec. 10, 1805

{Mr. Many is a friend and is influential in the government.}

I went to breakfast with him a few days ago and took the opportunity to mention our design to him adding that it was our wish if feasible to fix our Brethren as Missionaries and not as traders; I told him that we did not wish to conceal a single step that we took from the government, but that as things stand we were subject to innumerable hindrances from the magistrates of the districts, who in hindering us would be only doing their duty as things now stand . . . Mr M. in a very friendly manner desired me to state everything we wanted in a private letter to him, and said that he would privately communicate with Sir G. Barlow upon the subject and then give me his best advice. I have no doubt the government will give us all that they can.

Carey to Ryland, Dec. 25, 1805

. . . This year God has graciously blessed us with an increase of thirty persons, who have been baptised and received into the Church, viz. 27 native and 3 Europeans. Some of them have met with considerable opposition, and have had much of the malevolence of their ungodly neighbors to encounter, but have been hitherto upheld. The Church now consists of between 70 and 80 members in full communion. We hope soon to divide into four, two or three of which we hope to see native pastors ordained.- -

It has long been a favourite object with me to fix European Brethren in different parts of the country, at about two hundred miles apart, so that each shall be able to visit a circle of 100 miles radius, and within each of these circuits to place native Brethren at proper distances, who will till they are more established be under the superintendence of the European Brethren situated in the center. Our Brethren concur with me in this plan.

In consequence of this I thought it would be desirable to have leave of Government for them to settle, and preach without control in any part of the country. The Government look on us with a favourable eye, and owing to Sir G. Barlow, the Governor General's being up the country, Mr. Udney is Vice President and Deputy Governor. I, therefore, went one morning, took a breakfast with him and told him what we were doing and what we wished to do. He in a very friendly manner desired me to state to him, in a private Letter all that we wished, and offered to communicate privately with Sir G. Barlow on the subject and inform me of the result. I called on him again last week when he informed me that he had written upon the subject and was promised a speedy reply. God grant that it may be favourable. I know that Government will allow it, if their powers are large enough.

We have long since found a plan for translating the Bible into all the Languages of the East and have carried some of them on to a considerable extent at our own expence. But a Plan is now before Government (privately) to assist us by encouraging a publick subscription for that purpose. I trust it will take effect. We are engaged by the Asiatic Society & College of Fort William to translate the Hindu Books and print them, for which we have an allowance of 300 Rupees per month, and the whole profit of the sale. Sir John Anstruther has written to all the learned Societies in Europe to recommend the work.

Carey to Ryland, Apr. 27, 1808

My Dear Bro.

I received yours, (I think of Sept. last but the letter being at Serampore and I at Calcutta I cannot refer to the date) and one from Brethren Fuller and Sutcliffe. You can scarcely think the pleasure which letters from any of you afford us, as we therein see the interest which you feel in our labours. I perceive that you have been filled with fears on our account, and, as I suppose you have before this received the accounts sent by the Gen. Stuart, you have no doubt been in still greater alarm. Be not cast down on our account. The cause in which we are engaged is the cause of God and must prevail. I think, however, that a petition to Parliament might be presented, praying respectfully for leave to settle Missionaries, and for them to be allowed to pursue their labours among the Natives (subject in all civil matters to the laws of the country). I doubt not but with a little exertion, a million of signatures might be procured to such a petition, and I think the time to present it will be when the renewal of the charter comes before Parliament. In the meantime, however, do not think that we are concealed or afraid to shew ourselves, or to avow our work. Bro. Marshman and I waited twice on Lord Minto a little time ago, presented him with specimens of the translations, and solicited his subscription to them. He assured that the would cheerfully have subscribed if his political situation would have permitted it. Bro. M. then wrote a letter requesting his subscription to a translation of one of the works of Confucius which he has translated from Chinese, and is publishing in aid of the translations of the Bible. His Lordship wrote a very polite reply and subscribed for ten Copies. A subscription for this work is filling up well among all the higher officers of Government, and Bro. M. is now going from house to house to get subscriptions for this work and for the translations of the Bible. You will be surprised to learn that the Secretary Edmonston who raised up the late storm, has subscribed 300 Rupees for the translations of the Bible, besides subscribing to the other work. You will see the reason of this application from my letter to Bro. Fuller.

Carey to Jabez, undated but arrived in Amboyna Sept. 10, 1814

. . . new charter granted to the Christian Missions . . . are permitted to come out and settle for the purpose of instructing the natives in the Gospel. The battle was a hard fought one in the House of Commons. Mr. Prendergast asserted some gross falsehoods of me in the house but the spirit of the country could not be withstood; about nine hundred petitions were presented to Parliament to obtain this object, some them signed by a thousand or more persons.

TAKE ADVANTAGE OF EVERY OPPORTUNITY

Carey to the Society, Aug. 5, 1794

. . . but Mrs. Udney at Malda being very ill, thro grief on account of the Death of her Son, and his Wife, at Calcutta, who were both drowned in crossing the River in the Night. Mr. T. was sent to attend her. I was remarkable that Mr. Udney of Malda had just begun to erect two Indigo Manufactories at some distance North of Malda but without having any persons to Superintend them, he, therefore, engaged Mr. T. to take the oversight of one, and wrote to me to superintend the other. This appeared to me such a remarkable appearance of providence, so unexpected, unsought for, and furnishing us ample supplies for our Wants, and at the same time opening so large a Field for witnesses, putting us each in a state of direct or indirect influence over more than 1,000 people, that I could not hesitate a moment in concluding it to be the Hand of God. I, therefore, left my unfinished House, and Farm and set out to Malda, about 250 Miles. My place is about 30 Miles further North, and Mr. T. 16 or 17 further than me . . . the name of my Place is Mudnabati, that of Mr. T, Moypauldiggy. - Here then is the principal Seat of the Mission; and if any lose Caste for the Gospel we have good and profitable employment for them. Mr. Udney allows us each 200 Rupees per Month, Commission upon all the Indigo we make, and next year promises to present us each with a fourth Share of our respective Works.

In consequence of which I now inform the Society that I can subsist without any further assistance from them; and at the same time sincerely thank them for the exertions they have made, and hope that what was intended to support my Wants, may be appropriated to some other Mission. At the same time it will be my Glory & Joy to stand in the same near relation to the Society as if I needed supplies from them; and to maintain the same Correspondence with them.

Carey to Sutcliffe, Calcutta, Feb. 11, 1807

. . . After the disposition of Govt. to prevent our settling subordinate mission stations in their territories had been sufficiently manifested to show us the impropriety of attempting it under present circumstances; it one day occurred to my mind that the present was a fit opportunity to make a trial to introduce the Gospel into the Burman Empire, which lies east of Bengal, separated from it by impassable forests, and including the kingdom of Ava, Pegu, and Arakan. We had thought of this attempt before, but it only appeared as a distant object, and almost out of reach; but on my, now, mentioning it to Bros. Marshman and Ward, they thought the attempt eligible under present circumstances. The matter was, therefore, proposed to all our Brethren, and heartily approved; Brethren Mardon and Chater were chosen as the most fit persons to engage therein and after a proper time, accepted the call. Sisters M. and C. heartily agreed, likewise to the proposal. We thought if prudent, however, for our Brethren to go first and spend a few months there, and afterwards return and, if nothing made it absolutely improper, take their wives thither with them. Our Sisters were also just expecting to be confined in child bed.

{Carey follows this with the statement that they sailed and thinks they have arrived.}

. . . We have, besides making this a regular matter of prayer in our constant addresses to the throne of Grace, appointed an hour, the first Friday evening in every month, for the express purpose of seeking the divine blessing on this undertaking. This is a large empire, as you may see on the account of Col. Symm's embassy thither; I hope, if we can obtain proper men from England, that we shall be able to send Missions also to Malacca, Cambodia, Cochin China, and the western part of China; Diligent, mild, preserving, godly men are wanted for that purpose.

You must not, however, suppose that no attempts are making in Bengal; our native brethren are constantly employed; Six of them have a monthly allowance from us, and are continually out as itinerant preachers.

Carey to Morris, Feb. 7, 1806 Calcutta

There are materials for two, if not three more new Churches which I hope to see soon organized, one in Jessore, one at Ramkrishnapore, opposite Calcutta, on the other side of the River. Bro. Ward, more than three years ago, went to that Village to see our friend, Mr. Cunningham. On this occasion he went into the Market place, and distributed a few pamphlets, having but one New Testament, he left that at a shop for the use of the village, telling the shopkeeper to put it into the hands of any one who could read it. One of these papers fell into the hands of a devotee whose name is Jugummath, he employed a neighbor named Krishna to read it. This Krishna got information about it, and afterwards read it frequently to a few neighbors; the consequence was, that God begins a work of grace upon the hearts of several, and carried it on long without our knowing any thing of the matter: Sometime ago they came to Serampore when, having given satisfactory proofs to the Church of the work in their souls, seven of them were baptised, viz. Jugummath, and Krishna, with their wives, another man, named Goverham and his wife, and a . . . called Sebuhunam. Another member of the Church has since settled in that village, named Baluk-nam, so that their present number is eight, and four more at the same place shew hopeful signs of a work upon their hearts. Two of these four, A man and a woman, who had lived in a state of concubinage, previous to this change were married by me on Saturday last. This is the first instance of a couple married by us before they were joined to the Church, and is an action sufficiently abominable in the sight of all Hindus. Should these people be formed into a separate Church, it is highly probable that our Bro. Krishna, the first convert in Bengal (for I do not mean the Krishna just Baptised) will be their Pastor; He is a truly valuable man, grows in Scripture knowledge, and preaches Christ with great boldness. -

Carey to Sisters, May 4, 1810, Calcutta

. . . There has, of late, been a great awakening among the European Soldiers in several Regiments now in India. Bro. Chamberlain has baptised near fifty, mostly belonging to one Regiment. There are thirteen now in Fort William, who are under hopeful impression, who constantly attend worship at our Chapel in Calcutta. One of them, who has been long under very strong convictions is a native of Flower near Daventry, and another from the neighborhood of Bedford. Thus the Lord takes these people from a Land of Gospel light, to an land of gross Idolatry, and there reveals his grace to them.

Carey to Fuller, Jan. 20, 1811

. . . a glorious work was carried on among the Soldiers of the M. 22 Reg. under the ministry of Bro. Chamberlain. The whole of these Soldiers with several belonging to the 14th Reg. who belonged to the church at Calcutta, went some months ago on an expedition against the Isle of France. We have not yet heard from them, nor is the result of the expedition yet known. Our Brethren, should the island be taken, will probably be stationed there. If so, I consider their going thither as the introduction of the gospel into that Island. They are active men. One of them was called to the work of the ministry among them, and (chosen) as pastor of that their little church. He has good ministerial abilities, and will I trust be a useful man.

I have not heard from Rangoon since my last. That country is in a distracted state through war with the Siamese, and the unrelenting oppressions of its own government. Bro. Chater is here, waiting for an opportunity of returning. Since his arrival here two pamphlets have been printed in the Burman language, and if he stays long enough, we shall begin to print the Gospel by Matthew.

Carey to Sutcliffe, Calcutta, Mar. 20, 1811

Would to the Lord we had more men fit to engage in more missions. An Expedition has just sailed hence to take the Island of Java. We have more than one invitation, from those immediately under Govt. to send a mission there, and it has been said to us that the very reasons which have been urged against the policy of Missions in India, would be urged for them at Java . . . I greatly rejoice at the formation of the London Society for the sending the Gospel to the Jews.

Carey to Ryland, Nov. 17, 1813

This week we received a Letter from Government offering to afford facilities for the passage of any missionaries we might wish to send to Amboyna. This was in consequence of a representation from W.B. Martin Esq. who is the President there. About two months ago, I received a letter from Mr. Martin pressing us to send Missionaries thither. He observes to me that there are 20,000 native Christians there, with schools, places of worship, and everything that can be desired to afford facility of instruction, but no men to give Christian instruction. We are quite at a loss to know whom to send. We have thought of Bro. Rowe, but if he should carry himself with cold-hearted inflexibility towards the Malay that he did towards the Bengali, he would assuredly be murdered by them. I think, however, we shall try him. My mind is a little relieved by my son Jabez's offering himself last night to go to Amboyna. Jabez is articled to an attorney and has a very promising prospect if he pursues it, as it regards the world. This he must sacrifice if he goes to Amboyna. I am overjoyed at his proposal, as his conduct has for the last year and half given such satisfaction to every one as to leave no reasonable doubt of his conversion. I have, notwithstanding I heartily wish to see him sacrifice everything to the cause of God, thought it duty to set before him the whole of the prospects he sacrifices, and of the inconveniences and privations he must expect in the work of God that he may not engage in the building of a tower without having counted the cost. Jabez is active, and of a conciliating temper, and would, I trust, be useful there: My Brethren do not yet know of his offer, they only know generally that he has once or twice expressed his preference of the work of the Lord to every other work.

The openings of providence or rather the loud calls of providence, are now very numerous, and are continually increasing, but the want of labourers especially such as we could wish, is severely felt, so much so, that I sometimes almost sink into discouragement. Yet I must acknowledge that the Lord has done great things for us, and far surpassed our expectations. The leaven may be perceived to ferment in every part of India.

I trust Bro. Robinson is settled in Java, he has baptised a good number of soldiers there. Bro. Chater will, I doubt not, be useful in Ceylon, and Bro. Aratoon Carapeit at Surat. Bro. Chamberlain occupies a most important station in the north of Hindustan, almost within sight of the Himalaya Mountains, the highest range in the world. Felix is expected here in a few days, but I cannot say why, I only know that he is sent by the Government of Ava, and expects soon to return. Bro. Judson has joined the Rangoon mission: he is one of the right stamp. We sent a Printing Press to Rangoon about a fortnight ago. All these movements of providence surely indicate some good result.

As to the translation and printing of the Scriptures, it goes on as fast as so vast and multifarious a work can be expected to do. If I could learn languages faster it would be more rapidly got through the press: but some of the languages are very difficult and differ so widely from others as to occasion me much hard labour, for every translation goes through my hand except the Burman and Chinese.

Within the last month facilities have been afforded of beginning a translation into three new languages, two of them are spoken on the banks of the Indus, the one extending from the sea northward four or five hundred miles, and the other beginning where that leaves off and extending to the Punjabi. The most southern of these is called Sindi, and the northern Wuch, or more properly speaking the province of Sindi is divided into these two parts. The other language is that of the Kassal's a nation of mountaineers lying on the Eastern border of Bengal near Sylhet, and ranging along the north of the Burman Empire. This nation has no written character, and I suppose the person we have obtained, a Woman, is the only person in the country who can either read or write.

I hope Missionaries will come out, and that obstructions will be removed out of their way. But let them come, expressly for new countries, Siam, Cochin China &ct., &ct., where missions are not yet established, this being the very thing for which they are requisite. Give my love to all who know me.

I am very affectionately yours,
W. Carey

Carey to C. Stuart, M.D., Nov. 30, 1813

The work of the Lord in this country now embraces such a number of objects that I sometimes wonder at its magnitude, and stand humbled at my own unprofitableness while I am obliged to acknowledge the hand of the Lord in the success granted to every part. So has the Lord blessed our feeble undertakings that there is now a chain of stations belonging to this Mission extending nearly from the Himalaya mountains in the north, to Ceylon in the south, and from Java to Bombay, and even the Isle of France, East and West, the particulars of which you see in our printed circular letter.

About a fortnight ago we were applied to by the government to send men to Amboyna to superintend the schools on the Molucca Islands. This is a vast opening, Mr. Martin, the President there lately wrote to me pressing us to send Missionaries thither, and stating that the number of professing Christians there was not less than 20,000, with places of worship, schools, and every predisposing encouragement to expect success, but not ministers. We intend to send some one or more thither, and have written Brother Rowe to undertake it. My third son, Jabez, who is articled to an Attorney at Law, has also offered himself for this work. Jabez is, I trust, truly converted, and appears now to be decidedly on the Lord's side, as it respects the work of extending the knowledge of the Gospel.

Carey to Sister, July 20, 1814

The Cause of the Lord prospers with us. I last Lord's Day baptised eight Soldiers in H.M. 24th Reg. There is a Church in that Regiment of nearly one hundred members. They were in communion with us, but are now a distinct Church.

MISCELLANEOUS STRATEGIES

Without giving details, Carey alludes to various strategies for missions that complimented other things being done. Literacy training, medical aid, the practice of church discipline to keep the Indian church pure, house to house discipleship and evangelism, and agricultural improvement promoted the good of India and thereby the work of missions. In addition, the idea of allowing a missionary to enter a country based upon other skills than missions was promoted by Carey. This resembles the current movement in missions of entering a country as an engineer, English teacher, social worker, or other professional and then performing the work of a missionary in conjunction with that primary job.

Carey to Society, Hooghly River, Jan.10, 1799

Neighbouring Gentlemen have often supplied us. Indeed considering the distance we are from Medical assistance the great expensiveness of it - far beyond our ability - and the number of wretched afflicted objects whom we continually see, and who continually apply for help, we ought never to sell a pennyworth. Bro. Thomas has been the Instrument of saving numbers of Lives - This House is constantly surrounded with the Afflicted and the Cures wrought by him would have gained any Physician or any surgeon in Europe the most extensive reputation. - We ought to be furnished . . . by with at least Half a Hundred pounds of Jesuit's Bark - Other medicines we have plenty of for some time to come.

Carey to Fuller, Mar. 14, 1806, Calcutta

A few weeks ago nine members were detached from our church to form a new one at or near Dinajpur over which our beloved Bro. Fernandez is ordained Pastor. Notwithstanding this, and the expulsion of several for dishonourable conduct we have now eighty two members, all in full communion except six who are under suspension. But concerning most of whom we have hopes.

Carey to Fuller, April 20, 1808

Felix, who had before studied medicine, has introduced the Vaccine Inoculation there *{Rangoon}*, and has vaccinated the family of the Mayeraon Viceroy.

Carey to Fuller, March 25, 1813

{Difficulties with the government. The charter of the East India Company allowed them to send home all people not associated with the East India Co. Three of the missionaries had been ordered to England (Johns, Robinson, and Lawson). Carey argued that they had value to the India on other grounds than being a missionary.}

In the case of Lawson this was easy, for his abilities as an artist, and the advantage his ability would be to Oriental Literature was plausible. It would have, however, answered no purpose to have forbade Bro. Johns' abilities as a medical man or as a Chymist.

Carey to Jabez, Jan. 20, 1816

{Carey urges his son, Jabez, to win converts and then plant churches.}

I recd. yours with the report of the Schools and the secretary's letter to you in return. You have exceedingly gratified me by these communications and especially by the account of your having begun to preach in Malay. I hope you will be enabled to persevere in that work and in every other endeavour to convince the inhabitants of those islands of their sinful state and lead them to the church for salvation. Whatever you can do by translating simple and useful books, especially upon religious subjects, from English into Malay, I hope you will do and I am pretty sure that I shall have no great occasion to press this upon you. I trust the love of Christ will constrain you to do this, and everything else within the compass of your ability and opportunities to promote the best interests of the people among whom the providence of God has placed you. Should any of them be truly converted I hope you will baptise them and form them into a gospel church and watch over their interests in the Lord. The Malays of those islands are by the Providence of God committed to your charge. I expect but little from the labours of the Dutch ministers.

Carey to Jabez, Nov. 23, 1816

. . . I wish you to stay in Amboyna, at all events if it be possible. Your way of doing good may at first appear to be shut up but it will gradually open. Teach the people publickly and from house to house holding out to them the free tidings of Salvation through the Redeemer's Blood and teaching them to observe all things which he has commanded them. Have nothing to do with the Dutch or any other National church. National Churches are unknown in the word of God. Collect a church of true believers as soon as God gives you proper materials and nourish that church in the words of faith and sound holiness. Go forward in your work with holy disinterested zeal like Paul, and God will assuredly be with you and bless you. As for Mr. Kamm, be thankful he was the aggressor and not you; do not retaliate on him even in your mind. Take care not to do to him as he has done to you but cordially forgive him and pray for him. If you can unite with him in any plan to do good, do so, and do him all the good you possibly can. I fear his loose notions of church government will prove a millstone on the neck of his usefulness. If your resources fail, which I expect will be the case when the English leave the Island, it will be necessary to point out to us by what channel you can receive supplies. Perhaps the best way will be through Batavia and it is not unlikely that the house of Jesson and Co. - whom you know at Serampore - may be the best. Write about this and state your circumstance and the probable extent of your wants.

Carey to Jabez, Dec. 7, 1818

{Jabez has now moved and is in route to Ajmere. This letter was sent in care of Rev. J. Rowe in Digga near Patna.}

. . . The prospect before you is glorious and the work very great. You will have great need or prudence and firmness, both as it respects yourself and your Work, but keep your eye steadily upon the object and embrace every opportunity of doing good and I have no doubt but God will ultimately crown your undertaking with success.

I dined with Lord Hastings the Saturday before last when he wished me particularly to write to you to follow the direction of Sir David Ochterlony about setting up Schools; as he would be the best judge of the proper time to do it and the proper place where; you will I am sure do this with pleasure as it respects attempts to preach to the natives, I recommend you not to attempt to collect publick congregations yet. Converse in private with as many persons as your can, and recommend the Gospel to them and where you have opportunity (of) giving a Gospel to anyone with prospect of its being read, give one, but it is probable that any attempts to collect large congregations at present would defeat the very end you aim at. In private conversation be peculiarly serious and recommend Christ as the only Saviour of Sinners and look up with fervent prayer to God for a blessing.

Carey to Sisters, March 4, 1820, Calcutta

I am now engaged in promoting the establishment of an agricultural society - Indio. I have had several conversations with Lord and Lady Hastings about it, who both of them encourage it much. I was with Lady Hastings yesterday a couple of hours about it. She is uncommonly for its forming. This if it can be accomplished will be a great blessing to India.

Mission Support

Missions pertains to God's use of people to carry the gospel message to a lost World. That ministry requires support—prayer for God's power and money to take care of the human needs. Even prior to the formation of the Baptist Missionary Society Carey considered the needs for missionary endeavors and wrote about prayer and paying for missions in his *Enquiry*. He called the rich to give generously while modest members of congregations offer a penny or more a week as able.[1]

Carey embarked on the mission to India thinking through the idea of support more fully and developed new ideas specific to his situation. He wrote to the Society with detailed plans and requests. Carey engaged in active self-support as a teacher, Indigo planter, and publisher. The spreading of the good news could not be tossed aside for lack of means.

In addition, Carey needed and pleaded for prayer support and new missionaries to sustain the work. He sought support from unusual sources using the government, other missionaries, and the population at large to promote the pursuit. Subscriptions were solicited for schools and publications. Carey tirelessly pursued any means available to ensure the success of God's work in India and the surrounding countries. No stone was left unturned.

To Carey's credit, his plans not only involved spending but also economizing on the mission field. Carey demanded good stewardship and along with Ward and Marshman developed a scheme for getting the most out of each pound, dollar, and rupee. By establishing a family communal concept, the missionaries required fewer servants, pooled funds for better buying power, and served one another's needs.

Carey's proposals on support may be considered archaic now, but one must credit the missionary and his friends with creativity and initiative in discovering and maintaining ways of keeping the work alive. Surely a reading of Carey's thoughts on missions support can spur us in our own attempts to encourage missions in our day.

CAREY'S PLAN FOR SUPPORT

Carey to Fuller, June 17, 1796, Mudnabati

With respect to printing the Bible I fear the time of printing is distant enough; as in the aforementioned case at Debhatta as here we were perhaps too Sanguine - but tho means have hitherto failed we are as much resolved as ever to give our all to that work . . . I think it will be [better] for at least a Hundred pounds per annum to be remitted hither by the Society which shall be applied to the purpose of printing the Bible, and educating the Youth [and what we do shall be done as a contribution to the Society.]

Carey to Society, Dec. 28, 1796, Hooghly River

Should those who believe in Christ Join us by a publick reception of the Lord's Supper with us, they would immediately be outcasts from society. It, therefore, behooves us to devise some means for their support without being scattered all over the Country and exposed to publick derision, on the one hand, and without their being idle and useless members of the Community on the other.

This also is a situation so central that had we sufficient Men and proper means the Gospel might with ease, and small expence be sent from hence through all Hindustan, Persia, Bhutan, Assam, and what are generally called the Rajmahal Hills - on the west of the Ganges, and was a proper plan adapted, all the Educations necessary for this extensive design might be obtained in one situation in this Country, and a connection with the Mission here invariably, and regularly maintained.

Carey to Fuller, June 22, 1797

An acquaintance which I have formed with J. Rapburg, superintendent of the Company's Botanic Garden, and whose Wife is daughter to a Missionary on the coast may be of future use to the Mission, and makes that investment of vegetables more valuable.

{Carey describes the issues faced when sending materials to them. All must go through the Custom's house. He instructs the Society to include invoices and send copies to him. Some books and cutlery have been there for months.}

You some time ago mentioned a wish to contribute regularly to our assistance; but have sent no account to what amount, except for 1795. I, having drawn on the Society, it may raise some Jealousy up in Mr. Thomas's mind if they do not make him an allowance or otherwise, say what he is to expect. This I think I may venture to say that if you would determine to pay his allowance to his creditors in England, on his account, it might tend more to the advantage of him, and also to the honour of the Mission than any other method.

Carey to Ryland, July 6, 1797, Mudnabati

I hope the Society will send out more Missionaries to our help. The Harvest is great and from the amazing events which are now taking place, it is highly probable that nothing which is done will be done in vain. I also think some regular plan for a Missionary settlement should be thought of. I mentioned one last year. I think some such plan should be adopted, and perhaps it would be advisable to erect a small Indigo Manufactory on account of the Mission, not exceeding two Vats, in the best situation we could choose out. A Plan of this kind I intend to send to Bro. Fuller with my reasons for recommending it.

Carey to Ryland, Serampore, January 17, 1800

Serampore, the place at which we are, is an handsome town, belonging to the Danes: it stands on the banks of the Hooghly River about seven Cose from Calcutta, northward: and is the city of refuge for all who are in debt, and afraid of their creditors. On this account a degree of disgrace is attached to an inhabitant thereof, and indeed the natives appear to me to be some of the vilest of the vile. There are also many native Portugese who are full as bad. Europeans are so transitory in their abode here that little can be said about them: the most respectable are the Danes: and the Governor, Col. Bie has been peculiarly attentive to us.

We have a prospect of a tolerably good congregation of Europeans: I counted about thirty persons last Lord's day: among whom was Major Prowle, the officer I once mentioned at Barrackpore which is on the opposite side of the River, just facing this Town. He has constantly attended, and generally brings over some other officers with him. I have had several conferences with the natives, the particulars of which Bro. Ward is writing to Bro. Fuller, and as everything, being new, strikes him more forcibly. I think he will be more particular than I should have been. I, therefore, shall not say anything more respecting them.

I shudder at the heavy expences which we shall necessarily subject our Brethren in England to, and can only say that they are unavoidable. Tho I did to the best of my knowledge, and indeed acted originally for myself in the purchase of Kidderpore, yet should the Society think me to blame, I am willing to sink my own money which I have laid out, and which was all I had in the world. But this is gone - and the plane was all I had in the World - and the plane will require 30,000 Rupees more to clear it. Tho it would have suited me on account of its nearness to Mudnabati, yet it would never be salable to any body else, and the Vats for manufacturing are not erected. There is only the place, and an unsalable Crop on the ground. I believe it would have answered our purpose could we have all settled there, but providence forbad it.

The very heavy Rent we should have to pay here makes it advisable to purchase an House: which we have done, but this is an additional expence of 6,000 Rupees, and the purchase will require so much of our Money as to reduce us to very great distress, unless the Society send us a sum immediately.- - We need 3,000 Rs. For Kidderpore debt, 6,000 for our House, 4,000 for printing the Bible which is 13,000 Rupees, or 1,625 Pounds sterling, besides our support which I think cannot come under 750 pounds a year. We intend to teach a

School, and employ our Press which we hope may bring us in 2,250 Pounds per Annum. We have thought, and in this we are joined by those in the Country who wish well to our undertaking, that it will be well if the Society can agree to send all their money to this Country in dollars, and put it in the Company's funds, where it will produce 12 per cent interest. If you had 5,000 pounds to send into the Country it would clear off our encumbrances, which I calculate as follows.

Due Mr. Udney on account of Kidderpore	2,400
Bot a House _____ for _____	6,000
to compleat print 1000 copies of Bible	4,000
My own money expended for the Mission	1,000

13,400 or at 2/6 per Rupee, 1,675 Pounds sterling, then would remain 3,325 Pounds, which if by the sale of the Bible or any other means we could make up 4,000 - would produce us 480 Pounds per Annum. Sending dollars also will be attended with a good profit - for the difference between sending 5,000 pounds in dollars at 4/6 each and drawing for that amount will be 926 pounds at only two Rupees. The gain may be fairly estimated at 1,000 Pounds so that 5,000 Pounds sent out in dollars would pay off every encumbrance, print the Bible, purchase a good House and Garden for the Mission, in a situation where we shall be always safe and to which more missionaries may be sent without fear, and will also raise a Fund for the maintenance of the Mission, of nearly or quite 500 Pounds per Annum. This would make it comfortable both to us and to you for the mission would then be established without any more labour of begging and we should have a fund to resort to without the very precarious expedient of trading, viz. having Goods from England - or of drawing on England, and without any danger of loss. Our success may be long delayed tho all our Brethren are very hearty in their work and it is impossible to say that the publick mind will not be tired out, if hope be much longer delayed. Those also who have hitherto been pillars to this work may soon be cut off by death, and the work might thus fall to the ground: but in case of our having such funds in this Country the mission would be established. I have written thus to you, and to several others lest any of the letters should miscarry: and because we all think this plan so important: Money also is so scarce here that any one will advance it for the best bills in Europe.

Carey to Fuller, Feb. 5, 1800, Serampore

I fear dear Bro. Pearce is dead. You, Bro. Ryland and a few of the most active to provide funds for the Mission may soon die; and the work may fall through for want of active persons who will feel interested in it as you do.

The Publick mind may tire soon, especially if success is much longer delayed. In that case the Mission must be broken up for want of funds to support it and then all that is done will be lost.

Now if you can send out all your Funds to this Country, say 5,000 pounds it would pay all our Debts and be a fund for our support. Nay, I cannot say that 4,000 pounds might not suffice for the difference between drawing for 4,000 pounds at 2/8 per Rupee the present rate of exchange and receiving that sum in dollars will be at least 700 pounds. So that now we have paid for the House we should be nearly able to part out the 4,000 after Debts are paid which would be 480 pounds annum without touching the principal which with our School, and the profits of our Printing Press would, I trust, be sufficient for us. I think this would establish the Mission, so far as pecuniary help would be requisite, and you might then turn your thoughts to a new mission or to the enlargement of this, as it might appear eligible.

I have written so much about our temporal concerns in all our Letters, because I fear some of them (may) miscarry and also because I much wish to see this Mission settle on a permanent foundation.

Carey to Sutcliffe, Serampore, June 29, 1801

. . . We received the Dollars safe by Mr. Short who arrived a few Days ago to my great surprise. He also produced a Note for 100 pounds which he is to pay us at a month after Sight. Providence having appeared very remarkably for our support. We have come to a determination to put by the whole of this money as a fund for the future support, or extension of the Mission, as may be thought proper and have accordingly laid it out in Treasury Bills which bear an interest of 12 per cent. A Note on a Mr. John Rose sent out by Mr. King of Birmingham I have received but cannot find out Mr. Rose in Calcutta.

You will have heard long before this reaches you of the increase which God has graciously given us. We have baptised five Hindus; the last whose name is Gokul about three weeks ago and I hope his Wife who was a bitter persecutor of him a little time ago, may soon follow him. Very favourable symptoms appear on her. Krishna our first-born from among the Hindus, gives us much pleasure, both himself, and all his family are constantly talking to others about the ways of God, and we think seriously of putting Krishna out at Compound Interest, or as he is the fruit or interest of our Labours; encouraging his gifts to the uttermost that he may preach the Gospel to his countrymen.

. . . When you send again do think and send me one of Fuller's Letters on Socinianism, and one "Gospel, Its own Witness." A Dozen of each would soon be disposed of here and are greatly needed in this Land of Infidelity. Do also send me Mr. Ryland's three sermons at College Lane . . .

Carey to Fuller, Sept. 7, 1803

I mentioned to our Brethren what you wrote to me respecting supporting the mission for one year and presenting us with our own earnings. For my own part, I sincerely hope that such a step will never be taken. Our individual earnings may be very unequal and not proportioned to our ? and might therefore if given from the common stock occasion little uneasiness. The existence of the mission financially perhaps depends upon [as a mean] our having no private interest to serve but accounting all our publick stock. This prevents those separations which might take place if each looks to himself or his own family. Besides what have we to serve but the Mission and our gains are connected thereto, and as objects large enough to absorb all those gains. If they are a thousand times greater than they are pressed upon us on every side we shall find employment for all our funds of time, talents, and wealth to the end of our lives. We have, therefore, determined nothing upon the matter.

Carey to Sutcliffe, Calcutta, Aug. 22, 1805

{Carey lists the ten stations that the Mission has and then gives some clue as to his strategy for keeping them afloat.}

. . . Each station, if it could not do something to support itself would cost us 100 Rupees per month, and ought to be surrounded by ten subordinate stations occupied by native Brethren, each of which would cost Ten Rupees per month amounting to another 100 or 200 Rupees a Month for the whole. It is probable that sources of income for their maintenance may be opened, but these and many more such stations are absolutely necessary. Besides these expences Bibles, and Pamphlets will be wanted in much greater numbers than heretofore. We must look to you for much help, and we will ourselves contribute to the utmost of our Ability to the carrying forward of this Work. Some new sources of income are opening here which I shall mention bye and bye. But is it not possible to do much more in England? <u>Money must be turned into this Channel</u>. Would not an annual meeting in some central part of England, [say London] be of use to call the publick attention more to this point? The annual meetings of our Paedobaptist Brethren have this affect. Ought not more Ministers be engaged in the active part of the Society? I see that the whole rests on the few, Bro. Fuller, yourself, Dr. Ryland and one or two more. Were you to die who would be found that would take equal interest in the active parts of the work? Would it not be wise to get such men as Steadman, Burt, Saffery, Hinton, Blundell, Morgan, &ct. &ct., heartily engaged in it, and as it were broke in to it before your deaths. I think this is a very important object and should be attempted, and persevered in.

Carey to Sutcliffe, Calcutta , July 29, 1806

. . . We have, therefore, laid down an extensive plan which it is obvious can only be filled up by degrees, though it is highly desirable to do it as soon as possible. I fear you will be frightened at the calculated expence, though I think it very small compared with the object. Christians, however, must be very, very much more liberal, shall I say, nay ardently desirous of laying out themselves and their all for Christ, than they ever yet have done, as the Gospel will never be spread to any extent. The impact of "Ye are not your own, ye are bought with a price, therefore &ct." will I trust be more and more realised, and induce them to come, their Silver and their Gold with them to &ct. I consider the work of translating as the great work of my and Bro. Marshman's lives and that of superintending the printing as that of Bro. Ward's, besides our occupation for the support of the Mission, viz. the School, College, Translation & Publishing of the Hindu Shastras, &ct . . .

Carey to Sutcliffe, June 2, 1807, Calcutta

. . . It would be a good thing if you were to send us an acct. current every year - we have no advice respecting bills drawn on England, and know not whether they are paid or not. Those persons whose money we have received, of course come to ask us, but we can say nothing about it.

Carey to Ryland, Nov. 15, 1815

We have through several hands received the very afflicting news of the death of dear Bro. Fuller. I feel perhaps improperly depressed at the event, as it relates to the Mission on several accounts which I shall endeavor to state to you; but as it relates to himself his reward is great in Heaven, and I feel that no eulogium on him can add to his praise in the churches; the most that his friends can do is to weep over their own loss and that of the cause of God. I hope a good account of his life will be written by someone who will be able to do justice to his memory.

. . . We all sensibly feel the loss, and perhaps no one more than myself. I loved him very sincerely. There was scarcely another man on the Earth to whom I could so compleatly lay open my heart as I could to him.

I will not mention some things relating to the Mission which lie with much weight upon my mind, and you being the only person now living of those to whom my heart was formerly joined by the tenderest ties, I shall as long as we live freely disclose all my feelings to you.

1. I sincerely hope no childish aspiring to distinction and honour will occasion any difficulty in the choice of a secretary to the Society. Some hints which we have received in different letters make me apprehensive lest this should be the case. It will be distressing indeed if at a time when everyone ought to feel the importance of the most hearty union, bickerings, strife, and ambition for office should take place. There can be no want of proper persons, but those who are ambitious to shine should not be suffered to make that distressing circumstance which makes the selection of a secretary necessary, the occasion of doing so. (Qn. Would it not be advisable to enlarge your Committee still further? I fear there are but a few men in N-shire who are able to direct the affairs of the Mission.)

2. I am afraid lest Satan should take occasion under the pretence of Economy to lay fetters upon the work of God. The circumstances of the heathen world are such as absolutely to forbid the lessening the number of missions, and most pressingly to call for an increase of them. My fears on this head were awakened by a step which appears to have been taken even before dear Bro. Fuller's death, which by a letter from Bro. Ivimay to Bro. Lawson, I understand to be nothing less than the giving up the missions in the islands or some of them. A

letter written to us by Bro. Dyer, and signed also by Bro. Ivimay and Mr. Burls, does not go quite this length but yet strongly intimates the same thing. I hope nothing will be done precipitately of this nature. Bro. Trowt (who I find has been written to, to remove from Samarang, is not an expensive man). So far as I can learn, he lives upon as little as Bro. Robinson does, and no one can think him profuse. I doubt not but ways will open to lighten the burden, but if not, your great point must be to increase your collections. Bro. Trowt is likely to help himself a little by means of a school Te Udhiputy of Samarang, viz. the Sovereign prince, who had two sons educated at Serampore, has been to visit him and is desirous of encouraging the extension of useful knowledge among his subjects. He has probably by this time sent one of his sons to him (Trowt) as he proposed it. We cannot hold churches, viz. be preachers in national churches with a salary, as the missionaries of The M. Society do, because we cannot sprinkle infants. Otherwise Bro. Robinson and Trowt, and Jabez also might have had the situations and salaries which three of their men now occupy. Their men can wear gowns or supplices, and read the church liturgy and be under the direction of Carnal man, but I bless God our brethren cannot. You must not shrink from the burden and I doubt not but God will find supplies.

3. The work of translating the Scriptures is now a work almost surpassing calculation, and must be supported. God has bestowed upon us facilities for doing this work which are possessed by no other persons on the earth. The great advantages derived from employing natives from the different countries; the large establishment of those natives which we already have: the intimate dependence of the language of India upon the Sanskrit; the habit of translating which we must have in some measure as gained by so many years labour in that work; and the ease with which the versions can be printed by us, call loudly on us not to relinquish this work in any part of it. Bro. Marshman is preparing a memoir of translation. I shall, therefore, only say that I trust it will not sink for want of support. I desire to persevere inflexibly in this work to the end of my life.

4. The last circumstances I shall mention. We have conveyed a short notice of in a letter lately sent. I mean that of making all the missionary brethren dependent immediately on the Society for their support. This is what human nature makes necessary in the present enlarged state of the Mission. - While the mission confined to one station or to a few branching out from it, there was propriety in all the brethren receiving all their support through us: but as they increased this was attended with much difficulty. We are all brethren, all equal, but in many instances it was necessary for us to say, "Brother your expences have been too great this month, you have gone to unnecessary expence upon this or that head. You have not done this or that - or we wish such a thing had been done - or such a thing had not been done, &ct." The answer will of course be, who made you ruler over us? I shall not say whether we have always spoken with proper wisdom and tenderness. It would be wonderful if we had never erred. Nor shall I say whether what we have said has always been rightly received - but I do say that it would be much more for the advantage of the mission for

everyone to receive his salary immediately from the Society. And this appears to be the best time to do it as there was never a time when we had less of disagreeable collision than now. We shall write more largely upon this head soon, till that time let this be only considered as a private communication.

Carey to Jabez, March 13, 1820

Your last letter gave me considerable pain, because you have certainly misunderstood me, or perhaps the fault was mine in not understanding you. I thought you had applied to borrow 200 Rupees more on credit of your house at Amboyna, which we must have been unable to meet for we have been obliged to borrow considerably to support our current expences.

I showed your letter to Bro. Marshman who immediately thought the house at Ajmere ought to be the property of the publick in the same way, and that the 200 Rupees should be immediately sent to you to put it in repair. We have not finally settled to whom the house should belong, I think to the Mission Society, and that your settling there should be considered as the founding of a Mission station there, to which the establishment of schools should be counted an appendage, and that a part of your salary should be paid by the Mission Society and part from the School Fund. This will enable us to face the publick with more confidence than if the whole belonged only to the schools. It is impossible to say whether the Mission Society will sanction this but we will run the risk, and be answerable for the expences as they now be.

MORAL, PRAYER, AND PERSONNEL SUPPORT

Carey to Society, from the Hooghly River boat trip to Calcutta, Jan. 10, 1799

{He gives information on the preaching, translation, and printing and then gives information on what a new Missionary should do.}

. . . We want more Missionaries. Men of mild Temper, good sense, and genuine love to our Lord, and Zeal for his Glory. Bro. Pearce wrote to me wishing me to advise how they should be sent out - There are not difficulties here except at their first landing, and I know of no serious ones then, but I advise that they come out Cabin Passengers in a Foreign Ship and immediately on their landing at Calcutta to procure a Boat, and a Servant who understands English - and having purchased a few necessary Articles for the Journey such as Bread, Wine, Biscuits, Beds, Mosquito Curtains, set to proceed immediately to Mudnabati without saying anything to any person about why they come into the Country. They will get all necessaries in one Day; and must be very careful not to put any confidence in their Servant who will infallibly cheat them - They should send a Letter up to me the moment they Land (by Post) and I would take care of their every difficulty with Government *{which}* will be got through afterwards if they behave peaceably . . .

Carey to Fuller, March 27, 1809

I feel much the kindness of the society in their making poor Mrs. Short an allowance for her support. It has never been in my power till now to testify my sense of the disinterested part she acted in coming out with us. I, however, now request that you will, in addition to what the Society allows her, request her to accept of a small donation of five pounds a year from me. I will pay that sum here, together with what you pay to my own relations to this publick stock here. She contributed her utmost to make my coming out here comfortable, and if I can contribute in even so small a degree to her comfort, I shall be gratified thereby.

Let me have a share in your prayers, you are not often forgotten by me. - I suffer much through the decay of my sight. I am forced to use spectacles alas of high magnifying power.

Carey to Fuller, Dec. 1809

I have received several Letters lately from you, for which accept my thanks. Few things afford me more pleasure than your letters do. I, however, know that your numerous engagements must leave you but little time for epistolary correspondence, and by myself, judge of the difficulty you must have in corresponding so largely as you do. I also feel a pleasure when you write to any of our Brethren, especially our younger Brethren, as I know it contributes much to their encouragement. I wish you in particular, to write to Bro. Chamberlain to encourage him . . . I am not insensible of his natural temper, and of the great difficulty we have, more than once had to know how to act toward him, but I had forgotten that any report had been made to you on the subject. We, at one time felt very keenly, an account of some of the younger Brethren, and perhaps have expressed ourselves with (austerity), perhaps, also sometimes we have not been sufficiently tender towards them. I have always disapproved of some states which had a magisterial appearance, and I labored to the utmost of my power to bring about the present constitution of the mission, in which every station is independent of Serampore, and depends entirely on the Society. I am happy to say that this step has healed all our breaches, and that the younger Brethren are now employed in their different stations. I hope contented and happy. The sending an account of the amount of expenditures every year at each station, will in my opinion be a stronger check upon any want of accuracy, than any remonstrances from us could be; and will save us that very disagreeable part of our work, to which we were, as things formerly stood, bound by conscience. Bro. Chamberlain is not, as you intimate in one of your letters, excluded from our present constitution, nor is any Brother whatever. Indeed I am happy to say that Bro. C is one of the most active and successful of us all. He has this year baptised 33 European Soldiers . . .

I believe the number baptised within the last year, in all the Churches of Bengal, is sixty seven. Two or three of them have been excluded or suspended, but a greater number of those who had been formerly excluded, have given satisfactory proof of repentance, and have been re-admitted to the Lord's table. All the churches are supplied with pastors and have the Word regularly dispensed among them, and some new stations have been attempted, and old ones strengthened. Upon the whole, I cannot but rejoice in what the Lord has done and is now doing among us.

Carey to Burls, Jan. 3, 1821, Serampore

I regret to say that, as you will see by the report lately sent to England, we have been obliged to relinquish several of the versions of the Bible at present for want of funds. To me this is a very distressing thing but I trust God will appear and find ways and means by which that very, very important work may be carried onto its completion.

SELF-SUPPORT/BIVOCATIONALISM

Carey to Society, Jan. 11, 1796, Malda

{Carey has received a letter from the Society and some have complained about the Indigo business as a means of mission support.}

. . . I am from not having it by me, much incapacitated from answering it; and one part I acknowledge rather surprised me, I mean that respecting our engaging in employment for our Support - - I always understood that the Society recommended it, tis true they did not specify Indigo Business - - but the Trade in Timbers was recommended, and Cultivation of the Ground was also looked upon as eligible - - but I am astonished to find an Indigo Manufacturer called a Merchant - which is just like calling a Journeyman Taylor a Merchant. Were we proprietors the name might be proper but we have only had a Promise of a Share, and whether it will or will not be given we know not, nor do we trouble ourselves about it. We receive Wages, adequate to the maintenance of our Families; and now our Buildings are over. I think no line of Life could afford us more leisure, or Opportunity for doing good - - - to vindicate my own spirit, or Conduct. I should be very averse; it is a constant maxim with me that if my conduct will not vindicate itself, it is not worth vindicating - - but we really thought we were acting in Conformity with the universal wishes of the Society - - whether we are Indolent or laborious, or whether "the spirit of the Missionary is swallowed up in the pursuits of the Merchant" it becomes not me to say - but our Labours will speak for us. I only say that after my family obtaining a bare allowance - my whole Income, and some months more goes for the purpose of the Gospel in supporting persons to assist in the Translation of the Bible, write Copies, teach School, and the like. This is to me a certain and constant expence of 33 Rupees a Month - but this I rejoice in and would not lose the pleasure of it for 300 Rupees per Month. I only mention it to shew that the love of Money has not prompted me to engage in the plan that I have engaged in. I am indeed poor and shall always be so, till the Bible is published in Bengali, Hindustani, and the people want no further instruction . . ."

Carey to Fuller, June 22, 1797

. . . whether the Company will or will not molest us must be left to his care who holds the seven stars in his right Hand, and without whose permission a Sparrow does not fall to the ground, but that no human mean for our safety may be wanting I have it now in my power to engage in any line of Business, either nominal [that is I can take a dozen acres of Land, and cultivate a Row of Sugar Canes, and be called a Sugar Manufacturer; or any other Business for it is absolutely necessary to be nominally in some employment, if not really or actual which last I think will be necessary to a certain degree for our support; after the example of the Moravians; and in that case whoever comes may be denominated assistants to Mr. Thomas and myself on their first arrival; and as we are now permitted by the Company to live in the Country, and trade therein, and mutual covenants for that purpose are signed, we may with boldness pursue any line of conduct that may prosper - not to mention that I have reason to believe that we are respected by the Magistrates of the District who perfectly understand our errand. Indeed the judge of Diajpur expressed very great approbation of the translating the Bible . . .

Carey to Fuller, July 17, 1799, Mudnabati

You should also know that Europeans are not permitted to purchase or occupy more than 50 biggahs of Land, or about 20 acres, so that all Business is carried on by purchasing the produce of the Soil of the Natives and whoever engages in any Business must acquaint the Board of Trade therewith so that such a settlement as you propose for us to make, is impossible. I am, however, doing what will approximate as near to it as circumstances admit, if the Society approves of the Plan.

A little time ago I took a small Indigo Work near this place on my own Account. I took it of Mr. W. at the rate it stood out in his books, viz. with a Debt of 3000 Rupees lying on it. It was an appendage to Mudnabati but too distant to be of any use unless detached. My reasons were these. I have long thought that Mudnabati must be evacuated and have been expecting it every year. In that case it would be an asylum for my family. If I should [contrary to all expectation] remain here it would be a situation for my Sons in the neighborhood who are now large lads and must be brought up to Business. - Or if more Missionaries should arrive it might be converted into a Missionary settlement.

{On Sept. 28 the Indigo Works ceased because of inundation that destroyed the crop.}

Our difficulties also will not be small, but I am not discouraged if we are all of one Heart, and God grant his Blessing, all will be surmounted.

We are not necessitated to settle at Kidderpore (the name of the place I have taken) where I am erecting Houses, and other Buildings in expectation that our Brethren Ward and Brunsdon are not far off.

Carey to Sutcliffe, Apr. 8, 1801, Serampore

. . . We are waiting with considerable anxiety to hear whether our dear Society approve or not of the steps we have taken in purchasing the Mission House, keeping an English school for our support, &ct., &ct. - all of which we have given them an account. The Purchase was a heavy expence, but will be far cheaper and more convenient than hiring Houses, and as the whole Bible [Old and New Testament] will be printed for nearly the Sum which it was supposed it would require to print the New Testament alone. I hope our dear Friends will be able to answer the Bills drawn this year. We have a pleasuring prospect that our School will soon defray the current Expences of the Family. It increases more than we could have expected, and I hope we may look forward to some good Fruit being produced thereby of a spiritual kind. Should the Society send out more Missionaries, I would propose to them to have their Eye upon someone who would be capable, and willing to step into the School in case of the death of Bro. Marshman, and it will be necessary that he be a pious man who would have been capable of managing one of the first Boarding Schools in England. Bro. Marshman's Industry and hearty engagement in the Work is such as have raised the School to a good degree of Celebrity which must be maintained. Sister Marshman has also a School of Young Ladies which rises in reputation. I hope we may not be deprived of either of them for many years, but it would be well to provide against such an event. A Young Man thus qualified, especially if Married to a Woman thus qualified would be a great acquisition indeed. I hope you will be peculiarly careful respecting the Men you send out. They must be of mild accommodating temper to live peaceably in a common Family like ours, and they must not only be such who appear hearty in the Mission, but such who will not account it a hardship to be subject to Rules in all their conduct, and who will have no views of personal aggrandizement, but yet will labour diligently for the publick stock. I believe one of our family rules which forbids any Member of the Family to enter into Business on his private account, has done more than anything towards preserving our Peace, and I hope it will in no instance ever be broken in upon. This cuts off all ambitious Schemes, and yet secures industry in the body. Perhaps we may have not further occasion for help from England at present . . .

. . . A College has lately been instituted at Fort William upon a very extensive plan. Rev. D. Brown is Provost, Rev. C. Buchanan, Vice Provost and there are a number of Professors of all the Eastern Languages and the Sciences. Yesterday morning I very unexpectedly received a Letter from Rev. D. Brown, Rev. Buchanan attended, who with both Marquis Wellesley & and several Gentlemen of the Council, to Barrackpore just on the opposite side of the River from us. He invited me over to Gen. Posham's Bungalow to have some conversations upon the matter of the College, and about proposing to Marquis Wellesley to appoint me Professor of the Bengali language. Our Brethren thought that I ought to accept it, provided it did not interfere with the Mission, or break in too much upon my time. I had more scruples on account of my want of ability to fulfill such an engagement with propriety. I, however, went and we had much conversation upon the Subject. They thought that it would much contribute to the forwarding of our original plan; and that it would essentially serve the Mission. It would immediately introduce the Bengali New Testament into the College and any other Books also which I might recommend, and eventually would spread them into all parts of the Country. I pleaded my inability. They replied that (two or three Deists or Atheists excepted) there was no other person in Bengal who was qualified - and as the Morals of the Students must be well looked after, it would be a very improper thing to consign them to the management of such persons. On these considerations and others, such as the following, viz. that it would open a way to preach to the Hindus in Calcutta and its environs, and would put a number of respectable Hindus under my direction as Munshis, I agreed that they should propose me. What will result I know not. Should I be appointed it will bring about 600 Rupees a Month into the Family [I am not quite certain about the salary] and tho it would be an increase of expence yet it will put it in our power to enlarge our plans for publishing the Gospel, and will greatly relieve our Dear Society and friends in England, for whom we feel much in this time of almost Famine with them. Any of the Professors may if they please retire on a Pension of not less than 1/3 of their pay at the end of seven years.

Apr. 13 The Business of the Professorship is settled. Yesterday Rev. Buchanan came with the Governor of Serampore to our house to inform us of my appointment. . . . He informed our Brethren that when I was proposed to Marquis Wellesley he wished to be informed of two things. 1st. Whether I was well affected to Government. 2nd Whether I was capable of filling up the office properly. To both which they answered in the affirmative. To the first they might safely do it, but I very much doubt the latter. I will, however, do what I can. I was appointed by his Excellency as, in the character of, a Missionary, or in conjunction with the Mission so that our Friends in England may now be perfectly at ease respecting the safety of the Mission. For my own part I confess that I almost sink under the prospect. Without having seen College Discipline, to be called to so conspicuous a situation, [and in a College on so extensive a scale as that - I am credibly informed that the expence of it equals that of the whole University of Cambridge. Just under the eye of Government and without Books to print in the Work except such as I be able to compose myself. Halbed's Grammar is nearly out of print, and only one part, [viz. English Bengali] of Forster's Vocabulary is yet published.

Carey to Fuller, Jan. 21, 1802

We have made ourselves trustees for the Baptist Society in England in both these purchases. *{Carey is speaking here of some land and a house.}* Our school increases. It is not yet fixed what I am to have for my salary in the College but advances are made from time to time. We might get something considerable by our Printing Press but our Fount of English is too small for us to undertake any considerable Work. We were applied too to print the last Vol. of the *Asiatic Researcher*. Rev. W. Brown has now applied to us to finish several School Books and in short we have more in that line than we can do.

{They print NT, grammars, and histories. Sale of the grammars recoup costs.}

These are sold off except a very few copies of the two first. Government took 100 copies of each for the College.

Carey to Ryland, Calcutta, June 23, 1803

Mr. Colebrooke, one the Judges of one of the Courts of Appeal and translator of four Vol. of Hindu laws from the Sanskrit Grammar follows Sir. W. Jones' system. He is also printing a Sanskrit Grammar. He is a Professor of Sanskrit & Hindu Law in the College and the first Sanskrit Scholar in the World. I suppose one Press would not print his collection of Sanskrit Books in 100 Years - The *Vedas* which he has kindly offered to lend me to print from, would make about 20 Vol. Oct. of 500 pp. each, I mean merely the text for the Commentaries (without which they will be scarcely understood) would make it 100 such Volumes. We are making an application to Government or rather proposals to print them if Government will indemnify us for 100 Copies, at 4 Rupees the 100 Pages, several persons very high in office are friendly to the undertaking. It will be bread for the Mission.

Carey to Ryland, July 17, 1806

. . . By three Letters recd. from you by Bro. Marshman this week, I find that you are greatly distressed because we do not send more news and more accounts of the natural history, mythology, &ct. of Hindustan; You will soon have an authentic source of Information respecting the mythology, manners and customs of the Hindus in the *Ramayana*, the first volume of which will be sent to England by the next ships. I am afraid that the work will be stopped for a want of paper to print on, unless our order by the *Medusa* frigate be soon fulfilled. I hope the paper will be of the best quality. The Society has been egregiously cheated in that article. I suppose you know that Sir J. Anstruther (now in England) wrote to Sir Joseph Banks twelve months ago to forward a letter written by him, to recommend their work to all the literary societies in Europe. In India the Subscriptions has filled beyond our expectation. Sir G. Barlow, G.G. recommended it in a publick speech and subscribed for three copies. I hope the profits arising from this work manufactured by Satan, will enable us to support two or three stations to destroy his empire. I rejoice to say also that my enormous Sanskrit Grammar will accompany the *Ramayana* to England. It is printed, except a small part of the Index, and the Errata. The labour it has required has been great, but my situation demanded it. So much for these things.

Carey to Fuller, Aug. 26, 1806, Calcutta

Morris mentions another thing which had he not done it by way of conscience I should never have mentioned to any one. I mean my not contributing to the support of my dear afflicted Sister Mary. He blames me for giving my whole income to the mission and putting it out of my power to assist my relations saying that the Society cannot do it with propriety and several other things too long to mention here. It is not that I or my Brethren are inattentive to the wants of our relations that we have put it out of our power to assist them, but because it was necessary to lay down and adhere to the set of rules for the regulation of the mission, among these, "that all earnings shall go to the common stock and no one have any private property, except a small allowance for necessities," was one. And perhaps the rule on which the continuance of the Mission depends. Bro. Ward, Marshman, and myself think so. Now as we three contribute as much to the mission (I wish it were as much more) as all England and Scotland, and scarcely allow ourselves common necessities that we may save the cause . . .

Carey to Ryland, Jan. 20, 1807

. . . An order from the Court of Directors, has occasioned the new modeling of the College: this took place the beginning of this month. I was only teacher before, but am now appointed by the Gov. Gen. in Council, Professor of the Sanskrit and Bengali languages, with a Salary of 1000 Sica Rupees or 125 pounds a month. The date of my appointment is the first day of the present month. This is a great help to the Mission, thus the earth helpeth the women.

Carey to Sutcliffe, Calcutta, Feb. 11, 1807

. . . Till lately I was teacher of three languages in the College on a monthly Salary of 500 Rupees per Month; but on the 1st of January past I was, by the G. Gen. in Council appointed Professor of Sanskrit and Bengali Languages, (to which the Mahratta is added though not specified in the official Letter) with a monthly Salary of 1000 Rupees per Month. This will much help the Mission.

Carey to Sutcliffe, Mar. 31, 1812

{In this letter he repeats the calamity of losing seven people from the mission in various illnesses and the burning down of the printing office. He discusses the support of the mission.}

I have of late thought much about the future support of the Mission, and have endeavored to press the matter upon my Brethren. At present our supplies are drawn from my income and from the School, except a little from the Printing, but as most of the works we print are given away, we rather esteem the press as a vehicle of divine knowledge than of income. I have thought much of some kind of Cultivation of the Soil; but Europeans are prohibited from purchasing land. In a conversation I had some time ago with one of the members of the Supreme Council upon that subject I pointed out to him the advantage of planting Timber; and he then gave me one reason to hope that if we made an application to Govt., they would give us leave to purchase a thousand Biggahs for the purpose of planting Timber. I have well considered this matter and think we should at once secure the privilege, as that will cost us nothing. I *{believe}* such an Estate planted with various timber, with Coffee, and some other articles, would in a few years bring in a considerable income to the Mission, perhaps equal to one of the present sources. Our present Calamity has, however, for the present put it out of our power to go to any expence but it may be highly important to take some such step when we are able.

Carey to Sisters, Sept. 5, 1823

. . . I have lately been appointed to an office by Government, which brings in an additional thirty Pounds a Month: It is that of translator of the Acts and Regulations of the Governor General in Council, into Bengali. It has hitherto occupied much of my time, owing to my predecessor in office having suffered his work to fall in arrears which I have to work out. I have also this year received three works of Honour from different bodies in England, having been chosen a Fellow of the Linnaean Society, a member of the Geological Society, and corresponding member of the Horticultural Society of London: the latter was without any application on my part; to the other two I was proposed by my Friend H.T. Colebrooke, Esq.

Carey to Jabez, May 16, 1826

. . . I heard last Friday that the __________ Education came to a resolution to abolish __________ Schools. This is to me very unpleasant news, first because I entertained a hope that those schools would ultimately lead to the establishing of a Mission station in that important place and secondly because you would thereby be dismissed from an employ which though not lucrative, was a reasonable means of support to you (and your) family. Respecting the first of these particulars, I must leave it in the hand of God who is infinitely wise and good, and perhaps may overrule even this dark Providence for the very purpose to which it seems to stand opposed. With regard to the second I heard at the same time the office of Secretary to the College at Agra was open and as it was impossible to consult you I applied to Mr. Harrington for that situation for you. I have not received his reply but am in hopes of success. I do not know what is the salary of that office, nor whether you would like it, nor whether you can fulfill the duties thereof, but I suppose you __________ a punctual correspondence with all parties concerned in it, and __________ clear statement of accounts will be absolutely necessary. I consulted Jonathan about it and he concurred with me. We are all well, through the goodness of God and all unite in love to you and Eliza and the Children.

Carey to Jabez, Apr. 15, 1830

. . . My chief anxiety is about the Cause of God: the whole expence of maintaining all our stations, and paying an annuity to Sister Ward and Mrs. Randall (as was), lies almost entirely upon myself and Bro. Marshman. I give 600 Rupees a month to support our stations, and Bro. Marshman and John between them about 800. Our stations depend on us for the wicked opposition made to us in England, and the misrepresentations of Eustace and Mr. Yates, have done much towards hindering supplies from England. Some supplies we obtain, but not sufficient to supply the deficiency which will be occasioned by the abstraction of my Salary. And I know of nothing which will give me so much distress as the relinquishment of any one of our stations. I know the Lord can provide, and I trust he will, but at present our way is very dark.

Carey to Sisters , May 24, 1830 from Serampore

{Concerning Carey's retirement support}

. . . The Bengal Government has been for the last two years employed in reducing the salaries of the Civil and Military establishments, and about three months ago a publick letter was sent to the College Council saying that Government had resolved upon abolishing the Professorship of the College and only retaining the examiners at perhaps 500 rupees a month each. I concluded that if I accepted an office at the reduced allowance and afterwards applied for a Pension, it would be proportioned to the reduced allowance. I, therefore, well knowing that every member of the Government was favourable to me, waited on the Honourable W.B. Bayley and Sir Charles Metcalfe and stated my length of service, twenty nine years, and my requests. They advised my waiting on Lord W. Bentinck and stating the whole to him as I had done to them. I, therefore, immediately applied for a private audience and obtained one, at which I requested that, if possible, an exception might be made in my favour on account of length of service, and my office and salary continued as before under new management: but if that could not be acceded to, that a Pension, equal at least to half my income, might be granted me: but I observed at the same time that if this was refused, I must accept the office of examiner on the reduced allowance, of which it would cost me an hundred rupees a month to go up and down, and pay Palkee hire, and considerably more if I rented a house in Calcutta. I told him I should not want a pension long, being now near 69 years of age, and stated that I had not laid up a rupee, having regularly devoted my whole income, my household expences excepted, to the purposes of spreading the Gospel among the natives of India.

His Lordship said I was clearly entitled to a pension, and that I might make myself perfectly at ease, as every possible attention should be paid to my circumstances. I made the same application to the College Council who sent my letter in to Government and recommended the Pension. Thus the matter rested until about three weeks ago when it was determined that I should have a pension of 500 rupees a month. For this I am thankful both to God and them. I still also draw 300 rupees a month as Translator of the Regulations, but am informed that that office also is to be discontinued. The pension will be sufficient to maintain me comfortably either here or in England. My greatest distress has been that it would incapacitate me from doing anything toward the support of the Mission to which I have till now given 600 rupees monthly. I trust I laboured to commit my way to the Lord and prayed that my will might be bowed to his, and I feel tranquil and hope He whose cause this mission is will provide for its wants notwithstanding the base misrepresentations of its enemies in England.

ADDITIONAL SOURCES OF SUPPORT

The Mission at Serampore sought and received support from places other than the Society in England. From agreements with other organizations like the College, the Asiatic Society, and the Bible Society, funds were procured for translations and publications. Mission supporters from Scotland and America donated funds and often at the time of greatest need. Carey, Marshman, and Ward busied themselves in seeking subscriptions to support translation work and schools.

Carey to Fuller Dec. 10, 1805

The College and the Asiatic Society have agreed to allow us three hundred Rupees a month to translate and publish the Sanskrit Writings of the Hindus. The profits of the sale to be ours.

Another propitious circumstance will, I trust, enable us to do more. The British and Foreign Bible Society sent a letter to Mr. Udney wishing him, Rev. Mr. Brown, and Buchanan, Bro. Marshman, Ward, and myself to form a committee to co-operate with them in this country. In consequence of this Bro. Marshman drew up a memorial, which was much approved, showing the practicability of translating and publishing the Bible here for a comparatively small sum. From this Mr. Buchanan drew up an address which was immediately forwarded to the Governor General, and is intended to be circulated all over India to get subscriptions for this work, and I doubt not of its success. This will, if successful take off the heavy expence of translating and printing and enable us to employ the money in spreading the word when printed.

Carey to Fuller, Nov.18, 1806, Calcutta

America has sent 3,340 dollars, or thereabouts, to assist in translating the Scriptures. We are going on with this work with all our might. Jeremiah is just printed in Bengali. Matthew in Sanskrit and Mahratta, and Matthew is begun in Hindustan and Dorissa.

Carey to Sisters, Calcutta, Feb. 25, 1807

The Mission now wears a new face to what it did. Ten or twelve native preachers are constantly out in one direction or another. All these persons must be supported . . .

Our dear brothers in England, Scotland, America, and India have contributed largely to the translating and printing of the Bible, but after all we stand in need of more.

Carey to Fuller, Jan.14, 1808

Our friend W. William Grant who died some time ago left 20,000 Rupees to the Mission, which sum I have this day received from his executor Mr. Weston. He also left 10,000 to assist the translations and 10,000 more to a . . . formed at Calcutta, to maintain an evangelical minister at the Mission Church.

Carey to Fuller, April 20, 1808

{For support of the work of translations, Carey and Marshman confronted Lord Minto and showed him samples of the translation work and asked him a donation. He said after consulting with advisors and friends that it would not be good politically and wished them well.}

I asked him whether he had any objections to our making a collection from house to house. He said, none, but wished us success. He observed that it was an admirable thing that orders should be sent from home, to determine to what extent Christianity should be forced on the inhabitants, and added that he thought the best way was to use only persuasion, and to bring them over by . . . as we had done. I replied that I thought it would be wrong for government to use any force at all, and added that as conversions must arise from conviction in the mind, it was not possible that coercion should ever produce that, it might make hypocrites but could never make Christians.

Carey to Ryland, March 15, 1809

. . . We made an attempt on New Year's Day to raise a subscription for a charity school, and though our subscriptions were not great, we have begun one, and have forty boys already in it. It is under the care of one of our Members, Son of a clergyman in Huntingtonshire, whose name is Peacock. He was by the intolerance of the Managers, turned out of a similar situation in the Orphan School, because he had embraced the opinions of the Anabaptists. This school is intended for the benefit of the Portugese poor, but is not confined to them: and there is every reason to hope that it will be a blessing in this large city.

Carey to Harrington, July 7, 1812, Serampore

{Money came to the mission through an agreement with the Bible Society for publications.}

The only question for consideration, therefore, is whether the sum we receive shall be received in aid of one or two of the translations or of the whole. We are willing to agree to either mode; but we imagine the latter will be most agreeable to the Bible Society, both because they seem to have a view to the whole in voting the supplies and because we imagine they would rather receive a report of the whole annually than of one or two, to which the report must then be restricted as it could of course only include those which were aided.

Carey to Ryland, Oct. 4, 1818, Serampore

Could subscriptions be made in England for the Schools in Rajputana, or would churches or individuals maintain one or two schools at about 12 Rupees a month, or 18 pounds a year, it would greatly assist that most important work and put a power into our hands to do much more than can be done without it.

Carey to Jabez, Aug. 25, 1819

. . . Lord Hastings in his speech at the College disputations noticed the favourable reception your (proposal) of setting up schools in Rajputana had as mentioned in (your) first letter after your arrival there. I greatly wish you could make a beginning without delay. There is no need you should propose teaching anything yet but reading and writing and indeed it will be highly proper to avoid anything which may cause a prejudice against the schools (at) first setting out. You will have opportunities of gradually introducing other things as circumstances arise and which I doubt not you will improve to the utmost. It would, however, be highly gratifying to me to be able to report a beginning. All eyes are now upon us. There is not a little envy occasioned by the fact that Lord Hastings put this business into our hands and not into those of the Bishop of the Church of England Society or the London Society and I assure you that all parties are watching all we do with the closest attention and would I fear not be a little gratified (at) our miscarriage.

About an employment under Government - you are aware that Govt. never appoints any but their own covenanted servants to offices and that appointments to inferior offices are always made by the Judges, Collectors or other publick functionaries upon the spot. Let, however, your first care be to set up schools and God will provide all things needful.

Carey to Burls, July 7, 1820

We have received no accounts of the Translation Fund for a long time past and no communication from the Bible Society though we have heard that the 500 pounds for first editions of the N.T in several languages has been voted to us. We have had no authority to draw on them for the last two years, and no communication from the Secretaries nor do we know where to apply for the sums already voted to us. We have, therefore, been forced to relinquish several versions for want of funds, and must relinquish others also unless funds are provided . . .

Last Tuesday evening an Auxiliary Missionary Society was formed in the Church meeting at Lall Bazar. Five young men offered themselves as missionaries to the population around their dwellings. These act gratuitously. I hope the funds will enable us to do more at a distance from Calcutta.

Carey to Jabez, Jan. 16, 1821

. . . Bro. Ward intends to return with Sister Marshman and hopes to arrive here about September. I suppose he is now in America collecting for the College.

By the bye, the building of the College is nearly finished, some of the upper beams are on. There is still, however, much to be done before it will be compleat.

Carey to Jabez, Jan. 18, 1822

. . . It is our intention to apply to Government to support you in your present situation. Bro. Marshman and I intend to wait on Lord Hastings and ascertain his private feelings upon the matter before we make an application in a formal manner.

Carey to Jabez, Feb. 16, 1822

We made an application to Government about a fortnight ago requesting them to take the expences of the Rajputana Schools on themselves. Bro. Marshman and I first waited on Lord Hastings to know his mind and showed him a letter from Lieut. Dalzell to me in which he spoke highly of them. His Lordship was much gratified with that testimony from an indifferent person and promised to present the application to Council himself the next day. We applied for 300 Rupees monthly and stated that this would enable you to set up gradually to the amount of four or five schools in addition to those you have already. The application was successful and Government also agreed to refund us all we had advanced for your schools, nearly 4,000 Rupees. The pay for them by Government commences on the first of Feb. as you will see by the enclosed copy of the letter of Govt. to us. You will, therefore, from henceforth receive your pay - 300 Rupees a month - from the Ajmere Treasury, viz. from Mr. Wilder, who has orders from Government to pay it to you, and you are to make your reports to him. As, however, the direction of these schools is still considered as under us I hope you will from time to time send us regular reports that we my be able to answer all enquiries on that head. I shall also feel happy if you should soon be enabled to begin two or three more schools in addition to those you have already. I hope you will not write less frequently to me on account of this alteration for I feel a very lively interest in all your undertakings.

Carey to Ryland, May 7, 1823

. . . The late generous grant by the Bible Society and the sum sent by our Society in aid of the translations have eased us of a load under which we must otherwise have sunk. Through divine mercy we are all well. I am as well as I ever remember to have been, except the inconvenience felt from the intense heat, often more than 100 degrees of Fahrenheit (April and May being the hottest months in the year).

Carey to Sisters, Oct. 25, 1827

The Cause of our Redeemer gradually gains ground, and the accounts from various posts are highly gratifying, especially from Benares, Dinajpur, and Arakan. The Lord has wonderfully appeared also in pecuniary things. Last Year

The Benevolent Institution fell off so much in its Funds that it was Ten thousand Rupees in Debt. I made an application to Government for assisstance, and they agreed to allow 200 Rupees a month for it. And within the last month a Man died at Dilbee, who was utterly unknown to us all; nor do I know that he was a Professor of Religion. His name was Dunn. He left 60,000 Rupees to his Wife during her life, and after her death 30,000 of it is to go to the Calcutta Free School, 10,000 to the Benevolent Institution, 10,000 to the Serampore Mission, 5,000 to the female Asylum, and 5,000 to the Parental Academies Institution. Thus we are witness to the kindness of God in finding means to support his own cause . . .

ECONOMY ON THE FIELD

Carey outlined fairly specific plans regarding how the missionaries might live more economically in India. This included some savvy regarding the nature of the Indian people and business practices of the day. The programs included education for the children, shared resources, and various forms of industry. Methods for dispensing pecuniary aid to the individual missionaries was also part of the economic formulation.

Carey to Fuller, Nov. 16, 1796, Mudnabati

I must now just tell you my thoughts about the Mission. Bro. Fountain is safely arrived and gives us pleasure [but our affairs as a Mission are in a delicate situation. [I have written what I think of Bro. T's affairs]. This place I expect given up. Mr. M. has not mentioned anything but I have written to him all that I think about it, however, the experiences obtained here I look upon as the very thing which will tend to support the Mission. I now know all the methods of Agriculture that are used here. I know the tricks of the natives, and the nature of the lowest rate of housekeeping in this Country, having had a monthly allowance. I have made all those experiments on those heads which could not have been made without ruin had I not had those resources and I will now propose to you what I would recommend to the Society. You will find it similar to what the Moravians do. Seven or eight Families can be maintained for nearly the same expences as one, if this method is pursued. I then earnestly entreat the Society to set their faces this way and send out more Missionaries. We ought to be seven or eight Families together and it is absolutely necessary for the Wives of Missionaries to be as hearty in the Work as their Husbands. Our Families should be considered as nurseries for the Mission, and among us should be a person capable of teaching School, so as to educate our Children. I recommend all living together in a number of little Straw Houses forming a Line or Square, and of having nothing of our own but all the general stock. One or two should be elected Stewards to provide over all the management which should with respect to eating, drinking, working, Worship, Learning, Preaching excursions yet be reduced to fixed Rules. Should the above mentioned Natives join us all should be considered equal and all come under the same regulations.

The utility of this Community of Goods in the beginning of the Gospel Church here will be obvious by considering the following things -

1. Our finances being small it will be necessary to live economically, but one set of Stewards will do all the Work for the Whole if thus organized when if otherwise every separate family must have the same number as would be necessary for the whole if united, and if God converts the Natives they would in time supercede all want of servants, being partakers of the publick stock, and, therefore, bound to labour for the publick benefit. -

2. Education of our own and Converted Heathen Children is a very important Object, and is what might, if followed by a Divine Blessing train up some of them to be useful Preachers or other members of the Mission themselves.

3. The example of such a Number, would be a shining witness of the Excellence of the Gospel, and would contribute very much to the furtherance of the Cause of Christ. -

4. Industry being absolutely necessary, every one would have his proper Work allotted to him; and would be employed at his post. Some cultivating land, some instructing, some learning, some Preaching, and the Women superintending the domestic concerns - &ct., &ct.

In order to this I recommend about one or two hundred Biggahs to be cultivated for the Mission, which would produce, most of the Articles necessary for them, and their Cattle, - that all these people should not come at one time, but one or two families in a year, or in two years or so - but as Bro. T for obvious reasons could not join this Family, and for others as obvious to me would not, except he had the sole direction [in which case all would fail] and as there is often greater possibility of his being torn from the work, than not]. We are in immediate want of more - say one Family more of Missionaries - and I entreat the Society to send them [as the only way of keeping the Mission together. Best pray be very careful what stock Missionaries wives are of. Place - should this place be continued to me I recommend the seat of the Mission to be here, and my income, and Utensils will be immediately thrown into the common stock - or any part of Bengal would do tho the North is most agreeable, and will produce Wheat - a very necessary article. The heat also is more moderate. Should we go South, the neighborhood of Nuddea is most eligible but I fear too near Calcutta. All provisions are also much cheaper in the North, and by keeping a Small Boat which can be bought for 30 Rupees, two persons may travel any where at a time. Cultivation, and all except superintendence must be performed by natives. Expences- - The number of Servants kept would fall under 200 Rupees a Month. I think about 130 and the Expences of Planting and articles of Furniture would be near 100 for the number mentioned..." *{Carey then mentions the cost of everything from seeds to clothes.}*

Carey to Ryland, Serampore, Apr. 11, 1818

{In this letter Carey again recounts the problems at Calcutta with the Younger Brethren, especially Yates who accuses Mrs. Marshman of misusing the funds for a trip for health reasons. Carey explains the workings of the mission finances in this discussion.}

To understand this you should know that every person in the family has an allowance monthly to purchase clothes and other personal conveniences, and as soon as a child is born the allowance commences, and is increased at certain ages. The allowance is the same throughout the family. Sister M. providentially kept an account for and against each one under her charge; and upon examining it, the balance was in favour of Sister M.

Carey to Jabez, Jan. 18, 1820

. . . You must be aware my dear Jabez, that we shall be hardly pressed to raise funds for carrying on our schools and that we have no more to expect from Government. They may or may not give but they are under no engagement to do it, we must, therefore, be as economical as possible and must at any rate have no charges in the report which can be found fault with. You also know the load of ill will which the Brethren at Calcutta bear us. A false story has been already propagated about your going to Ajmere and the expences to which you ran, and the great passion for dress and finery in which Eliza has indulged have been bandied up and down, much to your prejudice. Indeed the permission of that has been mentioned by real friends in higher provinces as highly dishonourable to you. All say that you are bound as a Christian man to take care that such a dishonourably fine show should not be made in your family. As a parent who loves you most tenderly I feel all these things very keenly but were I to say nothing of what is said I should be a partaker of the evil. I often with much deep distress pour out my supplications for you to God and feel for you in the most tender manner.

Carey to Jabez, Apr. 18, 1821

I write today hoping to send the letter in a few days when I have got the order for your money. You must not suppose we neglect you if there should be a few days delay. The time you mention the Surkar kept the money a full week in his hands and the very next week I discovered that he had robbed us of more than 2,000 Rupees which I had sent in small sums to Alexander's house by him. He was seized, but when suffered to go to make up his affairs he took poison and killed himself. The publick made up my loss and lost about a thousand Rupees more by him. It was providential that I got your money from him.

A GRATEFUL HEART

Carey to Father, Nov. 24, 1813, Calcutta

The amazing sums that are now collected for Evangelical purposes in England alone surpass all credibility, and yet notwithstanding the enormous price of all articles of life, the depression of trade, and the heavy burdens under which all classes of people labor, they are certainly raised - Our great loss was made up . . . Weeks. The Bible Society, The Religious Tract Society, Mission Societies, Sunday Schools, Lancastrian education, and a great number of other benevolent purposes are supported and carried on. Almost every thing of this nature has been begun since the year 1792. Though trade was brisk, commerce flourishing, and articles of expenditure cheap, the attempt to collect a tenth part of what is now freely contributed to religious purposes would have been made in vain. A strong proof that the religious opinions and feelings of the people of England have received a powerful impulse in the ways of God . . .

Carey to Sisters, May 24, 1831, Serampore

Within the last fortnight we have received most cheering news from England of the beginning of a turn in the tide of publick feeling as it regards Serampore, and the strongest proof of the reality of this is remittances to a very large amount, 23,000 rupees and odd. This seasonable relief came at a time when we were much depressed, and were almost without hope of being able to support the stations dependent upon us. Now our burdens and our fears are removed, and I doubt not but the gross misrepresentations which have been so industriously spread abroad will give way and the truth be known. We may always and everywhere safely commit our souls and all our interest to God in well doing.

NOTE

[1]Timothy George, *Faithful Witness: The Life and Mission of William* Carey (Birmingham AL: New Hope, 1991) 56-57.

Relationship to the Missionary Society

In 1792 Carey issued a call to his fellow ministers pleading with them to join him in organizing for missions. In the fall of that year the Baptist Missionary Society began its work with Carey and John Thomas going to India as the society's first missionaries. A relationship with the home society ensued presenting challenges for the missionaries that perhaps Carey never expected.

Almost from the beginning Carey complained about the scarcity of regular communication with the home supporters. Due to distance and circumstance correspondence arrived slowly and sporadically, and Carey queried from time to time whether the new missionaries had been forgotten. He repeatedly encouraged the homefront to keep those cards and letters coming.

The problem of regular communication soon paled into insignificance. As new, younger missionaries arrived so did problems. From about 1815 to his death, Carey's relationship with the Society turned rather stormy. Commencing with Fuller's death change occurred and the once held confidence in the seasoned missionaries like Carey, Ward, and Marshman turned to distrust and favor for the newer missionaries. Criticism toward Carey and his associates became more common as the newcomers on the field clashed with the older generation. Carey sensed the Society sided with the younger brethren. This struggle caused Carey deep emotional pain, and he communicated that to Ryland and others.

The man whose vision promoted the first missionary society eventually separated from the same.

Carey to Sisters, Oct. 25, 1827

> You have undoubtedly heard of our separation from the Baptist Missionary Society. I have written to Mr. Dyer nearly twelve months ago, telling him my determination to separate from the Society unless they come to amicable terms with Bro. Marshman, so that my mind was quite made up to the separation . . .

Carey expected little support from the Society later in his life. Unfortunately, controversy often plagues men and women involved in God's work and hinders the task. This consequence concerned Carey the most.

COMMUNICATION

Communication with the Society at home was often frustrating to Carey and his companions. They longed to hear news from friends about the religious situation in England. At the same time Carey wished to keep the Society informed and wrote often to leaders with precise information about India and the work of missions there. Even with these best intentions, communication was inconsistent and Carey complained, undoubtedly, as did those in England.

Carey to Society, Mudnabati, Jan. 6 1795

. . . It is to me very wonderful that no Letter from any of my Friends in England has yet been received. I am afraid that they have been sent by private Hands . . . but Letters sent by the Post seldom miscarry; and Parcels sent in a regular Way are sure to be delivered safe, Direct to me at Mudnabati near Malda in Bengal . . . and I shall undoubtedly receive whatever you send me.. I long to know how all my Friends do . . .

Carey to Society, Jan. 12, 1796

Dear Brethren,

Since my last I have waited with anxious expectation to receive letters from you; [but Europe Letters are tardy in arriving, and those from the Society peculiarly so. This I hope will not always be the case; but on the contrary, I could wish them to be much more frequent than any others. -] I am, however, certain that the tie with which we are united cannot be broken by length of time, distance of place, or any of the common intervening incidents of Life; but that we shall continue to love one another in all situations whether prosperous or Diverse.

Carey to Fuller, Nov. 1800

I have formed a design of writing my Letters to you in the form of a Journal and by this means I may retain some of those circumstances which would otherwise be forgot or neglected and may also perhaps fill a Letter in a couple of Months as other correspondents may receive shorter letters on this account and some may have many inaccuracies in details, but I cannot suppose this will be a loss to anyone for my letters are generally uninteresting if not trifling.

Carey to Fuller Jan. 21, 1802

Our dear Brethren in England are not forgotten by us in our prayers, tho we have some reason to fear we are forgotten by them, it being now a year and a half, at least, since the date of the last letter we received.

Carey to Morris, Feb. 25, 1802 Calcutta

I have no inclination to retaliate or I should be a long time before I wrote to you again - but I am told by him who judges of all things aright "to do to others whatsoever I would that they should do to me". From all my Friends I have received two Letters only of a Date less than a Year and half ago - and each of them about twenty Lines. I think you would all write your Sheets as full as possible if you properly considered the expence of Postage with us. Last Week Bro. Marshman received one from Dr. Ryland, only a single Sheet and which only passed through the General Post Office at Calcutta and went on Stages to Serampore, the Postage of which was five Rupees, four Anas - or 13 Schillings of your Money. An hint is enough.]

. . . Last Week we got the Boxes &ct., which came by the *Sarah Christiana.* We feel delighted with the rich intelligence which they contain - but we wonder much that our dear Friends send us so few Copies of useful Works, [and even then so long after their Publications] - a dozen or a score Copies of the Evangelical and Missionary Magazines and at least a Dozen Copies of Periodical Accounts and the other religion periodical publications and other good &ct., yet have received more than one Copy (not compleat) of N. G. Periodical Accts. and] cannot possibly keep a Copy of any valuable work for ourselves - [I sincerely hope that you will learn to amend of these things] - our number of religious enquirers and consequently of readers, increases.

It is also a very unfortunate thing that the very Types which we are in greatest distress for, viz. Roman English were not sent, tho charged in the Bill. They are the only Types that will stand with our Bengali and Deo Najoree. We are just going to print my Sanskrit Grammar, every line of which must be scabbarded on account of this defect unless we can purchase some any where, and as it will be a work of almost 500 Pages (I expect) the Labour will be very great, and the work appear very bad.

Carey to Ryland, April 25, 1820

It is a very long time indeed since I received a Letter from you and I must have written at least two or three Letters of which you have taken no notice. I cannot, however, prevail upon myself to suppose that you have left off writing to me, and shall, therefore, continue my correspondence, as usual, only I shall not say anything respecting those differences which have for the last two years embittered my life. I have said all I ever wish to say upon them, my opinion is not altered in the least about them, and as all that can be either said or done is not likely to do anything except to aggravate the evil and destroy my own peace of mind, I am resolved to leave everything in the hands of God. He will do what is right and He can overrule everything for ultimate good.

Misuse of Carey's Communications

The Society regularly used the correspondence of William Carey and the other missionaries as the material for their periodical accounts informing British Baptists of the work in India. As is often the case, excerpts appear out of context and are misinterpreted. This happens both innocently and intentionally. This precipitated a recurring problem and Carey objected frequently.

Carey to Sisters, Aug. 24, 1803, Calcutta

I was sorry to see a letter which I sent to you published in the Biblical Magazine. I wrote to you in the simplicity of my Heart and just as my feelings suggested at the time, but there is too much about myself in it for any one else to see. I never wish to see anything like self complacency published in my Letters, for the truth is that I am always ready to fall by temptation and indeed do often so fall that if it were known others would be as much ashamed of me as I am of myself.

Carey to Ryland, Dec. 13, 1804

. . . I have felt very much at seeing several passages in my Letters printed both in the Periodical Accts. and in other publications. I am not conscious that they were dictated by vanity at the time I wrote them, but when I saw them in print I concluded and I believe others much think the same, that I am one of the vainest creatures upon the earth. But pity towards a foolish Bro. should have suppressed them. I generally begin and finish a letter at one sitting, and then write what is uppermost in my mind; and I suppose this may account for some unadvised expressions. All that has been said by me or by others about my situation in the College should have been suppressed and what I have written about my engaging in any literary works, as Grammar &ct., ought not to have been mentioned till the works are published. So many things may occur to change intentions, or to frustrate undertakings of this sort. This is actually the case with the Sanskrit Dictionary. H.T. Colebrooke, one of the Judges of the Sudder Dewany Adaulut being engaged in a dictionary I gave it up with great pleasure. I hope nothing of this kind will ever appear again: such things can be of no service to the Mission, but may do it much injury.

We sometimes express our hopes of certain persons in a very sanguine manner, who after all only disappoint our expectations. Whenever we write thus strongly, you should soften down the expressions, such things prove abortive, and should they prove equal to our or your hope, the pleasure would not be the less on that account.

Carey to Fuller, Aug. 11, 1807

Some asperities have lately passed between us and one or two of our Brethren in England for which I am heartily sorry. I am persuaded that the whole has arisen from misunderstanding one another. Nothing could be further from my heart than a wish to give you or any one else pain about the periodical accounts. I was sorry that I had written some things to England which appeared in print. I think, however, that I pointed them out in a long letter which I wrote to you. I might express myself improperly or even wickedly, for I am sinful enough to do so, but I have not the smallest recollection of what I wrote, and, therefore, cannot tell. I hope, however, that there is an end of that business; both myself and my brethren shall do all we can to furnish matter for the P.A. *{Periodical Accounts}* and I have the fullest confidence in your care respecting what you print.

Carey to Ryland, Oct. 7, 1807

I received yours dated in March yesterday. I wish you to be entirely easy respecting our views about the Periodical Accounts. It never was my wish, that I recollect, to do anything towards suppressing them: I thought that there were some things in them exceptionable, and wished that some expressions in my letters, which evidently savoured of vanity, had been expunged. It is probable that I might not express myself as I ought to have done, about them, and I assure you, I am very sorry to have wounded the feelings of my Brethren, whom I am sure I love with an unfeigned affection. I usually write a letter through at one time, and as I appropriate only a certain portion of my time to epistolary correspondence, usually write what is uppermost in my mind, and, therefore, do not wonder that I write many things of which I ought to repent.

You set your mind at rest, however, and supercede the necessity of any more of those flagellations which you have given us in some of your last letters. I will now inform you that we intend to contribute as much as we can to the P.A. Bro. Marshman, Ward, and myself intend, besides common Missionary intelligence, to furnish some papers, on different subjects, once a quarter, or oftener. We shall perhaps deviate from the plan which we have laid down: but it is intended that Bro. Ward shall send occasional pieces on the manners and customs of the Hindus, I on the Natural History and the state of the arts and sciences, and Bro. Marshman upon the languages. - He would have sent a long list now and then of difficulties which we meet with in the translations: but the light manner in which many of them were mentioned in a letter sent by someone of our Brethren on some formerly mentioned difficulties has nearly discouraged him: for however easy of solution many of them may appear to you, to us the difficulties are real and often great.

We are about to adopt, also, a new regulation by which all correspondence between us and our Brethren in different parts of India will be sent to you in detail, from which you may make such selections as will be fit for the P.A. I do not recollect having written a letter to Dr. Rippon this last ten years, except a note to introduce a person to him who was going to England. I have a very high esteem for him, but since you wished me not to write I have entirely desisted therefrom.

There appears from one or two expressions in your late letters to be some misunderstanding about our wish to receive missionaries from other quarters besides the Society. You may be sure that no such idea ever entered the mind of any of us: I fear the idea has arisen from some indiscretions of our friend Maylin in America, and perhaps in England, but we certainly never encouraged him to invite any person to come to India, nor should we think ourselves at liberty receive them, were he to bring any out with him. I can't conceive how you heard that we intended to invite one of Lady Huntington's preachers to come to India and preach in the new chapel in Calcutta. The first word we ever heard of it was by means of your letter to Bro. Ward. I suppose it must have arisen from someone's having confounded two ideas which are perfectly distinct. The Evangelical Episcopalians, conscious that the Gospel will not be long preached to them by any Clergyman in the service, have raised a fund for supporting an Evangelical Clergyman to preach in the Mission

Church, and in case such an one could not be obtained, to get one of evangelical sentiments of some other denomination, and would probably prefer one of L.H.'s connection: but the New Chapel for Protestant Dissenters (now nearly finished) will be principally thought not exclusively occupied by us; and I trust a Baptist Church will be soon formed in Calcutta there being now about twenty members of the Church at Serampore who live in or near Calcutta.

Carey to Jabez, Sept. 15, 1829

. . . I cannot give you a full account of the attacks made on us in England. The thing published there was eighteen of my private letters to Dr. Ryland. Two or more others ought to have (printed) with them but the Society refused to give them up for that purpose. They had lent them to Eustace and Mr. Yates who had published a garbled extract from one of them in which they have grossly misrepresented me. But as all on both sides is before the publick, they will form their judgment.

Carey to Society Committee, Date?

{Carey is upset that some excerpts from his letters were used as ammunition to discredit Marshman. Evidently the committee obtained them from one of Ryland's family members after his death. Since the letters were private, Carey believes they should remain confidential.}

. . . Private correspondence, as you well know, is always accounted sacred, and ought so to be; consequently no person had a right to make such use of my private letters, much less to publish them or any parts of them, without my consent. Had I been applied to, I could never have consented to permit other persons to make extracts from my letters, because that would have been commissioning them to make me say just what they pleased; and accordingly those Gentlemen have, by publishing garbled extracts from them, grossly and deliberately misrepresented me. I do not recollect the contents of those letters, but such is my confidence in my own integrity, and consistency in what I wrote about Bro. Marshman; that I think the letters should be published entire, for my justification or condemnation, as the case may be . . .

{Carey goes on to say he wants all the private letters to Ryland sent to Rev. Anderson, his friend who will do with them as Carey wishes. He even points out a particular issue of the Baptist Magazine (Nov. 1827) that has misrepresented him.}

REACTIONS TO SOCIETY ACTIONS

Halfway round the globe, the Baptist Missionary Society decided policy that affected the missionaries in India. Often these decisions pertained to issues like mission stations or support, and Carey felt missionaries on the field understood these things better. The India missionaries reacted to perceived Society blunders. Carey also promptly defended his associates, especially Marshman, when they received undue criticism.

Carey to Ryland, Oct. 4, 1815

Yours of May 2nd and a preceding one enclosing a letter from Attah to my wife, I received a few days ago, and at the same time received an extract from a Cambridge Paper, copied at Plymouth by an officer of the Ship (Mr. Johnston who is acquainted with us) informing us of the death of Dear. Bro. Fuller. By the same ship came a letter from Mr. Burls enclosing one from Mr. Dyer in the name of the Committee, saying that they found it necessary to remove Bro. Trowt from Java on account of the expensiveness of that Mission. To say the least I think this was sufficiently in haste, as our Dear Bro. Fuller was not then dead. - By the Bye, this step makes me tremble for the Mission to the East. The loss of Bro. Fuller is a great loss indeed. I must, however, make a few remarks on the affairs of the Mission, which I hope will not be superfluous.

1. Considering the extensive countries opened to us in the East, I entreat, I implore, our Dear Brethren in England not to think of the petty shop keeping plan of lessening the number of stations so as to bring the support of them within the bounds of their present income: but to hand all their attention and exertions to the great object of increasing their Finance to meet the pressing demand that divine providence makes on them. If your objects are large the publick will contribute to their support. If you contract them, their liberality will immediately contract itself proportionately. A subscription equal to one farthing a week to all the inhabitants of Great Britain who are grown up, viz. 8 millions of farthings, or a penny a week from a fourth of them would produce 8333. 6. 8 pounds per annum. Let only this sum come to the Baptist Mission (surely not too much to expect) and all the objects will be accomplished for which European subscriptions are at present wanted. (Translations excepted).

2. It is not agreeable to me to draw comparisons, but I know well that all which has yet been done by other missions may be put into a very small compass. - - Mr. Morrison has made the greatest noise, but Mr. M. did not translate the N.T. into Chinese. I have a letter from Mr. Burder's to me now in being, which informed me that he (M) took the copy of a considerable part with him from England. I do not say that he cannot translate with the helps which he can obtain: but the sentences which he has given as examples in his Chinese Grammar (formed from English ones) could not be understood by our Chinese teacher. They are English sentences in Chinese character. Mr. M. has, I am informed, made very few alterations in what he has printed, and most of them are for the worse. His publishing it, however, as his own translation, THE Society's blazoning it abroad as his are both unjustifiable. Vanity pervades all that whole society and nearly all connected with it. Some of their best missionaries are at Vizagapatam and Ganjam, but I fear they do little. At Madras Mr. Loveless is very usefully employed, but not as a Missionary to the Heathen. In Ceylon the names of their missionaries are scarcely known: - In Java much the same. They have got Dutch churches which their Paedo Baptist principles fit them for. Mr. Ham at Amboyna chose to spend a Lord's Day Evening in playing at chess rather than disoblige a few carnal acquaintances. I hope the Church Missionaries are in general better men, but they do not stand on their own legs, they

are up borne by the support of Government. The Methodists at Ceylon are Churchmen, and thus upheld. Abdul Mopee at Agra is I believe a good man, but now Mr. Corrie has left Agra I expect all will be silence from that quarter till someone else occupies his place. I fear considerable drawbacks must be made from these reports. They appeared true then to Mr. Corrie, but like others he must expect drawbacks, and I fear they are more than could be wished.

3. Our Brethren have no external support in their work. They cannot baptise infants, consequently they cannot occupy churches. Bro. Robinson relinquished the Dutch church at Batavia because they wished to prevent him from even saying anything about Baptism. That is given to one of THE M Society Missionaries. Jabez could not sprinkle children at Amboyna, but he spoke to the residents in favour of Mr. Ham and got him appointed to the Dutch church. Our Brethren, therefore, stand without any human support, all others by it.

4. Bro. Trowt occupies a very important situation, and is very diligent in it. He ought not to be removed. If in anything he is expensive, which, however, I do not see, he should be admonished. Both our Brethren at Java I think, suppose more horses necessary than are really so, but a man may as well be without legs as without a horse in the hot country. I think, however, one horse may suffice for one missionary. But the expences of a missionary in the islands, cannot, in my opinion be reduced below 250 rupees a month each. Living there is enormously dear.

5. No one of your missionaries lays up anything for himself, and I am sure that every one of them suffer many privations. When every exception is made I think our Brethren are men who labour for God, and devote their all to him, nor do they labour in vain. The fruits of their labours are also evident and I scarcely know any who will deny them. - But these men must not be capriciously removed from their stations, nor have their hands tied by a petty calculation of pounds, shillings, and pence.

6. The translations of Scripture are now become so numerous that the work is of the first importance. By constant attention to the object, and the smiles of God upon our undertaking, we have now collected at Serampore a large body of men from all parts of India who are employed in translating the word. These men write out the rough copy of the translation into their respective languages, some translating from the Bengali, others from the Hindustani, and others from the Sanskrit, as they are best acquainted with them. They consult one another, and other Pundits who have been for several years employed in correcting the Press and copy, and who almost know the Scriptures by heart. They, therefore, form the idiom, after which I examine and alter the whole where necessary: and upon every occasion have men born and brought up in the country themselves to consult. The number of these languages far exceeds what I thought it till very lately: for till lately I like almost everyone else thought all the North and West of India occupied by the Hindi or Hindustani, but I now doubt whether any country be exclusively so. What have hitherto been accounted varieties of the Hindustani and vulgar varieties of jargon, are in reality distinct languages, all derived it is true from the same source, the Sanskrit, and having all the same words, altered and diversified but easily recognisable to

one acquainted with Sanskrit; so differently terminated in inflection as to make them unintelligible to the inhabitants of the surrounding countries. The uniformity of the words in all these languages makes it comparatively easy for me to judge of the correctness of the translations, and makes that quite possible which to one unacquainted with Sanskrit, and the mutations of words in the current languages would be impossible.

I think you have been unreasonably severe with Bro. Marshman and have reiterated your complaints too frequently. He is not a perfect man but he is a good man. In your last to me, you mention something of introducing our *Cursed Caste* into the army. I confess I do not know what you intend. I have asked what circular letter you could possibly allude to, but no one knows. Bro. Marshman says he supposes you must allude to a letter either received from or sent to Bro. Whitworth of Berhampore, but no one knows what. I suppose you by the *Caste* mean Baptists, and I always thought you to be one. If anyone were to ask my opinion about that point I should tell him, and if necessary defend my sentiments, even if it were the Governor General. If you allude to the promiscuous communion of baptised with unbaptised persons, I confess I disapprove of it and if anyone were to ask my opinion of the matter I should give it without hesitation, but I *never will* engage in an unlovely controversy about it. Before we tried it, I did think it doubtful whether it might be lawful in certain cases to sit at the Lord's Table with unbaptised persons but since that I have not doubts left: there is no place left for the sole of one's foot. You receive persons by the Suffrage of the Church, or occasional communicants from Independent congregations, but we had to receive occasional communicants from the Church of England, or directly from their being converted from Heathenism or Mohammedanism. I do not think persons sprinkled in infancy or even at riper years ought to be baptised. Such persons, therefore, must be received to communion without the testimony of any Church to their Character, and without the Church which received them having anything more than a general and in most cases, very superficial acquaintance with them. No body of Christians except Mixt Communion Baptists commune with persons known and acknowledged to be unbaptised. The Heathen name *Caste*, therefore, should not be applied thus harshly to men who conscientiously act upon a principle admitted by Christians of every denomination except Mixt Baptists.

The Churches in India, also are as Independent as they are in England. We may give an opinion, or even advice to the Church at Berhampore, or elsewhere, but we have no authority over it: and we want none. Some time ago Mr. R. Hall wrote to me on the same subject, and I heard, for I did not see the letter, that he wrote to Bro. Ward in a manner which might have occasioned a very serious division in any other circumstances. I am sorry for it and only conclude that a man may be as truly bigoted to what he thinks liberality of sentiment as to anything else, and that as Witherspoon expresses it he "may be *Fierce for Moderation*."

I never intend to write one more line to you or anyone else from henceforth on this disagreeable subject. Be assured my dear Bro. that no man on earth lies nearer my Heart or has a larger share in my affections than yourself. Be assured we have in all things acted to the best of our knowledge in conducting the affairs of the Mission. We intend, however, to write to the Society immediately to relinquish the management we have hitherto had, and to request that all our Brethren at the Stations may depend immediately on them. The Mission was formerly one. There are now MANY, and human nature requires that we should ALL BE BRETHREN.

Poor Leonard has fallen into the sin of adultery and is excluded the church - a heavy blow - but his heart appears broken with his fall. We find it necessary that one or more brethren should live in Calcutta and be co-pastors of the Church, and have proposed my nephew Eustace and Bro. Lawson for that purpose. They have agreed to it, and I expect the church will declare its choice the next church meeting. They, particularly Eustace, will consider Calcutta as a Mission Station, and he will devote himself as much as possible to the work among the Heathen there. They have both removed to Calcutta. Bro. Yates is associated with me in the work of Translations. My dear Wife is with me on the River for her health, she has been unable to walk for three years, but we hope the river air may do her good. She has received from Attah a very agreeable and interesting letter and will reply to it as soon as she can, but the writing of a page brings on fainting fits which sometimes continue for a day or two. She unites with me in love to yourself and Mrs. Ryland.

Carey to Ward, Jan. 20, 1820, Serampore

. . . You mentioned somebody at Birmingham who had refused to subscribe to our object of the Mission, under the idea of our want of faithfulness. I think the publication of our accounts which have been regularly sent to England would clear up this matter, and think the Treasurer, or the Secretaries to the Mission should do that. As that, however, has not been done, we have drawn up a short statement of what has been disbursed here, which we have printed, and desire that it may be reprinted in England, and dispersed as widely as possible. If the Society with ample materials in their hands neglect to vindicate our reputations, we must do it ourselves.

I hope the regulations or whatever they may be called, which we have sent will meet your approbation. I am sure we have laboured unto the utmost to meet your wishes. The premises were bought and are held in trust for the Society. No attempt to alienate them has yet been made and were we, or any other trustee so unprincipled as to make such an attempt, it would be in vain. It is not in the power of the trustees to do that. It is possible that the Society itself might do it but the trustees cannot. As it respects the premises, therefore, there can be no ground of dispute, and the writings, viz. an attested copy of them, are in the hands of the Society. I suppose [for they have never acknowledged the receipt of them].

The only things to be feared are the perpetrations of the Mission by admitting new members into the family mission, the providing for the right applications of the unappropriated stock; the expulsion of occupants who are disapproved; and the cutting off all right of succession to them on the part of our descendants. We have laboured to secure these and all collateral points in the instrument we send to you; and if we have failed, it has been from out of further light, and not from want of inclination. I think Bro. M is sincerely desirous of the articles being such as will conciliate the minds of all parties, and I assure you that I would make any sacrifice, that of truth and righteousness excepted, to accomplish that end. I am sure we only need to understand one another better, to lay aside all these unlovely things which have arisen and which will eat as a canker, and destroy all that is dear to Christians.

Carey to Steadman, June 29, 1830, Serampore

I wish I felt a pleasure in writing letters, you would then hear much more frequently from me, but there is scarcely anything at which I feel so awkward, and out of my element as writing.

I am much discouraged at the almost entire want of cooperation with us in the work of the Serampore mission. I see there is a very serious balance against us in the accounts of our Treasurer, which he has advanced. The Society has become hostile to us, and has sufficient influence to prevent those supplies of a pecuniary nature without which we cannot meet the expences of the stations depending on us.

The spread of the Gospel in India was the first object of the Society and it has been the first and last with us, to that object Bro. Marshman, Bro. Ward, and myself have uniformly devoted all our time, our strength, and our income, except a pittance scarcely sufficient for our necessary expences can be called a reserve. When Bro. Ward died he left but little for his widow, and we have constantly paid her an annuity since his death. By a statement just sent to England, you will use our present circumstances, and the necessity we will be reduced to, of relinquishing some of our stations, the doing of which will be to me like having my limbs forcibly torn from me while living. I hope no person is so entirely lost to Christian feeling, or so much under the influence of a party spirit as to feel pleasure in the ruin of those stations, merely because they are connected with Serampore. The Society and all the friends of vital godliness formerly gloried in them; and they are the fruit of missionary exertions carried on, under many discouragements for a long series of years, and may God in mercy make such provisions for carrying them forward that our hopes may not be disappointed . . .

Answer to Criticism from the Society

The mission at Serampore received a great deal of criticism from the Society after 1815. New, younger missionaries disagreed with the older missionaries on issues of control. Evidently several in the Baptist Missionary Society sided with the younger group and complaints from home became more frequent. Carey was detailed in his reactions to those attacks. Much of the information in some very long letters to Ryland and Dyer chronicle the controversy. The problems centered on the ownership of the Serampore property and the management style of Marshman.

Carey to Sutcliffe, Aug. 5, 1812, Calcutta

It has been said by some in England "How can these men know so many Languages?". To this I reply let any one who makes this objection set himself as decidedly to study any ten or twelve of the modern languages of Europe, as I have done to study those of India, and he will easily account for it.

Carey to Ryland, Dec. 30, 1816

. . . You have heard evil things of several of our Native Brethren and cautions against receiving all the reports of the Circular Letters appear to have reached England. To this I can only observe that we could wish all our Brethren to be as able and diligent as the first Divines in Europe and America, but they are not so, and even in Europe and America there are many of inferior abilities, and very exceptional temper. We take all the care we can in selecting the persons, and are I think scrupulously exact in reporting the intelligence contained in the Circular Letters. But we have had a task of no small difficulty, and a burden of no small weight. Most of our European Brethren have a great degree of jealousy respecting our Native or country born Brethren and think the accounts from them occupy too much room, when their own names scarcely appear. But we have no remedy for this, as some of them, Brethren Moore and Rowe for instance, do nothing among the natives and I think will never be able to do anything, except the superintending of Native Preachers, and schools.

When my Nephew and Bro. Yates came out they saw some letters from these men to Bro. Lawson, and believed all the evil without giving us credit for knowing as much as they. They imbibed a strong prejudice against Brethren Marshman and Ward, and this was not a little strengthened by Bro. Lawson who had always been full of the same from the time when Bro. Johns left us or a little before. These two young men brought with them such notions of independence as at an earlier period of the Mission would have been its infallible ruin. Happily, however, we were enabled to concede to them every cause: and the step of placing Bro. Lawson and my Nephew at Calcutta and retaining Bro. Yates at Serampore met every cause.

Now all the accounts of Brethren Thompson and Kerr, and the summary condemnation of de Bruyn were received by them from above the quarter: and not only believed but propagated, and sent to England without giving us the credit of even caring about them. We had, however, heard all these reports more at full than they had, and before they did. We, however, thought it best to examine before condemnation. We did so, and obtained all the intelligence we could both from Friends and Foes, and in one instance sent a Brother to Chittagong to make enquiry on the spot. The result was that the reputation of the Brethren rather gained than lost by the enquiry. It must be observed that Kerr (of whom I have the lowest opinion) supported himself and laboured in the Mission. My son, William, has lately returned from a tour through the East of Bengal, and is as fully convinced of the innocence of de Bruyn, and of his value as a Missionary as a man can be. A hasty step, such as would have been in unison with our Brethren's feelings at that time would have torn up several important stations and have left us the mortification of seeing that we had done it without just grounds.

Carey to Ryland, Apr. 12, 1817, Calcutta

. . . We shall send you, without delay, attested copies of the Deed of all the Mission Property. I confess I am a little indignant at some of the hints in one of your letters, about our interested conduct. Our late Dear Bro. Fuller would with one scowl of his brow have dissipated a thousand such insinuations. I have devoted my all to the Cause and so have my Brethren and when my Son Felix obtained some sums of money which he had never paid, I became responsible, and with the little private property I possessed, paid the whole. Though I do not say that the society to whose interests I have devoted my life and property owe me as a debt of gratitude much more than that, I am now in my old age destitute of a Rupee, except that my Brethren have so accommodated things as to agree to a gradual liquidation of the Debt. My Wife likewise in her old age is in the same predicament though the greatest part of the property came to me with her. I do not complain; We are trusted for the Publick and for God. My Brethren could not remit the Debt if they would, nor could I have accepted it if they had. I confess I am become a fool in glorying but you have compelled me.

Carey to Ryland, Serampore, Apr. 11, 1818

I and Bro. Ward have now lived with Bro. M for 18 years; We have seen him in all situations, and I do not think either of us are blind to his faults. I have seen all his tortuousities and all his ambition, the two crimes Eustace charges him with. He is not a perfect man, any more than others, and I believe a certain kind of crooked policy is natural to him, it runs through all he does and says. He cannot walk straight on the road, he cannot preach straight forwards, but leads all his sentences with parentheses. I admit the whole of these things and every other Defect of his character; but I cannot caricature him, which I am sure our brethren do, that would be like publishing a caricature print of a man who had a long nose, by representing it as elongated to the extent of several yards. Bro. M's excellencies are such that his defects are almost concealed by them, and I believe him to be one of the finest friends the Mission ever had and I hope the Mission may never stand in want of one like him.

Carey to Dyer, July 15, 1819, Serampore

{One reason not to include the letters to the Society signed by Carey, Marshman, and Ward in this collection is the statement by Carey found in this letter. He tells us that Marshman was responsible for those reports.}

Bro. Marshman has always been ardently engaged in promoting the cause of God in India, and being of very active mind, has generally been chosen by us to draw up our reports, to write many of our publick letters, to draw up plans for the promoting of the objects of the Mission, founding and managing schools, raising subscriptions, and other things of a like nature, so that he has taken a more active part than Bro. Ward and myself in these publick acts of the Mission. These things placed him in the foreground, and it has been no uncommon thing for him, to bear the blame of those acts which equally belong to Bro. Ward and myself, merely because he was the instrument employed in preparing them.

You know that Bro. M., Bro. Ward and myself were some years ago chosen to be a committee to manage the concerns of the Society, to disperse its funds, to regulate the Salaries of the Brethren, and to choose their situations for labour, in short, to manage all the details of the Mission in India. Several of these were unthankful offices, and we always found it difficult to give satisfaction; indeed, I have no doubt that the circumstance of our being thus chosen excited jealousies among our other Brethren long before the present leaders arrived in India. They often thought us severe, and not unfrequently charged us with being unkind . . . and induced us several years ago to declare that we considered every station as independent of Serampore and of each other, and only dependent on the Society. The harsh and unkind letters we often received from our Brethren induced us to write Bro. Fuller and afterwards to Bro. Ryland, declining to manage the funds of the Society any longer till they could accommodate themselves, and recommending the House of Alexander & Co. in Calcutta. Much obloquy, therefore, was cast on Bro. M. merely from the suspicion that he was the moving cause in most of these transactions.

The charge of profusion brought against Bro. M is more extensive than you have stated in your letter. He is charged with having his House superbly furnished, with keeping several vehicles for the use of his Family and with labouring to aggrandize and bring them unto publick notice to culpable extent. The whole business of Furniture, internal economy, &ct., of the Serampore station, must exclusively belong to ourselves and I confess I think the question about it is an unlovely one. *{Someone had accused Marshman of having a more lavish table than the Gov. Gen. Lord Hastings. Carey had been at both tables.}* I suspect the informant never was at Lord Hastings table, as he could not have been guilty of such misrepresentation. Lord Hastings table costs more in one day than Bro. M's in ten.

The following statement may explain the whole business of Bro. M's Furniture for which you all have been so puzzled to account for and have certainly accounted for it in a way which is not the true one. We have you know, a very large school, perhaps the largest in India. In this school are children of persons of the first rank in the country. The parents or guardians of these children frequently call at the Mission home and common propriety requires that they should be respectfully received and invited to take a Breakfast or Dinner, and sometimes to continue there a day or two. It is natural that persons who visit the Mission Home upon business superintended by Bro. M should be entertained at his house rather than elsewhere. Till within the last four or five years we had no particular arrangement for the accommodations of visitors who come to see us; but as those who visited us on business were entertained at Bro. M's, it appears to be the most eligible method to provide for the entertainment of other visitors there also. But at that time Bro. M. had not a decent table for persons of the above description to sit down to. We, therefore, voted a sum to enable him to provide such articles as were necessary to entertain them with decency, and I am not aware that he has been profuse or that he has furnished anything not called for by the rules of propriety. I have no doubt Bro. Ward can enumerate and describe all these articles of furniture. It is, however, evident that you be very imperfect judges of their necessity unless you could at the same time form a just estimate of the circumstances in which we stand. It might also be considered that all of these articles are publick property, and always convertible into their fuller value in cash. *{Carey goes on to say he would hope the situation has not come to that point where a man and his wife who have for 19 or 20 years labored and sacrificed much and given many Rupees to the work would have their furniture taken from them.}* Surely I say, things are not come to that [place] that he or any other Brother must give account to the Society of every plate he uses and every loaf he eats.

{In explaining the mission vehicles, Carey notes that until recently there was only one horse chaise that was used to get back and forth to Calcutta. Sisters Marshman and Ward both had a liver disease and needed to exercise so another vehicle was purchased.}

I never ride out for health, but usually spend an hour or two Morning and Evening in the Garden. Other conveyances pulled by men and horse and saddle included. Marshman also has the most children and educating them requires more transportation.

Surely a Man's caring for his Family's health and his Children's education is, if a crime, a venial one, and ought not to be held up to blacken his reputation . . .

I wish I had half his piety, energy of mind, and zeal for the cause of God. These excellencies in my opinion so far unbalance all his defects that I am compelled to consider him as a Christian far above the common man.

I have said that "I never ride out for the sake of Health" and it may, therefore, be enquired why are vehicles but for the purposes of health more necessary for the other members of the Family than for you? I reply, that my health is in general good, and probably much benefitted by a journey to and from Calcutta two or three times a week. I have also a great fondness for Natural Science, particularly Botany and Horticulture. These, therefore furnish not only exercise but amusement for me. These amusements of mine are not, however, enjoyed without expence, any more than those of my Brethren, and were it not convenient for Bro. M.'s accusers to make a stepping stone of me, I would no doubt but my collection of plants, aviary, and museum, would be equally impeached as articles of luxury and lawless expence, though except the Garden, the whole of these expences are borne by myself.

. . . When I engaged in the Mission it was with a determination that, whatever I suffered, a breach therein should never originate with me. To this resolution I have hitherto obstinately adhered. I think everything should be done, every sacrifice made, and every method of accommodation or reconciliation tried before a Schism is suffered to take place. I confess I have no certain grounds for the suspicion, but I cannot help thinking that our Brethren were instructed by some person or persons, before they left England, to spy out our conduct. I do not think this was done by the society as a body, but the unworthy suspicions uttered by some, and the proposals actually made by the Society respecting the Trust for the Serampore property, connected with the high tone assumed by our Brethren on their arrival certainly concerned with each other in a manner inexplicable upon any other supposition. A Letter lately received by Bro. Pearce from a Friend I very highly respect, but whose name I will not mention, leaves no doubt on my mind that he was privately desired to spy out our conduct.

. . . you will see that I disapprove as much of the conduct of our Calcutta Brethren as it is possible for me to disapprove of any human actions. The evil they have done is I fear irreparable. And certainly the whole might have been prevented by a little conversation with either of us, and a hundredth part of that self denial which I found necessary to exercise for the first four years of the mission would have prevented this awful rupture . . . I certainly think a monstrous waste of strength, and money for four Missionary brethren, besides Pearce and Penny to be crowded together in Calcutta where there are besides them four Paedo Baptists, and four Evangelical Clergymen, besides four native Brethren and where we also preach.

. . . I have now only to recommend to the Society to send out all Missionaries hereafter, so that they may be independent of each other, and to appoint them to the stations they are to occupy naming, however, optional stations for them if any thing should make it impossible to occupy those first intended, and to fix their monthly or yearly income, including in all cases either a sum to erect a house, or an increased allowance for the rent of one. [In most cases, however, the latter will be scarcely practicable]. I consider this as the only means of preventing Missionaries from crowding together in a few large places, to the neglect of all the country around.

Carey to Ryland, Sept. 28, 1819

I was much grieved at the two letters you sent some time ago, one to me and the other to Bro. Marshman. I have no way to account for these letters than by supposing that you had just received some report from the Calcutta Brethren and while red hot with their representations wrote the letter. I suppose this to be the case because every complaint contained therein is an echo of the Calcutta slang.

The idea that if you had sent a letter to Bro. M. I should not have seen it originated in Calcutta. I despise that idea from my heart: but it is not true that communications have been with held from me. We act on no such principles of suspicion. Those young men found it necessary to say something, and they, therefore, in expressing their regards to me, made me appear either a tame fool or an unprincipled villain: for the purpose of having a cloak to their conduct.

In reply to your Queries - The whole premises at Serampore belong to the Society. I am one of the Trustees, and while I live and have the use of reason, they never shall be alienated from it. Nay, more, if the Society wish to expel me from the house in which I live, they have nothing to do but to appoint someone to inhabit it and I will, without a word, vacate it. - - And I wish you to rest assured that no part or particle of the Mission premises shall ever cleave to me or to my seed after me if I can possibly prevent it.

There are no writings made out for Cutwa. It belongs to the Society to have them made: but I will not be a Trustee to one more particle of the Society's property in India.

. . . Your letter to Bro. Marshman was absolutely insulting and I will confidentially say unmerited. You are bound as a Christian Man to acknowledge the evil of what you have said, and if you have mentioned such things to others you are bound as an act of simple justice to contradict what you have said.

In that letter, you seem to set it down as a principle that we have two principal heads in our accounts, Landed Property - Solid Landed Property - - and Dissipations. All the property at Serampore &ct., belongs to the first, and all the support of Missionaries, printing and distributing of Tracts &ct., to the latter. The first you say is ours, the latter yours.- - Now, my dear Brother be assured that neither I nor my Brethren have any objection to reversing this account. For though the Premises &ct., are actually the Society's and conveyed to them, yet as, generally speaking one part was purchased with money realised in India and the other with money sent from England, we cannot object to its appearing on record that the Baptist M.S. had laid out, all its funds from the beginning in the Purchase of Solid Landed Property, and that the money realised by their Brethren in India has been completely dissipated, viz. employed to support Missionaries, and to carry on all the work which has been done to spread the Gospel among the Heathen.

All the ill natured things said about John Marshman, I am sure Bro. M., however, much he feels it, will take no notice of - And I never shall more mention the Sneer about Poor Felix's having Cutwa. The younger Brethren have Children as well as we. They will I hope some time arrive at Man's Estate. But if you should then expect them to hate their children, and account it a crime for them to wish to see them employed in the work their Father's have chosen. If it should be expected that they should do as we have done, viz. devote their all to the Mission till they are unable to provide for their children - and after that if it should be a crime for them to receive their children when in want, or not in want, into their Houses and to feel the sentiments towards them. - It may be that you may find them as little ready to relish the bitter pill as we have been.

Be assured that Bro. M. will never think of replying to any letter till he is accounted an honest man. He has not deserved the treatment he has met with. I advised him to burn your letter and let no one see it, which he did. I hope you will say that these two letters were not written by order of the Society, but were entirely your own. Be assured, however, that such letters are not likely to do any good. I think it was unwise in the Society to desire Bro. Dyer to write to me. I would have shewn his letter to Bro. M. but he refused to see it. I replied to it but hope no such unlovely task will ever be impressed on me again. If that does not see things to rest I have no hope that they will be put to rest at all.

Sooner or later the truth will be understood, and nothing can prevent righteousness from being brought forth as the light. To that God who will finally set everything in a right point of view, and who will not be a party to any one's private or publick views, I wish to commit my cause.

You, in your letter to Bro. M. several times repeat an expression in our printed Letter; Are you Gods?, incorrectly. In that letter it was said that we had devoted our all to God: and the question was "But are you God?" It is a fact that we have devoted our all to God but not to Men. And I might ask, when, immediately after the death of Dear Bro. Fuller, the Society was divided, in which half did the Deity inhere? For if God and the Society are synonymous, it is of the utmost importance to determine this point, and it will be equally important should any division occur thereafter. But if they are not synonymous, we have only to do as we have all along done, and act independently of both parties. I have no doubt but my nephew and Bro. Yates were authorised by a party which did not think over highly of Bro. Fuller's measures, to take the steps they did. They traveled on steadily from the day of their arrival in the high road of Separation, without a single effort to prevent it, or to get the evils of which they have complained, redressed. I think they would not have done this without assurance of support. I have no authority for this I confess but cannot account for their conduct upon any other principle.

As to a right to govern their own Family and their Mission undertakings, they are as tenacious as we ever were, and were any one of us to live with them a much longer time than they did with us, and then take upon himself to censure them or to attempt to direct their affairs, I believe they would no more submit to it than we.- - Families must be independent of each other and Stations must be independent of each other, but if the Mission is of any use Missionaries must be spread through the country and must not act in hostility to each other. What are the Calcutta Brethren doing which we did not do before they came. With the assistance of their Auxiliary Society they have built four or five strong houses. We had built three long before they came without any aid. They charge us with unfairly representing the labours of our native Brethren in our reports, but they too can puff. See their reports. - - The truth is we represented everything as accurately as we could, but it is possible we might sometimes say more and sometimes less than the real facts. __________ - ever published the Letters we received. - - The C. Brethren make their own reports. If nothing were represented to be done subscriptions must fail.

I was in hopes that I should never more have had occasion to write upon this disagreeable subject again, but I thought these most unlovely letters required some reply. I have now for ever done with the business, and be assured that no one will henceforth draw from me one syllable about it.

Carey to Society, Jan. 21, 1820

From some rather vague reports which have reached us we understand that ideas have been entertained by some persons in England of our having acted unfaithfully in the management of the Funds entrusted to us; and that this has in some instances operated to the injury of the publick collection.

It should always have been easy for you, Dear Brethren, to have repelled such a Charge, as the accounts of our management of your Funds have been always sent to England and those of our management of other funds regularly published.

To prevent the evil, however, we have drawn up a statement, a few copies of which we send to you; but it is our desire that it be circulated as widely as possible throughout Great Britain.

Carey to Dyer, March 27, 1828

Two days ago the Baptist and Particular Baptist Magazines for Nov. arrived here. What can be the object of those malignant pieces invented in them against us? Did Bro. Marshman's statement call for anything in this spirit? We and the society have separated. What then can be the design of these intemperate attacks? Is it intended thereby to prevent the publick from supporting the stations and works connected with us? If so, I must say the object is not very benevolent, and I should suppose few would be to defend it, but what other object can the writers of these pieces have had? Surely they did not mean to vindicate the steps taken by the Society at our expence, and if they did, surely the Society must consider their interference as somewhat officious.

Carey to Jabez, Apr. 17, 1828

. . . From a letter of yours to Jonathan, in which you express a very indecent pleasure at the opposition which Bro. Marshman has received, not by the Society, but by some anonymous writer in a Magazine, I perceive you are informed of the separation which has taken place between them and us. What, in that anonymous piece you call a set down I call a falsehood. You ought to know that I was a party in all publick acts and writings, and that I never intend to withdraw from all the responsibility connected therewith. I utterly despise all the creeping mean assertions of that party when they say they do not include me in their censures nor do I wish for their praise. According to them, and according to your rejoicing at Bro. Marshman's set down, and I suppose Jonathan's, to whose information yours appears to have been an answer, I am either a Knave or a Fool. A Knave if I joined with Bro. Marshman, but if, as those gentlemen say, and as you seem to agree with them, I was only led as he pleased, and was a mere cats paw then, of course, I am a Fool. In either way, your thoughts are not very high as it respects me. I do not wonder that Jonathan should express himself unguardedly, his family connection with Mr. Pearce sufficiently accounts for that. We have long been attacked in this country, first by Mr. Adam, and afterwards by Dr. Bryce. Bryce is not silenced by two or three pieces by John

Marshman, printed in his own Newspaper, the *John Bull* and as to some of the tissues of falsehood published in England, I certainly shall never reply to one of them, and I hope no one else will. That cause must be bad which needs such means to support it. I believe God will bring forth our righteousness as the Noonday.

STRUGGLE WITH THE SOCIETY FOR CONTROL

Two key issues precipitated a struggle for control between the Serampore Mission and the Baptist Missionary Society. Who owned the Serampore property and who determined the makeup of the mission family at Serampore? The property, even though not purchased with Society money, became the Society's with Carey, Marshman and Ward as trustees. The decision concerning who could be part of the mission family in Serampore remained in the hands of Carey and his associates. They would not relinquish that right.

Carey to Ryland, Sept.1817

{In this letter Carey vents his anger and frustration at the Society and Ryland for accusations and lack of support economically and otherwise.}

. . . You know, My Dear Bro. that I and my two Brethren at Serampore have from the beginning devoted ourselves and our all to the cause of our Redeemer in India, and that we have laboured to the utmost of our Power to promote the work of the Gospel, but after twenty years labour I now see myself and My Brethren see themselves called upon to witness a distrust of our honesty, and an attempt to place us in circumstances in which we may be expelled from the premises for which we have laboured and the sphere of action in which we are placed, at the instance of a very few men on the opposite side of the Globe. Our Families are considered an encumbrance and our Widows, when we die, liable to any treatment which men placed in our situations think proper to subject them to.

My Dear Bro. We are yours to live and to die with you, but we are your Brethren, not your Servants. I beseech you not, therefore, to attempt to exercise a power over us to which we never shall submit. Bear with me a little, even if I should speak foolishly, for my heart is exceedingly wounded at the proposal of the Society and at several concomitant symptoms which accompany it. I have not myself examined the accounts, but as we are preparing a statement of all that has been done by you and by us for the cause of God here, I have heard some of the Items and may, therefore, without attempting numerical accuracy mention the gross sum at random . . ."

{Carey here gives a summation of all the property costs etc.}

. . . and entirely have we devoted our all to the cause, that My Sister was actually left to be supported by the Parish. I have two Sons whose conduct has been reprehensible, but I am their Father. I became responsible for one to a large amount, all of which I paid mostly from property which received with my Wife.

I am now accountable for another Son to a large amount, and if he fails of paying it I must make up my mind to go to Prison, and have made up my mind thereto. Were I to die today I have not property sufficient to purchase a Coffin, and my Dear Wife would be entirely unprovided for. I know my Brethren will provide for her, but I would not commit her to any one except my two elder Brethren for the Word. I know that it is being reported in England that we are making private fortunes. I, therefore, mention this circumstance as a confutation of it. We are coarsely clad, and, certainly, not over-fed, and I believe he among us who possesses the most, has not so much as he contributes to the publick stock in four months. I had 6,000 Rupees, but as I said before I have none of it left. In these things, I am become a Fool in glorying, but Ye have compelled me.

You mention that a Letter of ours made a great sensation among the members of the Committee; I can assure you that yours made such a sensation among us as I never wish to see repeated, and the greater numbers of us should certainly have immediately quitted the Mission Premises and have carried on our engagements for the Cause of God on other premises, had not a concern for the cause of God prevented our taking a precipitate step. We My Dear Bro. have laboured for these premises. We borrowed money to pay for them. We paid for them. <u>We bought them and became trustees for them on behalf of the Baptist Missionary Society</u>. And now we are required to associate with ourselves a large majority of persons in England as trustees for them, and the reason alleged is the <u>very delicate one</u> that our Children may perhaps become Rogues. They may, but what security have we that the Children of these persons named in England may not equally fail in virtue?

The fact is My Dear Bro. that WE not our Children are the suspected persons. <u>We can have no objection to a single individual of the persons</u> proposed as co-trustees. We have always entertained the highest esteem for their Character. But we <u>will never consent</u> to put it into the power of the best persons on the Earth, at the distance of 1/4 the Circumference of the Globe to appoint any person or persons they please to supercede us in the occupation of the Premises and the conducting of the large concern in which we are engaged. <u>The Premises belong to the Society. We have made a present of them to the Society</u> - but if the Society insists upon the measure proposed, we will, much as we are attached to the place evacuate it and purchase other premises which though they shall be given to the Lord shall not be given to the Baptist Missionary Society, and there we will carry on the Work in which we are engaged subject to no control but that of God's most holy Word. In this we are all of one mind, and here we shall make our stand.

I cannot see why our Wives and Children are to turned out into the wide World on our demise . . .

. . . We always thought ourselves masters of the funds produced by our own labour. We devoted the whole to the cause of God, and wish to do so till our dying day, but the Funds we produce though employed to promote the same object have never been so merged in to the funds of the Society as to put them under the control of others. We are your Brethren, but not your hired Servants. We have always accounted it our glory to be related to the Missionary Society and with them to pursue the same grand object and shall rejoice in it as long as you permit us - but we will not come under the Power of any so long as we can help it. I would hope the ideas of Domination which Dear Bro. Fuller never thought of; but which the society has simultaneously imbibed since his death, will be given up; as we shall never give place by subjections, no not for an hour.

This idea of the right of the Society to dispose of our funds, has predominated in the minds of our Younger Brethren, and If I am not mistaken, the opposition which they have shown to us has arisen from finding that we would not admit of their directing the use of them . . . I find them seize upon any fault or failing of our Native Brethren, especially those employed in the work of the Ministry with a malignant tenacity which can scarcely be equaled, but they themselves settle down into a course of preaching to Europeans, and aim at little more. My Nephew, Eustace, is an exception to this and would his Health permit, would have laboured much among the Heathen . . .

Were we to evacuate the Mission Premises at Serampore, (which we shall certainly do if the scheme of a majority of trustees in England be persisted in) what would be the consequence? We should carry with us the School, the Printing office, and the Translations, and merely leave the buildings. They would in that case lose all their value, for it is the use they are put to that makes them valuable. They might be inhabited by the younger branches of the Mission or any other you might nominate; but where would be the wisdom or the advantage of settling four or five persons at Serampore to do nothing? And where are any to be found who either could or would carry on the work, in which we are engaged?

Mr. Pearce is an amiable young man for anything I can see, but what could you mean by sending him to be Bro. Ward's coadjutor? Would you force a man upon us of whom we know nothing. Is he to be subject to Bro. Ward? or Bro. Ward to him? Are there to be two managers of the Printing office with equal powers? And in that case who will or can ensure their agreeing upon every occasion?

Oct.1. I had written thus far three weeks ago, and though I fear I have expressed myself with rather too much warmth and with much incoherence, and could on that account wish to write the whole again, Yet an impossibility of commanding time to copy it, on the one hand, and a strong desire to say something which shall convey something of my feelings upon the proposal of the Committee, on the other, prevail on me to let the whole go just as it is; I am writing to a Brother who will make no bad of me of it. I have the pleasure to say that our publick letter is now finished to my mind . . .

Carey to Burls, Aug. 19, 1818, Serampore

Assure yourself that no such thought as that of alienating the property at Serampore from the Mission Society ever entered our minds. We did think it wrong that after all our exertions the whole fruit of our labours should be at the disposal of Brethren just arrived, and that the Society should be able by a single vote, probably carried by a party among them, to cripple all our efforts and whatever we have said has been said to prevent others exercising a power over us which we never wish to exercise over them, but <u>we glory in our relation to the Society. We have forwarded its objects to the utmost of our powers and will do so. The property was but a trust from them and it is our wish it may always remain theirs.</u>

Carey to Ryland, Oct. 23, 1820

It is clear we have nothing to expect from the Society. We asked for a little assistance to support the Native Preachers who are the life and soul of the Mission, but by a resolution of the Committee I see it has been refused. I trust that God will enable us to support them without its help though we feared it when we made the application.

. . . As to the Veto upon our choice of Brethren to the family remains; my unalterable determination is all summed up in the word "no". And this not from obstinacy but from the fact that "two cannot walk together except they are agreed" . . .

All I had to say to the Society, therefore, I sum up in the following Declarations.

1. The three parcels of land with all the buildings on them (and certainly as much has been laid out on their improvements as they cost at first) commonly called the Mission House, are the property of the Society, and held in trust for it.

2. All the produce of our Labours, with certain exceptions for a provision for our Widows and private expences, is devoted to God, but forms <u>no part</u> of the funds of the Society nor is in <u>any sense</u> under their control.

3. The choice of our associates in this family union belongs to ourselves alone, and no Brother, however, excellent, can be imposed upon us without our consent. We have, however, in a document sent to England by Sister Marshman, mentioned circumstances in which the choice of Brethren for Serampore will revert to the Society. To these declarations we shall scrupulously adhere.

4. We are co-workers with the Society, but by no means, nor any sense, <u>its servants</u>."

{Carey threatens to withdraw from the Society if they do not retract a resolution that was put out by the Society Dec. 31, 1819. The resolution accused Carey and his associates of trying to alienate the property in Serampore from the Society. The Society stated its refusal to allow this. Carey defends himself, Marshman and Ward saying they never threatened to do such a thing and were offended at the accusation and demands the Society retract the resolution.}

Carey to Ryland, June 14, 1821

Yours of January 1, 1820 gave me much pain. If I had in any letter ever said or intimated that I felt the slightest diminution of affection towards you it must have arisen from inability to express myself clearly, or from inadvertence. My dear Brother I have always loved you since I knew you, and my love, I am sure, continues undiminished. These most distressing things which have occurred in the Mission may have extorted inconsiderate expressions from me, but nothing has altered my love for you. I did think an expression in that letter you sent contained a sneer at Felix: but you had only to say I was mistaken to satisfy my mind upon the subject. I now entreat your forgiveness for harbouring one single moment the idea that you were capable of doing so, and if I have ever written in an unkind or disrespectful manner, I request your forgiveness for doing so. Pray my dear Brother let nothing divide our affections in this world, and I am convinced then nothing will do it to eternity. The sentiments I have expressed concerning the Society, the younger Brethren in India, the unlimited condemnation of Bro. M. I cannot retract.

. . . As for the Society, its rapacious grasping for power will sink it. We gave it the property, and have improved that property to double its former value: and still more would have been given, had it not been for its rapacity. But this would not do. The Society must claim dominion over our family union, demand a veto upon the choice of members of the family and claim a control over the manner in which we spend the funds which we have earned with the sweat of our brows. This cannot be conceded. We never asked the Society whether we should form a family union at all; we never asked who should be included in it. Bro. Rowe was chosen, Brethren Mardon, Biss and Moore were not, and the same of others. We never asked the Society's opinion about these things nor ever intended to do so. Why then is this right demanded over us now?

The younger no more admit this right in their transactions than we do. They would not part with Bro. Adam at the remonstrances of the Society: when a dispute arose between him and them they separated without any reference to the Society, and ever made a division of (Mission) property. They received Mr. Stratham into their family union, though I fear the only object aimed at was a second division of the church in the Lall Bazar. I do not say this to reflect on them, they have a right to act according to their own judgment. But they have in their transactions justified everything in us for which they separated from us, and shew to the whole world how chimerical the principles are which they and the Society have demanded that we should recognize. Bro. Adam now denies or expresses <u>doubt equal to denial of</u> the proper deity of Christ - and if a letter I saw from him, is to be depended on, Bro. Yates has the same doubts. Adam is now engaged (not avowedly) with Ram Mohan Ruya, in writing against the Trinity. Ram Mohan Ruya is the avowed author of the work, but Adam who is always with him furnishes helps, to what extent I know not. The work is in the press of the younger brethren. Bro. Marshman will, if spared, reply to it in the "Friend of India". All this will work for good in the end. - Mr. Townley's party and the Church of England brethren are very friendly with us, and greatly strengthen our hands.

. . . A letter just received from Bro. Ward, written on his passage to America, fully confirms everything I ever expected about the Society, or rather Committee. After he had been in England for more than twelve months, they invited him to one of their sittings, where the determination that we should be their dependents was openly asserted. Bro. W. conceded more by far than ever I would have agreed to, but that was not enough. All our earnings are devoted to the cause of God in India, but not to the Baptist Society. To this point we have invariably cleaved, and I now possess somewhat less property of my own, than my late dear Wife brought me. We have in no instance appropriated these earnings, consecrated to God, to other purposes. The Society does not say we have: but thinks us such villains that we may probably hereafter do it. Would the Society be content to act with us, as it always did before the death of dear Bro. Fuller, it would immediately appear that we were in all we do, promoting the objects for which it exists, but if the Society is resolved to identify itself with God, and claim a control over that which we have devoted to him, it will find itself mistaken for I, for one, will never acknowledge any such right of control.

Mr. Burls wrote to me an ill natured letter some time ago, holding out a threat of resigning his office as treasurer, and magnifying his labours and disinterestedness. I certainly have no wish to detract from either of these, but Mr. Burls is under the same obligation as I am to devote himself to the cause of Christ. Unless he intends to prove that " he is <u>not</u> bought with a price", I must say he "<u>is not his own</u>", but is bound to glorify God "with his body and spirit which are his".

I cannot write to Mr. Dyer. All his communications are like those of a Secretary of State, and not, as was formerly the case with dear Bro. Fuller, those of a Christian Friend. In short, after Bro. Ward's return, unless his reports call for the contrary, it is my fixed intention to withdraw from all connection with the Society, though not from the Mission. And as all my letters, and all our publick documents have been suppressed by the Society, and nothing even replied to, I shall take steps which it cannot counteract, of circulating through the Christian World my reasons for the steps which I then take.

My dear Bro. pray for me that I may do all things right and in a right spirit. I wish not to be precipitate, but the ungenerous conduct of the Society in whispering suspicions through the Christian publick, or in suffering us to lie under these suspicions, when they had most abundant proof of their falsehood. In suppressing all our correspondence, and almost totally neglecting all care of the translations, the schools, and the College, the only things for which we wish their help - too plainly shew that they feel no interest in Serampore. Nothing but tenderness for a Society which was like my life blood, would have induced me to submit to such a series of injustice so long: but now I see no object to be accomplished by further forbearance.

. . . Jabez at Ajmere. I should have written to the Committee to consider him as a Missionary, which indeed he is: but their refusal of a small request about some money he had taken up from us on the credit of his House at

Amboyna, discourages me. They allow the younger brethren at Calcutta who are getting rich, an immense income for no earthly purpose than to oppose us and divide the church we had raised (for as to all their other labours they are nothing more than we had constantly engaged in for the last fifteen years) but if we apply for the most reasonable thing in the world it is refused.

Carey to Burls, Oct. 5, 1821

You mention a wish that the misunderstanding between us and the Society may be brought to a termination. I assure you I wish it most sincerely. Several years have now elapsed of most unprofitable contentions. We have declared as explicitly as we could that the Mission Premises belong to the Society, and have sent the Deeds of sale and trust to them and the Society has declared that it has no wish to intermediate in our management of our own concerns. What else does either party require? I am fully of opinion that all things hostile ought to cease; and I think neither party need be ashamed to acknowledge that there has been much wrong on both sides. I wish this long letter we received from the Committee yesterday dated sometimes in April, had contained something of this instead of the long history of its proceedings about the promises.

{Carey continues for another page and half speaking about the controversy. He believes the private letters written years ago are being used as ammunition for the controversy and accuses the Society of taking them out of context.}

LATE LIFE RELATIONSHIP TO THE SOCIETY

Unfortunately, the controversy with the society grew worse. Continual wrangling over these issues and especially criticism of Marshman eventually led Carey and the Serampore Mission to separate from the Society. Certainly this was a sad moment in missions history when the one whose vision helped form a missionary society became independent of it.

Carey to Ryland, July 4, 1822

. . . The Society must expect no communications from me. To you I will write my whole heart. The Society appears to have given up all concern about the translations. We have consequently been obliged to relinquish some for want of funds. Mr. Thomason and the churchmen feel very indignant that the work of translation is not in the church, and have tried twenty little contrivances to lessen the credit of them, but in vain. This very week they received such an overwhelming testimony in favour of the Assam version from a Gentleman to whom they had applied, and who was entirely in their interest, has put a stop to a source of vexatious delays in paying the sum voted by the Bible Society. Judson is going on well and I believe most of the converts.

Carey to Sisters, Oct. 25, 1827

. . . You have undoubtedly heard of our separation from the Baptist Missionary Society. I had written to Mr. Dyer nearly twelve months ago, telling him my determination to separate myself from the Society unless they came to amicable terms with Bro. Marshman, so that my mind was quite made up to the separation. The Society had left us to struggle beyond our strength with the Expences of the Mission . . . Bro. Marshman, Bro. Ward, and myself have jointly contributed at least about 4,000 Rupees a month, for the last twenty years to the Mission, besides giving them the Mission Premises at Serampore, and were in our old Age forced to take the extreme step of putting some of the Dist-stations upon them, or seeing them sink. Bro. Marshman knew this was a thing which nothing but the greatest extremity could have forced us to; and he very properly refused to agree to it . . . I now wish they may be a thousand times more successful than we have ever been.

Carey to Jabez, Oct. 27, 1827

. . . An entire change has taken place in our relations to the Baptist Mission Society; we are now entirely separated from them. They had left us to support all the out stations for many years, and when we applied to them for assistance, they gave it in such a manner as to cramp all our exertions; and as the Friends of the cause in Scotland, and the West of England, and many other parts promised us separate support, we have mutually agreed to act separately and do all the good we can.

Carey to Jabez, Dec. 16, 1829

. . . I am extremely grieved at the spirit of contention which has broke out among the Churches of every denomination. As it respects our own denomination, the ostensible excuse is the refusal of myself and Bro. Marshman and Bro. Ward to acknowledge a right in the Baptist Missionary Society to all the property which we realized by our own labours. We gave them the premises at Serampore, those premises belong to them but this does not satisfy them. Of late, however, things have taken such a turn in England, in consequence of a statement published by Bro. Marshman preceded by a preface by Mr. Forster, that large districts have separated from the Society and agreed to devote all their funds to the cause at Serampore. This has been the case at Exeter, Bath, Bristol, at several places in Yorkshire, at Newcastle and in every part of Scotland. The opposite party have shewed so bad a spirit, and have been guilty of such misrepresentations as have quite opened the eyes of a great part of the Baptist interest, and I hope great good will arise therefrom. Our cause is in the hands of God, who does all things right. The Independents and the Church of England are in much the same predicament, the Mission Societies appear to have assumed to themselves an extravagant degree of authority over the Missionaries to which the latter have refused to submit. This is a most distressing circumstance and has contributed greatly to injure the cause of God in the Heathen world. I hope a better spirit and a better understanding may soon take place.

Carey to Steadman, May 17, 1831, Serampore

All the stations connected with us are very dear to us, and the relinquishing of any one of them would be most a distressing circumstance. All our Brethren at those stations are tried and faithful men, and even those who have gone forth to the work within the last year give us as much pleasure as those who have been longer in the work.

Among other things in your letters both to me and Bro. Marshman you expressed a wish that I would pay a visit to England. To this, my dear Bro. there are many serious objections. The chief of these is the neglecting of my getting the edition of the Bengali Bible through the press which is now being printed. I am paying all the attention I am able to the making this edition as correct as possible of the Old Testament, the second Book of Kings . . . *{Carey also mentions the work on other Bibles that are soon to go to press.}* I could then leave India, so far as regards my work, but not before unless God should call me away by death.

With respect to myself, were I in England, all my friends would be greatly disappointed. I am now 70 years old within three months. My recollection is so shattered and gone that I am afraid to assert anything, and often fear that I shall be accounted a liar merely through my want of recollection. I am sometimes depressed under the idea that I shall soon be superannuated. I could not travel day and night as Bro. Ward and Marshman did. I have also sometimes looked over England and to me it presents a great blank; nearly all my old acquaintances are dead, and I should have a new set of religious connections to form.

I wish from my heart that success may attend all the efforts of the Society, but I cannot approve of many things in their proceedings and should be occasionally obliged to say more upon those subjects than I am disclosed to do. For these and other similar reasons, I think my going to Europe would neither be useful or comfortable.

I think the pieces written by Bro. Marshman, and Mr. J. Marshman were necessary and I hope the controversy may end there. Above all things I dread the stirring up again of the unlovely spirit which spread itself through the Churches when Bro Marshman was in England. I must leave all this with God, and shall trust as long as I live, pray for the peace of Jerusalem.

Carey to Sisters, Dec.16, 1831

As to the disputes with the Society, my advice to all is "Answer them not a word." I believe the fiercest fire will go out if not fuel be added to it. Eustace, who is very pugnacious, has written a large book, full of small talk, full four fifths of which might with the utmost ease be made to tell as forcibly for us, if brought forward by a friend, as it is intended to make against us by him, our sworn enemy. I do not wonder, My Dear Sisters, that you who live in the atmosphere of the Society should feel towards it as you do; but be assured there is nothing of religion in those hostile attacks, and the sooner they are relinquished on all sides the better.

Spiritual Life of the Missionary

Perhaps the most fascinating feature of William Carey and other great Christian leaders is their spirituality. How did Carey's relationship to God instill in him such a reliance on God in desperate and dangerous situations? How did he cope with disappointment and success? What did he believe about God and God's activity in the world? What kind of spiritual disciplines did Carey practice habitually?

Many of Carey's letters disclose, although indirectly at times, the character of his spiritual walk. Perhaps the clearest information surfaces in letters to family as he advises his Sisters, Jabez, and his Father to walk closely with the Lord. Although not explicitly speaking of himself, surely these excerpts clue us into Carey's notions concerning the faith and its practical application.

Carey asserted strongly the importance of possessing a personal faith in Christ. His expressions of dependence on God grew out of a clear Calvinistic faith that declared God's sovereignty and providence. That confidence in God was evidenced in Carey's belief in prayer and commitment to scriptural truth. One expects nothing less from a missionary of William Carey's caliber. The letters illuminate a bit of the heart of the man.

Another facet of Carey's character was humility, a trait common to many great spiritual leaders. He perceived himself unworthy and ill equipped for the task consigned to him by God. Yet, Carey refused to abandon it allowing God's strength to be his refuge. Several letters in this section describe how Carey drew his strength from God.

Faith in Christ

A personal relationship with Christ captivated Carey's attention above everything else. He spoke about it often when corresponding with his family. An interest in Christ was "of the utmost importance." A union with God provided the power, grace, and sweetness of life for Carey. Separation from God resulted in everything to be avoided in life.

Carey to Father Mother, Moulton, March 3, 1787

While we live in a Changing world, we must expect to feel its mutations, nothing here continues long in one situation. Probably God's design in permitting such a Varying Scene continually, is to excite us to set our affections on Things above, so that we may use this World as not abusing it, because it passeth away and the Fashion thereof. Here we never should expect to enjoy Quietness long, for this polluted place is not our rest! No Felicity here like that experienced by a Heavenly-minded person whose hopes are fixed on an unchangeable God. Religion is the only thing that can truly ennoble the soul and raise the mind above the Flattering Sweets, the mean Pursuits or pungent sorrows of the present state, as well as refine the Hopes, expand and dignify the Ideas, and truly Beautify the Actions of its real Professors. Religion!...If we profess all things besides we're wretched without that. As that secures the mind against all Dangers of the present time, supports in trouble; Humbles in Prosperity, keeps us from Lazy security and Sloth on the one Hand and from Wild Enthusiasm, or mad Presumption on the other.

Religion is far from being a Dry and formal Round, mere Externals. When we Pray, tis to the Almighty Governor of Heaven and Earth. When we Hear a Sermon it is for Eternity. The Solemn Thought that we are accountable immortal should on all occasions possess our minds. Probations for an eternal world - How should we live! By nature Children of Wrath and under Condemnation. How earnestly should we sue for mercy! Our Carnal minds (at) Enmity against God. How ought we to be sorry for our Sins! Repentance is absolutely necessary to salvation. Pardon, Justification, Adoption, Sanctification may all be obtained by asking for them, without them we're miserable; with them we shall be eternally Happy. How stupid are those who neglect them! I Hope all my Dear Relations know the truth of these Observations by their own experience . . .

How does Polly? How is she in her mind? Tell her to Retire and read her Bible to be Gay; that admirable Line of Dr. Young contains a Direction that will never Fail, in that Glorious Book are Medicines of every Case of every Wounded Soul.

Carey to Father, Apr. 26, 1788

. . . We are creatures of such a Constitution, that our minds are too capricious to be filled with any thing but God; tis evident to you that we are all fallen and Justly exposed to the Curves of that Law that is holy, & Just, & Good. But as the Bias of our minds is opposite to that which it ought to be, and which in the nature of things cannot satisfy us, it proves that they who have no better portion will meet eternal disappointments. Of what importance then is it for us to set our affections on things above so that we may Join with Jeremiah and say Jehovah is my portion; therefore will I trust in him.

Carey to Sisters, Bandel, Dec. 4, 1793

I hope your Souls are prospering, and pray you not to be too much attached to this present World. It will soon perish and then they who sow to the flesh will find that to be carnally minded is death. Embrace Christ with all the Consequences of

Christianity, and commit all your ways to the Lord. Choose Affliction always rather than Sin, and let it be your Daily Business to walk near to God and endure as seeing him who is invisible.

For my own part, I must confess my wretched carnal Indolence, and Worldliness; yet if I find satisfaction in a thing it is in the things of God, and the Exercises of Religion.

Carey to Sisters, Tangan River, Dec. 22, 1796

. . . and while I commiserate with you all in all your distresses, and difficulties; I yet praise God to find you all in the Land of the Living; and I think while we complain of the greatest distresses, we must after all put all to the score of Divine Mercy; and say, It is of the Lord's mercies that we are not consumed because his compassions fail not. This side of Hell, Door of Hope, Praying Ground, all these are astonishing expressions and while there is a propriety in these expressions, we have abundant cause for thankfulness.

Was I disposed to complain, I have enough both within and without to complain about. My Heart is as bad and in some respects worse than that of any other person in the world; my coldness in the ways of God amazing, . . . little carnality great; yet were I to do nothing but complain, it would greatly add to my criminality. If there are all these pull backs and so much opposition, what is the proper inference but this, that we ought to use so much the more diligence to make our calling and election past all doubt; and if the days are evil, let it be remembered that this is an encouragement for using the more diligence, circumspection, and care that we may redeem the lost, and misspent time of our past lives. Let me recommend the first verse of the 33rd Psalm to you for your consideration, and it will appear that it is comely to change your voice, and unite with the ransomed of the Lord in songs of praise to God, and the Lamb.

I don't say this because I don't sympathize with your afflictions, I do sincerely do that, but it is my sympathy that induces me to entreat you not to double all your afflictions by always pouring over your darkest side, but take a peep on the other side; see what God has wrought, what he has promised to do. Reflect on his power, and on this, that he knows all you have to conflict with. The Omniscience of God is a sweet Theme to a genuine praying Christian, as indeed are all the attributes of God.

I am very fruitless and almost useless but the Word and the attributes of God are my hope, and my confidence, and my Joy, and I trust that his glorious designs will undoubtedly be answered, and accomplished notwithstanding all my usefulness. It is incongruous to suppose that God needs a poor creature like me to fulfill his Word, and as inconsistent to suppose that any of his designs can fail tho my feeble efforts should be altogether useless. I don't use this language because I want a cloak for my Idleness. I think I truly desire the accomplishment of God's purposes which is the best preservative from Idleness.

Carey to Ryland, Jan. 30, 1801, Serampore

{Carey quotes a letter from a good friend of his named Cunningham, whom he esteems highly. Obviously, Carey agrees with Cunningham's words.}

. . . I think the following extract from a letter I very lately received from Mr. C will do you good; "I agree in theory with all that is advanced in your letter. I think it evident that no being who has been infected with Sin can be admitted to the Divine presence without a sufficient atonement; and on this account all that is contained in the Scripture regarding the mediation, death and suffering of Our Saviour, is worthy of all acceptation. I also think that our own works can in no sense be the foundation of our acceptance with God; for to maintain this would be at once to set the necessity of a Saviour, and to maintain either that we are innocent, or that God can regard the guilty as innocent, both which are false. But tho I thus agree with you in Theory, I find that my belief is very far from having that constant & effectual influence on my conduct, which I conceive essential to the Character of a Christian. However, as I think that only the contemplation and enjoyment of infinite Good can satisfy the wants of an immortal mind, I feel a desire to go on, and cannot rest satisfied with any system of happiness which should exclude religion; and I am the more confirmed in my conviction by observing the empty and unsatisfying nature of the pursuits of those who surround me.

"At the same time my own experience teaches me, that to expect any attainment in Religion by my own strength would be vain & extravagant.- - One of the members who has joined our Society since you left us is a strong deist, and at the same time a very able & well informed man. As I was arguing with (him) a few Days ago on the absurdity of rejecting Christianity without examination, he owned that he never knew a man examine Christianity, who did not receive it but excused himself from examining under the plea that to do so was analogous to drinking Brandy, which always produced intoxication. I have brought this so remarkable a confession as to be well worthy of being repeated to you. It is really honourable to Christianity to have enemies, who must give up the exercise of their reason before they reject it."

Carey to Father, Dec. 1, 1802

. . . May you, My dear Father, and may I learn to place a greater Confidence in that almighty hand which so carefully superintends the variegated affairs of this lower world. I am more and more convinced of the great importance of a life of real communion with God, not only as it is the preparatory step to everlasting happiness but as the only line of conduct which can be attended with real pleasure here. An interest in Christ the Saviour, and faith in his Death are the springs of holy life, and, therefore, of the utmost importance to us. May God grant to you and to me that Faith which purifies the Heart.

Carey to Father, Feb. 18, 1807, Calcutta

. . . Dear Father, let us renew our covenant with God, let us anew surrender ourselves to Christ, let us with redoubled ardor, trusting in the death and merits of our redeemer, go forward in the Christian course looking to Jesus the author and finisher of our faith. I am far from a confidence that I shall go to heaven when I die; but I wish to be found among them who will eternally love and serve God. I have no pleasure now in the society of the wicked, and think that it would be a hell indeed to be eternally in the company of the best of them. I do take pleasure in the society of them who fear God, and though one of the most unprofitable, and the lowest in spiritual experience, I wish to be in their society for ever and ever.

Carey to Sisters, Aug. 18, 1828, Calcutta

Yesterday I was 67 Years old and preached in the Evening upon the occasion from Luke 12 Ver. Let your loins be girded and your lights burning and ye &ct. The subject was the great importance of being ready for death for which I observed two things were necessary. First, an interest by Faith in the atoning Blood of Christ; or Justification by Faith, which includes the pardon of Sin, the reversal of the sentence of Condemnation under which we lay, and a title to the Blessings of the Gospel. Secondly, a mind united to the blessed Society of Heaven. I felt much seriousness myself, and hope others did also. I cannot expect to live many more years and, though my health is good, and I go through my labours with little difficulty, yet I am actually growing old. I can generally preach twice on the Lord's Day without much fatigue, but cannot do much more. I yesterday preached twice, once in Bengali at the Christian Village near Serampore, and once in English. Besides this I gave Lectures on Divinity in the College, ever since Bro. Swan left us, and Preach on Wednesday Evening once a fortnight.

Carey to Sisters, Serampore, Oct. 25, 1831

Through the good hand of God upon me I am now in health though a series of attacks of fever have kept me very weak through the greater part of this year. After three weeks or a month's silence I preached last Lord's Day at the Danish Church. My not preaching was not because of absolute inability, for I scarcely ever omitted attending at worship, but my friends thought it would be likely to bring on new attacks. I never felt myself so old as I now do, indeed I never, except in the very hot months of March, April, May, and June, felt the burden of age; and during those months almost every young person feels old . . .

When I look around me I see almost all those both in England and in India with whom I was formerly on terms of intimacy removed to another World. None of my former acquaintances in England are living, but Dr. Rippon and Mr. Goode. . . . Indeed I have no wish that anyone should write or say anything about me, let my memorial sleep with my body in the dust, and at the last great day all the good or evil which belongs to my character will be fully known. My great concern now is to be found in Christ. His atoning sacrifice is all my hope; and I know that Sacrifice to be of such value that God has accepted it as fully vindicating his government in the exercise of mercy to sinners, and as that on account of which he will accept the greatest offender who seeks to him for pardon. And the acceptance of that sacrifice of atonement was testified by the resurrection of our Lord from the dead and by the commission to preach the Gospel to all nations with a promise, or rather a declaration, that whosoever believeth on the Son shall be saved, shall not come into condemnation, but is passed from death unto life.

I trust the publick events now taking place in the world will ultimately bring about such a state of things as shall be for the glory of God. I wish to see Idolatry, Mohammedanism and all the political establishments of religion in the world swept from the face of the earth and also see slavery and war abolished, and infidelity cease. I account Socinianism and Arianism as nothing but modifications of Mohammedanism; or if you will Mohammedanism only a modification of what they choose to call Unitarianism. They must all stand or fall together.

DAILY SPIRITUAL DISCIPLINE

By analyzing the advice offered to family members concerning the proper Christian walk, one can piece together a picture of what Carey discerned as important to a spiritual journey. Prayer, Bible study, evangelism, meditation, and doing good to people all occupied key places in Carey's description of a spiritual person.

Carey to Society, Dec. 28, 1796, Hooghly River

. . . I have nothing more to add but my warm wishes for the prosperity of the Society, and its establishment on the most permanent Basis. I rejoice much in the mission to Africa - Pray convey my warm Love to Brethren Grigg and Rodway, and tell them that they are often remembered by us in our solemn meetings for Prayer; especially on the first Monday of the month when we meet constantly unless something unavoidable detain us from each other. I hope the Labours of those dear Souls may be far more successful than our own have been - and that they may be supported to labour constantly for God.

Carey to Sisters, Dec. 31, 1805, Calcutta

. . . Indeed I seldom omit to remember you both, and all my other relations after the flesh in my prayers, if my confused addresses to the God of all mercy can be called prayer.

Carey to Jabez, May 11, 1814

. . . Judson informs us that Rangoon has been nearly consumed by fire. The Mission house and the king's go-down, in which was the printing press, were, however, spared and no Mission property has been lost.

. . . I need not repeat what I have so often said to you about your work. I feel a confidence that the Lord will support you and bless you and make you a blessing. Fix your plan as soon as possible after your arrival and then steadily pursue it notwithstanding every discouragement. Never step much out of the way of truth and righteousness to secure favour or avoid disgrace but examine the word of God for every step you take. The Bible rightly understood will never lead you wrong. Serve the Lord and he will never leave or forsake you.

Carey to Jabez, June 9, 1814

. . . Supposing you to have now entered upon your labours, I feel a more than ordinary concern that you may adorn the Gospel of Christ in all things. I, therefore, with the affection of a Father entreat you to walk closely with God, and to cultivate diligently every grace of the Holy Spirit. Every one, however carnal or wicked he may be, expects you to be Holy, and should the men of the world see you lax or carnal or conformed to the world they will be disappointed in you and will not fail to report it to your disadvantage and to the discredit of religion. I do not say this because I have any suspicion of you, but I am jealous over you with a godly jealously and not only desire that you may be saved at last but that you may adorn the Gospel of God in all things. I am glad to hear that Eliza is happy. I trust you will both be more so when you become settled, and your affairs assume a domestic form. Give my love to her. Her Mother has been ill but I understand is getting better.

Carey to Jabez, Nov. 25, 1814

. . . I trust the work of God, the publication of the Gospel is your chief delight; if so I am sure your pleasure therein will increase more and more and have no doubt but you will see the fruit of your labours and prayers with great joy and pleasure. I trust you are instant in season and out of season, that you instruct, exhort, and where necessary, rebuke with all long suffering and patience. In all labours of love for the conversion of men be steadfast, immoveable, always abounding in the work of the Lord, for as much as you know that your labour will not be in vain in the Lord.

Carey to Jabez, Feb. 7, 1816

. . . Above all things, live near to God. If personal religion be in a lively flourishing state in your heart everything will go well and your work will be an enjoyment, but on the contrary, if personal religion be low, your work will be a burden and your situation unhappy and disagreeable. So great an influence has this one thing upon all we do and say that it may be always considered as the life blood of all our enjoyments and all our usefulness.

I see nothing to blame in the manner you have supplied yourself with a servant, only take care to have no more to do with slavery than necessity obliges you to; and be punctual to your engagement to set him free when he has earned his liberty. Labour also to do your utmost to communicate the saving knowledge of the Gospel to all the Malays and to collect them into churches of the living God formed on the Scripture model.

Carey to Jabez, Nov. 17, 1818

. . . I follow you with my prayers, not only for your personal support under all trials but for your abounding in all the Graces and Gifts of the Holy Spirit and for your being furnished by the Grace of God for that very important work which lies before you. You will need Zeal, Prudence, Tenderness of Conscience, Perseverance and Firmness at almost every step. The Lord, who has opened this important door for you in his Providence is able to supply all you wants out of the riches of his glory in Christ Jesus and to make you the instrument of evangelizing the Countries to which you are going, which are now enveloped in the grossest Darkness. Go forth, My Dear Jabez, in his strength. Make mention of his righteousness and of his only and leave it with Him to choose your Lot. It is of little importance whether we are poor or rich, admitted to the Society of the great men of this world or frowned upon by them if God give us a work to do, fit us for it and support us in it. That is sufficient. "Unto me who am less than the least of the Saints" said Paul, "is this Grace given that I should preach among the Gentiles the unsearchable riches of Christ."

Carey to Jabez, Mar. 9, 1819

. . . I know your trials are often severe, and should not wonder if the enemy of our Souls should try to discourage you in you work, and to tempt you from it. Be assured, however, that your work is the work of the Lord and that no other work can bear the smallest competition therewith. Difficulties you will find in this and every other undertaking and will stand in need of strength from above to enable you to persevere. The God whom you serve is, however, Almighty. He can support you in all he calls you either to do or to suffer, and can make all things work together for your greatest good. I hope that (you) will commit your way to the Lord, and go forward steadily in his work making mention of his righteousness even of his only . . .

Carey to Jabez, Feb. 20, 1821

. . . The Character of a minister of the Gospel is the highest character on earth. It is no less than that of the Ambassador of God commissioned to negotiate with sinful man concerning the great article of their salvation. We, therefore, as if God himself entreated sinners by us, beseech them to be reconciled to God. May you and I, My Dear Jabez, always keep in view our character, our obligations, and our vast responsibility and let us spend and be spent for God. Our reward is on high and God will acknowledge at last those who faithfully labour for him here.

Carey to Jabez, Feb. 16, 1827

. . . I hope, My Dear Jabez, you will most carefully for the future keep out of the way of Temptation. No one can assume himself that he shall stand in the evil day, and every one who is convinced of his own weakness will commiserate with the others when they are fallen, and will labour to restore them.

I am glad you see and acknowledge your sin, but let this be principally done to God. You are under no obligation to publish it to men, but labour continually to maintain a deep sense of the turpitude of Sin, of all Sin, but especially of the Sin which easily besets you. "If we say we have no Sin we deceive ourselves and the truth is not in us. If we confess our Sins, He is able to forgive our Sins, and to cleanse us from all unrighteousness." "He that hardeneth his heart shall fall into mischief but he that confesseth and forsaketh his sins shall find mercy." Take care of an indolent trifling habit, and devote yourself to the duties incumbent on you. This will be a great preservative and will also be a source of enjoyment to your mind.

Carey to Jabez, May 19, 1827

I received your last letter some time ago. The contents I assure you gave me great pleasure. In all I have ever written to either yourself or Eliza, my aim has uniformly been your happiness and spiritual advantage; and this is my constant prayer to God for you. I am certainly anxious about your future lot in this life; but my chief anxiety is respecting you spiritual state. If true Religion prevails in your soul, it will enlarge your views, strengthen you energies, give a substance and weight to your Character, and a dignity to all you say and do. Such a person will not often be left destitute in the present state, for even irreligious persons will see and duly appreciate the character of such a man; and prefer him in all their concerns to men of pleasure or fashion who are too frequently men of light minds and unsettled principles. But the last reward of true Religion in this life is not that connected with earthly advantage and respectability. There is an inward satisfaction invariably attends devotedness of the heart to God which is sought in vain from any other source: while at the same time the man who loves God will, and must, love his neighbour also; insomuch that a man who fears God will bear injuries with patience, will seek the good of those who seek his hurt, will not be overcome of evil but will overcome evil with good. A good man will labour to do good, and though repulsed or discouraged will not be weary of well doing. I need not say that great will be the reward of such in heaven; for all the glories prepared by God for those who love and fear him, will be bestowed on such when God comes to judge the world.

Carey to Jabez, undated

. . . I must now, My Dear Jabez, conclude with a reiteration of my earnest desire that you may always live a life of near communion with God in prayer and meditation, upon this your comfort and success will in great measure depend. God usually gives success to those who seek in the most simple manner his glory, and those who live most in the practice of prayer to him, dependence on him and meditation upon his ways and works especially those of redemption and providence, will be likely to seek his honour in all things more than any others do.

Labour also my dear son, to obtain a more compleat knowledge of the doctrines and duties of the Gospel . . .

. . . I rejoice that you have begun to preach in Malay. Consider this as your greatest work and labour to build up the people in Faith and Holiness but above all labour to lay Christ Crucified as the foundation on which you build for all that is not built on that foundation will fail. Walk worthy of the Gospel, be not conformed to this world but be transformed by the renewing of your mind. We would send more missionaries to Amboyna but we have none to send. If we send a printing press who can work it? Does anybody at Amboyna know how to do it? Must you have the Arabic or English letters for Malay printing? . . .

Carey to Sister Ann, no date.

Love solitude, seek to be alone and then examine your Soul with Holy severity in the Light of God and by the Word of God. Meditate upon the Character of God as a Holy, wise, powerful, gracious and merciful Being upon yourself, upon God's word, and Divine things. Contemplate the Beauties of Creation, the Wisdom of God, and more than all the Wonders of Redemption. Endeavor to set apart some time every day for prayer and Secret exercises of Religion at least Half an Hour as Circumstances allow. Consider yourselves as Christians in all Company and act and speak like such, in short make God's Word your Rule, for to lay down a system of Rules for the Conduct of every Person would be to introduce formality but the Bible is a competent Rule which may you always . . .

DEPENDENCE ON GOD

Facing the hardships of mission life, Carey developed a strong dependence on God. The disease, death, tragedies like floods and fire, as well as opposition and personal problems created a necessity for a missionary to find stability and refuge. Carey's ardent faith in God's power and sovereignty furnished that stability. He often wrote of this dependence on the Almighty.

Carey to Father and Mother, Ryde, Isle of Wight, May 2, 1793

. . . and I trust that God is indeed with me. That sense which I have of the importance of my undertaking is sufficient to support me under all the Sacrifices that I am called to make. Indeed I find that both by Land and by Sea, the presence of God is sufficient to support.

Carey to Fuller, Jan. 30, 1795

Having never yet received a Letter from England, I can only write you a dull account of what concerns myself; and am unable to engage in that kind of Conversation which people at such distance carry on.

Through the Mercy of God we are all well, except my eldest Son; tho we have had a considerable share of affliction in every Branch of the Family; and have lost a fine little Boy of five years of age. The Dealings of God are mysterious, but always end well, and oftentimes in our greater temporal felicity, and happiness [advantage]. This I trust it is with me, both in Body and Soul - During the time in which I could see very little else but sorrow, I was powerfully supported by the reflections I often had upon the goodness of the Cause upon which I [came] had undertaken; and by those Words [of Peter, "The God of all grace who hath called us unto his eternal glory by Christ Jesus."] "Now the Lord, after ye have suffered awhile, [Comfort], stablish, [and] strengthen, settle you." I saw that it was God's method, oftentimes, to lead his people through tribulation before he appeared for their Deliverance, and was enabled to rely upon his goodness, and trust in his grace. And now I have Light arisen out of Darkness, and a Wide field for usefulness [and] I pray that God may give me an heart to express thankfulness by a constant devotedness to his work [and service] and as I am devoted to his service may he preserve me from embezzling that property with which he has entrusted me, and which is properly his.

Carey to Sisters, Aug. 23, 1804

. . . As to myself I have great occasion to praise God, and to be ashamed of myself. It is always an useless, and often a hurtful thing to complain to our fellow creatures. I would, therefore, rather confess my guilt to God and seek him to strengthen the things which remain, which are ready to die. I am persuaded that God can make all grace abound towards me.

In a sermon "I defined Growing in Grace as consisting in frequently looking into ourselves, always seeking for more than we have already - and a continual seeking to lay out for God's Glory what we do obtain from him."

Carey to Sisters, Oct. 1, 1807

. . . The last month has been full of hurry, and alarm, and confusion so that I have scarcely been able to fix my mind upon anything like correspondence. We have received orders from Govt. not to teach or preach to the heathen any more in the name of the Lord Jesus, and you may suppose that we have been much distressed. In our afflictions we have called upon God, and I trust have fixed our only hope on him. For my own part, I was never more impressed with a sense of his love to his Church - his sovereignty, his power, and his Wisdom than on the present trying occasion. I must, however, confess that my mind was so agitated with tumultuous, rather than unbelieving thoughts, that after several days labour, sorrow and distress of soul, I felt like one quite exhausted, and incapable of thinking any more. I know not how the affair will end, but the clouds have seemed for some days past to be clearing away . . .

Carey to Fuller, March 25, 1812

We have been smitten in a very tender front . . . Poor Bro. Chamberlain has been bereaved of all his children; all three of them having been removed within the short period of nine months. Bro. Mardon has lost his (partner in life) and, last week his youngest child, Bro. Marshman, his youngest son and the week before last our Printing office with all that it contained was consumed by fire, nothing was saved except the presses which was in the adjoining room. The loss cannot be estimated at less that 70,000 pounds. By this providence several important manuscripts were lost. I believe, in my own case, it will require twelve months of hard labor to replace what has been consumed . . . Many very merciful circumstances, however, attended this providence, and I rather wish to record them than to dwell upon the gloomy side of the events. No life was lost, and no one's health injured, though Bro. Ward [was in very great danger of being suffocated by the smoke] through remaining in the place as soon as the fire broke out.

{He mentions also blessings of kindnesses of the neighbors both European and native, the quick recovery of the metal to recast the type, the purchase of type from a printing office in Calcutta, the availability of funds, and the support of God.}

. . . We have all of us been supported under this affliction, and preserved from discouragement. To me the consideration of the divine sovereignty and wisdom has been very supporting and, indeed, I have usually been supported under afflictions by feeling that I and mine are in the hands of an infinitely wise God. I endeavored to impress this our afflictions last Lord's Day, from Psalm XLVIE. 10 "Be still and know that I am God". I principally dealt upon two ideas, viz. 1. God has a sovereign right to dispose of us as he pleases, 2. We ought to acquiesce in all that God does with us or to us. To enable us to do which I recommended, realising meditations upon the perfections of God,-- upon his providence, and upon his promises including the prophesies of the extension of his kingdom.

Carey to Fuller, March 25, 1813

{With the threat of missionaries being sent home and applications being made to allow them to stay Carey states his faith. He does all he can to help but then . . .}

In all these distressing circumstances my hope is in God. Indeed, I have always found a firm confidence in the power and wisdom of God, and a deep sense of his sovereignty, the most powerful means of calming my mind, and supporting me in times of trouble. To him I commit these distressing things.

Carey to Jabez, Nov. 23, 1816

I am now mercifully recovering from a very severe bilious fever which brought me exceedingly low, my mouth now suffers severely from vast quantities of mercury which the doctor rubbed in and gave in other forms, but I am living to praise the name of the Lord and have this new mercy accompanied with many thousands more for which to glorify his holy Name.

During my illness I was enabled to review my hopes for when eternity opens before me. What can be so important as to have all clear so as to meet and welcome death? I think I found Christ to be the sole foundation of my hopes and though my life has been full of awful neglect of God and spiritual sloth and carnality . . . (but) sinful and imperfect as I am I can trust my soul in the hands of my dear Redeemer.

My Dear Jabez, let it be your practice often to examine the grounds of your hope, if that be clear and transparent, obedience to God and the most vigilant attendance on all the calls of Duty will be proportionately easy and delightful.

Carey to Ryland, Dec. 30, 1816

. . . How important is it to live in that state of continual communion with God and lively faith in Christ as to have the great point of our acceptance with God quite clear while we are in health. In my illness great weakness, and great stupor so prevailed that I found it impossible to do more than cast my sinful soul on the Redeemer, and hope in the mercy of God to eternal life. Now I am raised up may I labour in the work of the Lord with increased diligence! My Dear Brethren Pearce, Sutcliffe, and Fuller are gone to their rest. I am in my 56th year, and cannot expect many more years. Whenever I die may I through divine Grace join them in the World of bliss.

Carey to Jabez, June 12, 1819

. . . You seem discouraged at the introductory circumstances, such as the dilapidated state of the place, the dearness of provisions, and the difficulty of getting a house &ct. I hope, however, you will not sink under these difficulties, nor think of comparing Ajmere with Amboyna, but rather consider that Divine Providence had shut up your way for usefulness in Amboyna, and had opened a very extensive line for usefulness where your are. You must expect some difficulties and privations where you are but if your are the means of civilization, and final salvation to the inhabitants of that Country - an object of which I hope you will never lose sight - How glorious will be the reflection hereafter? It will be necessary for you to endure hardness as a good soldier of Jesus Christ. Consider that someone must be first in the attempt to spread the Gospel in the heart of India; and whoever is first must have many inconveniences to suffer . . .

Carey to Jabez, March 19, 1821

I wrote last month to you about the importance of doing everything in your power to spread among the inhabitants of the countries around you the knowledge of the Gospel. It is not because I think you remiss in this particular but to encourage you in it that I write. I know the difficulties of first engaging in this work are great and feel much for your standing alone in the vast field but I am sure the Lord can give you strength according to your day and that he will sustain all who with a single eye to his glory engage in his glorious work. It is equally the same with him to help with many or with a few and to effect his great designs by weak instruments as by those which are apparently the strongest for in truth all are weakness itself. The greatness of the power is in him and must always appear to be so. It is, therefore, not unlikely that he may give as great and even greater blessing to your labours who are working alone as to the combined effort of those who appear to have advantages. He is the Almighty God.

Carey to Jabez, Nov. 5, 1822

. . . Felix has been at the point of death with a liver complaint, he is now recovering very slowly but thinks his original disease no better. This is indeed a miserable dying world. O how important is it that we should fix our affections on things above and not on things on the earth and that while we live we should labour with all our might to live to the glory of God and for the good of men, everything short of this is an inferior object which we should hold with a loose hand, and consider that we are in daily, hourly danger of being separated therefrom, and called to give an account to God of our stewardship.

Carey to Dyer, March 18, 1824

{Carey had an accident when he fell on the bank of a river hurting his hip, and this was followed by a fever and lung condition. He was sick for six months and almost died. Carey received good medical attention from a Dr. Mellis.}

During the heaviest part of my affliction I had scarcely any mental exercises unless excepted by a tendency to deliriousness for one or two days. I (once assumed) my end to be near. I had no fear of death, nor any exalted joys. The language of David in the 1 and 2 verses of Psalm 51 was the language of my heart, and I requested those verses might be included in a funeral sermon for the good of others. I could rise no higher than "A Guilty, weak, and helpless worm, on Thy kind arm I fall" or "Hang my lifeless soul on thee". That afforded me a calm which in that important season was of the highest value. I have since more closely examined the grounds on which my soul then rested, and find this, so far as I am able to judge, to be substantial.

Carey to Jabez, Aug.17, 1831

I am this day seventy years old, a monument of Divine mercy and goodness, though on a review of my life I find much, very much, for which I ought to be humbled in the dust. My direct and positive sins are innumerable, my negligence in the Lord's work has been great, I have not promoted his cause, nor sought his glory and honour as I ought. Notwithstanding all this, I am spared till now, and am still retained in his work, and I trust I am received into the divine favour through him. I wish to be more entirely devoted to his service, more compleatly sanctified and more habitually exercising all the Christian Graces, and bringing forth the fruits of righteousness to the praise and honour of that Saviour who gave his life a sacrifice for sin.

Through the goodness of God I am now quite well, but I have within the last three months had five or six severe attacks of fever, which has greatly weakened me. Indeed, I consider the time of my departure to be near; but the time I leave with God. I trust I am ready to die, through the grace of my Lord Jesus; and I look forward to the full enjoyment of the Society of Holy men and Angels, and the full vision of God evermore.

Carey to Sisters, Dec. 16, 1831

. . . I was taken ill with a bilious attack, the day I heard Levi's illness, and was confined to my couch for several days. I am now, through mercy, getting better, but the repeated attacks I have had, viz. eight or nine within the last twelve months have much enfeebled me, and warn me to look forward to a change. This change, I through the mercy of God, do not fear. I know in whom I have believed, and that He is able to keep what I have committed to him, against that day. The atoning sacrifice made by our Lord on the Cross is the ground of my hopes of acceptance, pardon, justification, sanctification, and endless Glory. It is from the same source that I expect the fulfillment of all the prophecies and promises respecting the universal establishment of the Redeemer's Kingdom in the World, including the total abolition of Idolatry, Mohammedanism, Infidelity, Socinianism, and all the political establishments of Religion in the World; the abolition also of War, Slavery, and oppression in all their ramifications. It is on this ground that I pray for, and expect the peace of Jerusalem; not merely the cessation of hostilities between Christians of different sects and connections, but that genuine love which the Gospel requires, and which the Gospel is so well calculated to produce.

Carey to Jabez, Feb. 7, 1832

. . . You see My Dear Jabez, how uncertain everything in this World is. We have no hold on the next moment. How very important it is for us to live a life of faith in Christ and conformity to his commands, this will not only set us above the fear of death, but will secure our happiness let our circumstances here below be what they may. And without this trust in Christ all things in the present world, could we possess them, would be insufficient to make us happy.

Carey to Jabez, Sept. 3, 1832

. . . Through divine goodness, am now well, having had no attack of fever for the last three months, but I shall scarcely ever recover the strength I had before these attacks, and am exceedingly emaciated. This does not particularly appear in my face, but is so great in all other parts that my clothes are so large as to hang about me like bags. My mind is tranquil. I think I never had a greater sense of my sinfulness and of the evil nature of all my sins than I have had for some time past, but I see the atoning sacrifice of Christ to be full and compleat, to have been accepted of God, and to be a ground __________ the bestowment of all spiritual blessings, and I trust that I do daily and continually trust in Christ for acceptance into the divine favour, for pardon, and justification, and the entire renovation of my nature. Our Lord has said that "if we confess our sins God is faithful and just to forgive us our sins and to cleanse us from all unrighteousness". My conscience testifies that I do confess my sins; I, therefore, hope in time for pardon and sanctification. Christ has said, "He that cometh to me I will in no wise cast out". My conscience bears witness that I do come to Christ and I feel the enjoyment arising from confidence in His gracious declarations.

HUMILITY

Carey exhibited a remarkable characteristic that some might call self debasement. Rarely perceiving himself worthy to be a missionary or to receive God's favor, Carey often referred to his own sinfulness and inability to focus on the things of God. Undoubtedly, much of this rhetoric grew out of Carey's Calvinism. He feared he would disgrace himself or the cause of Christ due to his inclination toward temptation and sin. Carey even implied that he might be a cause for the lack of success on the mission field. This humility persisted to the end when Carey requested the epitaph for his grave stone: "A wretched, poor, and helpless worm, On Thy kind arms I fall."

Carey to Society, Jan. 12, 1796

. . . With respect to myself, I have the utmost reason to mourn over my deadness, and amazing indifference to eternal things; and for the encouragement of others I may say that if God should at all bless my Labours none need fear to lay themselves out for God. Yet I have lately had some comfortable revival of Soul; and find the Work of preaching of the Gentiles more and more pleasant. And when I find that people understand me, it gives me much hope. I will, therefore, still go in the Strength of the Lord God and make mention of his Righteousness only.

Carey to Fuller July 17, 1799, Mudnabati

I, therefore, only observe respecting myself that I have much proof of the sinfulness of my heart, much more than I thought of till lately; and indeed I often fear that instead of being instrumental in the conversion of the Heathen I may some time dishonour the course in which I am engaged. I have hitherto had much experience of the daily supports of a gracious God but am convinced that if those supports were intermitted but for a little time, my sinful dispositions would infallibly predominate. At present I am kept but am not one of those who are strong and do exploit.

I have often thought that a spirit of observation is necessary in order to our doing, as communicating much good, and was it not for a very phlegmatic habit, I think my soul would be richer. I, however, appear to myself to have lost much of my capacity of making observations, improvements or of retaining what I attend closely to. For instance, I have been near three years learning the Sanskrit language, yet know very little of it. This is only a specimen of what I feel myself to be in every respect. I try to observe, to imprint what I see, and here on my memory, and to feel my Heart properly affected with the circumstances. Yet my soul is impoverished and I have something of a lethargy disease cleaving to my Body. I feel not pain or decay of strength but an abundant inclination to sleep, attended with a great sense of weariness, even when I have not walked a Mile. I know that this country requires more sleep than a colder one, and a sleep in the afternoon, especially in the hot seasons relieves me more than anything. Indeed without it I could not do any thing. My inertness of mind may be in some measure owing thereto, tho many other causes can contribute to it. Perhaps my sinful propensity to ease and negligence; added to sameness of society and employment, and the few opportunities I have of varied religious discourse may act powerfully to the injury of my Soul.

Carey to Sisters, Serampore, Nov. 23, 1801

I have frequently at Night been very thankful to God that I have not been suffered to fall down the precipice on which I have stood, and for weeks together every day has appeared to be a day of remarkable preservation and escape. I am in a world of temptation and have an heart capable of any crime, so that I have frequently thought that my escape have been much more owing to the superintendence of God who in his providence has put it out of my power to act myself out, than to any true grace which I profess, and which might be supposed to influence me to flee from the Ways of sin. Indeed, I have been often so much depressed that I have concluded myself to be the real cause why this Mission has not been more successful, because it would be inconsistent with the Character of God to give a Blessing to the labours of one who lives so distant from himself and would appear to the world to be a sanctioning of indolence and disregard to his honour, and most holy commandments.

Yet I am preserved. Hitherto the Lord has helped me. I have lived to see the Bible translated into Bengali, and the Whole New Testament printed. The first volume of the Old Testament will also soon appear. I have lived to see two of my Sons converted, and one of them join the Church of Christ. I have lived to baptise five Native Hindus and to see a sixth Baptised and to see them all walk worthy of their vocation for Twelve Months since they first made a profession of faith in our Lord Jesus Christ.

Carey to Sutcliffe, Calcutta, Mar. 17, 1802

. . . A year or more ago, You, or some other of my Dear Friends mentioned an intention of publishing a Volume of Sermons as a testimony of mutual Christian Love and wished me to send a sermon or two for that purpose. I have seriously intended it, and more than once set down to accomplish it, but have as constantly been broken off from it. Indolence is my prevailing Sin, and to that are now added a number of avocations which I never thought of. I have also so continual a fear that I may at last fall some way or other so as to dishonour the Gospel that I have often desired that my name may be buried in oblivion, and indeed I have reason for those fears. For I am so prone to sin, that I wonder every night that I have been preserved from foul crimes thro the day. And when I escape a temptation, I esteem it to be a miracle of grace which has preserved me. I never was so fully persuaded as I am now that no habit of religion is a security from falling into the foulest crimes, and I need the immediate help of God every moment. This sense of my continual danger has I confess operated strongly upon me to induce me to desire that no publication of a religious nature should be published as mine whilst I am alive. Another reason is my sense of my incapacity to do justice to any subject or even to write a good sense. I have, it is true, been obliged to publish several things and I can say that nothing but necessity could have induced me to do it. They are, however, only Grammatical Works, and certainly the very last things which I should have written if I could have chosen for myself . . .

Cary to Ryland, March 1809

. . . With respect to myself, I have as great a show of health and domestic comfort as most people have. I long to see the conversion of my two youngest sons, but have not that happiness yet. They are, however, in other respects promising and steady lads. Jabez has a tolerable knowledge of Chinese, and writes it well, he is still studying it and will continue so to do. The greatest bodily calamity I have, is failure of sight. I am obliged to use spectacles of pretty great magnifying power. My Soul has always been like a brook, nearly dry, yet I trust it has still some communication with the fountain. If I am not much mistaken I see more need of Christ and more preciousness in him than I formerly did. - I have tried to persuade my Wife to correspond with Mrs. Ryland but she is rather timid: She thinks her knowledge of the English Language too imperfect, having always spoken either French, German or Italian till she came to this country. Give my Xn. love to all who know me . . .

Carey to Jabez, July 19, 1821

. . . I feel lonely since the death of your Dear Mother. Could I enjoy greater intercourse with God this solitude would be less felt; and undoubtedly were I with a single eye to seek more earnestly after communion with God there is no doubt but I should obtain it. A carnal mind is my great obstruction in the heavenly course. May the Lord graciously make me more spiritually minded.

Carey to Sisters, Jan. 15, 1823, Calcutta

I informed you in my last of my third marriage, and can now through much mercy add that this marriage is among my great mercies. My Dear Wife is a Woman who fears God. During my late illness her attention to me was unremitted; and I have the highest reason to be thankful for the Union. She does know of my writing, or she would write in love to you all. During the time of my affliction I was enabled to review my life, and to look into my evidences more closely than usual for Eternity; the result was a deep sense of my condemned and sinful state, and of my absolute need of the full and free pardon held forth in the Gospel. I can get no further than "hangs my helpless soul on thee." Indeed the language of David in the 51st Psalm has long been the habitual feeling of my heart. "Have mercy on me O Lord according to thy loving kindness and according to the multitude of thy tender mercies do away my transgressions" and again "Create in me a clean heart O God, and renew a right spirit within me. Cast me not away from thy presence, and take not thy Holy Spirit from me, Restore to me the joy of thy Salvation, and uphold me with thy free Spirit." I have derived Life from this passage. "If we say we have no sin we deceive ourselves and the truth is not in us, but if we confess our Sins He is faithful and just to forgive us our sins and to cleanse us from all unrighteousness." I am sure I am a great and constant sinner, I confess it, and so far as I can see or feel, with sincerity; Would God forgive my sins, and cleanse me from all unrighteousness, I should have all I could desire and want.

PERSONAL BELIEFS

Systematic statements of Carey's personal theology rarely surface in his letters. Several doctrinal beliefs are visible as pieces of theological tenets used in arguments, discussions, and descriptions of events. Carey's views relating to God, salvation and missions are not hard to find. The following letters reveal other beliefs that the missionary affirmed including ideas on doubt, God's faithfulness, the future, the military, war, and church discipline.

Carey to Sister, Mary Carey, Dec. 14, 1789

. . . You express in your letter very great gloominess and languor of soul, prevalence of sin and unbelief, and seem to question the sincerity of your pretensions to any share in the Christian character. But allow me to say: Wherefore didst thou doubt? Is it because you feel that which all the saints have complained of? Zion saith the Lord hath forsaken me and my God hath forgotten to be gracious - Jeremiah.

Behold all ye that pass by is there any sorrow like unto my sorrow. He covereth himself with a cloud that my prayer cannot pass through. Paul's flesh warred against the spirit and the spirit warred against the flesh and he mourned a law in his members warring against the law of his mind and bringing him into captivity to the law of sin which was in his members. Do you doubt then because your case is singular? But there is no need for that for some of the brightest saints in all the world have felt the same, or do you doubt of God's ability or God's Will? I say he that withheld not his own Son but freely gave him an offering for us all, how will he not with him freely give us all things. To purchase Salvation cost the Saviour's groans, strong grief and tears and life itself, but to bestow it will not occasion a repetition of any of these. Had he Goodwill enough to die for sinners and will he not bestow upon them the purchased benefits? No, His mercy is as great as ever and his compassion as abundant, tis a dishonourable thought of God to suppose that he bestows his favours as a Miser does his gold. He waiteth to be gracious and while this is the case despair is as absurd on the one hand as boasting on the other.

Now sister suppose a person was to come to you and say I once had a notion that the Christian life was a conflict and that saints mourned a body of Death and daily opposition to God in their hearts. I believe from God's Word that this was the experience of all Christians but now things are altered. I not only believe it but I feel it. I feel cold and dead and wicked, the good that I would I do not but the evil that I would not that I do. What would you say to such an one? Be honest now, for you ought in matter so momentous! Why according to your principles you must say Ah! had you kept the last part of your complaint back I should have some hope of you, but no Christian can feel so much sin &ct. Would you not be ashamed of such an objection respecting others and would you rather look on it as a favourable indication that their faith and feelings correspond together? But is there one rule laid down for you and another for others? Or dare you hope for another on those principles that you doubt for yourself? Consider that the Bible is our rule and if we would fetch our evidence from that we should do well.

Again do you doubt because you have not seen visions, heard voices, or felt impulses? This I know is what many Christians placed dependence upon. But suppose that you have felt nothing of all this, there is no reason for you to despair and if you have been favoured with repeated instances of this nature this is no proof of your Christianity. I apprehend that too many people place too much confidence in things of this nature and make a shining light, an audible voice, or the sudden application of a passage of Scripture an evidence of their being the children of God. But where is the part of God's Word that informs us of any such evidence of religion as these are? Or if a person had no other evidence than such would you, could you encourage him to depend or take comfort from this? That these are extraordinary interpositions of Divine Power upon extraordinary occasions I don't deny but tis God and not us that must judge of the emergency of our case and even if he does interpose in a singular way tis the matter and not the manner of his interposition that we ought to depend upon, and that not as an evidence of grace but as Divine support in the path of duty. No doubt but the tempter is aware of the taste of the age and, therefore, endeavors to seduce us by things miraculous to which the mind of man is much prone, and while we thus listen to his devices and limit the Holy One of Israel we distress ourselves and dishonour him.

But we have a more sure word of prophecy whereunto we do well that we take heed. I don't know that you expect any such appearances, but I am not certain that you don't feel troubled because you don't feel something of that nature. You will, therefore, excuse me if I attempt to set the matter in a clearer light and, therefore, I observe that all the operations of the Holy Ghost are by illumination and impulse but Divine illumination does not suppose that my new discoveries are made of unrevealed truths, but that the soul is enlightened to see the radiance and innate beauty of those things which are contained in the Holy Scriptures. As for impulses some are unnecessary, as to administer comfort when there is no distress &ct. Some are childish and absurd, such as are interpreted contrary to the manifest intent of the Scripture, as for instance a person has the words "he for our profit" and thence is filled with pleasure because the office of Christ is so wonderfully displayed to him. Or who from this being impressed on his mind "Son of Man prophecy among the thick boughs" should from thence conclude it his duty to leave a small congregation in the country and go to preach the Gospel in London? This kind of pious trifling is very hurtful and lays a snare for the souls of many.

Some impulses again are of good tendency but are very transient and short lived, like as the seed sown on a rock appeared very promising but soon withered away, so the fault of many good impulses is not in their tendency but in their duration. Were they permanent they would be useful but they are exceeding defective and do die away. But Divine and useful impulses are more steady, more permanent, and more effectual, the often more unperceived.

You will observe the conviction flows from illumination to see our sin, and the demands of God's righteous law; comfort from a discovery of the correspondence between our state and the Divine Representative of the Christian character, consolation of hope from a view of the promises of God as suited to remove our miseries and a fiducial dependence on them, and obedience from such view. Thus the excellence of all the ways of God, and impulsive operations to a compliance with them in a most cordial manner which will necessarily excite sorrow and distress on account of defect. Real religion consists in all these, conviction, repentance, faith, obedience, submission, zeal, and consolation, sometimes one may be predominant and sometimes another, but there they all are. Learn, dear Sister to make proper distinctions. Go on in the path of duty and undoubtedly the Judge of the whole earth will do right.

Carey to Father, Calcutta, Nov. 25, 1793

I doubt not but you are very anxious to hear from me before now, and indeed I am desirous to write to you. You no doubt was (were) much surprised to hear of my return from the Isle of Wight, and of my Wife and Family going with me. The Ways of God in this were mysterious, but all right and well. I cannot sufficiently admire the goodness of God, but this is to me a striking proof that he who forsaketh any earthly comfort for God will have it restored an hundred fold, and indeed the faithfulness of God is such that no one will ever be a loser by trusting in his Word.

Carey to Sisters, Mudnabati, Jan. 10, 1798

. . . Poor Mr. Sharman. I still hope that a merciful God may recover him from the Snare of the Devil into which I find he is not only fallen, but as his Letter to me proves, dreadfully entangled. I shall not answer his Letter but observe to you that his enjoyment of Peace under affliction is no proof that he is right, for Tom Paine in that abominable piece, *The Age of Reason*, speaks of his having enjoyed great consolation on what he thought a dying bed from reflecting that he had written that impudent Book. Calvinists, too, as well as he have peace in afflictions and I think peace which is built on a surer foundation.

Carey to Sisters, Aug. 24, 1803, Calcutta

We have great reason to bless God for his great favour towards this Mission. He has protected and cared for it in all its stages so that it has not yet failed either through the opposition of enemies, or the misconduct of those engaged in it. We have, if I recollect right twenty five baptised members of our Church, and fourteen Europeans &ct . . .

My own extreme liability to fall, and the continual apprehensions which I have respecting it make me willing to judge perhaps too favourably of others who are guilty of improprieties; but notwithstanding this it has sometimes been my painful office to pronounce the censures of the Church upon such as have acted inconsistently. The good Lord grant that I may never have occasion to do that painful work again.

Carey to Fuller, Jan. 14, 1808

Yesterday an Armenian proposed to join the Church. Oh! - what is proper respecting baptising Armenians. They are baptised in infancy by triune immersion, ought they to be rebaptised on a profession of faith?

Carey to Ryland, Aug. 16, 1809

. . . I did not expect, about a month ago, ever to write to you again: I was then ill of a severe fever, and for a week together, scarcely any hopes were entertained of my life. One or two days I was supposed to be dying, but the Lord has graciously restored me, may it be that I may live more than ever to his glory. Whilst I was ill I had scarcely any such thing as thought belonging to me, but, excepting seasons of delirium, seemed to be nearly stupid, perhaps some of this arose from the weak state to which I was reduced, which was so great, that Dr. Hare, one of the most eminent physicians in Calcutta, who was consulted about it, apprehended more danger from that than from the fever. I, however, had scarcely a thought of death, or eternity, or of life or of anything belonging thereto. In my delirium, greatest part of which I perfectly remember, I was busily employed in carrying a commission from God to all the princes and governments in the world, requiring them instantly to abolish every political establishment of religion, and to sell the parish and other churches to the first body of Christians who would purchase them. Also to declare war infamous, to esteem all military officers as men who had sold themselves to destroy the human race, to extend this to all those dead men called heroes, defenders of their country, meritorious officers &ct. I was attended by Angels in all my excursions, and was universally successful. A few princes in Germany were refractory, but my attendants struck them dead instantly. I pronounced the doom of Rome to the Pope, and soon afterwards all the territory about Rome, the march of Acona, the great city and all its riches sunk into that vast bed of burning lava which heats Nero's bath. These were considerably more than the delirious wanderings of the mind, but I hope I feel force, to pray and strive for their accomplishment to the end of my life. But it is now time to attend to something not merely ideal.

Carey to Sisters, Dec. 21, 1809, Calcutta

. . . If I had money to purchase a commission for Peter, I could not do so conscientiously. Thinking as I do that War is one of the greatest plagues with which a righteous God scourges a wicked world, and that in perhaps nine instances out of ten, it is unlawful, also that every person who gets a commission in the Army does actually sell himself for the purpose of killing men wheresoever he may be sent for that purpose, and that his will must be wholly under the control of another, from whom he receives orders, so that he is not in that instance a free agent; I cannot be accessory to Peter's gaining a commission by my means as a purchaser. And were there no difficulties on those two heads, yet there is another which could scarcely be surmounted. I mean the pride of the Army, which will scarcely ever permit an man to hold a commission who has served in the ranks.

Carey to Jabez, April 15, 1814

. . . I hope the war in Europe will now come to a close. Bonaparte is everywhere defeated and scarcely a doubt remains but peace is concluded ere now. I do not think it will continue long but most heartily rejoice in even a short cessation of these desolating wars. I look with pain upon the last twenty two years when I consider how much blood was shed in them. Surely the Lord has better things in reserve for the world.

Reason for Trials

Carey possessed a theological construct that allowed him to address the many trials he and his companions faced in India and survive. He reflected true Calvinism with his emphasis on God's sovereignty and providence asserting that God uses and sometimes causes the disagreeable situations to teach, discipline, and accomplish his purposes.

Carey to Father, Leicester, Nov. 27, 1792

. . . We have need of afflictions here to lead us to the Lord. Our minds are naturally prone to revolt from him, and lose sight of those glorious excellencies that compose his Character which is sure to produce a spiritual lassitude, and make the ways of God toilsome, and burdensome, while at the same time it lays us open to every temptation, and we soon fall an easy prey to the artifices of our adversary, the Devil. "Let us then lay aside every Weight, and the Sin that so easily besets us, and let us run with Patience the race that is set before us." . . . Polly tells me that you are afraid lest I should go as a Missionary. I have only to say to that, that I am at the Lord's disposal, but I have very little expectation of going myself, but I have a very considerable offer, if I want to go to Sierra Leone in Africa. I, however, don't think I shall go.

Carey to Father, Sept. 11, 1804, Calcutta

. . . Trials of a great variety we must expect in this mortal state, but they are all sent by the hand of that gracious God who pities us as a father pities his Children, not to please a capricious disposition but for our ultimate good, and that we may be thereby weaned from this present world and may have our minds set on things above. This is peculiarly necessary on account of the habitual tendency of our minds to secular objects, and to coldness in our attachment to the Saviour who has done so much for us. It, therefore, becomes us to commit all our ways to the Lord, and to serve him in our situation be it what it may for we cannot be in any circumstances which render it unnecessary, or impossible to act out the Christian Character, but on the contrary every circumstance calls on us to set forth the high praises of God who daily loadeth us with benefits.

Carey to Sisters, July 17, 1805

. . . Painful as afflictions are they may be reckoned among the most useful teachings of the Spirit of God. Who can tell the carnality, worldly mindedness, spiritual sloth, and actual falls into open sins which are prevented by them? And who is able to say how far they operate to restore us when we have departed from our God? We may be sure that he does not willingly afflict nor grieve the Children of men, and that some important purpose is always to be answered thereby.

Carey to Jabez, Feb. 1, 1815

. . . We are every day expecting Felix. I long to see him but fear he has much declined in divine things. He is coming in some official situation, for which I am sorry. Had Felix continued firm to his object and laboured for the spread of the Gospel I could have met every distressing providence with confidence that all would work for good, but I am now at every step full of apprehension and anxiety respecting what may be the next stroke of divine providence for the Lord is a jealous God and no one can be indifferent to his interests with safety.

My dear Jabez be faithful until death and the Lord will give you a crown of Life. The more unreservedly you devote yourself to the cause of God the more you will feel of that joy which passes all understanding. I long to hear a particular account of the school, and the state of religion as it respects the inward experience of it in the heart among the people of Amboyna. Seek their good by all means in your power and whatever disappointments you may meet with be not weary in well doing, for in due season you shall reap if you faint not.

Carey to Sisters, Oct. 1818

Be assured that I have borne a share of all your trials and afflictions, and have blessed the Lord for supporting you so graciously. I have no doubt but the present dispensations of Divine Providence are those which are the most united to your good of all others, had it not been so you would not have been exercised with them; for no good thing will be withheld from them who walk uprightly. We are the worst possible judges of what things are really good things, for we generally suppose ease, prosperity, friends, and external enjoyments health and plenty to be good things, whereas they may be either good or evil according to circumstances.

God's judgement of what things are good, therefore, frequently differs from ours, for he often bestows those external, apparently good things on his Enemies, and visits his saints with poverty, disappointment, afflictions, contempt, and many other things supposed by us to be evil. He, however, well knows these external evils to be necessary to the substantial good of his servants; and were not this the case they would not be exercised under them; for he doth not willingly afflict nor grieve the Children of Men. I rejoice that you have both been enabled to commit your ways to the Lord; persevere in that cause and all will be well. The Joy of the Lord will be your strength.

Carey to Jabez, Dec. 19, 1820

Two or three days ago I received your welcome letter, for so it was indeed to me. Your former one had given me such an account of your family afflictions that I was full of anxiety to hear again. Blessed be God who has been so much better than my fears. I rejoice in the restoration of Eliza and her Mother. Poor little William! I feel much distress for him. I hope his feet will soon be healed. Well it is for us My Dear Jabez, when our afflictions are sanctified and lead us nearer to our God. This is the fruit God expects from the discipline with which he visits us; he chastises us for our profit that we should be made partakers of his holiness; let us learn to say from the heart "I will bear the indignation of the Lord because I have sinned against him." Let us examine our ways and turn again to the Lord, and devote ourselves more entirely to his service.

LOW TIMES

Spiritual lethargy plagued Carey after the death of his wife, Charlotte. He describes his house as a wilderness, and it is evident depression had taken over. Carey ascertains that if he could only be more spiritual he would better cope with this grief. It appears Carey did not do well living alone.

Carey to Sisters, Feb. 16, 1822

. . . Since the death of my Dear Wife, which I recount the greatest loss I ever suffered, I am lonely, and frequently very unhappy, my house seems a wilderness; and the gloom of having no one to whom I can communicate my feelings is very great. I wish I was more spiritually minded and felt more of the power of divine things in my own soul that would more than fill the void which I now feel and would turn my mourning into rejoicing . . .

Carey to Sisters, May 18, 1822, Serampore

With respect to myself I am a poor melancholy creature, I am the most unfit creature on earth to live alone, and every thing about me fills me with the most lonely sensation. To which must be added the low state of my mind as it respects divine consolations. - I can seldom rise higher than "Hangs my helpless Soul on thee". The language of the 51st Psalm is the language of my Soul. Have mercy upon me according to thy loving kindness, according to the multitude of thy tender mercies blot out my transgressions, send me loving kindness, mercies, tender mercies, a multitude of mercies, nothing short of this could reach my case. Often do I walk about alone and turn this psalm into a prayer, but further than this I do not presume. I hope all my friends pray for me, for I much need their prayers.

NEED FOR CHRISTIAN FELLOWSHIP

One of the blessings for which Carey longed and needed was Christian fellowship. Early in the mission endeavor circumstances provided little opportunity for relating to other Christians. This was remedied somewhat with the arrival of new missionaries allowing companionship with fellow believers. Carey cherished the privilege.

Carey to Sisters, Mudnabati, March 11, 1795

. . . Many changes have taken place with me since I left England, but I find that all have been conducive to my Good, and I trust will be found so to the promotion of the knowledge of the Gospel of our Lord Jesus Christ. Tho I have abundant Cause to complain of my leanness from Day to Day; and the exceedingly ungrateful returns that I make to God for all his very great goodness, and bounty towards me; I am surrounded with favours, nay they are poured in upon me. Yet I find the rebellion of my Heart against God to be so great as to neglect nay forget him, and live in that neglect day after Day without feeling my soul smitten with compunction. I trust that I am not forgotten in the prayers of my friends and perhaps it is in answer to their requests that the spark of love to God is not quite extinguished.

The inestimable blessing of Christian Society is enjoyed but scantily here, to what it is in England; for tho we have very valuable Christian friends, yet they live 20 or 30 miles distant from us; and as traveling is very difficult here, there being no High Roads, or Inns, to call at, and in the Rains no way of traveling but by water, we have the pleasure of seeing each other but seldom. Tho when we do it makes our meetings much more sweet and agreeable than they might be if we met oftener. We have in the Neighborhood about fifteen or sixteen serious persons or those I have good hopes of, all Europeans. With the Natives I have very large concerns. Almost all the Farmers for near 20 miles round cultivating Indigo for us, and the Labouring people working here to the number of about 500, so that I have considerable opportunity of publishing the Gospel to them. I have so much knowledge of the Language as to be able to preach to them for about half an hour, so as to be understood but am not able to vary my subjects much. I tell them of the evil, and universality of Sin, the misery of a natural State, the Justice of God, the incarnation of Christ and his sufferings in our stead, and of the necessity of Conversion, Holiness, and Faith in order to Salvation. They hear with attention in general, and some come to me for instruction in the things of God. I hope in time I may have to rejoice over some who are truly converted to God.

Family Life of the Missionary

Family life on the mission field presents the missionary with unique challenges resulting in both joy and anguish. William Carey experienced the apparent worst of familial situations and the best according to his own appraisal. His three wives, all different in personality and temperament, provided him with marital bliss (the last two) and with an anguish (Dorothy) that can only come from a less than ideal marriage circumstance. Carey's letters open a window into that area of his life and allow us a peak.

Carey's children provided some deep satisfaction and disappointment to their father. He concerned himself seriously over their spiritual condition, and Carey often issued advice to them relating to spiritual and marital matters. Some of this counsel provides information about his own views concerning marriage and family.

The extended family remained in Carey's thoughts and prayers from the beginning of his work in India. He helped provide for their physical needs when possible and was ever vigilant in his care for their spiritual needs. Carey's letters to his Sisters, Father, and Brother betray the heart of a man ultimately committed to missions, but unwilling to forsake totally the welfare of his family in England. Carey undoubtedly loved them.

Family News

Carey to Father, Dec. 1802

> I have great reason to bless the Lord for his goodness to my Family. My two Eldest Sons I trust are now converted by divine grace. They are now nearly grown up, indeed Felix is quite so, and they are a great source of consolation to me. Both of them are become Printers and should you live another year I hope to be able to send you a large work written by myself and printed by Felix, viz. a Sanskrit Grammar. Jabez, and Jonathan are fine lads, and as we have the advantage of an excellent school in our own Family, they are in it under the tuition of Bro. Marshman. Poor Mrs. Carey has been long deranged in her mind. She is obliged to be confined or closely watched continually. There is I fear no reason to hope that she will ever recover.

Carey to Ryland, Calcutta, June 23, 1803

I cannot recollect the exact ages of my sons, when I go to Serampore I will look at my Memoranda, and send you word as soon as I can remember. I certainly remember you, and yours in my poor addresses to the throne of Grace - my love to them all & all others who care for Zion.

Carey to Sutcliffe, Calcutta, Mar. 20, 1811

. . . Through mercy we are now all well; My wife has been at the point of Death with the measles, but is nearly recovered; more than 50 in our family have had that disease and are mercifully recovered without one single death.

Carey to Jabez, July 4, 1823

. . . Having but little time I must give you some account of the state of our Family. Through mercy I and your Mother are well. I expect she will be baptised in about two months more, an event which is a great consolation to me. We live in great happiness, and I believe she is a truly pious person. Amelia lives with us. She and the children are well, Lucy lives with Mrs. Ward, Dolly is on a visit to us, and little Margaret is a fine lively child. I have not heard very lately of William, but hope he is not worse than when he wrote. He complains of a pain in his side, which he fears is the Liver. Jonathan is well, and busy at the Court, it being now the assizes.

CONCERN FOR FAMILY IN ENGLAND

Carey grew up in a very modest setting and was himself a cobbler who often scraped to make ends meet. His parents, brother, and sisters played heavily on his mind, and he corresponded with them frequently. He worried about their physical and economic situation. Carey's letters express this concern in a very affectionate and substantial way as he provides monetary help when possible.

Carey to Sisters, Aug. 24, 1803, Calcutta

. . . I am extremely distressed to hear of the heavy afflictions of my dear Sister Polly - Might not the removal to a warmer climate do much towards restoring her Health, and could she not come to India with some female Missionary if there be any possibility thereof, I will thankfully pay the expences of her passage. I confess that I have for several Years thought this step impracticable or I should otherwise have proposed it, but a Lady who is a member of our Church and who after having lost her voice and the use of her legs and feet was recovered in a great measure by a voyage to this place has so pressed it upon me that I should feel guilty if I did not propose it. She encloses a letter to confer in this.

Carey to Father, Calcutta, July 11, 1805

. . . I have thus shortly given you a history of our affairs, and this is all I can do. My heart often flies into England, and I frequently visit the house, the Orchard, and Garden where I passed my juvenile years. I trust that I often remember you and all my other relations when I approach the throne of divine Grace . . .

Carey to Sisters, Calcutta, Feb. 25, 1807

Could I receive incredible accounts of the conversion of my dear Father and my Brother, and of the Children of my brother and Sister it would be an occasion of great joy to my soul.

I can truly say that neither of you, nor my Father, brother, or many others of my friends, have been forgotten by me for a long time back in my poor addresses to the throne of Grace, but perhaps it would be presumption in me to expect that prayers so mixed with selfish and corrupt feelings, and which are often times almost void of that which is the spirit and soul of prayer, should be answered. I, however, feel much for your afflictions and must bear them on my mind.

I have no doubt but you often think it strange that I do not send you some pecuniary assistance. You may be assured that had I been in other circumstances I should have done it; but the day in which I embarked in the work of the mission I considered my self and my all as devoted to God. This is also the sentiment which is entertained by us all. While I was at Mudnabati, before our other brethren arrived, there was no opportunity of forming a family which should have a common stock. A small sum which I had laid by at that time was, therefore, accounted as private property, but this has been gradually diminishing. The whole of our income is, therefore, thrown into one common stock, and happy is he who can contribute the most to it. My income from the College has been doubled since Jan. the first, this year; and the School under Bro. Marshman is also increasing. This is to us both a matter of great pleasure, because the work in which we are engaged requires all that and much more.

Carey to Fuller, Jan. 14, 1808

You will oblige me by paying twenty pounds to my Father, and thirty to my Sister Hobson. (I intend the fact for both my sisters but as they live together it will be the same to which sister it is paid.) I shall pay that sum to the Mission here. I wrote to you last year requesting you to pay something to my relations but I forget how much, and to whom. I will thank you to send me the account in your next and I will repay it here.

Carey to Fuller, Oct. 25, 1809

I write now principally to request that you will on receipt of this pay on my account 30 pounds to my Brother Thomas Carey, this which sum I will pay to the Mission fund here upon receiving advice of its being paid.

Carey to Fuller, Dec. 1809

I have, in my last ordered a sum of money to be paid to my Bro. I hope you will pay it for me. I think it was 50 pounds. I have somewhat exceeded my ability this year in these little donations, but I could not be easy to propose property and know my Bro. to be in a state of distress. I have donated nearly the income of what I received with my wife on our marriage, to the relief of my relations, and hope it will be found sufficient, as I do not intend to give any permanent relief to my Brother, but do this at present, to assist him in getting into some kind of business.

CONCERN FOR SPIRITUAL LIFE OF THE FAMILY

As would be expected, Carey's greatest desire for his family, extended and nuclear, regarded their spiritual well being. As a son, a brother, and father, the missionary encouraged, advised, and pleaded with the family members to walk closely with God and make their salvation sure. Perhaps Carey's greatest joy expressed in his letters grew out of spiritual victories within the family.

Carey to Ryland, Dec. 13, 1804

Oct. 23, last, my son Felix was married to a pious young woman of this place, Sister to Mrs. Edmonds, who is also a very pious woman. I hope she will prove a valuable acquisition to the Mission family. Both Felix and William have I believe felt the real power of divine grace, but they will never shine in gifts, nor do I expect they will have that activity which is so necessary in their situation. They inherit the taciturn spirit and too much natural inactivity of their Father, which will be to them a great impediment in every important undertaking.

Carey to Sutcliffe, Sept. 28, 1809

. . . I have as great a degree of domestic felicity as, perhaps any man in the World; and have only two more family blessings to desire, viz. the conversion of my two younger sons, and their being employed in the work of God. Our American Friends sent out by conveyance 2,000 Dollars or somewhat more, to assist in the translation and printing of the Word of God. Thus God appears for his own cause.

Carey to Brother, Oct. 25, 1809

. . . You, my dear Brother, will greatly oblige me, if you will communicate to me unreservedly the state of your soul. I have never had satisfactory information from any quarter respecting your conversion and though, from several of your letters, and from some expressions in those of my Sisters, I have encouraged a hope that you are a believer in Christ, and a lover of Holiness, yet I have no such information as sets my heart at rest respecting you . . .

Carey to Sisters, Dec. 21, 1809, Calcutta

. . . Nothing now lies nearer to my heart as it respects my family affairs than the conversion of my two youngest sons. They are fine lads, and will have such an education as may fit them for any station in life, if they are industrious, nor have I any reason to find fault with their want of affection to me; but they are not converted; and when I have said this, I have said enough to shew you that my solicitude on their account is not unfounded . . .

Carey to Jabez, Jan. 12, 1815

. . . We are daily expecting Felix here. I am impatient to see him and yet greatly fear his coming. He has been sorely chastised but whether it has been sanctified is to me a matter of doubt. He was greatly hurt in his mind when he was here last. I think he was blameable, and the Brethren harsh. He now intimates his intention of withdrawing from the Mission and is coming in a publick capacity. I anticipate some further calamity to him for God is a jealous God, but I must leave Felix In the hands of him who is infinitely wise and good. I trust Felix will continue his translation and though separate from a formal connection with us will still not be separated from God and his work.

Carey to Jabez, undated

. . . Felix is in Calcutta. He was sent by the Burman Government ambassador to the Supreme Government at Calcutta but was not received as properly accredited. (Govt.) has, however, allowed him and his people adequate support. I am glad he was not received. I hope it is felt by him. Felix is in my opinion very much sunk as regards divine things. He has withdrawn from all connection with the Mission, has married a third wife, a young woman of French extraction. I hope a worthy person - but of this I can say nothing. He is absolutely shriveled up as it regards divine things. I believe he will go on with the translation of the Scriptures into Burmese and Chinese and I hope the Lord will be merciful to him and restore him to a sense of what he has relinquished.

Carey to Brother, Serampore, May 9,1815

. . . The concerns of your Soul have my dear Brother long been very near to my heart, and often have I supplanted the Father of Mercies on your behalf. But I never before could ascertain whether you made a practice of attending on the preaching of the Gospel or no. You have now explicitly informed me of your attendance on the Word and of the inward sentiments of your mind on divine things. I hope you will continue to the end of your life to communicate freely with me upon that most interesting subject, and let us henceforth mutually rejoice in the goodness of our God towards us and seek to the utmost extent of our powers to serve the God whom we owe all our hopes, to whom we are under the highest obligations, and whose service will, if we attend on it with simplicity of heart be in itself a very rich reward, a source of unsullied joy far superior to every other pleasure.

Carey to Jabez, Nov. 21, 1820

Your last letter has given me much uneasiness on account of the affliction of your family. I trust you and yours have been frequently remembered by me at the Throne of mercy on that account. Indeed, I have my stated times of interceding with God for my Children and for all the Brethren in the Mission and upon these occasions my mind is often much engaged on your account, that you and your family may enjoy all the blessings of the present life, but more especially that you may be preserved in the fear of God, and may be made an useful minister of the Gospel of our Lord Jesus Christ. Indeed this is my first and chief concern for you and for all who are near and dear to me. I hope ere this Eliza and her Mother and little William are restored, give my love to them.

Carey to Jabez, Apr. 11, 1829

. . . I was much gratified with the account you sent me of the Schools. I hope you will continue to send me accounts from time to time of all your concerns, for be assured, I feel a deep interest in them. I am most of all anxious to hear of the Spiritual state of your mind. I hope you live near to God, and set him always before you. Next to that I am concerned for your domestic peace. I hope an end has been put to your domestic differences. An account of Eliza's true conversion to God, and of your being fuller heirs of Eternal life would be most grateful to me. How do the dear Children? I think much of them. Pray do not neglect their education. I shall always be gratified to receive accounts of everything which concerns __________ I trust you and yours are much in my (supplications to) __________ The Throne of Grace. Your Mother unites in love to Eliza, yourself and the Children. Be assured that I am

Your truly affecte Father

THOUGHTS ON MARRIAGE

William Carey has received both criticism and defense concerning his marriage to Dorothy. In the journal we see her struggle with taking her family to India. The move affected her deeply emotionally and mentally. Dorothy Carey never recovered and remained in an incapacitated state and occasionally required restraint until her death. She verbally abused Carey in front of the children and even tried to kill him. This relationship resulted in great anguish for the missionary, his family, and friends.

The next two marriages to Charlotte Rumohr and Grace Hughes provided Carey much conjugal happiness. He described these women with glowing terms and enjoyed immensely his time with them. In addition, his second and third wives, despite their illnesses, served well in support of the mission work.

Carey to Sutcliffe, May 4, 1808

. . . I have resolved on a second Marriage, and expect by the end of June to be united to Miss Charlotte Emilia Rumohr. She is a person about my own age, and of whose purity and attachment to the Mission I have the strongest praise. She is of a noble family in the duchy of Schleswig. Her Father died when she was young, her Mother, the Countess of Alfeldt died about three years ago. She has a Sister living near Schleswig, who is the wife of the Graff (Chevalier) Wamstedt Chamberlaine to H. D. Majesty and Ranger of the Royal Forests. Another Sister is married and settled in Marseilles. I do not know of any except Mrs. Wamstedt, who are serious, though the family is very numerous.

Carey to Sisters, Aug. 9, 1808, Calcutta

I must now give you a short detail of the few occurrences which have taken place since I wrote my last. I was married May the 9th to Lady Charlotte Rumohr. We had designed to have deferred it till a longer time but her ill state of health made me determine an earlier time that she might be delivered from that neglect which sick persons must expect from native Servants. In her I have a very affectionate partner, and a true help meet.

Carey to Sisters, Mar. 8, 1809, Calcutta

My dear wife has had an affliction, having been ill ever since our marriage. She is now much better and indeed nearly recovered. She is a woman of great piety, and no man can be more happy in that connection than I am with her.

Carey to Sisters, Aug. 8, 1809, Calcutta

{Carey was very ill and almost died. Several doctors were consulted. One Dr. Darling ordered Carey to drink a glass of port wine every quarter of an hour. He drank nearly two bottles a day. His wife was very faithful during this time.}

My wife, who though very weak, attended me continually through my illness, and even though others watched me, never took off her clothes to go to rest for three weeks in a month was most surprisingly supported, and while I was thought in danger, was carried beyond her usual strength. As soon as I was declared out of danger, immediately began to fail. She has since been very ill, and though considerable recovered, is still very weak. I have now as great a share of domestic happiness as I can reasonably desire. My wife has been all her days in the school of affliction, and has been a great sufferer, but this climate serves her constitution, and she has a greater share of health than she ever had. My great wish now is to see my two younger sons converted and employed in the work of God. They are affectionate, obedient children, but want the chiefest of all things.

Carey to Sister, Anne Hobson, Oct.15, 1812

{Carey has just recovered from a horrible fever that he thought was going to kill him.}

. . . On the bed of affliction and in the prospect of death I was enabled to examine my evidence on an interest in the Redeemer. I saw plainly that everything in myself called for the deepest repentance and humiliation but thought I could trace a trust in the Lord Jesus for pardon and acceptance and, I think, I did thus commit my soul to him. My affliction was such as to sink my spirits to a very low degree of depression and to produce a degree of mental stupidity which I scarcely ever felt before.

My dear wife had for some time, I believe nearly three months before, been confined to her couch unable to stand or even lift her feet upon the couch without help. During my affliction she was one Lord's Day morning much depressed at not being able to stir or yield me any assistance. This led her to pour out her soul in secret before God and very earnestly to pray for such a recovery of strength as to be able to walk and attend upon me. Her request was granted, for before she had done praying her knees were strengthened and she was in less than a quarter of an hour able to walk about as usual, which has continued till the present time, and she is much better in her general health than for some months past. I mention this because I am not willing that God should be deprived of the honour of having done it in answer to prayer, especially as I find an inclination in many truly serious persons to attribute too much to second causes such as excitation, sudden pleasure or pain and the like and too little to God.

Carey to Jabez, June 16, 1821

I believe Felix (wrote to you) an (account) of the death of your Dear Mother. I was not able then to write upon the subject so very afflicting to my mind. She was one that truly feared God; her soul was continually engaged either in meditating on or praying to God, or in reading his holy Word, and next to that she lived wholly for me. She never did a thing during the thirteen years we lived together without consulting me, even though she was sure of my consent. She watched every change in my countenance with the utmost solicitude and often was full of anxiety if she perceived the least sign of weariness, illness, grief or distress. Often has she come to me and requested me to forgive her everything in which she had unknowingly offended me. She certainly had no occasion for such a request but her heart was exceedingly tender upon that point. My loss is irreparable, but her gain is . . .

Carey to Jabez, Jan. 18, 1822

My life is solitary and melancholy. I shall I think, endeavor to marry again, after some time but at present I know not where to look for a woman who will be a suitable partner for me. I hope the Lord will direct me in that matter as he has done in everything from my youth till now.

Carey to Sisters, Sept. 1822, Serampore

. . . I was married again on the 22nd of July last, to a Widow Lady, Mrs. Grace Hughes. She is a careful, serious Woman about 46 years of age. She is a native of a village in Essex called Ilscome or Elscome about three miles from Holstead. Her maiden name was Ellis. She had by her own industry brought up a family of four Children with which she was left on the death of her late Husband; two of whom are married and settled. - I have the prospect of happiness in my new relation, and have in that respect very great cause for gratitude to God. -

Carey to Sisters, Jan. 15, 1823, Calcutta

I informed you in my last of my third marriage, and can now through much mercy add that this marriage is among my great mercies. My Dear Wife is a Woman who fears God; During my late illness her attention to me was unremitted; and I have the highest reason to be thankful for the Union. She does know of my writing, or she would write in love to you all.

FAMILY PROBLEMS

Family crises always demand attention, and Carey dealt with several unhappy circumstances during his ministry in India. Early on his most pressing family problem was Dorothy's insanity and its effect on Carey and his children. Later Carey faced trials with his sons as they struggled with their faith and marriages. After losing his wife and children in a drowning accident, Felix caused his Father grief with his prodigal activities. Jabez fulfilled Carey's dream of becoming a missionary, but he too experienced marital problems with his wife, Eliza.

Carey to Sisters, Oct. 5, 1795 Mudnabati

I told you before I believe of the Afflictions of my Wife, and Felix, and the Death of Peter - the two first are through mercy recovered; and Mrs. Carey is near having another little one, but I have greater Afflictions than any of these in my Family; known to my Friends here, but I have never mentioned it to any one in England before - - in my poor Wife - who is looked upon as insane to a great Degree by both Natives and Europeans. I believe there may be something of that, and perhaps much; but I have been for some time past in some Danger of losing my Life. - -Jealousy is the great Evil that Haunts her mind - tho blessed be God. I never was so far from temptation to any evil of that kind in my Life.- - But her misery, and Rage is extreme. Europeans have repeatedly talked to her, but in vain, and what may be the end of all God alone knows. Bless God all the dirt which she throws is such as cannot stick, but it is the Ruin of my Children to hear such continual accusations.

Carey to Sisters, Mudnabati, Apr. 10, 1796

. . . I am very glad that Polly is recovered from her illness in some measure but it is very desirable to be always ready for Death which is I trust the Case with you both habitually. We are often apt to trust to flesh and sensible appearances but could we cease thus anxiously to look on the things that are seen and fix our minds upon invisible objects we should not only be ready to drop this tabernacle, but should also triumph over all the distresses of the present Life. I also have some distress. My poor wife must be considered as insane; and is the occasion of great sorrow. I have been obliged to confine her some time back to prevent murder which was attempted, but she now shews no disposition to commit such violence, and is at Liberty. In January last she was delivered of another Son whom we call Jonathan - him and Jabez are now ill with the Hooping Cough.

Carey to Fuller, Nov. 16, 1796, Mudnabati

Poor Mrs. Carey cannot I think be a greater burden than she is. She has even attempted my Life. Mr. T. has been a too unhappy witness of this conduct . . .

Carey to Fuller, March 23, 1797, Mudnabati

To say any thing of my own personal exercises would only be filling up paper with a long tedious tale about myself. I, therefore, decline it and only say that I have daily cause to complain, yet complain in reality but little; and am what I have been for many years, that poor, sluggish, phlegmatic creature, who made all the advantages of Godly society to set the springs in motion; yet have lost little of that . . . My family trials, of which you intimate, you have heard, continue, and increase, some attempts on my life have been made, but I hope nothing of that kind is to be feared now. God has graciously preserved me, and given me support, that I have not been remarkable retarded in my publick work thereby. I am sorely distressed to see my dear Children, before whom the greatest indiscretions and most shocking expressions of saga are constantly uttered; and who are constantly taught to hate their Father; tis true they don't regard what is said, yet is insensibly impressed (on) their minds with a kind of British ferocity, and viciousness which is to me very distressing.

Carey to Sisters, Mudnabati, Jan. 10, 1798

. . . Poor Mrs. C is as wretched as insanity can make her almost and often makes all the Family so too, but we are supported by a gracious God.

Carey to Sisters, Serampore, Nov. 23, 1801

. . . Mrs. Carey is obliged to be constantly confined. She has long got worse and worse, but fear both of my own life and hers, and the desire of the police of the place, obliged me to agree to her confinement.

Carey to Father, Sept. 11, 1804, Calcutta

I and my family am, through the good care of God, as well as I ever remember; except my poor Wife who continues in the melancholy situation which she has long been in. You seem to think that the climate of this country has contributed to her derangement, I have no such Idea. On the contrary I have every reason to suppose that it was gradually coming on for several Years before she left England tho then unsuspected by me, but I now recollect numerous instances of conduct which are best explained by referring them to this source. The enjoyment which I have in our Family, which is one of the happiest in the world, and in my Children, two of whom I have had the pleasure of baptizing with my own hands, more than compensates for the distress which I have from any other quarter. I expect that Felix will be married before this reaches you. He is under engagement to a young Lady (Miss Gunn) whom I think truly pious, and highly approve of.

Carey to Sisters, July 17, 1805

. . . I have, through divine goodness, as good health as I ever had, but my eye sight fails me much. I can scarcely see by candle light, with spectacles, and can read but very little without them by daylight. I feel this to be a great inconvenience, as so much of my business consists in reading and writing, but I ought not complain. I ought rather to spend my remaining strength more to glory of God. Poor Mrs. Carey is a very distressing object. Her whole life is a life of fear and rage, arising from ideal troubles, indeed her insanity is of that distressing nature that she never has any of those pleasing illusions which many in that unhappy state have, but seems to be wholly under the influence of malevolent impressions. A solicitude for her children, an Idea that they are ill or injured, &ct., constantly occupies her mind, and fills her with almost boundless rage against supposed enemies of her offspring.

Carey to Jabez, Feb. 7, 1816

. . . Give my love to Eliza, in which your mother joins very heartily; we very frequently think and converse of you both and I trust your steadfast adherence to the cause of our dear Redeemer will occasion us always to converse about you with joy. Not so Felix. The thought of him rends my heart. I received a short note from him since his arrival at Rangoon and a bill drawn on me for 4,500 rupees, which I, of course, refused to honour.

Carey to Ryland, Apr. 12, 1817, Calcutta

My Family trials are as much as I can, nay more than I can stand under without extraordinary support from above. Felix has lately been to see us, and appears in a very hopeful state, but he is a ruined man as it respects this world. I am, however, greatly comforted to see the great change which appears in his conduct. My youngest Son Jonathan is, however, an awful profligate; living in adultery with another man's Wife. I greatly need the sympathy and prayers of all who love God. My Wife is as well as she has generally been.

Carey to Jabez, March 13, 1820

. . . Felix has received word from Mr. Judson that his child is dead and his wife on the point of being married to another man, the Portugese Priest having declared the marriage null because it was not celebrated after the manner of the Church of Rome. The consequence is that Felix considers himself at liberty to marry again and has pitched upon a cousin of young Mr. Kierulf. I do know how it will end. I have advised him at any rate, to wait till he is free from debt, but Felix seldom thinks on what is to come.

Carey to Jabez, Apr. 21, 1820

. . . Felix is well but is thoughtlessness itself. He has heard that his wife was on the point of being married to another man, and has, therefore, considered himself as under no further obligation to her. In consequence of this he paid his addresses to a young lady, native of Norway, cousin to Mr. Kierulf. The worst of it was that he not only did not inform her of his true circumstances, but represented them as very different from what they were. The lady had actually given her consent when it came into their heads to ask me about Felix's actual circumstances. It certainly was a foolish thing in them to defer consulting me till the lady's consent was given, if they intended doing it at all, but when they did do it I could do no other than give them a just and true account. This I did and this broke off the match.

Carey to Jabez, March 19, 1821

. . . Through mercy we are as usual as it regards health. Felix has fixed his eye on a young lady in Mrs. Lawson's school and hopes to obtain her in marriage, how it will end I know not. From him I hear a good account of her and believe it to be just. Dolly has been so wicked that we are obliged to send her to Cutwa, to William, to prevent her ruin. A years residence there did Lucy much good and we hope it may have a similar effect on Dolly.

Carey to Jabez, Apr. 23, 1825

Eliza with the two children and, I believe Mr. Mills, left Calcutta for Ajmere last Wednesday.

I assure you that neither I nor anyone here ever heard anything of what you alluded to in your last letter, I mean that reports injurious to Eliza's character had been circulated and I believe I may say that no such report has ever been heard in Calcutta. In a letter from you to Eliza, I find she thought Lieut. Dalzell was the author of those reports. Lieut D. was at our house a few days before Eliza's arrival, but he mentioned nothing to me or any one else, detrimental to her or you. He is gone to Singapore, in a consumption, and I have no expectation of his recovery.

I am sorry to say that Eliza put it entirely out of my power or Jonathan's to pay her the attention we wished. We had arranged matters previously to her arrival for her residing with us, but she took a small house without saying why, and went to live with her mother. When I spoke to her about it she alleged a wish to have her servants well accommodated as the reason.

She made an application to Jonathan for money almost immediately after her arrival. It was not in his power to comply with her wishes, and he wrote her as affectionate a letter upon the subject as he could and which I believe you have seen. He shewed it to me before he sent it, and I thought it highly proper; but Eliza was highly offended at it and, certainly, scarcely treated Jonathan or his wife with common decency. Jonathan was about to advance her money for her return, when your bill arrived, the amount of which he immediately gave her; and which she laid out in purchases. She then offered her jewels for sale to pay the expences of her journey back at a price far beyond their value and after she had waited a month beyond the time she had appointed for going she made an application to Mrs. Wright of Agra to borrow 300 Rupees. Mrs. Wright immediately to Jonathan, and he immediately advanced her the 300 Rupees. She said many unlovely things to Mrs. Wright and others about Jonathan, and indeed about us all, every one of which was without foundation, and I fear only arose from resentment at not having her wishes about money complied with, which was impossible.

I tried what I could to persuade her __________, but to no purpose; and now she is gone in a way that fills my heart with distress. She intended going in a Palkee and had bought one, but I am sorry to say expended her money till she had not enough left to pay the bearers, and is gone I understand, in a hackery. I wish your mind may be prepared for the worst; but if she survives the journey, I have not expectation that the children will.

It would have been easy to have sent her baggage to Agra by Mr. Wright's luggage boat, or by Barber's boat, and to have employed the hire of hackeries to pay bearers. But Eliza would consult no one who wished her well.

I hope you will excuse my writing thus, but I am compelled so to do in vindication of ourselves. Jonathan I am sure felt it to be a luxury to provide for the education of William, and all he has done or proposed to do was wholly out of affection to you, and certainly did not deserve the return it was met with from Eliza. May the Lord grant that she and the children may get safely back, and may it be for your comfort and happiness. I trust you will be supported and directed from on high and be enabled to persevere in the work of the Lord.

ADVICE TO JABEZ

William Carey took the role of father seriously, especially when dealing with issues pertaining to missions. Jabez served in Amboyna and then Ajmere. Eliza, Jabez's wife possessed certain qualities Carey felt inappropriate for the mission field. Eventually, the stress of being on the field caused marital problems for Jabez and Eliza and Father Carey writes to give advice.

Carey to Jabez, Mar. 9, 1819

. . . I have never yet touched the very delicate subject of Eliza's excessive love of finery and her tawdry appearance. I would write to her about it if I did not despair of doing good thereby. Her expensiveness and tawdriness are very lamentable things, the first will ruin you in your circumstances the other in your reputation. I am fully sensible of her good qualities, and only wish you to keep a mild but resolute guard against these two great evils. I (hope) you set about remedying them and the spirit of the Gospel God will be with you and you will finally succeed.

Carey to Jabez, July 19, 1825

. . . I was sorry to see from (your letter that) you thought Eliza's journey hither with it's (attendant) circumstances would affect your future harmony __________ it may not. I hope you will always treat __________ both for her comfort and your own, you ought to act firmly and decidedly. Domestic happiness is too great a blessing to be lightly sacrificed but in your case I fear it will never be secured by yielding to all the wishes of Eliza. Yet, if you govern your house with firmness you may still be happy. I request you will overlook all the distance of her behaviour here. I was sorry for it a thousand times more on her account than ours.

Carey to Jabez, Oct. 11, 1826

I recd. yours of Aug - accompanying one from Eliza, and saying you had made up all differences. I had no expectation from that childish step and, therefore, did not wonder at receiving a letter from Eliza about a fortnight afterwards to inform me that you were as disunited as ever. I have written very severely to Eliza upon the subject and must now address a few lines to you.

The thing which most of all distresses me is you yielding to Sin. I hope God will give you deep and genuine repentance for it. Turn from it My Dear Jabez, with abhorrence, and seek for mercy. "If we say we have no sin we deceive ourselves and the truth is not in us but if we <u>confess our sins</u> God is <u>faithful and just to forgive our sins and to cleanse us from all unrighteousness</u>. 1 John 1st Ch 8, 9. Consider My Dear Jabez, that nothing is an excuse for Sin and that there is no reason why we should Sin, that there can be no safety in Sin, but that the way of mercy is open, and God is ready to receive everyone who returns to him.

I was afraid something was wrong when you gave up the ministry. Your reasons appeared very weak and insufficient. May God so restore you that you may in future time, devote yourself entirely to him. Thus David did "Restore to me the joys of thy Salvation and quicken me with thy free Spirit, then shall I teach Transgressors thy ways and Sinners shall be converted to Thee". Psalm 51. 12, 13. Be not contented without feeling the odiousness of your crime and loathing yourself for it in the sight of God.

In this affair you have nothing to say to men. I am astonished at you submitting to go to Rev. Mr. Palmer whoever he may be. What has he to do with you? I would with the utmost contempt have refused his interference. He assuredly will never write to me about it, unless he is as weak as you shewed yourself in suffering an appeal to him. The matter is between you and God, and he will yet restore you.

You, My Dear Jabez, have been to blame in yielding up the government of your family to Eliza. I did not choose to mention this disagreeable subject because I thought it might widen the breach but now things are come to a crisis. I advise you never to hear one word about a separation from your Wife. Declare this to her and stick to it. Never suffer her to go to visit anyone without your full consent. Her visiting her relations will only open the breach wider. Never furnish her with money or means of any kind to take a journey without you. You have had too fatal proof that you cannot live separately, therefore, never try it. Govern your own house with firmness, with temper and in the fear of God. Never yield in the smallest degree to Eliza's violence, but if she plays the mad woman keep her under proper restraint. If her mother interferes forbid her your house and take care she never enters it. Take the management of the children out of her hands and above all that of the purse and persevere till she acts a better part, but never strike her, or return low and vulgar abuse for hers. Hold your tongue. Act firmly. Pray much to God, and I may say, act kindly but not tamely or weakly. I know a reform in your family is difficult but it is not impossible. I am truly grieved for the children, if you could by any means put them to School, that would be the best thing you could do.

DEATH OF FAMILY MEMBERS

Death, all too common in nineteenth-century India, became a common grief for the new missionaries in the hot and disease infested land of India. Carey lived to a ripe age but buried several family members on foreign soil. Accidents and illness constantly plagued the Carey family. Carey experienced grief as little Peter, Dorothy, Felix and his family, and Charlotte all died on the mission field. Carey dealt with death in an interesting way. See also the Spirituality of the Missionary section for a more complete picture of Carey's coping ability in times of grief.

Carey to Sutcliffe, Nov. 22, 1796, Mudnabati

My family are well. I have another son named Jonathan, instead of Peter, who died.

Carey to Fuller, Jan. 14, 1808

On the 8th of December past, it pleased God to remove my wife by death. She, poor woman, had been in a state of the most distressing derangement of mind for this last twelve years; indeed *{terms}* of her mind was such, as prevented her from feeling even those ideal pleasures which sometimes attend maniacal persons. She was attacked with a fever which terminated in about a fortnight. My eldest son with his wife and youngest child and Brother and Sister Chater with their son sailed from Calcutta the 28th of November, and left the Pilot the 2nd of December on their way to Rangoon; The interfering hand of God was evidently stretched out for their protection, considering the dreadful havoc made among the Shipping of this port by one French Privateer, which has taken about thirty ships.

Carey to Sisters, Jan. 20, 1808, Calcutta

The last year has been one of the most eventful in my whole life, and has been marked by some of the strangest features of any period. I have received the greatest proofs of publick respond *{response}* and have felt the strongest effects of publick jealousy that have ever been shown to me before. I have had some of the most painful experiences, and felt some of the greatest supports that I ever recollect.

. . . In the last year the Lord bestowed upon me unspeakable favour of calling my son Felix to engage in an attempt to begin a new Mission to the Burman Empire. Felix and his wife, and Bro. Chater with his wife sailed from here for Rangoon the 28th of Nov. and left the Pilot De. 2nd. Little Lucy stayed with us. O that the Lord may now send prosperity.

A day or two before Felix left, my poor wife was taken poorly, but no danger was apprehended. She, however, grew worse and worse till Dec. 8th in which day she died. Her disorder was a fever. The affectionate attendance which my sons paid to her made a deep impression upon my mind.

I am aware that there is a degree of indelicacy in mentioning so early my design to marry again after a proper time, but as I shall not be able to write to you very often, and as some things connected therewith may contribute to your comfort, I shall inform you, that I do intend after some months, to marry Mrs. Rumohr. I have proposed the matter to her, and she has testified her agreement thereto. She is one of the most pious and conscientious persons with whom I am acquainted, and is two or three months older than myself. Her Father was a German Nobleman, his mother Countess of Alfeldt, and she a follower of the Lord Jesus Christ. She possesses some property which will enable me to do something for my Relations, and it is in consequence of a wish which she expressed, that I communicate my intentions to you so early.

Carey to Jabez, Nov. 25, 1814

A little time ago I wrote to you by way of Java particularly informing you of the distressing providence which had befallen Felix. On the eleventh or twelfth of August as he with his family were going to Ava on a brig purchased for him at Calcutta, a squall came on and overset the vessel. Felix's wife and two children, a female servant and four men were drowned. Felix and the rest of the people swam to shore. Felix, I am informed, proceeded to Ava, but no news from him has yet reached Rangoon when the last accounts came away. I mourn for Felix in silence, and still tremble to think what may be the next stroke. I am dumb with silence because God has done it.

Carey to Jabez, Oct. 6, 1815

. . . This week a letter arrived from Bro. Judson at Rangoon informing us that Felix with his wife and family had left that place for Ava. They had proceeded several days and were on the great river where they went on board a brig which we __________ to carry Felix to Rangoon and which had been purchased by the Burman Govt. to take him to Ava. He had not __________ himself, family and property on board above three hours when a squall arose in which the brig overturned and went down immediately. Felix swam to shore but his wife and two children were lost and several of the people . . . the newspaper says that Felix took his eldest child, little William, in his hands and swam with (him) till he was exhausted when he delivered him to a Lascar who swam with him till he was also spent when they were forced to relinquish him to save their own lives. He was supplied with clothes, money and necessaries by the governor of the Province and when the accident happened and when in this situation, the king's boat which was sent for him hove in sight . . . he went on to Ava. Bro. Judson says the people who returned with the jolly boat brought the news. Felix, I suppose, has neither pen or ink or paper or anything else left and was undoubtedly too much distressed to write so that we have not a line from him. We are all overwhelmed with distress at this most heavy tidings. I am dumb with silence because God has done it. May the Lord abundantly sanctify to dear Felix.

Carey to Ryland, June 14, 1821

I am now called in Divine providence to be a mourner again having lately suffered the greatest domestic loss that a man can sustain, my dear wife was removed from me by death on Wednesday morning, May 30th, about twenty minutes after midnight. She was about two months above 60 years of age. We had been married thirteen years and three weeks during which season I believe we had as great a share of conjugal happiness as ever was enjoyed by mortals. She was eminently pious, and lived very near to God. She lived only for me, her solicitude for my happiness was incessant, and so certainly could she at all times interpret my looks that any attempts to conceal anxiety or distress of mind would have been in vain. Nothing, however, but tenderness for each other's feelings could induce either of us for a minute to attempt to a concealment of anything. It was constant habit to compare every verse she had read in the various German, French, Italian and English versions and never to pass by a difficulty till it was cleared up. In this respect she was of eminent use to me in the translations of the Word of God.

She was full of compassion for the poor and needy: until her death, supported several blind and lame persons by a monthly allowance. I consider them as a precious legacy bequeathed to me. She entered most heartily into all the concerns of the Mission, and into the support of the schools, particularly those for female native children, and had long supported one at Cutwa of that kind. My loss is irreparable but still I dare not but perfectly acquiesce in the divine will. So many merciful circumstances attend this very heavy affliction as still yield me support beyond anything I ever felt in other trials.

1. I have no domestic strife to reflect on and add bitterness to affliction. 2. She was ready to depart. She had long lived on the border of the heavenly land, and I think lately became more and more heavenly in her thoughts and conversation. 3. She suffered no long or painful affliction. 4. She was removed before me, a thing for which we had frequently expressed our wishes to each other: for though I am sure my brethren and my children would have done the utmost in their power to alleviate her affliction if she had survived me, yet no one nor all united could have supplied the place of a husband. I have met with much sympathy in my illness.

Carey to Brother, June 18, 1821

I have now the sad office of informing you of the Death of my Dear Wife who was removed from this life on Wednesday morning, the 30th of May last. She was always in an afflicted state from her childhood; and frequently suffered much; but she was one of the best of Wives. During the thirteen years in which we were united, we never had a single thing which either of us wished to conceal from the other. She was eminently pious, and next to God. I believe all her care and anxiety was for me. I suppose that man's conjugal happiness was never experienced by any two mortals than by us. My loss is great, very great, but hers is eternal gain. Since her death I have been very unwell, especially occasioned by the great heat, which has this year exceeded any thing I ever recollect, but through divine mercy I am now quite well.

The dealings of God with respect to me have been remarkable in many respects. I have seen much affliction, and have experienced perhaps as much mercy as most men. Sometimes during the trial, I have been ready to sink under it; but I now see that The Lord has led me by a right way and, no doubt, should I at last arrive in Glory. I shall see that all which now to me appears dark, is done in infinite wisdom. I desire to cast my care upon the Lord, and commit all, both Soul and body to his care.

Carey to Burls, Oct. 5, 1821

. . . had I died and left a widow, she must have been unprovided for. God, however, who does all things well, however painful to us, has seen good to remove my dear partner to a better world; I was deprived of her on the 30th of May last. My loss in inescapable. If there ever was a true Christian in the world she was one. We had frequently conversed upon the separation which death would make and both desired that if it were the will of God, she might be first removed and so it was. Her illness was short and her trust in the Redeemer sincere and firm.

Carey to Jabez, Nov. 12, 1822

Last Tuesday I wrote you word that Felix was getting better. I did not then know that his disease had returned with more force. On my arrival at Serampore I heard was worse. I went immediately and found that he was seized with a Dysentery and Fever. I got a good medical man from Barrackpore, Dr. Chalmers. He saw him on Wednesday evening. On Thursday ten leeches were put on his side but he declined so fast that on Lord's Day at three in the afternoon he sank under the disease, and was buried yesterday morning close to the tomb of your Mother. Jonathan was with him when he died and William arrived in the evening. He could not speak a sentence the last two days, only three or four times a single word. He pronounced my name and Jonathan's about ten minutes before his death and appeared to make great efforts to speak to me but could not utter a word. I trust the Lord has been gracious to him. Amelia, who is near her time, is coming to live with us, Lucy goes to Bro. Ward's and Jonathan, who has generously stepped forward to support the whole family, as far as pecuniary aid is wanting, is going to put Dolly to Bro. Lawson's School.

Thus, mysterious, afflicting and yet merciful are the dealings of God. It is our part to be dumb with silence because the Lord has done it.

Carey to Sisters, Jan. 15, 1823, Calcutta

About two months ago I was called to mourn the loss of Felix, who died of a diseased Liver. Few men were more robust and strong than he was previous to his being seized with that disease. He was ill about six months from the time he first called in medical help, for I believe he suffered a long time before he said any thing to any one . . .

Miscellaneous Topics

Carey was a man of broad interests and learning. He regularly attended lectures on science and philosophy and delighted himself in horticulture both as a hobby and a help to India. He studied and experimented in natural sciences and was acknowledged publically for his contributions, even having some newly discovered species of plants named for him. Carey also received honors for his work. The following excerpts present a variety of traits not normally considered when studying Carey.

Carey the Naturalist

Carey to the Society, Aug. 5, 1794

The only Favour that I beg is that I may have the pleasure of seeing new Publications, that come out in our Connection and the Books that I wrote for before, viz. a Polyglot Bible, Arabic Testament, Malay Gospel, and Botanical Magazine . . . I wish you also to send me a few instruments of Husbandry, viz. Scythes, Sickles, Plow Wheels, and such things, and a yearly assortment of all Garden & Flowering Seeds and seeds of Fruit Trees, that you can possibly? . . . as it will be a lasting advantage to this Country and I shall have it in my power to do this for what I now call my own Country - only take care that they are New and dry.

Carey to Ryland, Calcutta, June 23, 1803

. . . I did not know that you had any friend a Nurseryman or I would have plentifully furnished you with seeds &ct. in hopes of some return, especially Bulbous roots (N.R. all such things should be sent so as to arrive here from September to the beginning of December - and should not be put in the ship's hold. They are best hung up in Nets or baskets in a cabin or the Steerage). I will send you plenty - I have never yet received a Copy of your funeral sermon for Mr. Francis - only one Copy of No. 6 Periodical Accounts, and one of Fuller's "Backsliders".

Carey to Sutcliffe, Jan.1, 1806, Calcutta

I must draw to a close. I have often desired to have Seeds Books &ct. sent out, but few have been sent. I will, therefore, give you a commission which I beg may be done at my private expence. I wish you Yearly in June or July to send an assortment of Culinary and flower Seeds, as great a variety of the latter as you can possibly procure, both indigenous and foreign. Also an assortment of Roots, viz. Tulip . . . Daffodil or Narcissus . . . The seeds must always be in a distinct box from the Roots and should never be put in the hold, which will infallibly spoil them. I wish the order to amount to Ten pounds per Annum. - . . . If I do not bear the expence I shall feel unhappy of receiving them. We received the Air-Pump and Electrical machine, but the Air pump leaks, and I fear will be useless. Perhaps we may get it rectified. The Electrical machine was sent without a large Jar, a Battery, a universal discharger, or even a discharging rod, on a chain. We have got a discharging rod made here and can get a Jar or two, and Chain, but very dear compared with the price of these things in England. We have lately purchased a good Apparatus, containing a Planetarium, a five foot Achromatic Telescope, a double, single, and Solar microscope, in one. The mechanical Powers, in brass, a Woolfe's apparatus for distilling - and a few more articles. I lecture in Nat. Phil. to the family and the higher class of Scholars once a fortnight. A few glass retorts, proper for concentrating Sulphuric Acid would be a great acquisition.

Carey to Ryland, Dec. 10, 1811

You wish me to send seeds of the *Careya* to England. It certainly is not modesty which prevents me from doing so, but the almost impossibility of doing it. The species found by me, from which the Genus was named, viz. *C. herbacea*,, seldom produces seeds, and when it does, they usually vegetate in the capsule, so that it would be impossible to send them to England. I may, however, perhaps succeed in getting seeds of the other two species, viz. *C. arborea*, and *C. Sperica*. These, however, become pretty large trees.

I have for a long time been describing the birds of Asia, and have already described, perhaps, almost one half of them, and some of the Quadrupeds: with a few of the insects. I shall perhaps publish them in a series of papers in the Asiatic-Researches, but have not yet determined. I have but little time to spare, for these pursuits, for which I have a strong natural inclination, and also find it very expensive, as nothing can be done without books, animals, correspondents in different countries, and the society of learned men. These I have in good measure, but yet the work goes on very slowly. I mention this because you mentioned in yours a wish that our Brethren might know something of the natural History, and geography. I certainly wish so too, and to shew that I do make this attempt to fill up that department.

Carey to Jabez, Feb. 1, 1815

. . . Tell Eliza that I expect her to dry seeds for me and butterflies, also to pick up stones, shells and crabs. You have many curious crabs and prawns. Send them but when you send seeds or dried birds - send me some stuffed birds - be careful to pack them very close, that no cockroaches can come at them. Send me bulbous roots and more parasitical plants. Send ugly shells as well as pretty ones. I ought not, however, repeat these things as I know your willingness.

Carey to Ryland, Nov. 17, 1813

Our friends Capt. and Mrs. Kemp are going to England with their family, I believe they will leave their children there for education, but they of course intend to return, as he goes in command of the *Moira* which is indeed his property. They are both members of our church, by them I send you a box containing plants, most of them if not all, new to the English Gardens. I enclose a list, numbered to correspond with the numbers on the sticks put down by the side of each plant. In order to secure them to the English gardens, I recommend your giving them to some Gentleman, or Nurseryman who has a stove, with a stipulation to receive one or more plants of each sort when they increase. I hope to receive some pretty liberal supplies of plants and seeds by the return of Capt. Kemp, I want your common field flowers, weeds, and shrubs, but nothing in the vegetable world will come amiss. I shall also be glad of a few cages of birds. We have here in common with England, the sparrow, the crow, the domestic duck, goose and fowl, and I believe no other birds. A few fragments of stone from the neighborhood of Bristol will be an acceptable present for my museum. Thus much for nature.

Carey to Sisters, Oct. 28, 1817

You ask about my ash tree. I really thought it one for a year or more but at last it produced flowers and undeceived me. I shall, however, always be glad to receive a few seeds or roots from my dear Nephews or Nieces. Blue-bells and Daffodils and Snowdrops or any other bulbs, if dug up after the flowers and leaves have decayed, and then well wrapped round with moss, ten or a dozen in a bundle, afterwards put into a box and nailed down, will come safe. I received a great number from Liverpool with other plants packed in this way which came with the utmost safety.

Carey to Dyer, July 15, 1819, Serampore

I have said that "I never ride out for the sake of Health" and it may, therefore, be enquired why are vehicles but for the purposes of health more necessary for the other members of the Family than for you . . . I reply, that my health is in general good, and probably much benefitted by a journey to and from Calcutta two or three times a week. I have also a great fondness for Natural Science, particularly Botany and Horticulture. These, therefore, furnish not only exercise but amusement for me. These amusements of mine are not, however, enjoyed without expence, any more than those of my Brethren, and were it not convenient for Bro. M.'s accusers to make a stepping stone of me, I would no doubt but my collection of plants, aviary, and museum, would be equally impeached as articles of luxury and lawless expence, though except the Garden, the whole of these expences are borne by myself.

Carey to Jabez, Jan. 26, 1824

The President of the Agricultural Society having found it necessary to go to the Cape for his health, the Society at it's (Annual) meeting unanimously chose me to be President. I was not at the meeting nor did I know that any one intended to propose me till I received the information from the Secretary the next day. This brings me out to publick view in a manner I would gladly have avoided but I had no choice.

Honors

Carey to Brother, Oct. 21, 1807, Calcutta

Last Year the University of Rhode Island America, conferred on me the Degree of Doctor in Divinity.

Carey to Jabez, Feb. 20, 1821

. . . The King of Denmark has written letters signed with his own hand to Bros. Ward, Marshman, and myself and has sent each of us a gold medal, as a token of his approbation. He has also made over the house in which Major Wickedie resides between Sarkie's house and ours to us three in perpetuity for the College. Thus divine (goodness) appears for us, and surpasses our expectations.

Carey to Sisters, Sept. 5, 1823, Calcutta

I have also this year received three works of Honour from different bodies in England, having been chosen a Fellow of the Linnaean Society, a member of the Geological Society, and corresponding member of the Horticultural Society of London: the latter was without any application on my part; to the other two I was proposed by my Friend H.T. Colebrooke, Esq.

Personal Life

Carey to Ryland, Dec. 10, 1811

In compliance with your wish, though not with my own, I have sat for my portrait, which the Painter informed me last night will be dry to send by the January Fleet. Bro. Ward had a great desire that I should be drawn as engaged in translating the Scriptures. The artist, Mr. Home has, therefore, introduced the Pundit whom I employ as an amanuensis as sitting by me. The likeness of the pundit is a very good one, his name is Gopala Nyayalankara. He has also introduced a number of books such as I use in translation, and in short has made it as much as possible like my translating table. He has introduced one conceit of his own, which, however, nobody will understand, having copied part of Acts 2.ch. 11 ver. from the Sanskrit N. Testament into a Mss. which lies before me.

BIBLIOGRAPHY

Secondary Sources

S. Pearce Carey. *William Carey.* London: The Wakeman Trust, 1993.

Mary Drewery. *William Carey: A Biography.* Grand Rapids: Zondervan Publishing House, 1978.

Timothy George. *Faithful Witness: The Life and Mission of William Carey.* Birmingham: New Hope, 1991.

Primary Sources

William Carey. *Journal.* Baptist Missionary Society Archives on permanent deposit in the Angus Library, Regent's Park College, Oxford. Property of the Baptist Missionary Society.

Carey Letters—All the letters cited in the work are housed in the Angus Library, Regent's Park College, Oxford. Property of the Baptist Missionary Society. Letters will be listed by the archive box or bound volume according to recipients, in chronological order. A notation of RPC (Regent's Park College) or BMS (Baptist Missionary Society) will be attached to designate the collection source.

Box IN 13 (1 of 2)

Carey to Fuller

January 30, 1795 BMS
June 17, 1796 BMS
November 16, 1796 BMS
March 1797 BMS
March 23, 1797 BMS
June 22, 1797 BMS
July 17, 1799 BMS
February 5, 1800 BMS
November 1800 BMS
August 4, 1801 BMS
January 21, 1802 BMS
September 7, 1803 BMS
February 27, 1804 BMS
December 10, 1805 BMS
March 14, 1806 BMS
August 26, 1806 BMS
November 18, 1806 BMS
February 13, 1807 BMS
August 11, 1807 BMS
October 1807 BMS
January 14, 1808 BMS
April 20, 1808 BMS
March 27, 1809 BMS
August 24, 1809 BMS
October 25, 1809 BMS
December 1809 BMS
January 20, 1811 BMS
August 2, 1811 BMS
March 25, 1812 BMS
March 25, 1813 BMS
May 5, 1813 BMS

Carey to Morris

February 25, 1802 BMS
February 7, 1806 BMS

Carey to Ryland

January 30, 1801 BMS
September 1817 BMS
April 11, 1818 BMS
October 4, 1818 BMS
March 30, 1819 BMS

October 23, 1820 BMS
June 14, 1821 BMS

Carey to Sutcliffe
November 22, 1796 BMS
January 16, 1798 BMS
October 10, 1798 BMS
April 8, 1801 BMS
June 29, 1801 BMS
March 17, 1802 BMS
August 22, 1805 BMS
January 1, 1806 BMS
July 29, 1806 BMS
February 11, 1807 BMS
June 2, 1807 BMS
May 4, 1808 BMS
March 8, 1809 BMS
September 28, 1809 BMS
May 11, 1810 BMS
March 20, 1811 BMS
February 5, 1812 BMS
March 31, 1812 BMS
August 5, 1812 BMS

Carey to Society
August 5, 1794 BMS
January 6, 1795 BMS
March 18, 1795 BMS
August 13, 1795 BMS
January 11, 1796 BMS
December 28, 1796 BMS
December 9, 1797 BMS
December 1797 BMS
January10, 1799 BMS
January 21, 1820 BMS

Box IN 13 (2 of 2)

Carey to Bentley
January 8, 1807 BMS

Carey to Brewin
March 12, 1795 BMS

Carey to Burls
February 22, 1814 BMS
August 19, 1818 BMS
July 7, 1820 BMS
January 3, 1821 BMS
October 5, 1821 BMS

Carey to Carapeit Aratoon
July 2, 1819 BMS

Carey to Dyer
July 15, 1819 BMS
March 18, 1824 BMS
December 24, 1824 BMS
March 27, 1828 BMS

Carey to Harrington
July 7, 1812 BMS

Carey to Moxon
January 3, 1816 BMS

Carey to Pearce
January 15, 1812 BMS

Carey to Steadman
June 29, 1830 BMS
May 17, 1831 BMS

Carey to Stuart
November 30, 1813 BMS

Carey to Ward
January 20, 1820 BMS

Carey to ?
February 7, 1819 BMS

Box F. P. C. E19

Carey to Brother
August 18, 1802 RPC
October 21, 1807 RPC
October 25, 1809 RPC
May 9, 1815 RPC
December 17, 1817 RPC
June 18, 1821 RPC

Carey to Father
October 13, 1787 or 88 RPC
August 8, 1794 RPC
November 23, 1801 RPC
December 1802 RPC
September 11, 1804 RPC
July 11, 1805 RPC
February 18, 1807 RPC
May 4, 1808 RPC
May 3, 1810 RPC
November 24, 1813 RPC

Carey to Sisters
Carey to Sister Ann, no date RPC
October 5, 1795 RPC
January 10, 1798 RPC
August 24, 1803 RPC
August 23, 1804 RPC
July 17, 1805 RPC
February 25, 1807 RPC
October 1, 1807 RPC
August 9, 1808 RPC
March 8, 1809 RPC
December 21, 1809 RPC
May 4, 1810 RPC
July 20, 1814 RPC
January 31, 1816 RPC
April 1818 RPC
October 1818 RPC
March 4, 1820 RPC
February 16, 1822 RPC
May 1822 RPC
May 18, 1822 RPC
September 1822 RPC
January 15, 1823 RPC
September 5, 1823 RPC
February 6, 1824 RPC
October 27, 1824 RPC
August 20, 1825 RPC
February 20, 1826 RPC
October 25, 1827 RPC
August 18, 1828 RPC
December 17, 1829 RPC
February 21, 1831 RPC
May 24, 1831 RPC
October 25, 1831 RPC
December 16, 1831 RPC
December 6, 1832 RPC
April 3, 1833 RPC
September 25, 1833 RPC

Bound Volume F. P. C. E20

Carey to Father
March 3, 1787 RPC
January 12, 1788 RPC
April 26, 1788 RPC
November 27, 1792 RPC
May 2, 1793 RPC
November 25, 1793 RPC
October 6, 1800 RPC
December 1, 1802 RPC

Carey to Sisters
December 4, 1793 RPC
March 11, 1795 RPC
April 10, 1796 RPC
December 22, 1796 RPC
November 30, 1799 RPC
November 23, 1801 RPC
April 11, 1805 RPC
December 31, 1805 RPC

January 20, 1808 RPC
August 8, 1809 RPC

Box IN 15 (2 of 6)
[Typed transcripts of letters belonging to College Street Baptist Church, Northhampton]

Carey to Fuller
April 23, 1796

Carey to Ryland
December 26, 1793
November 26, 1796
July 6, 1797
April 1, 1799
January 17, 1800
August 17, 1800
March 7, 1801
June 29-30, 1802
August 31, 1802
June 23, 1803
Date Unknown -
Sometime between
June 1803 and December 1804
December 13, 1804
August 1, 1805
December 25, 1805
June 12, 1806
July 17, 1806
November 11, 1806
January 20, 1807
October 7, 1807
January 22, 1808
April 27, 1808
March 1809
March 15, 1809
August 16, 1809
October 13, 1809
October 24, 1810
December 10, 1811
April 14, 1813
November 17, 1813
October 4, 1815
November 15, 1815
May 30, 1816
December 30, 1816
April 12, 1817
September 28, 1819
April 25, 1820
July 4, 1822
May 7, 1823
June 7, 1825

Box IN (3 of 6)

Carey to Sisters
December 14, 1789 BMS
October 15, 1812 BMS
October 28, 1817 BMS
May 24, 1830 BMS
October 25, 1831 BMS

The Jabez Collection

Carey to Jabez
Undated RPC
January 24, 1814 RPC
March 31, 1814 RPC
April 15, 1814 RPC
May 11, 1814 RPC
June 9, 1814 RPC
Undated -
arrived September 10, 1814 RPC
November 25, 1814 RPC
January 12, 1815 RPC
February 1, 1815 RPC
October 6, 1815 RPC
January 20, 1816 RPC
February 7 1816 RPC
September 17, 1816 RPC
November 23, 1816 RPC
February 3, 1817 RPC

November 17, 1817 RPC
December 7, 1818 RPC
March 9, 1819 RPC
May 5, 1819 RPC
June 12, 1819 RPC
August 25, 1819 RPC
September 13, 1819 RPC
November 16, 1819 RPC
December 16, 1819 RPC
January 18, 1820 RPC
March 13, 1820 RPC
April 21, 1820 RPC
August 15, 1820 RPC
September 19, 1820 RPC
October 12, 1820 RPC
November 21, 1820 RPC
December 19, 1820 RPC
January 16, 1821 RPC
February 20, 1821 RPC
March 19, 1821 RPC
April 18, 1821 RPC
May 15, 1821 RPC
June 16, 1821 RPC
July 19, 1821 RPC
August 18, 1821 RPC
January 18, 1822 RPC
February 16, 1822 RPC
July 16, 1822 RPC
November 5, 1822 RPC
November 12, 1822 RPC
April 2, 1823 RPC
July 4, 1823 RPC
January 26, 1824 RPC
August 3, 1824 RPC
January 4, 1825 RPC
January 31, 1825 RPC
April 23, 1825 RPC
July 19, 1825 RPC
April 16, 1826 RPC
May 16, 1826 RPC
October 11, 1826 RPC
February 16, 1827 RPC
May 19, 1827 RPC
October 27, 1827 RPC
April 17, 1828 RPC
April 11, 1829 RPC
September 15, 1829 RPC
December 16, 1829 RPC
January 16, 1830 RPC
April 15, 1830 RPC
June 6, 1830 RPC
March 2, 1831 RPC
August 17, 1831 RPC
February 7, 1832 RPC
September 3, 1832 RPC

Other Accessions

Carey to William
April 27, 1813 RPC

INDEX